WIDE AREA HIGH SPEED NETWORKS

Dr. Sidnie Feit

MACMILLAN
TECHNICAL
PUBLISHING
U·S·A

International Standard Book Number: 1-57870-114-7

Library of Congress Catalog Card Number: 99-62123

03 02 01 00 99   7 6 5 4 3 2 1

Interpretation of the printing code: The rightmost double-digit number is the year of the book's printing; the rightmost single-digit number is the number of the book's printing. For example, the printing code 99-1 shows that the first printing of the book occurred in 1999.

Composed in Galliard and MCPdigital by Macmillan Computer Publishing

Printed in the United States of America

Trademark Acknowledgments

Warning and Disclaimer

Feedback Information

At Macmillan Technical Publishing, our goal is to create in-depth technical books of the highest quality and value. Each book is crafted with care and precision, undergoing rigorous development that involves the unique expertise of members from the professional technical community.

Readers' feedback is a natural continuation of this process. If you have any comments regarding how we could improve the quality of this book, or otherwise alter it to better suit your needs, you can contact us at networktech@mcp.com. Please make sure to include the book title and ISBN in your message.

We greatly appreciate your assistance.

PUBLISHER
David Dwyer

EXECUTIVE EDITOR
Linda Engelman

MANAGING EDITOR
Patrick Kanouse

ACQUISITIONS EDITOR
Karen Wachs

DEVELOPMENT EDITORS
Linda Laflamme
Lisa M. Thibault

PROJECT EDITOR
Theresa Wehrle

COPY EDITOR
Anne Owen

PROOFREADER
John Rahm

INDEXER
Lisa Stumpf

ACQUISITIONS COORDINATOR
Jennifer Garrett

MANUFACTURING COORDINATOR
Brook Farling

BOOK DESIGNER
Anne Jones

COVER DESIGNER
Karen Ruggles

PRODUCTION TEAM SUPERVISOR
Daniela Raderstorf

PRODUCTION
Wil Cruz
Liz Johnston

Dedication

To my husband Walter.

Acknowledgments

I wish to thank Linda Engelman, executive editor of Macmillan Technical Publishing, for giving me the idea of writing this book, and for helping to get the project started. Linda Laflamme, the development editor, read every word of the text (twice) and made hundreds of useful suggestions. Jennifer Garrett, the acquisitions coordinator, kept us focused on exactly where we were and what needed to be done, and cheered everyone on to the finish line.

I also wish to express my gratitude to the technical reviewers, A. G. Carrick, Shahram Davari, Joel Halpern, and Mark J. Newcomb, who weeded out many errors and confusing statements, and gave generously of their time and knowledge.

Network Associates provided current Sniffer Pro monitor software, and Tom Rice of Network Associates supplied many interesting traces and insights.

Richard Willey and Lazlo Szabo provided the most recent versions of the GN Nettest WinPharoah LAN and ATM monitors, and many interesting traces.

About the Author

Dr. Sidnie Feit is a chief scientist for the Standish Group, which provides consulting services to computer vendors and end users. She is an analyst, lecturer, writer, and systems architect with more than 29 years of data communications and information processing experience. Dr. Feit has designed, tested, and reviewed numerous communications products. She also has developed training programs in communications standards and computer systems for vendors and academic institutions. During several years with the ITT Network Design and Architecture Group, Dr. Feit participated in planning for a corporate network and designing international x.400 mail services. Dr. Feit holds a B.A., M.A., and Ph.D. from Cornell University, and has written books and articles in the areas of computer science, data communications, and mathematics. Some of the books she has written include *TCP/IP: Architecture, Protocols, and Implementation with IPv6 and IP Security*, *SNMP: A Guide to Network Management*, and *The LAN Manager's Internet Connectivity Guide* (McGraw-Hill).

About the Technical Reviewers

These reviewers contributed their considerable practical, hands-on expertise to the entire development process for *Wide Area High Speed Networks*. As the book was being written, these folks reviewed all the material for technical content, organization, and flow. Their feedback was critical to ensuring that *Wide Area High Speed Networks* fits our reader's need for the highest quality technical information.

A. G. Carrick has more than a quarter century of experience in the information processing industry. His career spans the spectrum of the industry, including end user organizations, hardware manufacturers, software publishers, third-party maintenance firms, universities, and research and development firms. His industry experience began with the operation of tabulating machines with punch cards and proceeded through programming, systems analysis, systems engineering, LAN administration, network design and installation, software development management, MIS management, and consulting. He is nearing completion of a master's degree in computer science at the University of Texas at Arlington.

Shahram Davari is a systems engineer in the Product Research Department at PMC-Sierra, Inc. PMC-Sierra is a leading provider of networking semiconductor solutions that emphasizes ATM, SONET/ SDH, T1/E1, T3/E3, and Ethernet applications. He received his bachelor's degree in electrical and electronics engineering in 1988 and his master's degree in data communications from the University of British Columbia in 1998. Shahram is a member of the IEEE and is an active participant in the IETF. His current research interests are Multiprotocol Label Switching, Differentiated Services, and Integrated Services.

Joel Halpern is an entrepreneur in residence working with Institutional Venture Partners and John McQuillan. He came to that role after four years with Newbridge Networks where he was the director for internetworking architecture. Prior to joining Newbridge, Joel spent 11 years with Network Systems Corporation working as an in-house consultant to the IP router development group. Joel has been an active member of the IP and ATM standards communities. He recently completed four years as the routing area director at the IETF. Also at the IETF, Joel was an active contributor to the IP over ATM activities. In the ATM Forum, he was one of the key designers of the PNNI routing protocol for use by ATM switches. He also was active in the Multi-Protocol Over ATM specification effort. Joel served for a year as the chair of the ATM Forum Technical Committee Advisory Group, which reviewed all new work item proposals to the Technical Committee.

Mark J. Newcomb is the IS operations supervisor for a major medical laboratory in the Pacific Northwest, where he is directly responsible for both data and telephony communications to more than 600 remote locations. He holds certifications from both Microsoft and Cisco and has more than 18 years experience in the microcomputer industry. Mark's efforts are currently focused on frame relay, ISDN, and Microsoft networking systems. He also is a freelance consultant for numerous independent clients regarding network design and implementation. He can be contacted at mnewcomb@paml.com.

OVERVIEW

CONTENTS

INTRODUCTION

A new framework that encompasses voice, video, and data transmission is under construction in the world's communications networks. This converged framework is built on a transmission capacity that would have been unimaginable only a few years ago. Exciting changes are underway, and this book charts those changes.

Fiber optic SONET transmission and Asynchronous Transfer Mode technology are the cornerstones of the emerging high speed network structure. However, the new structure does not stand alone. ATM devices and switches, raw SONET lines and rings, frame relay circuits, ISDN facilities, and conventional telephony are all components that will have a role in private and public networks for a long time to come.

Network planners and implementers are faced with the task of deciding when and where to use these components and of integrating them into a stable, manageable network. There never have been more choices in the way that networks can be constructed than there are today, and there has been a corresponding growth in the body of information that is needed to make well-informed choices and to build and operate robust networks.

It is the goal of this book to provide a solid understanding of each component technology, explain how they interwork, and establish the appropriate role of each in the high-bandwidth, wide area networked world that is emerging. To achieve this goal, this book describes each technology from top to bottom. Technologies are explained in simple language, avoiding "standardspeak" wherever possible. Figures illustrate every major concept.

Audience

You can benefit from this book if you are responsible for planning, implementing, or supporting voice, data, or converged voice/data networks.

Network planners and architects will obtain insights into the features of available technologies, and discover the factors that need to be taken into account if a network is to grow and evolve without disruption.

Network implementers can gain a solid understanding of the protocols and mechanisms that operate beneath the surface and a comprehension of the configuration processes for many types of network equipment.

Network support staff are provided with details relating to standardized network management facilities for frame relay and ATM, and are introduced to methods that have been devised to simplify ongoing maintenance. Some insight into troubleshooting is provided by the inclusion of traffic traces that are explained in full detail.

Consultants, systems engineers, and sales engineers who design corporate networks for clients also can benefit from the technical information in this book. The material also can be used as a reference resource for personnel that operate public voice or data networks, or Internet service provider networks.

Organization

The book is organized into four parts. The first part describes conventional voice transmission, ISDN voice and data transmission, and high speed SONET transmission. The second part includes a detailed exposition of frame relay technology. The third part describes Asynchronous Transfer Mode (ATM). The fourth part provides some reference information.

Part I: Traditional Telephone Networks

The high speed network infrastructure that is under construction is not displacing older network components; it interworks with them. It is important to understand these older components and how they plug into a high speed network.

Chapter I-1 provides general background information required to understand voice and data networking.

Chapter I-2 outlines the evolution of the voice network and presents the conventional digital signal hierarchy. It includes detailed descriptions of transmission signal formats, multiplexing, and signaling.

Chapter I-3 explains the Integrated Services Digital Network (ISDN) and Signaling System 7 (SS7).

Chapter I-4 introduces the new SONET voice/data digital hierarchy that is at the heart of the new high speed infrastructure, describes its signal formats and multiplexing mechanisms, and explains how conventional signals are carried within SONET signals.

Part II: Frame Relay

Frame relay networks provide cost-effective data transfer and currently are the popular choice for wide area transmission, supporting access speeds of up to 20Mbps.

Chapter II-1 introduces data networks and virtual circuits.

Chapter II-2 reviews X.25 packet data network technology.

Chapter II-3 describes the expanding set of services offered by frame relay providers.

Chapter II-4 examines the meaning of the fine print in service level agreements.

Chapters II-5, II-6, II-8, and II-9 explore frame relay technology and protocols from the users' and the network service providers' points of view.

Chapter II-7 presents frame relay network management.

Chapter II-10 presents solutions to special problems that arise when IP, IBM SNA, and voice traffic are carried across frame relay circuits.

Part III: ATM

Asynchronous Transfer Mode (ATM) is the technology that has been chosen to support the converged, high speed voice/data networks. ATM switches already are used in public telecommunications networks and Internet service provider networks, as well as within an increasing number of private networks. ATM networks carry traffic types ranging from real-time voice to best-effort background data transfer.

Chapter III-1 introduces ATM and broadband ISDN.

Chapter III-2 presents basic ATM concepts and protocol sublayering.

Chapter III-3 explores ATM network internals.

Chapter III-4 represents the way ATM traffic is carried across several types of physical media.

Chapter III-5 describes the way information is packaged at the ATM Adaptation Layer.

Chapter III-6 analyzes the complex traffic contracts that nail down the performance and quality of service of each permanent or switched virtual circuit.

Chapter III-7 examines the signaling protocols used to set up switched ATM circuits.

Chapter III-8 presents ATM ILMI and SNMP network management mechanisms.

Chapter III-9 deals with ATM routing and signaling protocols.

Chapter III-10 presents the *LAN Emulation (LANE)* protocol, which enables current applications to run on top of ATM and supports virtual LAN services. It also introduces MPOA, the basis of a high speed network fabric that integrates routing with switching.

Part IV: Appendixes

Part IV includes acronyms, a glossary, and pointers to standards groups, consortia, and other information resources.

PART

I

Traditional Telephone Networks

1

Communications Concepts

The migration to new voice and data technologies that is described in this book is happening rapidly, but rapid change and growth has been characteristic of telephone and data networks since their beginnings.

The first commercial telephone exchange opened in New Haven, Connecticut, in 1878. In 1900, there were more than 800,000 telephones in the Bell system. A mere five years later, there were over 2,000,000 and by the 1990s, there were hundreds of millions of telephones installed across a global network.

Many technological improvements were introduced along the way. As the number of telephone subscribers grew, automatic switching replaced manual operations performed by human operators. The 1960s saw the beginning of digital transmission within the telephone backbone, which was assisted by the introduction of computer-based telephone switches in 1965.

The invention of the computer affected the telephone network in other ways. Customers wanted to use the telephone network to connect terminal devices to remote computers or to transfer information from one computer to another. Initially, analog voice lines were used for computer communications. Later, digital transmission was made available and businesses leased digital lines to carry their data traffic. The telephone network matured into a general telecommunications network.

Many of the behind-the-scenes mechanisms that enable telecommunications networks to operate involve computers and data communications. This chapter introduces data communications terminology and concepts that apply to both traditional telecommunications networks and the new, high-speed telecommunications infrastructure. These elements need to be understood before the other topics in this book can be tackled.

Voice and Data Transmission Requirements

Voice and data may flow on the same phone lines, but they have very different transmission requirements. When voice is transmitted, losing or altering a few bits along the way does not cause a problem. Minor blemishes are not even noticed. But, it is important to deliver voice content promptly and in order. Therefore, voice networks are designed so

- The loss of a chunk of digitized voice is handled by ignoring it.

- If a digitized voice bit stream contains a few errors, it still can be delivered to its destination.

- Prompt in order delivery is preserved by reserving a constant bandwidth for a voice call along a fixed circuit.

> **Note**
>
> The requirement to set up a fixed circuit and use that path throughout the period of transmission is the feature that characterizes *connection oriented* communications.

In contrast to voice transmission, it is not acceptable to lose transmitted data or deliver corrupted data.

The basic mechanism for safeguarding against data loss is

- Number data payloads.

- Before transmitting a numbered payload, set a timer.

- Wait for an acknowledgment. If none arrives within the timeout period, retransmit the data.

The sender performs a function called a *cyclic redundancy check (CRC)* on each data message and tacks the result onto the end of the payload. To protect against accepting errored data, the CRC is recalculated at the receiving end of the line. If the recomputed value does not match the original value, some of the bits have been corrupted. The data is discarded and is not acknowledged.

On the other hand, data communications can tolerate conditions that are not acceptable for voice transmission. For example, delays that would be totally unacceptable for voice are permissible for data transfer. And, a data receiver can deal with out-of-order data because data payloads are numbered.

Because strict timeliness and ordered arrival are not needed for data, the use of a fixed path with constant reserved bandwidth is not an absolute requirement for data communications.

> **Note**
>
> *Bandwidth* is a measure of the information carrying capacity of a transmission medium. Bandwidth is measured in thousands of bits per second (kilobits per second [Kbps]), millions of bits per second (megabits per second [Mbps]), or billions of bits per second (gigabits per second [Gbps]).

The HDLC Family of Data Communications Protocols

Data payload numbering and CRC error checking mechanisms are two of the techniques used to support reliable data communications. However, many more mechanisms and rules are required in order to accomplish intelligible data communications. These mechanisms and rules are called *protocols.*

One of the oldest data communications protocols still in use today is IBM's *Synchronous Data Link Control (SDLC)*. SDLC defined rules for transmitting data across a digital line and was used for long distance communications between terminals and computers or between pairs of computers.

IBM submitted SDLC to standards organizations. They revised and generalized it into the *High Level Data Link Control (HDLC)* protocol. HDLC is the basis of a family of related protocols. Among these are

- **Link Access Procedure on the D-channel (LAPD)**—Used with ISDN and described in Chapter I-3.

- **Link Access Protocol Balanced (LAPB)**—Used with X.25 and described in Chapter II-2.

- **Link Access Procedures To Frame-Mode Bearer (LAPF)**—Used with frame relay and discussed in Chapters II-5 and II-9.

- **Point-to-Point Protocol (PPP)**—Used for general data communications across wide area lines and discussed in the next section.

For each of these protocols, data is transmitted in a formatted unit called a *frame.* Figure 1.1 shows the general format of an HDLC information frame:

- **Address field**—Contains an address that matches a frame to its "conversation." It is important for SDLC, LAPD, and LAPF because multiple devices may share the same communications line, and several data conversations can go on concurrently.

- **Control field**—Contains payload numbers and acknowledgment numbers when reliable data transmission across the line is required.

- **Frame check sequence (FCS) field**—Contains the result of a CRC calculation that is performed by the sender.

Figure 1.1   HDLC frame format.

PPP

The point-to-point protocol strips HDLC to the bone for the purpose of transmission. Extra functionality is defined in add-on capabilities that are distinct from transmission. The PPP protocol includes a startup procedure during which the capabilities to be used are negotiated.

PPP frames are not numbered and are not acknowledged. The address and control fields have no function, and during negotiation, the partners can stipulate that these fields will be omitted. Various compression mechanisms are available for use with PPP, and PPP is an efficient, low-overhead data link protocol.

The information field in a PPP frame starts with a protocol identifier that indicates the type of data that is carried in the frame. This enables a receiver to identify the type of payload in each frame, so PPP can carry data for several different protocols across a single link.

The Birth of Packet Switching

Reserving constant bandwidth on a telecommunications line is wasteful because data usually is transmitted in bursts that vary in size. Often, there are inactive periods between bursts, as shown in Figure 1.2.

Figure 1.2   Bursty data transmission.

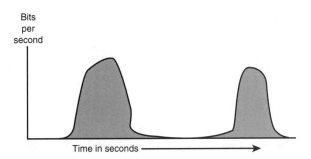

Modern wide area data communications began with the invention of *packet switching*. As shown in Figure 1.3, in a packet-switched network

- Data is packaged in units traditionally called *packets*.

- Each packet has a header that indicates where it is going.

- A packet passes through a series of switching nodes on its way to its destination. Each switch forwards the packet toward its destination based on the information in the packet header.

Packet switching was the result of a research project sponsored by the U.S. Advanced Research Projects Agency of the Department of Defense (ARPA) and first was implemented in 1969, on an experimental network called the *ARPANET*.

Packet switching allows traffic originating from many sources and bound for many destinations to share the bandwidth of the telecommunications lines in the network.

Figure 1.3   A packet-switched network.

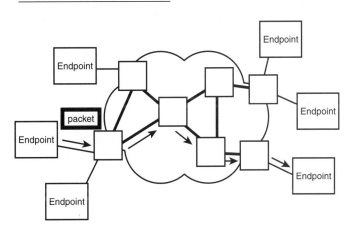

Virtual Circuits

A person using a telephone cannot carry on two separate conversations at exactly the same instant. Hence, a telephone supports only one active speech connection.

However, it makes perfectly good sense for two or more processes within a computer to carry on simultaneous data conversations. Packet switching networks enable an endpoint, such as a computer, to engage in several concurrent communications by means of *virtual circuits*. While a telephone circuit fully occupies a fixed physical bandwidth, virtual circuits share bandwidth.

For example, endpoint A in Figure 1.4 has opened up virtual circuits to endpoints B and C. These virtual circuits share the access line that connects the endpoint to the packet network and share lines within the network with data being transmitted across other virtual circuits.

Each packet transmitted from endpoint A onto the access line that connects to the network has a header that identifies its virtual circuit number. The network uses this number to deliver the packet correctly.

Figure 1.4   Virtual circuits.

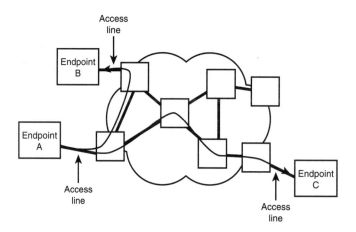

X.25 and Frame Relay Packet Switching

In the 1980s, the capable X.25 family of packet switching protocols was created by the standards organization responsible for international telecommunications: the *International Telegraph and Telephone Consultative Committee (CCITT)*, predecessor of the current *International Telecommunications Union Telecommunication Standardization Sector (ITU-T)*. Many commercial data networks that conformed to the X.25 specifications were built and support for X.25 spread to countries all over the world. X.25 packet switched networks are still used today, and are described in Chapter II-2.

X.25 packet switching is confined to low bandwidth applications. Where higher bandwidth is needed, X.25 has largely been displaced by the faster, leaner *frame relay* packet switching technology.

DTE and DCE

X.25 standards refer to an endpoint device as *data terminal equipment (DTE)*. A DTE connects to *data circuit-terminating equipment (DCE)* in order to access an X.25 network. X.25 protocols describe how a DTE interacts with a DCE.

The terms DTE and DCE have been reused for other types of data communications. For example, when a computer uses a modem for dial-up communications, the computer is called a DTE and the modem is called a DCE. The computer connects to the modem (DCE) in order to access the switched telephone network.

The DCE acronym sometimes is translated as *data communications equipment*.

Building Complete Data Communications Protocol Stacks

Packet switching is helpful, but lacks many capabilities needed to support robust and reliable data communications. During the 1970s and 1980s, several computer vendors defined more comprehensive data communications protocol suites. However, these suites were proprietary and were confined to each vendor's product family. There was a need for open standards that would enable any pair of systems to communicate.

Two parallel efforts aimed at open, standardized data communications were initiated in the 1970s: the development of the TCP/IP Internet suite and the definition of the International Standards Organization (ISO) protocols.

TCP/IP and the Internet Protocol Suite

In 1974, Vinton Cerf and Robert Kahn wrote a landmark paper that outlined what later became TCP/IP. TCP/IP was received favorably, and the decision was made to convert the ARPANET packet switched network to TCP/IP. The conversion was completed in 1983, and the evolution of the ARPANET into the Internet began.

TCP/IP flourished and the Internet evolved quickly because of the work performed under the umbrella of the *Internet Engineering Task Force (IETF)*. IETF committees are formed of volunteers. The work is focused on solving Internet problems and adding new functionality to the Internet.

Preliminary and final IETF standards are published in documents called *Requests For Comments (RFCs)* that are freely available on the Internet. IETF committees also often provide free software implementations of new protocols. Quick development, testing and rollout are characteristic of Internet protocols.

IETF activities are supervised by members of the *Internet Engineering Steering Group (IESG)*. General strategy and final review of standards are performed by the *Internet Architecture Board (IAB)*.

ISO OSI and the OSI Model

At the same time that the Internet was getting its start, the *International Organization for Standardization (ISO)* initiated its Open Systems Interconnect (OSI) effort. OSI's goal was to develop a set of international standards for open data communications.

The OSI data communications model was approved in 1982. Figure 1.5 displays the TCP/IP and OSI communications models.

Figure 1.5   The TCP/IP and OSI communications models.

TCP/IP Model	OSI Model	
	Application Layer	7
APPLICATIONS	Presentation Layer	6
	Session Layer	5
Transport Layer TCP and UDP	Transport Layer Classes 0 - 5 plus connectionless	4
Network Layer IP	Network Layer Connection oriented and connectionless	3
Data Link Layer	Data Link Layer	2
Physical Layer	Physical Layer	1

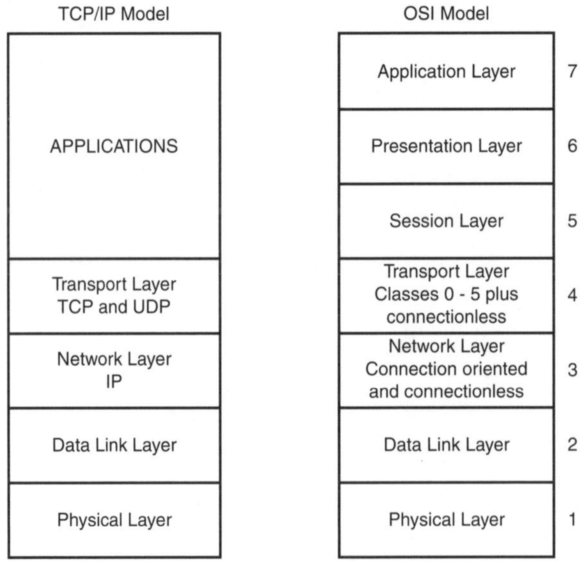

OSI committees set to work turning each layer of their model into a concrete set of protocol standards. The pace was slow, because ISO standards must be established by international consensus. Serious objections by voting members must be resolved before a standard can be adopted. This often results in lots of optional protocol features being wrapped into a standard.

Free documentation and software were not made available, and no testbed network was established until the standards were complete, so no one had any idea how the protocols would perform and whether implementations would interwork. In the end, OSI products were slow and expensive, and were adopted only where mandated by government requirements.

However, the model remains useful, and the sections that follow sketch the functions at layers 1 through 4, as they are commonly understood and used today.

Layer 1: The Physical Layer

Physical layer standards describe the hardware components used with a communications medium, the method used by a sender to encode 0s and 1s onto the medium, and the procedures followed by a receiver to extract 0s and 1s from the medium.

The physical layer usually performs some additional functions that require that some overhead bits be transmitted in addition to the data.

For example, in the local area network arena, a seven-byte preamble signal is sent onto an Ethernet cable to establish timing before an Ethernet frame is transmitted.

Extra overhead bits also are used in wide area communications. T1 transmission is a basic building block of today's wide area networks. In addition to carrying digitized voice, a T1 line carries some extra streams of bits. One stream is used to align the voice signal while others are used for error detection and network management chores. T1 is described in Chapter I-2.

Layer 2: The Data Link Layer

At the data link layer, 0s and 1s are organized into formatted units called *data link frames*, or just *frames*.

Frames that belong to the HDLC family and are used for wide area communications were discussed earlier. Other frame formats have been defined for Ethernet, Token Ring, and Fiber Distributed Data Interface (FDDI) local area networks (LANs). However, these local area network frames share common elements with HDLC frames, such as address fields, a control field, and a frame check sequence field.

For a long time, it was common wisdom that data link frames should be numbered and acknowledged. However, implementing reliable data link communications slows down throughput. This is not acceptable on high-speed LANs and WANs. In most cases, frame numbering at the data link layer was abandoned and reliability became the responsibility of a higher layer—usually layer 4.

Nonetheless, the *Institute for Electrical and Electronics Engineers* (IEEE) standards group, whose 802 committee is in charge of several LAN technologies, has defined a protocol called *Logical Link Control 2* (LLC2) for those who wished to use a reliable data link protocol across a local area network.

For the most part, unnumbered layer 2 transmission is the norm today across both local and wide area links. For example, frame relay and PPP data frames are unnumbered.

Note

"Reliable" data link protocols actually are not reliable. They only can recover from one problem situation—namely, if a frame is lost, the sender retransmits after a timeout. However, other problems can arise and when they do, these protocols simply restart, usually throwing away some data in the process. (Chapter II-2 provides more details.)

Thus, to support truly reliable data transmission, it is always necessary to number, retransmit, and perform additional error recovery chores at a higher protocol layer.

Data Link Layer Addresses

Data link layer addresses only make sense to systems that belong to the same link. For example, if you gave someone the address "number 31, just down the street," it only would make sense to someone that was on the same street. Similarly, SDLC or LAPD addresses are useful only to systems connected to the same line. LAN destination addresses enable you to deliver data only when you are on that LAN.

Note

The addresses on LAN network interface cards are under the control of the IEEE, and consist of six hexadecimal bytes. Every LAN card is preconfigured with one of these six-byte addresses. The first three bytes identify the vendor that created the LAN interface card.

A vendor must assign a unique address to each LAN network interface card that it manufactures. A LAN administrator can override that address with another, but must be careful that interfaces attached to the same LAN are assigned different addresses.

LAN network interface card addresses are called *Media Access Control* (MAC) addresses or *physical addresses*.

Bridging at the Data Link

On a conventional LAN, the transmission medium is shared by all stations, and only one station may transmit at any given time.

One way to improve performance on a LAN is to split the LAN into workgroup segments and connect the segments with a *bridge*, as is shown in Figure 1.6. A bridge prevents traffic whose source and destination are on the same segment from entering another segment. If most traffic stays within each workgroup segment, the overall traffic on each segment is reduced and this improves performance. On the other hand, when a system on one side of the bridge needs to communicate with a system on the other side, the bridge will carry traffic between the segments quickly and efficiently.

Figure 1.6   A Bridged LAN.

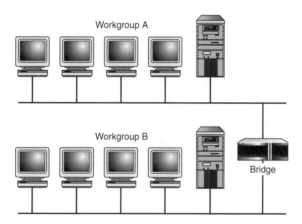

Some organizations find it convenient to bridge segments that are located at different sites, as is shown in Figure 1.7. Today, the bandwidth of the wide area line between two bridge devices often is far less than the LAN bandwidth, and the line can turn into a bottleneck. In the future, it may be possible to get a low cost, high-bandwidth line that supports high-speed access to a distant segment.

Data Link LAN Switches

A LAN switch is like a box full of bridges. Multiple LAN frames can pass through a switch at the same time.

When high-speed performance is needed, each station on the LAN can be given its own segment.

Figure 1.7 Bridging across a wide area line.

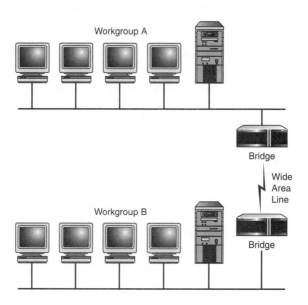

As shown in Figure 1.8, a LAN switch can provide generous bandwidth to its connected systems. Each segment is full duplex—data can be sent and received at the same time. Many LAN frames can be in transit concurrently.

Figure 1.8 A LAN switch.

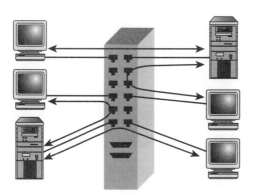

Layer 3: The Network Layer

Figure 1.9 shows a LAN desktop station accessing a server on a remote LAN. Data passed between the desktop station and the server traverses three links: a Token Ring, a wide area line, and an Ethernet. Each step on the way to the destination is called a "hop."

A data link carries data across a single hop only—for example, from one end of a telephone line to the other end of the line, or from one system on an Ethernet to another system on the same Ethernet. A *router* is a layer 3 device that forwards traffic from link to link until it reaches its destination. Routers cooperate to learn the topology of their network. They can shift the path that data follows based on current network conditions.

Figure 1.9   Multihop communications.

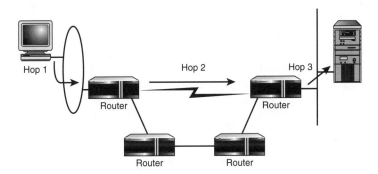

The network layer supports routed multihop communications by

- Defining global address assignments; each system has an address that identifies where it is.

- Supporting protocols that describe how data should be forwarded to its destination.

- Supporting protocols that enable routers to learn network topology and the current status of network links and routers.

Currently, IP, the Internet Protocol, is the most popular layer 3 addressing and forwarding protocol. IP is *connectionless*, which means that a fixed path from the source to the destination is not put in place before communications start, nor is bandwidth explicitly reserved for the communication. A router examines and forwards each layer 3 data unit as it arrives, according to what looks like the best decision at the time.

However, there is a trend toward using a mixed forwarding strategy. If there is a steady stream of traffic to a destination, a path is locked in place, and traffic in the stream is processed very rapidly.

Open Shortest Path First (OSPF) is a popular protocol that is used to learn network topology and maintain up-to-date knowledge of the status of network facilities. OSPF was created to determine layer 3 routes. However, it has been adapted for use within a layer 1 telecommunications network, to assist in determining the paths to be followed by voice or data calls. (Chapter III-9 describes this adaptation.)

Layer 4: The Transport Layer

The transport layer often is called the end-to-end layer. It is implemented in the endpoints that are the sources and destinations of data traffic. When reliable transmission is needed, this is the layer that contains the mechanisms that support it.

The transport layer for the TCP/IP protocol suite includes the transmission control protocol (TCP) for reliable communications. It also includes the *user datagram protocol (UDP)*, a simple, unreliable message based protocol for applications that can tolerate occasional loss of data and data that is delivered out of order.

More About OSI Layers and Standards

The actual nature of the OSI protocols often is misunderstood. This section outlines the OSI protocols defined at each layer for the benefit of readers who may be curious about OSI data communications.

For layers 1 and 2, OSI references other generally accepted standards, such as HDLC, Ethernet, and Token Ring.

Connection-oriented X.25 circuits were the first choice for an end-to-end layer 3 protocol, although there also is a specification for a connectionless alternative that is similar to IP.

There are five OSI layer 4 transport service classes that support reliable sessions, four of which are based on an underlying layer 3 connection-oriented (X.25) service, while the fifth is based on a connectionless layer 3. An additional service similar to UDP was added later to support unreliable transport of standalone messages.

The OSI session layer protocol provides mechanisms that support peer-to-peer transaction processing. One mechanism controls peer-to-peer conversations and can assure that only one party "speaks" at any given time. Another mechanism sets synchronization points that can be used to recover or roll back transactions. The session layer protocol followed IBM's logical unit 6.0 (LU 6.0) quite closely. (LU 6.0 originally was designed to support an IBM transaction processing product called CICS.)

The OSI presentation layer enables applications to negotiate a standard format in which data can be transferred, and assists in translating local data formats to and from that standard format.

The OSI application layer defines several standard services, such as support for *remote operations* (basically remote procedure calls) and for *2-phase commits*, which ensure successful completion of transactions such as funds transfer.

OSI Terminology

Along with its model, ISO introduced terminology that has become a standard part of the language of data communications. The terminology is formal and not very intuitive, but occasionally is useful. Common OSI terms include

- **Protocol data unit (PDU)**—A formatted unit of data. Most PDUs consist of a header followed by a data payload. Some PDUs have a trailer that follows the payload. There are protocol data units defined for layer 2, layer 3, and so forth. The data link layer frames described earlier are layer 2 PDUs.

- **Service data unit (SDU)**—A unit of data that is passed down to a lower layer for transmission, or is delivered to a higher layer for reception. As shown in Figure 1.10, a higher layer PDU is viewed by the adjacent lower layer as an SDU. For example, after the transport layer has prepared a transport layer PDU, it is passed to the network layer. The network layer views this block of information as an SDU and adds its own header and trailer to turn it into a layer 3 PDU.

- **Service access point (SAP)**—A point at which data is passed from one layer to the next. SAP identifiers enable incoming PDUs to be passed to the correct higher layer process.

Figure 1.10   PDUs, SDUs, and SAPs.

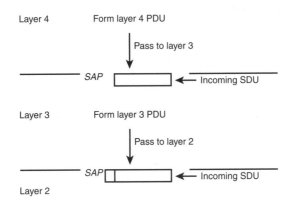

Note

It should be noted that Figure 1.10 describes a formal model that may have little relationship to the way that a particular communications protocol actually is implemented.

Multiplexing

Telecommunications lines are usually costly and often are underused. One way to improve the return on investment is to place several streams of traffic onto a line. The packet networks and virtual circuits discussed earlier illustrated one way that bandwidth resources are used more effectively by sharing lines.

The procedure of placing multiple information streams on a shared line is called *multiplexing*. There are three types of multiplexing:

- Line sharing on a packet network is an example of *statistical multiplexing*. Packets belonging to different virtual circuits arrive at a switch in a fairly random fashion and are transmitted on a first-come-first-served basis. The likelihood that a bottleneck occurs is reduced by putting a limit on the average transmission rate of each circuit.

- *Time division multiplexing* is completely predictable. Each information stream is assigned a time slot and data belonging to a stream only may be transmitted during its time slot. If no current information needs to be sent for a particular stream, its time slot is wasted. Telephone calls share long distance lines using time division multiplexing.

- *Frequency division multiplexing* divides the overall capacity of a communications medium into bands of frequencies that carry information in parallel. For example, when you switch channels on a cable television set, the television receiver locks onto a band of frequencies assigned to a specific station. This method also is used to send parallel streams of data down a fiber optic cable.

Several different instances of statistical, time, and frequency multiplexing occur in later chapters.

SNMP

One factor common to all types of networks is the need for network management capabilities—and the use of the *Simple Network Management Protocol* (SNMP) to meet at least part of this need. SNMP plays an important role in several technologies described in this book. Its main features are outlined below.

SNMP originally was created to introduce network management functions into the Internet. It was designed by an IETF committee, and its continued development has been controlled by the IETF. Use of SNMP is widespread, and today computers, bridges, routers, telephone switches, packet switches, and other devices can be managed with the help of SNMP.

SNMP Architecture

SNMP follows a database model. All devices contain information that a network administrator would like to see, including

- Configuration settings
- Status information
- Performance statistics

With the help of an SNMP *network management station*, an administrator can read this information and can update configuration or status settings.

Figure 1.11 shows the elements of the SNMP model. At the request of applications in the management station, an *SNMP manager* reads or updates management variables at a remote device by sending requests to the device's *SNMP agent*. The manager communicates with an agent using the SNMP protocol.

If a significant event such as a reboot or a serious error occurs at a device, the agent in the device can report it using a message called a *trap*.

Figure 1.11   The SNMP model.

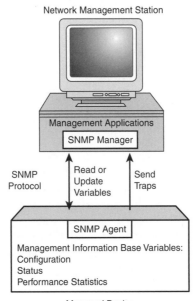

Network Management Station

Management Applications

SNMP Manager

SNMP
Protocol

Read or
Update
Variables

Send
Traps

SNMP Agent

Management Information Base Variables:
Configuration
Status
Performance Statistics

Managed Device

Device vendors and third-party software developers enhance the usability of a management station by writing applications that display management information in a graphical form. For example, the administrator may be shown a picture of a device and be able to troubleshoot or configure a specific component by clicking on it.

Management Information Base

A collection of network management variables is called a *Management Information Base (MIB)*. Examples of MIB variables include

- The description of a device

- The number of network interfaces in a device and the type of each interface

- Counts of incoming or outgoing frames

The standardization of MIB variables is an important part of the SNMP effort. A standard MIB variable value has the same format and meaning independent of which vendor has built the device.

MIB Documents

Many documents describing standard MIB variables have been published as IETF Request for Comments documents. In addition, vendors have written MIBs that describe variables that are specific to their own devices and are not covered in the standards.

A MIB document includes a set of related definitions that are organized into a unit called a *MIB Module*. These days, as soon as a new technology is introduced, a group of experts writes a MIB Module for the technology.

A major factor in the success of SNMP is that MIB documents are written in a formal language that can be understood by a management station. An administrator simply copies a MIB document to a management station's hard disk and enters a command that adds the MIB definitions into the set of definitions already understood by the management station. The station then will be able to read and update the variables defined in the document.

The usability of a new MIB is enhanced by installing an application that automatically gathers the MIB information and presents it in a succinct form.

SNMP Transports

SNMP queries, updates, responses, and trap messages can be carried between systems using any convenient communications protocol. Because SNMP was created to meet Internet needs, the Internet UDP transport protocol is a popular choice. However, there are several other protocols that are commonly used to carry SNMP messages, including one that is used in ATM networks.

Standards Body Overview

Several important standards groups have been mentioned in this chapter. The ITU-T is responsible for standards that relate to the global telephone network and packet data networks. The ISO has published many documents relating to data communications.

These international organizations are supported by national and regional standards organizations. Many standards result from technology submissions made by member organizations. For example, the *American National Standards Institute (ANSI)* has contributed to many ITU-T and ISO efforts, as has the *European Telecommunications Standards Institute (ETSI)*.

The IETF publishes standards relating to the Internet, and the IEEE supervises the evolution of LAN standards.

A relatively recent—and welcome—development is the formation of vendor groups that limit or adapt standards in order to promote interworking and user groups that provide feedback on the functions and features that they really need. The National ISDN Council, Frame Relay Forum, and ATM Forum exemplify this type of activity.

Appendix A, "Standards Bodies," contains summary descriptions of standards groups and provides pointers to their World Wide Web sites.

CHAPTER 2

Traditional Telecommunications Networks

Today's high speed networks did not come out of nowhere. They are a stage in an evolution that began in 1876, when the telephone was invented. It is not possible to leave old technologies behind and leap into new ones. There are strong ties between the old and the new, and it is important to understand how the old and new coexist and cooperate.

This chapter introduces telephony background, concepts, and terminology, and describes the conventional digital telecommunications infrastructure. Most of the discussion relates to North American telecommunications. Understanding these concepts will provide a strong foundation when you reach Part III, "ATM," of this book, which presents the changes being made to the worldwide telecommunications infrastructure to support today's and tomorrow's high speed wide area communications networks.

Telephone System Background

The telephone was invented to carry voice conversations and the structure of the telephone network was based on the needs of voice. Telephones were designed as *analog* devices: they converted sound wave patterns to analogous electrical wave patterns at one end of a call, and converted the electrical wave patterns back to sound at the other end.

Originally, the entire telephone network was based on analog transmission. If you are old enough to remember what analog long distance telephone calls were like, you may recall straining to hear what the other party was saying through a haze of crackling static, and shouting back across the line to make yourself understood. Your call suffered from the two flaws of analog transmission. Because of resistance on a copper line, a signal attenuates (diminishes) as it travels down the line. If the line is too long, the voice signal that is delivered becomes inaudible. Furthermore, the line picks up static and other noise. The attenuation problem was solved by inserting amplifiers along sections of wire. Unfortunately, noise gets amplified along with the voice signal.

In the 1960s an important transformation of the telephone network was initiated—the conversion from analog to digital technology. Today, when you place a call from Boston to San Francisco, the sound quality usually is just as good as the quality of a call to a neighbor down the street. The reason is that the voice signal has been converted to digital 0s and 1s within the telephone network, and amplifiers have been replaced with smart signal regenerators.

Figure 2.1 shows how a voice wave pattern can be distorted by noise when it crosses an analog network. The pattern becomes worse as it crosses multiple lines. There is no way for the network equipment to re-create the original wave form.

Figure 2.1   Distortions in an analog voice signal.

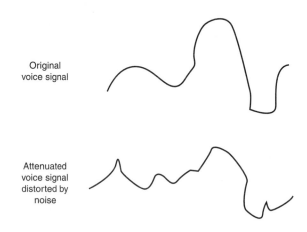

Original
voice signal

Attenuated
voice signal
distorted by
noise

However, if the wave form is digitized, then only 0s and 1s need to be transmitted across a line. As shown in Figure 2.2, a signal still will be distorted, but a regenerator only needs to be able to distinguish between a 1 and a 0. It then transmits clean 1 and 0 signals onto the next line.

Changing the telephone network from analog to digital transmission did not just clean up the voice network. It also opened the way to transforming telephone networks into telecommunications networks that support both voice and data transmission in digital form.

Figure 2.2   Regenerating a digital signal.

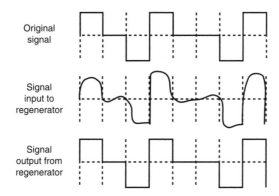

The Local Loop

For the most part, one element of the modern telecommunications system has remained analog: the *local loop.* The local loop connects telephones, fax machines, and computer modems in a home or small business with a telecommunications network.

A telephone, fax machine, or modem in your home is called a *terminal* or *station.* Your terminals plus the telephone wiring inside your home add up to your *customer premises equipment (CPE).* Somewhere in a box in your basement there is a demarcation point (DEMARC), which is the boundary between your house wiring and the telephone network. The telephone company is responsible for maintaining the equipment and telephone wire on their side of the DEMARC. Everything located on the other side is your problem.

A pair of wires connects your DEMARC to a central point that is called a *central office, local exchange office, switching center,* or *telephone exchange.* Wire pairs are combined into bigger and bigger bundles as they approach the central office. The wires in a pair are twisted together because this reduces their tendency to pick up signals from other wires in the bundle—hence, the name *twisted pair.* A twisted pair is called the *local loop, subscriber line, user line,* or *the last mile.*

Note
One of the characteristics of telephony is that almost every component has two, or three, or four names.

Although transmission across most local loops remains analog, end-to-end digital service is available in many areas. Chapter I-3 describes Integrated Services Digital Network (ISDN) technology, which supports switched digital telephone and data service.

A more recent technology called *digital subscriber line (DSL)* supports high speed digital transmission across the local loop. There are several variants of DSL technology. DSL standards have not yet solidified and, at the time of writing, DSL has not yet been deployed widely.

Local Exchange Carriers

The central offices within an area are owned and operated by a *local exchange carrier (LEC)*. Large numbers of wire pairs converge at each central office. Facilities at the central office send a dial tone to phones, switch calls to their destination, and forward ringing signals.

If a call is directed to a telephone connected to the same central office, then the central office switch connects the two local loops to form a *circuit*, which is a path between the two telephones. If a call is directed to a telephone that is not served by the same central office but is in the area served by the local exchange carrier, the switch routes the call—either directly to the destination's central office switch or to a switch in a *tandem office*. (A switch in a tandem office is called a *tandem switch*.)

Tandem means "one after the other." Tandem switches connect to central offices and to other tandem switches. A tandem switch connects a line that is part of a telephone circuit to the next line that will be part of that circuit.

Older telephone switches were electromechanical devices. Up-to-date switches are computers.

Note
In telephony language, a line joined to another in order to build a circuit is called a *cross connection*. This term is inherited from the earliest telephone networks, when an operator created circuits manually by plugging in a cable that connected two local loops.

Figure 2.3 illustrates connectivity within a local exchange carrier area. The lines that connect switches together are called *trunks*. The telephone system includes copper, fiber optic, microwave, and satellite trunk lines.

The figure includes trunk connections to *private branch exchange (PBX)* switches located at business premises. A PBX is a private switch that provides telephone service within a business, and also enables internal telephones, fax machines, and modems to connect to the outside world via one or more trunk connections.

| Figure 2.3 | Connectivity within a local exchange area. |

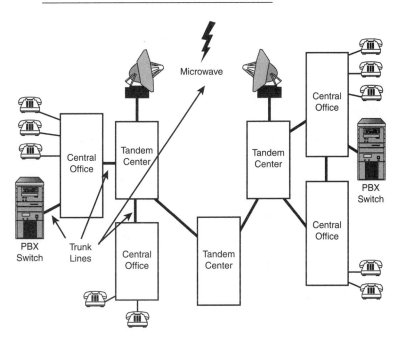

Interexchange Carriers

A long distance call whose destination is outside the local exchange carrier's area has to be routed across a long distance carrier to reach the called party's local exchange carrier. The formal name for a long distance carrier is *interexchange carrier* (*IEC* or *IXC*). Many people have been made aware that they can choose their interexchange carrier by frequent telemarketing calls from competing carriers!

When you make a long distance call, your number is looked up in a database to determine which interexchange carrier you have selected. Then the call is routed to a *point of presence (POP)* for that carrier, which sets up the route to the destination local exchange carrier. Figure 2.4 shows POP sites that are connected to a tandem center and to central offices.

Figure 2.4   Connecting to interexchange carriers.

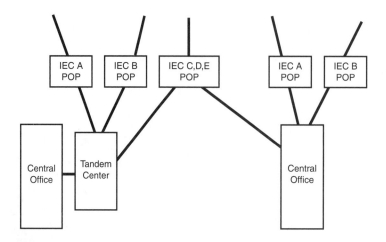

Digital Transmission in Telecommunications Networks

The architecture of digital telecommunications networks was scaled to voice transmission. An analysis of voice signals indicated that satisfactory quality could be achieved by taking a voice sample every 125 microseconds, and representing the sample digitally as 8 bits. This means that 8,000 8-bit samples—a total of 64,000 bits—must be transmitted each second.

These numbers became the magic constants of the telephone system:

- All transmission was performed in multiples of 64,000.

- 125 microseconds became a commonly used timing interval.

A 64Kbps circuit, which supports one voice call, is called *digital signal 0* or *DS0*.

The T-Carrier System

The United States transmission system designed to carry voice in digital form is called the *T-carrier system*.

The T-carrier system became the cornerstone of wide area data communications. Today, a T-carrier is as likely to transport data as to carry voice. Businesses routinely lease T-carrier lines, which bring digital service directly to their premises.

The T-carrier system evolved into a hierarchy that includes several bandwidth levels, but it all started with T1.

T1

A *T1 line* (which also is called a *T1 carrier*) is a full-duplex transmission facility. Physically, it consists of

- Cable segments made up of four wires (two twisted pairs). Two wires are used to transmit and two to receive.

- Regenerators that clean up and repeat the signal from one segment onto the next.

Channels

Digitized sound for a call is carried from its source to its destination on a 64Kbps *channel*. Two channels are needed for a call—one in each direction.

The T1 system was designed to carry 24 digitized telephone calls. Hence the capacity of a T1 line is divided into 48 channels—24 in each direction. Figure 2.5 shows the 24 channels used for one direction of each call.

Figure 2.5   Unidirectional channels on a T1 line.

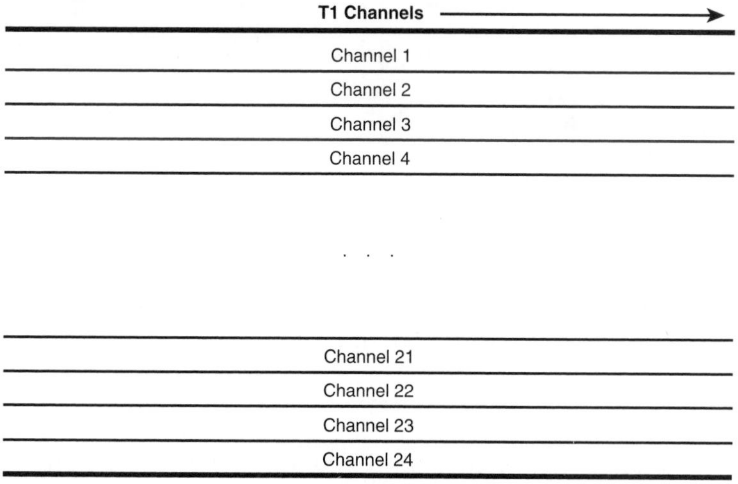

Multiplexing

Although we often think of these channels as flowing across the line together, bits actually are transmitted onto a line one at a time. One byte (8 bits) from the first call is sent, followed by a byte from the second, and so forth.

This is done using *time division multiplexing*. Each call is assigned a 1-byte *time slot*. The transmitting device sends one byte for a channel each time the channel's time slot comes around.

Note

In general, the process of combining two or more communications channels onto a common transmission medium is called *multiplexing*. When channels are assigned time slots, the process is called time division multiplexing.

Figure 2.6 shows a telecommunications device combining channels onto a T1 line. As shown in the figure, the device transmits a byte from call 1, followed by a byte from call 2, and so forth.

Figure 2.6   Time division multiplexing for a T1 line.

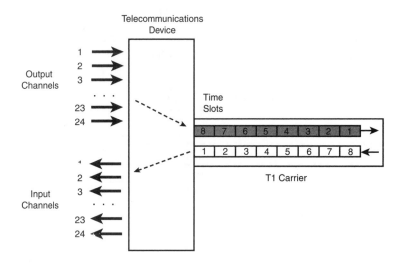

Note that the T1 line is full-duplex, and incoming channel bytes are being delivered at the same time as outgoing bytes are being transmitted.

DS1 Frames

It is important to know where each channel is located in the incoming stream. To track the channels, they are placed into a formatted package that includes extra bits. The basic unit of the package, called a *Digital Signal 1 (DS1) frame*, is shown in Figure 2.7.

A DS1 frame consists of a framing bit followed by 24 bytes—one for each of the 24 channels. Thus, a frame consists of 193 bits. Eight thousand frames are sent per second, giving a total signal rate of 1,544,000 bits per second. This signal is called *digital signal level 1 (DS1)*.

The terms T1 and DS1 often are used interchangeably. However, strictly speaking, a T1 line is a physical implementation, while DS1 defines the format of the signal transmitted on a T1 line.

| Figure 2.7 | A DS1 frame. |

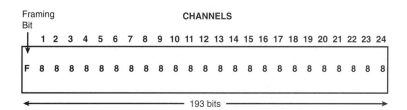

That one lonely framing bit in Figure 2.7 does not look like much overhead, but 8,000 of them are sent per second, which adds up to a respectable amount of throughput. Later, you will see that this overhead is put to work very effectively in modern telecommunications networks.

Note

It is not unusual for a word to be used in several very different ways in the world of communications technology, and this is true of the word "frame."

A DS1 frame is an example of a physical layer (layer 1) frame. It provides alignment for T1 channels.

In contrast, *data link frames* are layer 2 protocol data units used in data communications. Data is packaged in data link frames when it is transmitted onto a local area network (such as an Ethernet or Token Ring LAN) or across a wide area data link connection.

Packaging the DS1 Signal: DS4 and ESF

The original packaging that was defined for a DS1 signal was called a *D4 superframe*, and consisted of 12 consecutive frames. The 12 framing (F) bits in a D4 superframe contained the pattern

1 0 0 0 1 1 0 1 1 1 0 0

Telecommunications equipment locked onto this pattern to locate D4 superframes and maintained alignment.

An improved *extended superframe (ESF)* format was adopted later. An extended super-frame is made up of 24 consecutive frames. Its framing bits are used for three purposes:

- **Alignment**—Framing bits from six of the frames repeat the pattern 0 0 1 0 1 1. (This consumes 2Kbps.)

- **Error checking**—Framing bits from six of the frames contain a cyclic redundancy check (CRC) computed on the previous extended superframe. (This consumes 2Kbps.)

- **A messaging link**—Framing bits from 12 of the frames are used to form a messaging channel called a *facility data link*. (This consumes 4Kbps.)

Table 2.1 shows the layout of the extended superframe framing bits.

Table 2.1	Extended Superframe Framing Bits		
Frame Number	Framing Bits	CRC	Facility Data Link (m=messaging bit)
1			m
2		C1	
3			m
4	0		
5			m
6		C2	
7			m
8	0		
9			m
10		C3	
11			m
12	1		
13			m
14		C4	
15			m
16	0		
17			m
18		C5	
19			m
20	1		
21			m
22		C6	
23			m
24	1		

The CRC code enables receiving equipment to detect that bits have been corrupted during transmission. If this happens frequently, it is a sign that some diagnostic and repair work needs to be scheduled.

The introduction of the facility data link was a major step forward in network operations, administration, and maintenance (OAM). This link is used to report immediate errors, gather performance and error reports, and activate loopback tests.

Clear Versus Restricted Channels

The bits on a T1 line are represented by voltage pulses encoded using a method called *alternate mark inversion (AMI)*. For AMI, 0s are represented by 0 voltages, while 1s alternatively are represented by positive and negative voltages. Figure 2.8 illustrates the encoding scheme.

| Figure 2.8 | Code 0s and 1s with alternate mark inversion. |

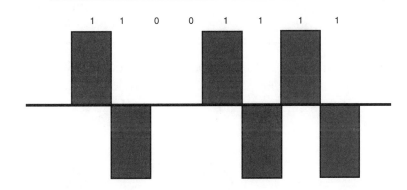

The trouble with this scheme is that when a device receives a long string of 0s, it loses bit time synchronization. The solution originally used to solve this problem was to convert some 0s to 1s, following a set of rules that required

- No more than 15 consecutive 0s.
- At least N 1s in every time window of $8 \times (N+1)$ bit time slots, where N can equal 1 through 23. (For example, if N=1, then there must be a 1 bit in every window of 16 bits.)

No harm is done by sprinkling an occasional 1 into a string of 0s in a voice call. However, it is not acceptable to change payload 0s to 1s on a leased line that is used for data communications. Network service providers solve this problem by restricting the user data payload to the first 7 bits of each time slot byte and coding a 1 in the last bit, as shown in Figure 2.9. This *restricted service* reduces the capacity of a 64Kbps channel to 56Kbps.

Figure 2.9   Restricted service on a data line.

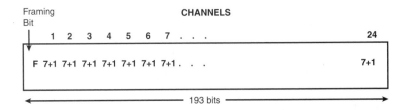

Up-to-date telecommunications equipment solves this problem by representing a bit pattern consisting of a 1 followed by eight consecutive 0s with one of the "illegal" voltage patterns shown in Figure 2.10.

If, as shown in the top half of the figure, the preceding 1 is represented by a positive voltage, then 00000000 is replaced by 000+-0-+. If, as shown in the bottom half of the figure, the preceding 1 is represented by a negative voltage, then 00000000 is replaced by 000-+0+-. These patterns do not occur in normal traffic because -0- and +0+ are not permitted.

This procedure is called *bipolar with 8-zero substitution (B8ZS)*. It enables a network provider to offer *clear channel service*. However, even today, it is not always possible to obtain clear channel service in all locations.

Figure 2.10   B8ZS representations of 100000000.

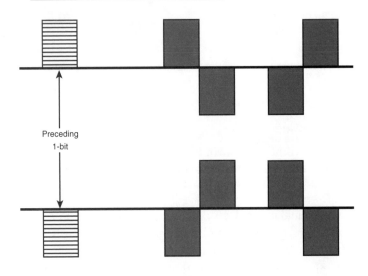

Digital Signal Hierarchies

DS1 multiplexes 24 channels together. The American National Standards Institute (ANSI) T1 committee defined formats for several higher level multiplexed signals. These form the North American Digital Hierarchy. The North American digital signal levels are listed in Table 2.2. Table 2.3 shows a similar hierarchy that is used in Japan. The *Conference of European Postal and Telecommunications (CEPT)* administrations defined the signal levels shown in Table 2.4.

The networks based on these three hierarchies are called *plesiochronous*. The nodes in a plesiochronous network are allowed to time their signals using separate clock sources with almost the same timing. Thus, timing at different nodes may vary by some limited amount.

Plesiochronous is not exactly a household word, and plesiochronous signals occasionally will be referred to as *legacy signals* in this book.

Note

Some of the signal levels correspond to bandwidth levels that are sold to subscribers, while others describe multiplexing arrangements that are used only by network provider equipment. For example, in the United States, a subscriber can order a T1 line that carries a DS1 signal or a T3 line that carries a DS3 signal. However, DS2 is a multiplexing pattern that occasionally is used within network equipment as an intermediate step when multiplexing DS1s into a DS3.

Table 2.2   The North American Digital Signal Hierarchy

Level	Number of Channels	Payload Bit Rate (Mbps)	Total Bit Rate with Overhead (Mbps)
DS0	1	.0064	0.0064
DS1	24	1.536	1.544
DS1C	48	3.072	3.152
DS2	96	6.144	6.312
DS3	672	43.008	44.736
DS4	4032	258.048	274.176

Table 2.3	The Japanese Digital Signal Hierarchy		
Level	Number of Channels	Payload Bit Rate (Mbps)	Total Bit Rate with Overhead (Mbps)
J0	1	.0064	0.0064
J1	24	1.536	1.544
J1C	48	3.072	3.152
J2	96	6.144	6.312
J3	480	30.720	32.064
J3C	1440	92.160	97.728
J4	5760	368.640	397.200

Table 2.4	The CEPT Digital Signal Hierarchy		
Level	Number of Channels	Payload Bit Rate (Mbps)	Total Bit Rate with Overhead (Mbps)
E0	1	.0064	0.0064
E1	30	1.920	2.048
E2	120	7.680	8.448
E3	480	30.720	34.368
E4	1920	122.880	139.264
E5	7680	491.520	565.148

Multiplexed Signal Bit Rates

A DS2 signal is made up of 4 DS1 signals. A DS3 signal is made up of 28 DS1s or 7 DS2s. As shown in Table 2.2, the DS2 payload rate is equal to 4 times the DS1 payload bit rate, but the total DS2 bit rate is almost 4.09 times the DS1 rate. Similarly, the DS3 payload is 28 times the DS1 payload, while the total DS3 rate is almost 29 times the DS1 rate. The extra bandwidth comes from two sources:

- Overhead bits are introduced to frame each multiplexed bundle and to support an alarm channel for the multiplexed signal.

- At a multiplexer, incoming bit times are not perfectly matched with outgoing bit times. Hence, a multiplexer needs some leeway in forming a combined signal. This is accomplished by two methods: storing a few early incoming bits in a memory buffer for a short time, and inserting "stuff" bits into a multiplexed signal when the incoming stream is too slow.

> **Note**
> The term *jitter* describes unwanted variations in a signal rate that cause bits to arrive a little too early or a little too late.

DS3 Frames

The basic unit of DS3 packaging is called an M-frame. Overhead bits are introduced into an M-frame to indicate the presence of stuffed bits and to support operations, administration, and maintenance channels.

Figure 2.11 shows the format of a DS3 M-frame. Each M-frame contains 4,760 bits, and is made up of seven 680-bit *M-subframes*.

Each M-subframe contains 8 overhead bits. This adds up to a total of 56 overhead bits in an M-frame. The M-frame overhead bits appear in the following order:

X1 F1 C1 F2 C2 F3 C3 F4

X2 F1 C1 F2 C2 F3 C3 F4

P1 F1 C1 F2 C2 F3 C3 F4

P2 F1 C1 F2 C2 F3 C3 F4

M1 F1 C1 F2 C2 F3 C3 F4

M2 F1 C1 F2 C2 F3 C3 F4

M3 F1 C1 F2 C2 F3 C3 F4

The M bits are used for M-frame alignment, and repeat the bit pattern 010. The F bits are used for M-subframe alignment, repeating the bit pattern 1001. The P1 and P2 bits, which are set to either 00 or 11, and provide a parity check on the previous M-frame. The X bits form an alarm channel. X1 and X2 are set to 1 to signal an alarm. The C bits either form an OAM channel, or are used to indicate whether stuffed bits are present.

Multiplexing Lower Level Signals into a DS3 Signal

Lower level signals can be multiplexed into the payload of a DS3 M-frame in a number of ways. For example, in Figure 2.12, the input to a multiplexer consists of 28 complete DS1 signals. Each consists of 1.544Mbps, and includes the T1 framing bits. These signals are being byte interleaved—along with some framing and OAM bits—into a DS3 signal at a multiplexer. This direct multiplexing scheme is called the *synchronous DS3 M13 multiplex format*.

Figure 2.11   Format of a DS3 M-subframe and M-frame.

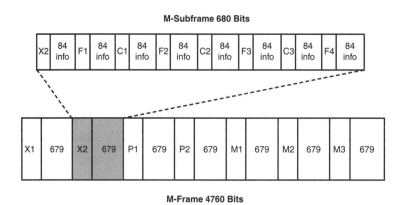

M-Subframe 680 Bits

| X2 | 84 info | F1 | 84 info | C1 | 84 info | F2 | 84 info | C2 | 84 info | F3 | 84 info | C3 | 84 info | F4 | 84 info |

| X1 | 679 | X2 | 679 | P1 | 679 | P2 | 679 | M1 | 679 | M2 | 679 | M3 | 679 |

M-Frame 4760 Bits

Figure 2.12   Multiplexing digital signals.

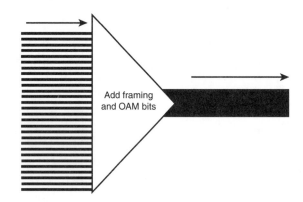

Add framing and OAM bits

An alternative way to pack DS1s into a DS3 is to bit-interleave groups of four T1s into DS2 signals, and then bit-interleave seven DS2 signals into a DS3 signal. This is called the *M23 multiplex format*.

Switching

Often a call must pass through several switches and traverse several T1 carriers. The complete bidirectional path used by a call forms a *circuit*. The pair of channels used for a call on a particular T1 is just a *segment* of a circuit.

In Figure 2.13, T1 carrier A between Switch 1 and Switch 2 is linked up to T1 carrier B between Switch 2 and Switch 3. The channels on carrier A match up exactly with the channels on carrier B.

However, calls on T1 carrier C between Switch 1 and Switch 2 are routed onto different T1 carriers at Switch 2. These channels are *cross connected*. Note that the time slots used for the circuits in the figure can change when channels are cross connected.

Figure 2.13   Switching.

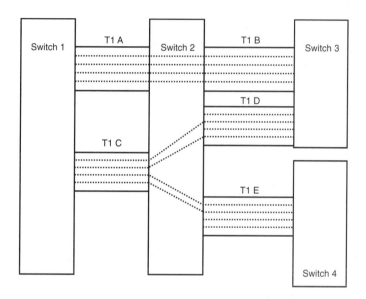

Signaling

Making telephone calls is such a routine process that we give little thought to what goes into setting up a call. Figure 2.14 illustrates the call setup steps that were followed until fairly recent times—and still are used in some places. To set up a call

- Signals are exchanged between a terminal and its adjacent central office switch.

- Signals are exchanged between switches.

- The switches reserve a circuit through the telephone network for the exclusive use of the telephone call.

The details of how this is done have changed over the years. Originally,

- The first switch would choose the second switch for the call path.

- The first switch would select and seize an unused circuit segment connecting to the second switch.

- The first switch would send signaling information to the second switch across that circuit segment.

- Successive switches repeated these steps.

Figure 2.14   Setting up a telephone call.

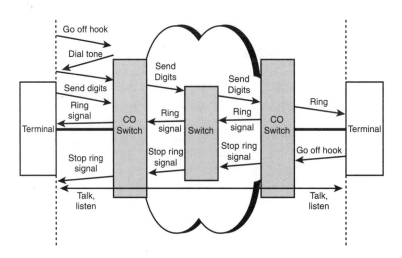

The circuit made up of these segments was used for the voice call—and for additional signaling (for example, to terminate the call). For this reason, every voice channel carried signaling as well as its voice payload.

This model continued to be followed after the T1 carrier system was implemented. Bit 8 in every sixth frame of a T1 channel was set aside for signaling. This was called *robbed bit signaling.*

Note

Robbed bit signaling is one way to perform *channel associated signaling*. Channel associated signals are transmitted either within the channel used for the call, or on a separate channel permanently associated with it.

North American telecommunications administrations chose the first option, while European telecommunications administrations selected the second. In Europe, an E1 carrier contains a separate signaling channel used to set up calls across the E1's 30 working channels.

Table 2.5 shows the signaling robbed bits within the old 12-frame superframe format. The robbed bits can be used to form a single 1,333 bits per second (bps) signaling channel (designated A) or two 667bps signaling channels (designated A and B).

Table 2.6 shows the signaling bits for the extended superframe format. Robbed bits can form one 1,333bps signaling channel (designated A), two 667bps signaling channels (designated A and B), or four 333bps signaling channels (designated A, B, C, and D).

Table 2.5 Signaling Bits for the Superframe Format

Frame Number	Payload Bits	Signaling Bit	One Signaling Channel	Two Signaling Channels
1	1-8			
2	1-8			
3	1-8			
4	1-8			
5	1-8			
6	1-7	8	A	A
7	1-8			
8	1-8			
9	1-8			
10	1-8			
11	1-8			
12	7	8	A	B

Table 2.6 Signaling Bits for the Extended Superframe Format

Frame Number	Payload Bits	Signaling Bit	One Signaling Channel	Two Signaling Channels	Four Signaling Channels
1	1-8				
2	1-8				
3	1-8				
4	1-8				
5	1-8				
6	1-7	8	A	A	A
7	1-8				
8	1-8				
9	1-8				

continues

Table 2.6	Continued				
Frame Number	Payload Bits	Signaling Bit	One Signaling Channel	Two Signaling Channels	Four Signaling Channels
10	1-8				
11	1-8				
12	7	8	A	B	B
13	1-8				
14	1-8				
15	1-8				
16	1-8				
17	1-8				
18	1-7	8	A	A	C
19	1-8				
20	1-8				
21	1-8				
22	1-8				
23	1-8				
24	7	8	A	B	D

Moving to Message-Based Common Channel Signaling

There are flaws in channel associated signaling:

- It is slow and it wastes bandwidth during call setup. A series of circuit segments must be reserved during the call setup procedure. These segments are unusable during the period that call setup is attempted, even if it turns out that the path cannot be completed.

- Robbed bits may be used by the network at any time. Hence, to provide an end-to-end switched service (switched 56Kbps), data payload is restricted to the first 7 bits of each byte.

- It is limited and inflexible and cannot be used as the basis of new services.

Common channel signaling, which moves signaling onto dedicated network links, was introduced in the 1970s. The initial common channel signaling system used in North America was based on an international standard, Signaling System 6 (SS6), but did not interwork with the SS6 implementations of carriers in other regions.

The move to a faster and far more powerful switching system, *Signaling System 7 (SS7)*, got underway in the 1980s. SS7 improves on the speed and functionality of SS6 network signaling. The North American implementation interworks across national boundaries. SS7 has an another important capability: support for ISDN.

Chapter I-3 outlines the capabilities of Signaling System 7 and explains how ISDN enables voice and data terminals to set up switched digital calls.

Digital Lines and Data Communications

56/64Kbps circuits and T1 and T3 carriers were created for internal use within the telephone network. However, telecommunications carriers eventually offered direct access to these digital facilities to business subscribers.

It is common today for organizations to use leased T1 carriers to transport voice, data, or both. Several T1 channels—or all 24 channels—can be combined into a single data pipeline.

An organization that does not need a full T1 can contract for a fractional part of the bandwidth. Typical bandwidth levels that are offered include 128, 256, 364, and 512Kbps.

If more bandwidth is needed, then a T3 or fractional T3 can be leased.

CSU/DSU Interface Equipment

A computer connects to an analog local loop via a modem, which converts digital symbols to analog form. A computer (or router) connects to a 56/64Kbps or T1 digital line via a device called a *channel service unit/data service unit* (*CSU/DSU*). Figure 2.15 shows a computer connected to a leased line via a CSU/DSU. The CSU/DSU

- Terminates the line from the telecommunications network. A 2- or 4-wire line is used for 56/64Kbps service. A 4-wire line is used for T1 service.

- Places signals on the line and controls the strength of the transmission signal.

- Supports loopback tests.

- Provides timing or synchronizes with timing received on the line.

- Frames the signal for T1.

- Optionally applies an algorithm that *scrambles* a signal. A signal is scrambled to improve the density of 0s and 1s.

A special DSU device is used to connect to a T3 line. T3 is implemented across coaxial cable.

Figure 2.15   Interfacing to a digital line via a CSU/DSU.

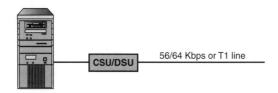

References

The North American digital hierarchy is described in the ANSI T1 series of documents. Some of the documents of interest include

- T1.107, *Digital Hierarchy—Formats Specifications* (1995)

- T1.102-1993, *Digital Hierarchy—Electrical Interfaces* (1993)

The European digital hierarchy is described in ITU-T G series documents. For example:

- G.702: *Digital hierarchy bit rates* (1988)

- G.703: *Physical/electrical characteristics of hierarchical digital interfaces* (1998)

- G.704: *Synchronous frame structures used at 1544, 6312, 2048, 8448 and 44 736 kbit/s hierarchical levels* (1998)

- G.706: *Frame alignment and cyclic redundancy check (CRC) procedures relating to basic frame structures defined in Recommendation G.704* (1991)

- G.707: *Network node interface for the synchronous digital hierarchy (SDH)* (1996)

CHAPTER 3

ISDN

When the original telephone networks were built, the focus was on analog voice, and telephone switching was done manually for each call by human operators. Gradually, switching became automated and the backbone of the network was migrated to a digital implementation. Many new business and residential services were added, and to accommodate them, the network architecture was altered in a piecemeal manner.

By the 1980s, the telecommunications network structure clearly needed an overhaul. The ITU-T (then called CCITT) spent several years developing the blueprint for an all-digital *Integrated Services Digital Network (ISDN)*. An upgraded network signaling system—signaling system 7 (SS7)—was designed as part of this process.

ISDN provides a component that was missing from traditional telecommunications networks: The ability to set up and terminate calls that can be used for either voice or data on an ad hoc basis.

There are two different forms of ISDN:

- Basic rate

- Primary rate

Basic rate ISDN extends digital transmission across a local loop to a residential or small business subscriber:

- An ISDN telephone digitizes voice at its source.

- A computer communicates across an ISDN line without the need for a modem that transforms its digital output to an analog representation.

The local loop is converted into a digital line that can be shared across several devices and supports two concurrent calls. Either call can be voice or data. Furthermore, with the right equipment, the two call circuits can be combined into a 128Kbps data circuit that can support a small data network, provide a telecommuter with excellent response time, or make Internet browsing a more satisfying experience.

Primary rate ISDN enables a larger business to use its bandwidth for voice or data on an as-needed basis:

- Circuits that are needed for voice communications during daytime peak hours can be shifted over to data transfer, browsing, or video conferencing applications at off-peak hours.

- Bulk data transfers can be scheduled for nighttime hours, when the telephones are silent.

Many businesses use ISDN for extra bandwidth on demand or for backup when conventional leased lines fail. The ability to dial up digital connections enables business-critical networked applications to proceed without interruption.

ISDN was designed to be a vehicle that enables telecommunications providers to offer additional services. For example, many telephone features that are useful to businesses have been implemented.

It also was anticipated that X.25 and frame relay packet data services would integrate with ISDN service. Thus, when setting up a call, a user could request voice, a digital data circuit, an X.25 packet service, or a frame relay packet service. This has happened to a lesser degree.

Note

ISDN is now sometimes called *narrowband ISDN* or *N-ISDN*. N-ISDN was an evolutionary upgrade to the telecommunications infrastructure.

In contrast, *broadband ISDN (B-ISDN)* is a revolutionary change in the structure of the world's telecommunication networks. This change is being implemented today. B-ISDN is based on a technology called *Asynchronous Transfer Mode (ATM)*. B-ISDN and ATM are discussed in Part III, "ATM," of this book.

ISDN Standards Groups

The ITU-T is the primary ISDN standards group. The ITU-T published its first set of ISDN specifications in 1984. Numerous additions and updates have been published since then.

ISDN standards define a broad array of services and features, and new ones are being added all the time. The standards are very complex. This hampers interworking and makes product configuration a difficult task. Three North American organizations were formed to simplify ISDN and guide future enhancements.

- **The National ISDN Council**—A forum of telecommunications service providers and switch suppliers coordinated by Bellcore. The council defined National ISDN (NI) standards that have been well accepted by product vendors.

- **The North American ISDN Users' Forum (NIUF)**—Founded in part by the U.S. National Institute of Standards and Technology (NIST), which continues to act as coordinator for that organization. Forum user and manufacturer members work together to make sure that ISDN applications and options meet user needs.

- **The Vendor's ISDN Association (VIA)**—A group dedicated to accelerating the deployment of ISDN products, services, and usage. To do this, it tries to find ways to bring ISDN closer to being a plug-and-play technology.

ISDN Signaling

ISDN service enables a residential or business ISDN subscriber to choose whether a circuit will be used for voice or data and to select special call features on a call-by-call basis.

To support these capabilities, signaling messages exchanged between the subscriber and the network are placed on a channel that is separate from the channels used for voice or data transmission. This signaling exchange is called user-network signaling, to distinguish it from the SS7 signaling used within the network. SS7 also is message-based.

User-network signaling between a subscriber device and a network switch is described in *Digital Signalling System 1 (DSS1)* standards. DSS1 interworks with the network's SS7 signaling to set up and terminate calls and to provide a number of other features and supplementary services. Figure 3.1 shows the scope of the DSS1 signaling standard.

Between them, DSS1 and SS7 set up calls very quickly—less than a second for voice calls, and usually within one or two seconds for data. Users accustomed to long dial-up delays when they use analog modems appreciate the quick connection setups they obtain after converting to ISDN.

Message-based signaling systems open the way to adding just about any new feature or service that a telecommunications provider can think up and implement—and that subscribers are willing to buy.

Figure 3.1   Scope of DSS1 signaling.

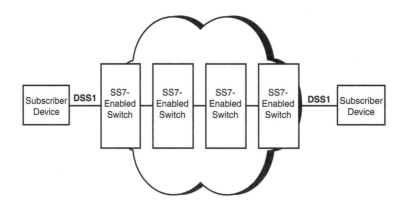

ISDN Interfaces

ISDN service is aimed at both residential or small office/home office (SOHO) users and larger business users. A separate user-network interface is defined for each target:

- **Basic rate interface (BRI)**—Connects a subscriber to the network across an ordinary local loop.

- **Primary rate interface (PRI)**—Operates across a leased T1 carrier connecting a subscriber to the network.

The Basic Rate Interface

The basic rate interface supports three digital channels across the local loop. As shown in Figure 3.2, there are two digital 64Kbps bearer (B) channels that actually carry calls, and a 16Kbps data (D) channel that carries signaling messages, and also can be used for general data applications.

The T1 channels discussed in Chapter I-2 carried information in only one direction. Two channels were required to form a bidirectional circuit segment.

The term "channel" is used differently in the ISDN world. ISDN B-channels and D-channels are bidirectional.

Figure 3.2   Basic rate interface channels.

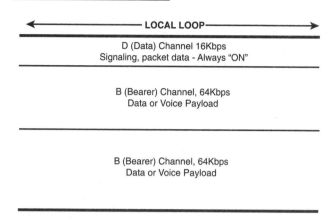

Note

Full-duplex (bidirectional) transmission is supported using a method called *echo cancellation*. If both sides send concurrently, each end of the transmission subtracts its own signal from the combined signal.

The D-channel always is active and ready for use. When a customer premise device wants to set up a call, it sends a message to the network switch at the other end of the D-channel.

BRI Physical Configuration

ISDN is not for everyone. Ideally, an ISDN subscriber should be within 18,000 feet (about 3.4 miles) of a central office switch that supports ISDN.

Many copper local loops are not of a quality that can support ISDN. A telephone company may refuse service, or may have to delay installation until it can send out maintenance staff to resolve line problems.

A local exchange carrier that is eager to market ISDN can make it accessible to more users by maintaining the local loops, installing repeaters so that far-away subscribers can access the service, and setting up T1 lines that carry ISDN channels from central office switches that do not support ISDN to switches that do support it.

Note

The presence of loading coils or bridged taps may make it impossible to run ISDN over the local loop.

A *loading coil* reduces signal attenuation by cutting off high frequencies. However, these frequencies are needed for ISDN transmission.

A *bridged tap* is a section of cable that is not on the direct electrical path from the user's premise and the central office. It may be the remnant of an old connection. A bridged tap degrades transmission.

If you are a telecommuter and qualify for service, ISDN offers some attractive features. A typical home office includes a telephone, fax machine, and one or more computers. With ISDN, any of these devices can set up or receive calls intermittently throughout the day. ISDN is designed so that up to eight devices can share the channels that are provided by an ISDN basic rate interface.

Figure 3.3 shows four devices—two digital telephones and two computers that have ISDN network cards—sharing a basic rate interface. These bona fide ISDN systems are called *terminal equipment 1 (TE1)* devices. (They also are called, more informally, *ISDN stations* or *ISDN systems.*)

A *network termination type 1 (NT1)* device provides the physical interface between a four-wire (two twisted pair) local network that connects to the devices and the two-wire local loop. An NT1 needs a power supply. This means that unlike plain old telephone service (POTS) telephones, ISDN telephones will be dead if power is lost!

In Europe, the NT1 device belongs to and is provided by the telephone company. In the United States, the subscriber has to buy the NT1.

Some ISDN devices have a built-in NT1. This eliminates sharing and restricts ISDN access to that one device. However, this is not a problem for the configuration in Figure 3.4. A small LAN is connected to an ISDN basic rate interface line by a router that has a built-in NT1.

separate NT1 that gives you a U interface. Knowing the alphabet can prevent hassles and may even save you some money.

Supplemental Services

Setting up calls via messages exchanged across a D-channel enables a user to ask for a lot more than just "voice" or "data." ITU-T committees put a lot of work into defining a large set of *supplemental services*. Supplemental services include such capabilities as call forwarding, call waiting, call hold, call retrieve, call transfer, call drop, call rollover, and conference calls.

A user often invokes these services by pushing special combinations of keys on an ISDN telephone. These keyed commands are translated to messages that are sent on the D-channel.

Ordering Basic Rate Service

The early years of ISDN were difficult for basic rate subscribers, especially in North America. Switch implementations differed, and often subscriber equipment could interface to only one type of telephone switch. Eventually, customer premise equipment vendors built the ability to work with several switches into their products, but the product configuration process still differed greatly depending on the type of central office switch that was at the other end of the ISDN line.

The very richness of ISDN features was—and still is—a barrier to quick and easy installation. A subscriber has to select a set of functions and features from a broad range of offerings. After the selection is complete, the functions and features for the subscriber's line must be entered into a *service profile* at the adjacent central office. Service providers call ISDN line settings *translations*.

Data entry errors are common and can cause the service to fail. Often, the customer has to perform the troubleshooting needed to resolve problems.

A subscriber may be able to choose a different feature set for each terminal. In this case, the network provider must create a separate service profile for each subscriber terminal— creating an even greater opportunity for error.

National ISDN Standards

Bellcore and the National ISDN Council developed the National ISDN 1 (NI-1) standards to solve these problems. A second generation of the standards (NI-2) also has been published. Switch products that support the NI standards interwork with any NI-capable customer terminal.

National ISDN Capability Packages

The NI standards define a set of *capability packages* (also known as generic *ISDN order codes* or *IOCs*) that are aimed at simplifying the BRI order process. Each capability package supports a different set of features. Special capabilities that go beyond simple voice or data call support include:

- **Call transfer**—Enables a user to transfer a call to a third party by depressing a button.

- **Call hold**—Allows a user to place a call on hold by depressing a button.

- **Call drop**—Allows a user to drop the last party added to a conference call or disconnect a two-party call by depressing a drop button.

- **Three way conference calling**—Enables a user to sequentially contact two parties and add them together to make a three-way call.

- **Calling number identification (CNI)**—For a voice call, the calling number is displayed on a screen. For a data call, the calling number is made available to a computer program. The service can be enhanced with *redirecting number delivery*, which delivers the incoming call to a different location based on the calling number.

- **Call forwarding variable**—The user can forward all calls made to a line's primary directory number to another number by pressing a call forwarding-variable feature button. The user activates or deactivates the forwarding function via an access code or a feature button. (Note that an ISDN line may be given more than one directory number. One number is identified as primary.)

- **Flexible calling**—Includes three-way conference calling, call drop, call hold, and call transfer.

- **Call appearance call handling electronic key telephone service (CACH EKTS)**—Supports more than one directory number and allows multiple call *appearances* on each directory number. An extra appearance allows you to put a call on hold while you continue an active call.

- **Additional call offering**—Provides two additional appearances of the primary directory number for making or receiving voice calls. That is, one call can be active and two calls can be on hold.

Table 3.1 describes the National ISDN capability packages. Note that package M fits the needs of many home subscribers.

Although packages A-V in Table 3.1 may appear to contain every imaginable combination of services, the North American ISDN Users' Forum has created additional packages (W, X, AB, AC, and EZ-ISDN 1, 1A, 2, 2A, 3, and 3A) that add features to NI packages.

Table 3.1   National ISDN Capability Packages

Capability Package	Description
A	Basic D-channel packet services. (No B-channels.)
B	Circuit switched data on one B-channel.
C	Alternate voice/circuit switched data on one B-channel. Basic voice only—no extra voice features are provided.
D	Basic D-channel packet services. Voice on one B-channel—no extra voice capabilities.
E	Basic D-channel packet services. Voice on one B-channel. Voice capabilities include three-way (conference) calling, call hold, call drop, and call transfer.
F	Basic D-channel packet services. Voice on one B-channel. Voice capabilities include three-way (conference) calling, call hold, call drop, and call transfer, and support for the CACH EKTS multiple call appearance service.
G	Voice on one B-channel and circuit switched data on the other B-channel. Voice capabilities include three-way (conference) calling, call hold, call drop, and call transfer.
H	Voice on one B-channel and circuit switched data on the other B channel. Voice capabilities include three-way (conference) calling, call hold, call drop, and call transfer, and support for CACH EKTS.
I	Circuit switched data on both B-channels. No Voice or packet capabilities are provided.
J	Alternate voice/circuit switched data on one B-channel, and circuit switched data on the other B-channel. Only basic voice—no extra features are provided.
K	Alternate voice/circuit switched data on one B-channel, and circuit switched data on the other B-channel. Voice capabilities include three-way (conference) calling, call hold, call drop, and call transfer.
L	Alternate voice/circuit switched data on one B-channel, and circuit switched data on the other B-channel. Voice capabilities include three-way (conference) calling, call hold, call drop, and call transfer, and support for CACH EKTS.
M	Alternate voice/circuit switched data on both B-channels. Only basic voice (no extra features) is provided.
N	Alternate voice/circuit switched data on one B-channel, circuit switched data on the other B-channel, and D-channel packet service. Voice capabilities include three-way (conference) calling, call hold, call drop, and call transfer.

continues

Table 3.1   Continued

Capability Package	Description
O	Alternate voice/circuit switched data on one B-channel, circuit switched data on the other B-channel, and D-channel packet data. Voice capabilities include three-way (conference) calling, call hold, call drop, and call transfer, and CACH EKTS.
P	Alternate voice/circuit switched data on both B-channels, and D-channel packet. Voice capabilities include three-way (conference) calling, call hold, call drop, and call transfer.
Q	Alternate voice/circuit switched data on both B-channels, and D-channel packet. Voice capabilities include three-way (conference) calling, call hold, call drop, and call transfer, and CACH EKTS.
R	Circuit switched data on two B-channels. Data capabilities include calling number identification. No voice is provided.
S	Alternate voice/circuit switched data on two B-channels. Data and voice capabilities include calling number identification.
T	Voice on two B-channels and basic D-channel packet data. Only basic voice capabilities are provided, with no extra features.
U	Alternate voice/circuit switched data on both B-channels. Voice capabilities include non-EKTS voice features including flexible calling, call forwarding variable, additional call offering, and calling number identification (which includes redirecting number delivery). Data capabilities include calling number identification (which includes redirecting number delivery).
V	Alternate voice/circuit switched data on two B-channels. Voice capabilities include non-EKTS voice features including flexible calling, advanced call forwarding (that is, call forwarding variable, call forwarding interface busy, call forwarding don't answer, and message waiting indicator), additional call offering, and calling number identification (which includes redirecting number delivery). Data capabilities include calling number identification (which includes redirecting number delivery).

SPIDs

A terminal must identify itself to its adjacent central office switch so the switch can activate the correct service profile. To do this, the terminal sends a *service profile identifier (SPID)* to the switch when it initializes.

In some cases, as long as all terminals use the same features, only one SPID is needed per telephone line. But sometimes a provider assigns a different SPID to each B-channel.

For much existing equipment, a customer must enter the SPIDs into the premise equipment. A SPID looks like a telephone number with some extra digits added.

Unfortunately, in the early years of ISDN deployment, each switch vendor designed a slightly different SPID format. This added extra confusion to an already difficult setup process. SPIDs caused (and still cause) endless trouble. A SPID may be entered incorrectly at the switch or at the customer's device. Sometimes the customer is given only a telephone number, and has to find out what kind of switch is in use in order to append the extra digits correctly.

National ISDN Generic SPID Format

One of the first chores performed by the National ISDN Council was to define a generic SPID format. As shown in Figure 3.6, the generic SPID is 14 digits long and consists of a

- **Directory number** (DN, 10 digits)—A telephone number, starting with the three-digit area code, assigned to the ISDN line.

- **Sharing terminal identifier** (2 digits)—A value that can range from 01 to 32. Terminals that are contracted to have the same capabilities are given the same directory number and the same two-digit sharing terminal identifier. Their configuration data is stored in a shared *terminal service profile (TSP)*.

- **Terminal identifier** (TID, 2 digits)—Used to distinguish between terminals that have the same directory number and sharing terminal identifier. A terminal that does not share a terminal service profile with any other terminal always is given the "01" TID value. TID values (01 to 08) are assigned in sequential order.

Figure 3.6   Generic SPID format.

Directory Number (Telephone Number) 10 Digits	Sharing Terminal Identifier 2 Digits	Terminal Identifier 2 Digits

For the second generation of National ISDN standards, NI-2, a SPID is a free-formatted numeric string whose length may range from 3 to 20 characters. However, vendors can continue to use the generic SPID format if they wish.

Simplifying the Configuration Process

The main goal of the Vendors' ISDN Association is the simplification and automation of ISDN customer premise equipment configuration, operation, and management. This group has backed some successful technologies. For example:

- **AutoSPID** automates the terminal initialization process. When a device connects for the first time, the central office switch sends down one or more SPIDs. If there is only one service profile for the interface, the terminal can use the unique SPID. If there are several service profiles, user interaction is needed to select the correct one. The terminal then stores the SPID in non-volatile memory. On subsequent initializations, the terminal identifies itself by sending its SPID to the switch.

- **Non-initializing terminals** (NIT) do not require SPIDs. There is a single service profile for the interface.

- **Switch identification** enables a customer device to automatically learn the switch type, switch manufacturer, and the National ISDN protocol version supported by the switch.

The Primary Rate Interface

Physically, a primary rate interface operates across a leased T1, J1, or E1 line.

For countries that use a T1 or J1 carrier, the primary rate interface supports 24 bidirectional ISDN channels. As shown in Figure 3.7, there are 23 64Kbps bearer (B) channels that actually carry calls, along with one 64Kbps data (D) channel that carries signaling messages and can be used for general data applications.

Typically, a primary rate interface connects a digital PBX switch, a remote access router, or a computer to a central office.

Note

A site with up to 20 separate primary rate lines can use a single D-channel to set up calls for all the lines. Each line after the first carries 24 B-channels.

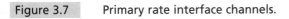

Figure 3.7   Primary rate interface channels.

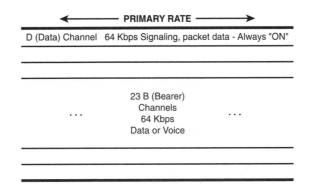

In Europe, a primary rate interface runs on an E1 carrier and carries 31 bidirectional 64Kbps channels. Of these, 30 are bearer (B) channels and one is a data (D) channel used for signaling and other applications.

PRI Physical Configuration

For many years, every vendor that built digital PBX switches for businesses implemented proprietary digital telephone interfaces, ensuring that customers would have to buy all of their telephones from the PBX vendor. ISDN can provide a standard interface between digital telephones and a PBX, as well as between the PBX and the network.

Figure 3.8 shows ISDN and non-ISDN devices connected to an ISDN PBX switch. The PBX is connected to the network switch via a primary rate interface. A subscriber device that connects to a PRI line is called *network termination type 2 (NT2)* equipment. In addition to a PBX, a remote access router, host, multiplexer, or other communications device also can assume the NT2 role for a primary rate interface.

In Figure 3.8, the PBX connects to a T1 carrier via a CSU/DSU that performs the NT1 line terminating role.

Primary Rate Reference Points

Figure 3.9 shows the reference points for a PRI interface. Note that instead of the combined S/T interface shown in Figure 3.5, there is an S interface between the ISDN devices and the NT2 (PBX) device, and a separate T interface between the NT2 and the CSU/DSU that acts as an NT1.

Figure 3.8   Primary rate interface configuration.

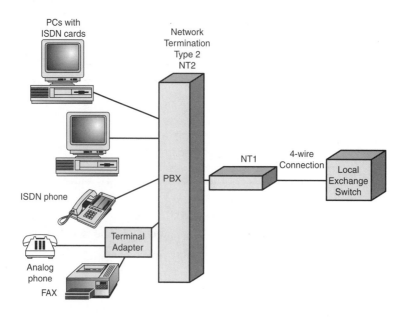

Figure 3.9   PRI reference points.

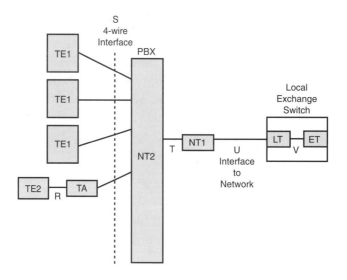

Combining Channels

Several B-channels can be combined into a higher bandwidth channel. This is done for a call used for a videoconference or some other high bandwidth application.

H-Channels

The ITU-T has defined several standardized high-level channels (H-channels). An additional H-channel level was added by ANSI. These are listed in Table 3.2. Using H-channel levels may be superfluous, because a general multirate Nx64Kbps service that allows a subscriber to request data bandwidth in any available multiple of 64Kbps instead of at a few prescribed levels has been defined.

Table 3.2   H-Channels

Channel Name	Equivalent Number of B Channels	Bandwidth Mbps
H0	6	0.384
H10 (ANSI)	23	1.472
H11	24	1.536
H12 (E1 only)	30	1.920

Inverse Multiplexers

Not all telecommunications providers support H-channels or Nx64K multirate channels. There also is the possibility that some providers that do support these services might charge a hefty premium price for using these channels. In either case, a user can obtain aggregated bandwidth by using devices called *inverse multiplexers*.

While multiplexers combine several channels into a single high-bandwidth channel, inverse multiplexers enable several low-speed channels to be given the appearance of a single high-bandwidth channel. To do this, a pair of inverse multiplexers have to coordinate their actions to deliver data in the same order in which it was sent.

Figure 3.10 illustrates inverse multiplexing. The multiplexer may be a separate device, or might be implemented by a communications card installed in a router, PBX, or computer. An inverse multiplexer may combine multiple ISDN channels that traverse a single line, or may combine transmissions that are carried across several separate lines.

Note

Videoconferencing, H-channels, and Nx64Kbps channels have a performance advantage over inverse multiplexed channels. The telecommunications provider will route an H-channel or Nx64 channel across its network as a single unit. In contrast, the individual inverse multiplexed channels may follow different paths. Some may even cross a satellite link, causing big variations in transmission delay.

Figure 3.10   Inverse multiplexing.

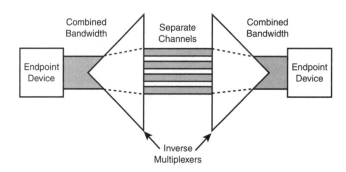

Until recently, there were no standards for inverse multiplexing. Vendors built proprietary products, and the only way to be sure that a pair of inverse multiplexers could work together was to buy compatible models from the same vendor. However, two inverse multiplexing standards recently have been proposed.

BONDING

The first solution is called *BONDING*, which stands for *Bandwidth ON Demand INteroperability Group*. BONDING is a solution designed for digital dialup environment. It enables communicating devices to turn multiple digital calls into a single, high-band-width communications link.

BONDING has some drawbacks. A subscriber must invest in conforming inverse multiplexer devices or add special interface cards to endpoint devices. Once a bandwidth level has been selected for a connection, it cannot be changed during the lifetime of a connection. All of the channels must be maintained.

But for some customers, this is exactly what they want. BONDING can provide constant bandwidth that is needed for a videoconference. It is a simple hardware-based solution.

A BONDING inverse multiplexer is configured with the telephone number of an inverse multiplexer at a remote site. When a call is made to the remote device, it sends back a list of other numbers that can be called. The originating multiplexer calls as many numbers as are needed.

The circuits that are set up may have different bandwidths and different delay characteristics. The partners then perform a *training* procedure that discovers the channel delays and establishes the order of transmission.

PPP Multilink Protocol

A different approach was taken by an Internet Engineering Task Force (IETF) committee, which designed a flexible software implementation of inverse multiplexing. The IETF design is suitable for *point-to-point protocol (PPP)* based data transmissions. PPP is a wide-area data link protocol that is familiar to many people because one of its uses is Internet dial-up access.

The IETF solution consists of a set of extensions to PPP, including the

- PPP multilink protocol (MP)

- Bandwidth allocation protocol (BAP)

- Bandwidth allocation control protocol (BACP)

Together, these protocols enable resources to be added and dropped as they are needed, which makes this a very cost-effective bandwidth management method.

The IETF protocols have several advantages. They are free, and can be implemented via a software upgrade to a computer or router. They can be used across any kind of wide-area line, and can combine different types of wide-area connections. For example, ISDN channels could be combined with one or more analog dialups, or an overloaded frame relay circuit could be enhanced with ISDN channels.

On the negative side, this solution is fairly complicated to configure and troubleshoot.

LAPD

Signaling between an ISDN terminal element or PBX and a network switch is carried out across reliable data links that are set up on the D-channel. A data link protocol called *link access procedure on the D-channel (LAPD)* is used to carry ISDN signaling messages.

Carrying signaling messages is just one of the LAPD applications. Additional LAPD links can be set up and used for data transfer.

The LAPD Protocol

LAPD belongs to the *High-level Data Link Control (HDLC)* family of protocols. One or more HDLC *flag* bytes separate each pair of transmitted LAPD frames, as is shown in Figure 3.11. Contiguous flags are sent out by an interface during idle times, when there are no LAPD frames awaiting transmission. The flag pattern, 01111110, was defined in the HDLC protocol standard.

Figure 3.11   LAPD frames separated by flags.

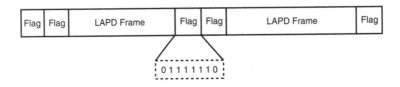

A frame's data may contain a bit-pattern that is identical to the flag bit pattern. A transmitter prevents confusion between data bits and flag bits by means of a procedure called *bit-stuffing*. The transmitting interface alters the data bits in a frame before sending them onto the medium. The sender inserts a 0 after any sequence of five contiguous 1s in the frame. The receiving communications interface restores the frame to its original state by removing a 0 that follows five 1s.

For example:

Original	0 0 1 1 1 1 1 1 1 0 1 1
Transformed	0 0 1 1 1 1 1 0 1 1 0 1 1
Restored by Receiver	0 0 1 1 1 1 1 1 1 0 1 1

There are three types of HDLC/LAPD frames:

- **Information frames**—Used to carry the ISDN signaling messages (or other data)

- **Supervisory frames**—Used for acknowledgments and flow control, and to report an out-of-sequence frame

- **Unnumbered frames**—Used to initiate and terminate a LAPD link, to negotiate parameters, and to report errors

For convenient reference, the HDLC/LAPD frame types are summarized in Table 3.3.

> **Note**
>
> The same frame types are used for the LAPB link protocol used with conventional X.25 service. For more details about the protocol behavior associated with various frame types, see Chapter II-2, which contains a detailed discussion of LAPB.

Table 3.3   HDLC/LAPD Frame Types

Type	Name	Description
Unnumbered	SABME	Set asynchronous balanced mode extended. Initiates a link.
	UA	Unnumbered acknowledgment of link setup or termination.
	DISC	Disconnect. Terminates a link.
	DM	Disconnected mode. Refuses a SABM or SABME, or just announces a disconnected state.
	FRMR	Frame reject. Announces a non-recoverable error. The link must be reset (reinitialized).
	XID	Exchange identification. Used to negotiate parameters when a link is established.
Information	I	Carries information.
Supervisory	RR	Receive ready. Indicates ready state and acknowledges data.
	RNR	Receive not ready. Indicates busy state and acknowledges data.
	REJ	Reject. Indicates that one or more frames need to be retransmitted.

LAPD Frame Format

The general format of LAPD frames follows the pattern that was established by HDLC. As shown in Figure 3.12, each type of frame has an address field, a control field, and a frame check sequence field that is used to determine whether data has been corrupted in transit.

Control field formats conform to standard HDLC conventions. All control fields identify the frame type. The control field in an information frame also carries a *send sequence number* for the frame and the *receive sequence number* that identifies the next information frame expected from the partner. Sequence numbers range from 0 to 127 and then wrap around—that is, modulo 128 numbering is used.

The control field in a supervisory frame contains a receive sequence number. Hence, supervisory frames can be used to acknowledge received data.

Figure 3.12   Format of HDLC/LAPD frames.

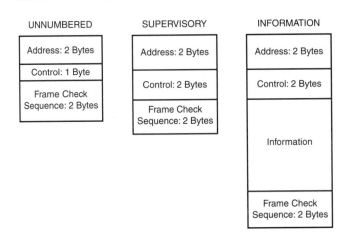

LAPD Address Field

Any BRI station on a bus that connects to an NT1 has access to the D-channel. However, the ISDN physical layer bus protocol allows only one station to send a frame at any given time, and ensures that each station gets fair access to the D-channel.

Each station can set up one or more LAPD data links across the D-channel. Frames for the various data links are interleaved. Figure 3.13 illustrates how frames for several separate LAPD links share the bidirectional D-channel.

Figure 3.13   LAPD links on a D-channel.

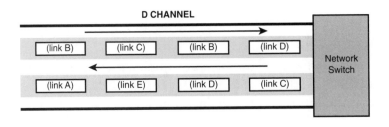

The LAPD address field is used to sort out these links. Each link corresponds to one application within one subscriber station. The LAPD address field contains a data link identifier consisting of a:

- **Terminal endpoint identifier (TEI)**—Identifies the subscriber terminal that is using the link.

- **Service access point identifier (SAPI)**—Identifies the terminal process that is using the link.

Each subscriber station that has access to a D-channel must be assigned a unique terminal endpoint identifier.

Note

Sometimes it is convenient for a subscriber system to have more than one TEI. From the point of view of the network switch, the system will appear to be two separate stations.

TEI assignment can be done automatically by the network switch when the system starts up its ISDN interface. However, some products cannot perform the automated procedure, and the TEI has to be entered manually.

The TEI occupies seven address bits, and hence corresponds to a decimal number in the range 0–127. Table 3.4 shows how these numbers are used.

Table 3.4	TEI Values
TEI	**Description**
0–63	Available for manually entered addresses
64–126	Available for automatic assignment
127	Broadcast address. Used during the automatic TEI assignment procedure

The SAPI occupies six bits, and hence corresponds to a decimal number in the range 0–63. SAPI 0 is used for the signaling link. Some of the remaining numbers have been assigned to specific uses. For example, SAPI 63 is used for the automatic TEI assignment procedure and SAPI 16 is used for a LAPD link that carries X.25 packets.

> **Note**
>
> Because LAPD is very similar to the X.25 LAPB link protocol, there was no difficulty in adapting the X.25 packet service to run on top of LAPD instead of LAPB.
>
> X.25 service across the always-available D-channel has proved to be a very useful service for applications such as credit card verification and bank automatic teller machine transactions.

Always On/Dynamic ISDN

Always On/Dynamic ISDN (AO/DI) is an innovative service that is attractive to telecommuters and Internet surfers—and to ISDN service providers. AO/DI enables a user to remain continuously connected to a remote network around the clock, and to transparently obtain ISDN bandwidth when it is needed.

Figure 3.14 illustrates how it works. The D-channel connection to a neighboring central office switch always is active. Every ISDN switch has a built-in packet handler that supports the LAPD protocol. The user can open a low-speed (9.6Kbps) X.25 data channel to the remote network. This channel provides enough bandwidth for background retrieval of email and low-level interactive applications.

When the user downloads a file or accesses a Web page, one or two B-channels will be activated to increase the bandwidth by 64 or 128Kbps. The inverse multiplexing capabilities of the PPP multilink protocol along with the bandwidth allocation protocol and bandwidth allocation control protocol are used to do this.

Figure 3.14   Using packet and switched services to support AO/DI.

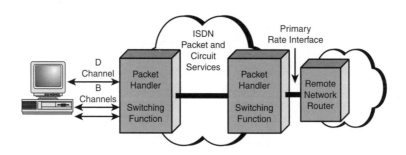

This scheme benefits telecommunications providers as well as users. Central office equipment was engineered for call holding times of four to eight minutes. Circuits used for Internet browsing and telecommuting are held for much longer times. The old model does not fit, and the result has been overload.

With AO/DI, the user maintains a sense of always being connected, but unused circuits are released automatically.

ISDN is faced with potentially formidable competition from Digital Subscriber Link (DSL) services and cable modem data transfer services. Until these services mature, AO/DI enhances the usability and convenience of ISDN data services.

Digital Signaling System 1

Many of the signaling messages that are carried across the D-channel mimic the call setup procedures of the traditional telephone network (see Chapter I-2, Figure 2.14). Figure 3.15 shows a minimal message exchange that can be used to set up an ISDN call. Only the DSS1 messages exchanged between user endpoint devices and their adjacent network switches are shown. SS7 messages would be used within the network to set up the call.

Figure 3.15   ISDN call setup.

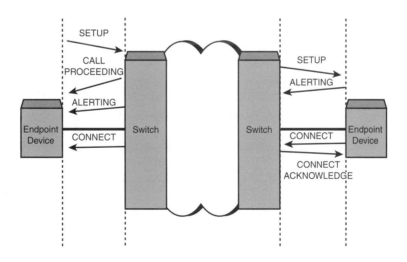

Figure 3.16 shows a sequence of messages that disconnect a call. Either party can initiate the disconnect.

Figure 3.16 ISDN call termination.

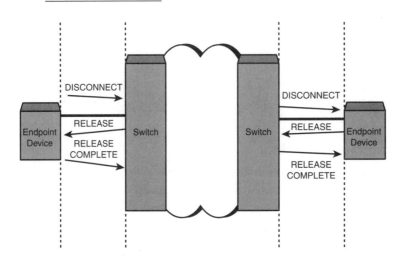

Messages are carried in the payloads of LAPD information frames. Each message has the format shown in Figure 3.17, and contains parameters that are encoded within formatted *information elements.*

Figure 3.17 Format of a DSS1 signaling message.

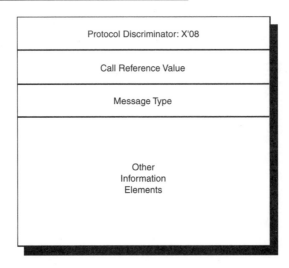

DSS1 Information Elements

A DSS1 information element contains one or more parameters relating to a call.

Each information element includes an identifier that indicates its type. The use of self identifying elements is a good idea. It adds flexibility to message design and makes it possible to add—or drop—information elements according to their usefulness. Table 3.5 lists and describes information elements.

There are two information elements that are included in every message:

- **Message type**—Identifies the type, such as SETUP or CONNECT.

- **Call reference**—A numeric identifier assigned to a call. It is a local value. The caller picks an unused identifier for its end of the call when it sends a call SETUP message. The switch at the called party's end picks an unused identifier to be used at that end when it delivers a call SETUP message. Either endpoint can be involved in more than one active call. The identifier is used to match messages to their calls.

Many messages from the network to the user include the *display* element. This element carries information to be presented to a user on a display panel.

Human users can enter information to be sent to the network using a keypad or special function keys. International ASCII code 5 (IA5) characters are entered at a telephone (or computer) keypad and are sent in *keypad facility* information elements. The network can prompt the user to enter information using the display.

Table 3.5   ISDN Information Elements

Element Name	Description
Bearer capability	Requests capabilities such as support for speech, video, restricted digital, unrestricted digital, or the use of a high bandwidth (H) channel.
Call identity	Identifies a suspended call.
Call reference	Identifies the call to which a message relates.
Call state	Describes the current status of a call.
Called party number	Identifies the called number.
Called party subaddress	Carries information such as a PBX number for voice, or a network address for data.
Calling party number	Identifies the calling number.
Calling party subaddress	Carries information such as a PBX number for voice, or a network address for data.

continues

Table 3.5   Continued

Element Name	Description
Cause	Includes an error code that indicates the source of a problem.
Channel identification	Identifies the channel to be used.
Congestion level	Indicates the congestion status of a call.
Date/Time	Used by the network to timestamp a message.
Endpoint identifier	Includes a user service identifier that corresponds to a service profile identifier and a terminal identifier.
Facility	Provides supplementary service information. An extended facility element is used if the length of the information is bigger than 255 bytes.
Feature activation	Invokes a supplementary service that is part of a user profile.
Feature indication	Used by the network to report the status of a supplementary service.
High layer compatibility	Carries information for the remote terminal. It indicates the type of communication desired; for example, Group 3 or Group 4 FAX, or a specific network protocol.
Information request	Carries a request for information such as the terminal identification or address digits.
Keypad facility	Carries IA5 characters entered by a user.
Low layer compatibility	Carries information for the remote terminal. Identifies characteristics such as the type of information (voice, video, or unrestricted data), the desired information transfer rate, and the use of flow control.
More data	Indicates that more information will follow.
Network specific facilities	Contains a network identifier and a field encoded according to rules set by that network.
Notification indicator	Indicates a change, such as: a call has been suspended or resumed, a party has been added to a conference call, or a party is using a supplementary service.
Progress indicator	Provides call progress information when interworking with a non-ISDN network.

Element Name	Description
Repeat indicator	Can indicate that one choice should be made from several information elements of the same type that follow.
Restart indicator	Indicates whether specific channels, one specific interface, or all interfaces controlled by this D-channel should be restarted—that is, returned to idle, breaking all calls.
Segmented message	Indicates that this message is part of a longer, segmented message, and reveals the number of segments that still have to be sent.
Sending complete	Indicates completion of the called party number.
Service profile identification	Identifies a user service profile stored at the network.
Shift	Signals a change to another codeset. After a shift, the information element types will correspond to definitions made within a different (e.g. national) codeset.
Signal	Reports on tones (off hook, dial tone, busy tone, and so on) and alerting signals when the ISDN network interworks with a conventional network.
Switchhook	Indicates on or off-hook state.
Transit network selection	Identifies one or more transit networks through which the call should pass.
User-user	Carries information to be passed to the remote terminal.

Note

An X.25 packet data circuit is set up following the same steps as an ordinary call, but using other information elements such as the maximum packet size, the desired information rate, and the maximum acceptable end-to-end transit delay.

DSS1 Messages

ISDN standards identify the information elements that may be used in each message. Some elements can be used in both the user-to-network (user→network) and the network-to-user (net→user) directions. Others may be used in only one direction. For example, SETUP message information elements are listed below, and the direction is marked for elements that may be used in only one direction:

Call reference	Feature indication (net→user)
Message type	High layer compatibility
Bearer capability	Keypad facility (user→net)
Called party number	Low layer compatibility
Called party subaddress	Network specific facilities
Calling party number	Progress indicator
Calling party subaddress	Repeat indicator
Channel identification	Sending complete
Display (net→user)	Signal (net→user)
Endpoint identifier	Transit network selection (user→net)
Facility	User-user
Feature activation (user→net)	

Obviously, the called number is a very important SETUP parameter. The number actually can be conveyed in two different ways. A smart device will wait until the user has entered all of the called digits before sending a SETUP message that contains the whole number. This is called *en-bloc* mode. A basic ISDN telephone or other manually dialed device may use *overlap* mode. The number is sent out one digit at a time. To do this, the original SETUP message is followed by INFORMATION messages that carry the digits of the called number.

Figures 3.15 and 3.16 displayed just a few of the ISDN messages. Tables 3.6 through 3.9 provide a more comprehensive list. Wherever possible, groups of messages in Tables 3.6 through 3.9 are arranged in an order intended to suggest the way that they would be used in a signaling transaction.

The direction of flow of a message also is suggested (for example, user→net, net→user). "User" in this case means the ISDN terminal that sends or receives the message.

The tables list some of the information elements used with each message. The purpose of including these information elements is to give a better idea of the meaning of each message. Many of the information elements are optional. See ITU-T standards Q.931 and Q.932 for details.

The *message type* and *call reference* information elements, which are carried in every message, are not listed. Other general parameters also have been omitted. For example, the *display* and *signal* information elements are used in many messages and are not specific to the purpose of a message. The *facility* information element optionally can be included in any call setup, clearing, hold or retrieve message, and has been omitted from the parameter lists for these messages. The facility element is listed for messages for which it is a key information element.

A few message types do not require any information elements beyond the general ones listed above. In the tables that follow, this will be indicated by entering "No others" in the Information Elements column.

Table 3.6   ISDN Call Establishment Messages

Message Name	Description	Information Elements
SETUP user→net→user	Initiates a call.	See list earlier in this section.
SETUP ACKNOWLEDGE net→user, user→net	Indicates that more setup information is needed.	Channel id. Progress ind.
CALL PROCEEDING net→calling user, called use→net	Call establishment has been initiated and no more setup information will be accepted.	Bearer capability. Channel id. Progress ind. High layer compat.
PROGRESS user→net→user	Indicates call progress, e.g., when networks must interwork to complete the call.	Progress ind. Bearer capability. Cause (used to include additional information). High layer compat.
ALERTING user→net→user	The called user indicates that alerting (e.g. ringing) has been initiated.	Bearer capability. Channel id. Progress ind. High layer compat.

continues

Table 3.6   Continued

Message Name	Description	Information Elements
CONNECT user→net→user	The called user accepts the call.	Bearer capability. Channel id. Progress ind. Date/time. Low layer compat. High layer compat.
CONNECT ACKNOWLEDGE net→called user, calling user→net	The called user has been awarded the call.	No others.

Table 3.7   ISDN Call Information Phase Messages

Message Name	Description	Information Elements
USER INFORMATION user→network→user	Enables a user to pass information to the remote user.	User-user. More data.
SUSPEND user→net	Requests that a call be suspended.	Call id.
SUSPEND ACKNOWLEDGE ne→user	The call was successfully suspended. The B-channel has been freed, but the call can be resumed later.	No others.
SUSPEND REJECT net→user	The network failed to suspend the call.	Cause of rejection.
RESUME user→net	Requests resumption of a suspended call.	Call id.
RESUME ACKNOWLEDGE net→user	Acknowledges that a suspended call has been resumed.	Channel id.
RESUME REJECT net→user	Indicates that the network has failed to resume a suspended call.	Cause of rejection.
HOLD user→net→user	Requests a hold function for a call. The holder's B-channel may be used for another call.	No others.
HOLD ACKNOWLEDGE net→user, user→net	Indicates that the hold was performed.	No others.

Message Name	Description	Information Elements
HOLD REJECT net→user, user→net	Indicates that the hold was denied.	Cause of hold reject.
RETRIEVE user→net→user	Reconnects the user to the held call.	Channel id.
RETRIEVE ACKNOWLEDGE net→user, user→net	Indicates that the call has successfully been retrieved.	Channel id.
RETRIEVE REJECT net→user, user→net	Indicates that the retrieve failed.	Cause of retrieve reject.

Table 3.8   ISDN Call Clearing Messages

Message Name	Description	Information Elements
DISCONNECT user→net→user	Request call termination (or indicate that the call has been cleared).	Cause of termination. Progress ind.
RELEASE net→user, user→net	Indicates that the call has been disconnected.	Cause of release.
RELEASE COMPLETE net→user, user→net	The channel has been freed.	Cause of release.
RESTART user→net, net→user	Return specified channels, or an entire interface, to idle.	Restart indicator. Channel ids.
RESTART ACKNOWLEDGE net→user, user→net	Restart is complete.	Restart indicator. Channel ids.

Table 3.9 ISDN Miscellaneous Messages

Message Name	Description	Information Elements
INFORMATION user→net, net→user	Includes or completes a called party number when the SETUP does not contain a complete called party number, or provides miscellaneous information.	Called party number. Sending cmplt. Keypad facility.
NOTIFY net→user, user→net	Report information pertaining to a call (e.g., user suspended).	Notification indicator. Bearer capability (net→user).
STATUS ENQUIRY net→user, user→net	Requests status information relating to a call.	No others.
STATUS user→net, net→user	Sent in response to a STATUS ENQUIRY, or spontaneously, to report an error.	Cause (used to include additional information). Call state.
FACILITY user→net, net→user	Requests or acknowledges a supplementary service.	Facility.
REGISTER	Assigns a call reference to a non-call transaction.	Facility.

Signaling and Supplemental Services

DSS1 signaling supports supplemental services such as call forwarding and call waiting by

- Controlling them. DSS1 messages can carry information elements that enable, disable, or configure supplemental services.

- Invoking them for actual use.

Three mechanisms enable a user to control or invoke supplementary services by entering data that is converted to appropriate information elements:

- **Keypad protocol**—The user requests a service by entering IA5 characters via the device keypad. The entered string is carried to the switch in a *keypad facility* information element. The keypad and screen can be used in an interactive dialog. The entered information may be delivered in either en bloc or overlap mode.

- **Feature key management protocol**—The user can activate or control a service by pressing a feature key. *Feature activation* information elements are sent to the network in SETUP and INFORMATION messages. The network responds with *feature indication* information elements.

- **Functional protocol**—Unlike the keypad and feature key protocols, the functional protocol is not triggered by telephone set buttons pushed by a user. The functional protocol is used by an intelligent device that can originate FACILITY messages or other messages that include *facility* information elements.

Signaling System 7

An important transformation of the telephone system had to be performed before ISDN could be implemented. The complex and sophisticated signaling system 7 (SS7) network and protocol had to be put in place.

Like DSS1, SS7 is a message-based signaling system. SS7 signaling takes place on a set of network links that are dedicated to signaling. These links and a set of SS7 nodes form a separate, dedicated packet-switched data communications network. Nodes in this packet-switched network route messages that are used to set up and terminate calls, support a variety of extra subscriber services, and carry network management and maintenance information.

SS7 adds intelligence to a network. The messaging capability used to set up and terminate calls also has been the basis of new end user services. Some examples of functions supported by SS7 include:

- 800- and 900-number service

- Mobile telephone service

- Mobile subscriber authentication

- Caller identification

- Charging calls to a credit card

- Charging calls to a calling card

SS7 Databases

An SS7 signaling network can perform complicated functions because it contains a set of databases. For example:

- When a user dials an 800 number, the user's central office switch sends a query to an 800-number database requesting the destination's "real" telephone number. The number that is returned may depend on the caller's number (to choose a location near the caller) or the time of day (to route calls to locations that handle calls after local business hours are over).

- A prepaid calling card lookup checks the validity of the card number and returns an indication of the time remaining on the calling card.

SS7 standards include a standard client/server transaction protocol (called the *transaction capabilities application part*, or *TCAP*). This protocol defines the way that an SS7 client interacts with a database server.

SS7 Network Node Types and Topology

There are three types of nodes in an SS7 signaling network:

- **Service switching point (SSP)**—A central office or tandem switch that supports SS7 protocol software and can connect to SS7 signaling links.

- **Signal transfer point (STP)**—A message switch that routes SS7 message traffic.

- **Service control point (SCP)**—A computer that hosts one or more databases.

As shown in Figure 3.18, an SS7-capable telephone switch (SSP) is connected to a *signal transfer point (STP)*. A telephone switch forwards all of its signaling messages to an STP and receives incoming messages from an STP. The STP is responsible for routing each message to its destination.

Each *service control point (SCP)* database node also is connected to an STP. It sends and receives all messages via its STP.

SSP switches and SCP databases are the signaling endpoints—that is, the sources and destinations—of signaling messages. The link between an STP message switch and a signaling endpoint is called an *access link (A-link)*. A link between STP message switches that serve different areas is called a *bridge link (B-link)*.

Replication of SS7 Network Elements

You don't expect your phone calls to "mostly" get through or your calling card to "mostly" work. The SS7 signaling system has to work around the clock with virtually no down time. To safeguard the signaling system, every node and line in the signaling network is replicated. Figure 3.19 shows a typical configuration:

- Every STP message switch is duplicated. The two message switches are called a *mated pair.*

- Each SSP or SCP signaling endpoint is connected to both STPs in a mated pair.

- The STPs in a mated pair are connected by a pair of cross links (C-links).

- An STP that connects to another area is connected to both STPs for that area.

- An SCP database node usually is replicated. (In any case, every database is replicated in an SS7 network.)

- The diagonal links (D-links) in Figure 3.19 connect to other STPs. For example, they might connect local exchange carrier STPs to interexchange carrier STPs.

Figure 3.18   SS7 nodes and links.

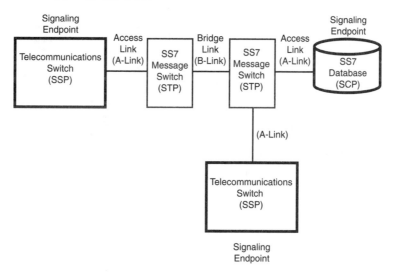

Setting Up Calls Using SS7

Switches set up circuits by exchanging messages across the signaling network formed by STP nodes. Figure 3.20 shows a call being set up with the help of the SS7 network:

- Switch A chooses Switch B to be the next node to be traversed by the circuit that will connect to the called number.

- Switch A sends a message to Switch B via the SS7 network. The message identifies the called number, (optionally, the calling number), and other information elements, and reserves a circuit segment between A and B for the new call.

- Switch B agrees, and chooses Switch C as the next switch to be traversed on the way to the called number.

- Switch B sends a message to Switch C via the SS7 network. The message identifies the called number (and optionally, the calling number) and reserves a circuit segment between B and C for the new call.

- Switch C agrees. If the destination is an ISDN telephone, Switch C sends a DSS1 SETUP message to the device. If the destination is an ordinary telephone, Switch C sends a ringing tone to the called device.

- When the called party picks up the phone, Switch C sends an answer message to originating Switch A via the SS7 network. Switch A makes sure that the calling party's line is connected to the reserved circuit.

Figure 3.19   Redundancy in an SS7 network.

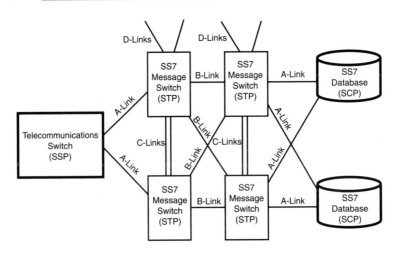

Figure 3.20   Using SS7 messages to set up a call.

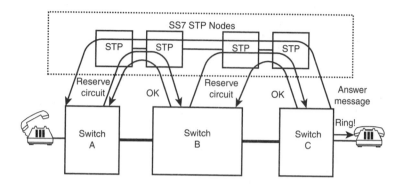

ISDN's Halting Start

The ITU-T ISDN standards-making process had some serious flaws. The participants put aside such mundane matters as a standard technology for the local loop; promoting interworking; simplifying installation procedures; and defining practical operations, administration, and maintenance procedures, and spent years developing a long list of supplemental services and features for which they might charge subscribers. One can imagine representatives from countries whose residential customers had to wait a year for a home telephone enthusiastically suggesting a dozen or so new features for a non-existent ISDN service.

The standards process stretched out over years. In the end, the realities of ISDN implementation were grim for both subscribers and telephony service providers.

First of all, telephone companies had to invest in costly new central office switches in order to support the service. Second, at minimum, BRI installation requires a visit to the customer site, and may also require work on the local loop. Many maintenance personnel have to be trained and made available to do these chores.

In North America, the first generation of switches supported ISDN in different ways. Different subscriber equipment had to be used with each. Vendors eventually built user equipment that could work with switches from the major vendors (AT&T and Northern Telecom), but the configuration process remained different, and installation glitches were commonplace. Furthermore, the process of configuring ISDN lines at the switch was manual, lengthy, and error prone. Botched ISDN installations have produced many angry customers.

Improvements finally are being implemented, and telephone companies are becoming more skilled at ISDN installation and support. However, the use of ISDN for data transfer is being challenged by higher speed cable and DSL technologies, and ordinary voice call service is being challenged by technologies such as Voice over IP and voice over cable.

ISDN's future depends on the industry's ability to streamline installation and support and offer attractive tariffs.

References

Some key ITU-T ISDN documents include:

- Q.920: *ISDN user-network interface data link layer—General aspects* (1993)
- Q.921: *ISDN user-network interface—Data link layer specification* (1997)
- Q.930: *ISDN user-network interface layer 3—General aspects* (1993)
- Q.931 *ISDN user-network interface layer 3 specification for basic call control* (1998)
- Q.932: *Digital subscriber signaling system No. 1 – Generic procedures for the control of ISDN supplementary services* (1998)

Signaling system 7 is described in the ITU-T Q.7xx series of documents. There also are many ANSI documents that deal with signaling system number 7: for example, ANSI T1.110—T.116.

ISO 3309 and ISO 4335 describe High-level Data Link Control (HDLC).

The PPP multilink and bandwidth allocation protocols are described in

- RFC 1990 *The PPP Multilink Protocol (MP)* (1996)
- RFC 2125 *The PPP Bandwidth Allocation Protocol (BAP) / The PPP Bandwidth Allocation Control Protocol (BACP)* (1997)

4

SONET

Only a few years ago, a computer was a costly piece of equipment that only a large organization could afford to buy. At that time, it was unimaginable that far more powerful computers soon would be found on office desks or in homes. The way we view computers is very different today from what it was in the early years.

The way we think about bandwidth is changing, too. Recently, a team from Bell Labs transmitted data at a trillion bits per second onto a single strand of optical fiber across a distance of almost 250 miles. That's *1,000,000,000,000* bits per second.

Advances in silicon chip technology enabled computer engineers to pack more and more circuits onto a chip. A series of advances in *wave division multiplexing (WDM)* have enabled communications engineers to pack more and more parallel streams of data down a strand of optical fiber. Wave division multiplexing is a technique that enables multiple parallel optical signals to be transmitted across one optical fiber using different wavelengths of light.

Since its introduction as a transmission medium, optical fiber has been valued because of its immunity to noise, low error rates, and security from eavesdropping, as well as its capability to provide high capacity transmission. The increased bandwidth provided by wave division multiplexing has accelerated the creation of a fiber optic communications infrastructure.

The old plesiochronous telecommunications hierarchy did not match the needs of this new, bandwidth-rich, high-speed optical transmission environment. The environment needed a new architecture that included the capability to

- Support high capacity signals

- Scale up to ever higher capacities easily

- Multiplex and demultiplex signals with minimal processing

- Integrate the plesiochronous signals to support coexistence for as long as it is needed

In the early 1980s, Bellcore proposed the *Synchronous Optical Network* (*SONET*) transport system to satisfy these requirements. SONET quickly became a North American standard maintained by the American National Standards Institute (ANSI) T1X1 committee.

ANSI uses the term SONET to embrace the entire system: the hierarchy of line speeds; the format of the signals placed on lines; and the media, connectors, and other physical layer attributes.

The ITU-T published its own version of the SONET carrier system called the *synchronous digital hierarchy* (*SDH*). Originally, the ITU-T standards differed in some details from the ANSI SONET standards.

Note
The ITU-T standards do not use the term *SONET*.

ANSI and ITU-T have cooperated to align their standards. Due to this cooperation the ANSI SONET optical carrier system and the ITU-T synchronous digital hierarchy now have only minor differences and are interoperable.

However, the two bodies continue to use different terminology. The initial sections of this chapter describe the optical carrier architecture using the ANSI SONET vocabulary. Later sections explain the ITU-T language and framework.

ANSI SONET standards define a network with precise timing. In contrast to a plesiochronous network, all nodes in a SONET network derive their timing signal directly or indirectly from the same primary reference clock. In a public SONET network, the primary reference clock is based on a cesium atomic clock with an accuracy of better than 1 part in 10^{11} (a hundredth of a nanosecond in every second).

SONET standards define a new signal multiplexing hierarchy—and a lot more. In the early years in which optical fiber was used in telecommunications networks, the physical interface equipment, line codes, signal formats, and operations, administration, and maintenance procedures were not standardized. It was difficult to connect equipment from different vendors, and to communicate between different networks.

SONET standards address all of the components needed to create working networks and interconnect multiple networks.

The SONET Interoperability Forum

SONET equipment is manufactured by many different vendors. The SONET technology cannot succeed unless equipment from different vendors interoperates without problems. Standards are the first step in attaining interoperability.

However, standards sometimes are ambiguous or overlook elements that need to be nailed down in order to ensure interoperability. Sometimes standards err in the opposite direction. They define too many options, resulting in products that support different, incompatible sets of features. Many of these problems are not discovered until vendors implement the standards and attempt to interconnect their devices.

The *SONET Interoperability Forum (SIF)* is an industry group that was formed in 1994 to promote SONET technology and resolve interoperability problems. There are several Forum working groups that develop and publish interoperability requirements documents.

The New SONET and SDH Hierarchy

A series of new bandwidth transmission levels for communications lines have been defined for the high-speed digital hierarchy. The ANSI bandwidth levels are called *optical carriers*. The ITU-T refers to the bandwidth levels as *synchronous digital hierarchy bit rates.*

Just as there were formatted signals (such as DS1 and DS3) for each level of the old plesiochronous digital hierarchy, there are formatted signals for the new hierarchy. ANSI calls these formatted signals *synchronous transfer signals (STSs)* and ITU-T calls them *synchronous transfer modules (STMs).*

Table 4.1 shows the relationship between the SONET optical carrier hierarchy and the SDH hierarchy. The names are different, but essentially the same levels and formats are used by both.

> **Note**
> There are electrical carrier lines that are capable of carrying an STS-1 51.84Mbps or STS-3 155.52 signal, and they are used when it is convenient. Higher level STS-N signals often are assembled within electrical equipment (such as a computer or a switch) and then are transmitted as optical signals.

The main difference between SONET and the SDH is that the low-speed SONET frame format, STS-1, is not included in the official ITU-T synchronous digital hierarchy. However, the ITU-T has defined a 51.84Mbps subframe format (STM-0) that is identical to the STS-1 format.

Table 4.1	The SONET and SDH Hierarchies		
SONET Signal	Optical Carriers	SDH Signal	Line Rate (Mbps)
STS-1	OC-1	STM-0	51.84
STS-3	OC-3	STM-1	155.52
STS-9	OC-9	STM-3	466.56
STS-12	OC-12	SRM-4	622.08
STS-18	OC-18	STM-6	933.12
STS-24	OC-24	STM-8	1244.16
STS-36	OC-36	STM-12	1866.24
STS-48	OC-48	STM-16	2488.32
STS-192	OC-192	STM-64	9953.28

SONET Multiplexing

Unlike the complicated multiplexing structures used in the old digital hierarchy, multiplexing STS signals is very simple:

An STS-N is equal to N byte-interleaving STS-1s.

It is very easy to combine STS streams. Figure 4.1 shows three STS-1 signals (A, B, and C) being combined into an STS-3 signal.

Figure 4.1   Multiplexing STS-1s into an STS-3.

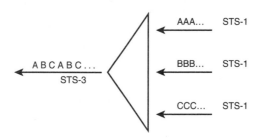

As signals are forwarded through a network, they often are multiplexed with other signals before being transmitted across a high-bandwidth link. Figure 4.2 shows signals that are combined in two stages.

At the top right of Figure 4.2, an STS-3 is formed by multiplexing three STS-1s labeled A, B, and C. The streams are multiplexed by taking one byte from each STS-1 in the order

> A B C A B C A B C . . .

A network device that processes an STS-3 signal knows exactly where the bytes for the first, second, and third enclosed STS-1s are located.

In the lower right of Figure 4.2, an STS-9 is formed by multiplexing nine STS-1s. The streams labeled D–L are multiplexed by taking one byte from each STS-1 in the order

> D E F G H I J K L D E F G H I J K L . . .

Again, a device that processes an STS-9 signal knows exactly where the bytes for the first through ninth enclosed STS-1s are located.

In Figure 4.2, the STS-3 and STS-9 signals then are multiplexed together to form an STS-12. The streams are combined by taking one byte from each STS-1 enclosed in the STS-3 and each STS-1 enclosed in the STS-9 in the order

> A B C D E F G H I J K L A B C D E F G H I J K L . . .

Figure 4.2   Multiplexing an STS-3 and an STS-9 into an STS-12.

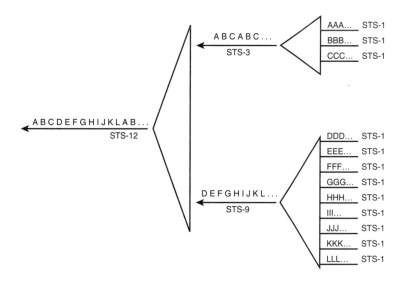

There are many ways of combining STS-1 signals into a high capacity STS-N signal. The nice thing about SONET is that it does not matter how you do it—the final signal format will be the same.

For example, in Figure 4.3, ABC, DEF, GHI, and JKL each are initially multiplexed into STS-3s. Then these four signals are combined into an STS-12. Again, the signals are multiplexed by taking one byte from each of the original STS-1 signals. The resulting STS-12 is identical to the one in Figure 4.2.

This is a very simple and flexible multiplexing scheme. Demultiplexing is equally straightforward. It is easy to extract one or more STS-1 signals from an STS-N.

In contrast, it is impossible to extract a DS1 from a DS3 without demultiplexing the entire DS3—an operation that requires a significant amount of computer processing.

Figure 4.3   Multiplexing four STS-3s into an STS-12.

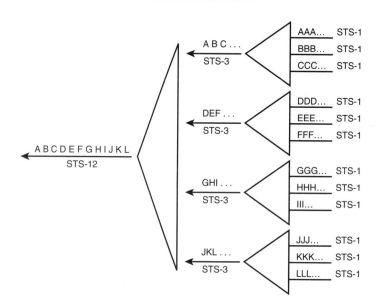

SONET/SDH Transmission Media

SONET and SDH links are full-duplex by definition. Full-duplex transmission is implemented in several different ways.

Information usually is transmitted across an optical fiber in one direction only. When this is the case, full-duplex communication is achieved by using two fiber optic strands or via a special ring configuration. SONET ring configurations are described later in this chapter.

There is some equipment that supports bidirectional traffic on a single fiber, but currently this is a costly technology.

SONET Network Devices

SONET can be used for a single point-to-point circuit or as the basis of a large, multi-site network. SONET devices are being used today to rebuild the public telecommunications infrastructure.

A variety of equipment is available to meet the needs of SONET users:

- *Terminal devices* define the boundaries of a SONET network. They gather bytes to be sent out onto the SONET network and deliver bytes arriving from the SONET network.

- *Regenerators* re-create a signal so that it can be sent across great distances.

- *Add/drop multiplexers* combine and split signals.

- *Digital cross-connect switches* route traffic and enable complex and robust networks with a lot of redundancy and backup capacity to be constructed.

Terminals and Terminal Multiplexers

The endpoint of a SONET transmission is called a *terminal* or *terminal multiplexer*. A terminal simply is any source or destination of SONET signals. A terminal multiplexer is a device that operates as a relay point between an electrical network and a SONET network.

A terminal multiplexer inserts signals from the classical plesiochronous hierarchy into outgoing SONET signals and extracts them from incoming SONET signals. For simplicity, from now on, the word "terminal" will be used to mean either type of SONET endpoint.

As shown in Figure 4.4, formatted bundles of data are transmitted across an optical carrier—and received from an optical carrier—at a terminal. In the figure, each DS3 signal arriving at terminal A is inserted in an STS-1 signal. These are multiplexed into an STS-3, which then is transmitted on an optical medium.

At terminal B, the STS-3 is demultiplexed into three STS-1s, and a DS3 is extracted from each. These then are output onto an electrical medium.

Figure 4.4   SONET transmission between terminals.

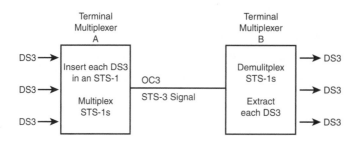

Regenerators

If the distance between the two terminals is large, then the signal will have to be regenerated at one or more points between the terminals, as is shown in Figure 4.5. A regenerator also is called a *repeater*.

Figure 4.5   Regenerating a signal.

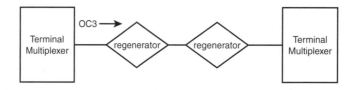

Add/Drop Multiplexer

STS-1 signals are easy to multiplex into or extract from an STS-N. The SONET add/drop multiplexer takes advantage of this feature. At an add/drop multiplexer, some STS-1s can be extracted and replaced by other STS-1s. Or, several signals can be reorganized into new multiplexed combinations very quickly.

A set of add/drop multiplexers connected by SONET transmission lines is a lot like a line of subway stations connected by subway trains. Passengers get on at a station (signals are added) and get off at other stations (signals are dropped).

There is one important difference. An add/drop multiplexer can clone a passenger. A copy of a payload can be dropped off at multiple stations.

An add/drop multiplexer

- Passes some of its signals straight through, simply repeating the bits onto a new fiber.

- Accepts new signals and combines ("adds") them into its flow onto the next fiber.

- Extracts selected signals and outputs ("drops") them locally.

- Performs "drop and repeat" for a stream—such as a cable TV channel—that needs to be copied to multiple destinations. The selected signal is dropped locally, but also is repeated onto a new fiber.

Figure 4.6 shows traffic passing into and out of multiplexers A, B, C, and D. The figure depicts multiplexers connected in a double ring configuration. Traffic flows around one ring in a clockwise direction and around the other in a counterclockwise direction.

Some multiplexing and switching products operate very efficiently on SONET light signals, manipulating the optical signals without converting them to electrical signals. Other devices that are not as efficient must first convert the optical signals to electrical signals before manipulating them and then must re-convert the signals to optical form.

| Figure 4.6 | Add/drop multiplexers. |

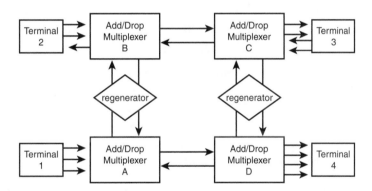

Digital Cross-Connect Switches

An add/drop multiplexer is a very simple device that only picks up and drops off formatted signals. A digital cross-connect switch has a lot more intelligence. As illustrated in Figure 4.7, it can receive SONET signals on many input ports, demultiplex signals, choose an output port, and remultiplex the signals exiting each port.

Vendors sometimes use the term *wideband* digital cross-connect to describe a product that can multiplex and demultiplex traffic that includes low bandwidth streams, such as DS1 or E1. They use the term *broadband* digital cross-connect to describe a product that can multiplex and demultiplex only DS3 and higher level STS (or STM) signals.

Figure 4.7   A digital cross-connect switch.

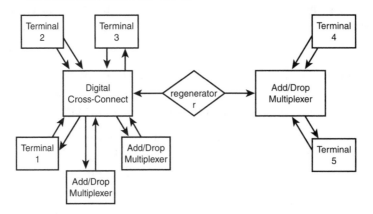

Sections, Lines, and Paths

Terminals, regenerators, multiplexers, and digital cross-connect switches all are types of SONET nodes. Peer SONET nodes "talk" to one another across *sections*, *lines*, and *paths*:

- **Section**—The span between any two adjacent nodes.

- **Line**—A span that does not have a regenerator as an endpoint. A line may cross one section or several sections.

- **Path**—A span whose endpoints are terminals. A path may cross one section or many sections. It may cross one line or many lines.

Figure 4.8 illustrates how this terminology is used. Note that the span between add/drop multiplexer B and regenerator r is a section. The spans between add/drop multiplexer B and C, and between the two terminals at the top of the figure also are sections, because there is no intervening device.

The span between add/drop multiplexers A and B is a line, as is that between add/drop multiplexers B and C, and between the two terminals at the top of the figure.

In Figure 4.8, the direct connection between the two terminals at the top of the page is a path. There are several other paths in the figure. Each of them passes through two or three intermediate nodes. For example, the path that originates at terminal 3 and terminates at terminal 4 passes through multiplexer C, regenerator s, and multiplexer D and is made up of four sections and three lines.

Figure 4.8   Sections, lines, and paths.

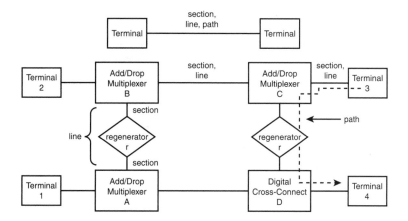

SONET Layering

The processing performed by a SONET node is broken into layers. The layers are displayed in Figure 4.9.

- Every node has to perform some low-level functions in order to put a signal onto a fiber. These functions belong to the *section layer*.

- Smart nodes perform additional multiplexing (and sometimes switching) functions. These functions belong to the *line layer*.

- Terminal endpoints must convert external signals to SONET format. These functions belong to the *path layer*.

Each layer performs additional chores that relate to network operations, administration, and maintenance (OAM). SONET signals include section, line, and path OAM overhead bytes. These bytes provide framing patterns and error monitoring, and form management message channels. Each layer must process its own overhead bytes.

Note

The term *operations, administration, management, and provisioning (OAM&P)* sometimes is used instead of OAM.

Figure 4.9   Layered view of section, line, and path processing.

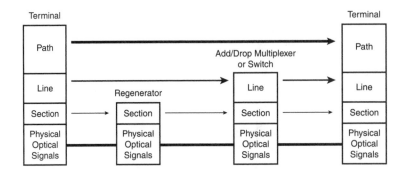

Layer Functions

It is worthwhile to take a closer look at the processing within each layer.

Every device performs section layer functions, which include

- Preparing a framed outgoing signal and inserting section overhead bytes

- Applying a scrambling formula to an outgoing STS to ensure that the signal has a sufficient density of 1 bit

- Unscrambling an incoming STS signal

- Processing the section overhead bytes for an incoming STS signal and handling any errors that are detected

Line layer functions are performed by each line endpoint and include

- Adding line overhead bytes to an outgoing STS signal

- Multiplexing and demultiplexing signals

- Switching traffic from a failed line to a backup line (called a *protection line*)

- Processing line overhead bytes arriving in an incoming STS signal and handling any errors that are detected

Path layer functions performed by a terminal include

- Preparing payloads for transmission. For example, packaging legacy (plesiochronous) signals so they can be carried inside a SONET payload.

- Adding path overhead bytes to an outgoing STS signal.

- Processing incoming path overhead bytes arriving in an STS signal and handling any errors that are detected.

As shown in Figure 4.9, a terminal has to perform section, line, and path overhead processing. An add/drop multiplexer or a switch performs section and line overhead processing. A regenerator performs only section overhead processing.

SONET and STM Formats

SONET transmission formats were designed to enable add/drop multiplexers and digital cross connects to work very efficiently. SONET formats

- Make it easy to add or drop formatted signals into a SONET payload

- Are scalable to high speeds

- Include ample bandwidth for administration, operations, and maintenance

The formats include a fair amount of overhead. However, enormous bandwidths are available with optical fiber. Reserving bandwidth for a strong network management capability is a good investment.

The STS-1 Frame

The STS-1 frame is the basic building block of the SONET hierarchy. As shown in Figure 4.10, an STS-1 frame is structured as an array of bytes that contains 90 columns and 9 rows. The first three columns contain *transport overhead* bytes. The transport overhead is made up of 3 rows of section overhead and 6 rows of line overhead.

The remaining 87 columns contain the payload area, which contains the path overhead and the payload.

Figure 4.10   Overall STS-1 frame format.

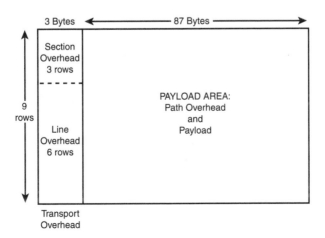

An STS-1 frame is transmitted every 125 microseconds (that is, 8,000 per second). The frame consists of $9 \times 90 = 8,100$ bytes, or 64,800 bits. 8,000 frames per second translates to the STS-1 line rate, 51.84Mbps.

The Floating Synchronous Payload Envelope

Data is transmitted in a *synchronous payload envelope (SPE)* that is made up of 87 columns—one column of path overhead bytes followed by 86 columns of data. Figure 4.11 shows the format of an SPE.

Figure 4.11   Format of a synchronous payload envelope.

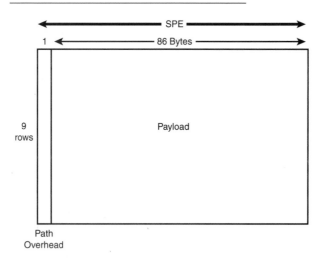

An SPE matches the size of the STS-1 payload area perfectly. However, an SPE is not aligned with the boundaries of the payload area. Instead, it is dropped into the payload area at a convenient point.

Figure 4.12 shows how an SPE floats in the payload area. A heavy black line has been drawn around the SPE. A pointer in the line overhead region points to the beginning of the SPE.

As shown in the figure, the first row of the SPE (that is, its first 87 bytes) wraps around to the next row of the payload area.

The capability to adapt and move the starting location of the 783 SPE payload bytes gives SONET equipment a welcome degree of flexibility. Electrical signals (DS1, E1, DS3, E3, and so on) arriving at a terminal multiplexer do not have the tight synchronization that SONET signals have.

SONET uses pointers and floating to solve timing problems. SONET payloads always are easy to locate, and can be inserted into the signal—or removed from the signal—with ease.

Figure 4.12   An SPE floating in a payload area.

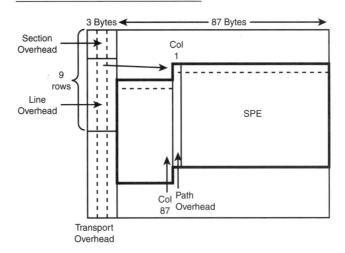

STS-1 Transport Overhead

The STS-1 transport overhead contains bytes that form the channels that are used to configure, manage, monitor, and troubleshoot the network—in other words, to handle the OAM functions.

Figure 4.13 presents a detailed view of the three rows of section overhead and six rows of line overhead that make up the transport overhead.

The section overhead bytes are processed by all device types—line terminating equipment, regenerators, add/drop multiplexers, and digital cross-connect switches. The line overhead bytes are processed by all devices except for regenerators.

The overhead bytes that contribute to managing, monitoring, and troubleshooting the network are briefly described next. (A few complex or very specialized functions are not explained in full detail.) Bytes with "Z" names (Z0, Z1, Z2) are reserved for uses to be defined in the future, and are called *growth bytes*.

The STS-1 section overhead bytes include

- **A1 and A2**—Framing bytes. They enable SONET equipment to locate and lock onto STS-1 frame boundaries. (These bytes are not scrambled during transmission.)

- **C1/J0/Z0**—Under ANSI, this byte originally was named C1 and a combined sequence of the C1 bytes contained an identifier for the source of the signal. The byte was used differently by ITU-T, and later was redefined by both ANSI and ITU-T.

The new definition is a little complicated. An STS-N is made up of N STS-1s. The byte now is called a "section trace" byte (J0) in the first STS-1 in an STS-N. It is called a "growth" byte (Z0) in the remaining STS-1s (if N > 1). "Growth" bytes are just bytes that currently are unused.

Figure 4.13 Section and line overhead.

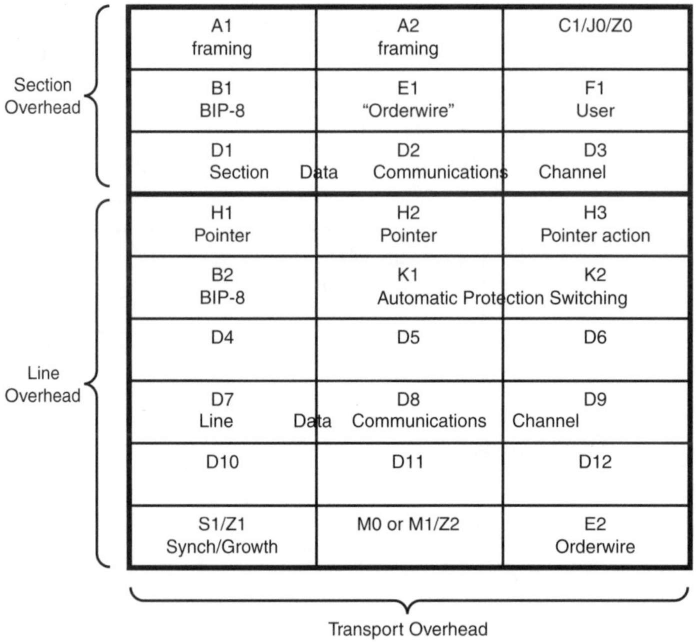

A1 framing	A2 framing	C1/J0/Z0
B1 BIP-8	E1 "Orderwire"	F1 User
D1 Section Data	D2 Communications	D3 Channel
H1 Pointer	H2 Pointer	H3 Pointer action
B2 BIP-8	K1 Automatic Protection Switching	K2
D4	D5	D6
D7 Line Data	D8 Communications Channel	D9
D10	D11	D12
S1/Z1 Synch/Growth	M0 or M1/Z2	E2 Orderwire

Section Overhead / Line Overhead / Transport Overhead

- **B1**—Section bit interleaved parity code (BIP-8) byte. B1 carries an even parity check code computed on the bits of the previous STS-1 frame (after scrambling). The code is generated at the transmitting end of a section and is checked by the node at the other end of the section.

Note

To compute the value of the nth bit in the bit interleaved parity, add up the bits in position n for all the bytes that are covered. Set the value of the nth bit to 0 if the sum is even and 1 if it is odd.

- **E1**—Section "orderwire" byte. This bandwidth supports a voice channel for technicians. In general, an orderwire circuit is a voice or data circuit used by technicians to configure, activate, test, and maintain communications equipment.

- **F1**—Section user channel byte. A channel whose purpose is vendor- or network-specific. For example, it could be used to download software upgrades.

- **D1, D2, D3**—Section data communications channel bytes. A 192Kbps bandwidth channel used to pass OAM messages across the section, this channel carries alarms, control information, performance monitoring data, and other administrative data.

The line overhead bytes include

- **H1 and H2**—STS payload pointer bytes. A pointer to the start of the SPE. The right-most 10 bits indicate the offset in bytes between the pointer and the first byte of the SPE.

- **H3**—Pointer action byte. H3 is used as an extra payload byte in order to make up for a small timing discrepancy between incoming legacy streams and the outgoing multiplexed SONET stream. The section titled "Negative Stuffing" contains a more complete explanation.

- **B2**—Line bit interleaved parity code (BIP-8) byte. An even parity code computed on the line overhead and SPE of the previous STS-1 frame. The code is generated at the transmitting end of a line and checked by the receiver at the other end of the line.

- **K1, K2**—Automatic protection switching bytes. Used for information needed to repair a broken SONET ring.

- **D4-D12**—Line data communications channel bytes. A 576Kbps bandwidth channel for OAM messages between SONET line-level network equipment. This channel carries alarms, control information, performance monitoring data, and other administrative data.

- **S1 or Z1**—Synchronization status byte. A byte located in the first STS-1 of an STS-N. Bits 5–8 of this byte contain a code that reports the synchronization status of the transmitting network node. The byte is a growth (Z1) byte in other STS-1s in an STS-N (if N>1).

- **M0 or M1/Z2**—If this is an STS-1 signal, then this position holds an M0 byte and bits 5–8 contain a line remote error indication (REI-L), which reports an error count.

  For an STS-N, an M1 byte holds the REI-L. The M1 byte is located in the third STS-1. The bytes in this position in the other STS-1s are growth (Z2) bytes.

- **E2**—Line orderwire byte. 64Kbps bandwidth used for a voice channel for technicians.

STS-1 Path Overhead

Path overhead bytes are processed by the terminal devices at path endpoints. There are nine path overhead bytes per SPE, located in the first column. Figure 4.14 shows the path overhead column.

Figure 4.14   Path overhead bytes.

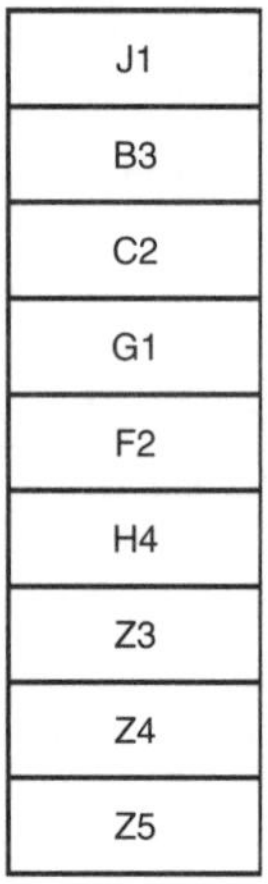

J1
B3
C2
G1
F2
H4
Z3
Z4
Z5

Path overhead bytes include

- **J1**—Path trace byte. Used to repetitively transmit an E.164 string that represents the network address of the originator of the SPE payload.

- **B3**—Path bit interleaved parity code (BIP-8) byte. An even parity code computed on the bits of the SPE of the previous STS-1 frame. The code is generated at the originating terminal and checked by the receiving terminal.

- **C2**—STS path signal label byte. An identifier that indicates the type of payload that is carried within the SPE.

- **G1**—Path status byte. Used by a receiver to signal a remote error indication (REI) or a remote defect indication (RDI) to the sender. An REI reports that an errored block has been detected. An RDI can report loss of signal, loss of frame, and other problems.

- **F2**—Path user channel byte. A vendor-specific "user" channel for communication between path elements.

- **H4**—Virtual tributary multiframe indicator byte. Legacy DS1, E1, DS1C, and DS2 streams are packaged inside an SPE within a subframing format. The H4 byte provides subframe alignment.

The Z3-Z5 growth bytes are reserved for future uses.

Positive and Negative SPE Stuffing

Data to be transmitted in an STS-1 may arrive a little too slowly. A correction can be made by adjusting the pointer on the next SPE, but sometimes just a small immediate adjustment is needed. A slight slowdown is handled by stuffing a dummy byte immediately after the H3 transport overhead byte. This is called *positive stuffing*. The H1, H2 pointer field will contain a special coding that indicates that a dummy byte is going to be stuffed into the flow, and that the next pointer offset will be 1 greater than the current one. Figure 4.15 illustrates positive stuffing.

Figure 4.15   Positive stuffing.

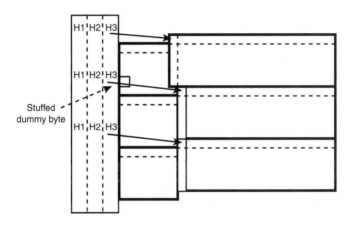

The opposite problem can also occur. Data to be transmitted in an STS-1 may be arriving a little too quickly. In this case, the H3 position is recruited to hold an extra data byte. This is called *negative stuffing*. The H1, H2 pointer field will contain a special coding that indicates that the H3 byte contains data and the next pointer offset will be 1 less than the current one. Figure 4.16 shows negative stuffing.

Figure 4.16 Negative stuffing.

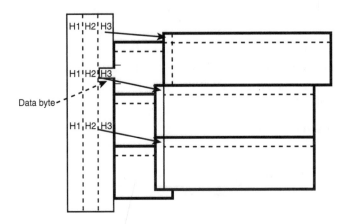

Higher Level Signals

Now that a fairly detailed picture of the STS-1 format has been presented, it is time to examine the formats of the signals at the higher levels of the hierarchy. These include

- STS-N signals formed by multiplexing STS-1 signals

- STS-Nc signals, which are not multiplexed, but are *concatenated* units designed to carry bigger payloads

- Synchronous transfer module STM-N signals, used within the ITU-T synchronous digital hierarchy

Multiplexed STS-N Signals

An STS-N frame carries N multiplexed STS-1 signals. For example, Figure 4.17 shows the general layout of an STS-3 frame, which carries 3 STS-1 signals. The STS-3 is an array of 9 rows and 3 × 90 = 270 columns, made up of 3 byte-interleaved STS-1 frames.

- The first nine columns contain the three interleaved transport overheads. (Note that a J0 byte is used for the first STS-1 and Z0 growth bytes are used in the second and third.)

- The remaining 261 columns contain the three interleaved payload areas. Each payload area contains a path overhead column and 86 payload data columns.

The gray columns belong to the first STS-1. The first pair of H1 and H2 bytes points to the J1 path overhead byte that starts the first SPE. An asterisk (*) marks the first byte of payload data for this SPE.

The figure can be a little confusing on first view. But note that the first STS-1 "owns" all of the gray columns, namely columns 1,4,7,10,13,16,19,22,..., and 268. If you discard the remaining columns, you will see an ordinary STS-1 with a pointer that locates its SPE floating within its own payload area columns.

The second and third SPE areas also float within their own payload area columns. Each has its own SPE, whose position is located via the H1 and H2 bytes in its own transport overhead columns.

Figure 4.17   STS-3 frame format.

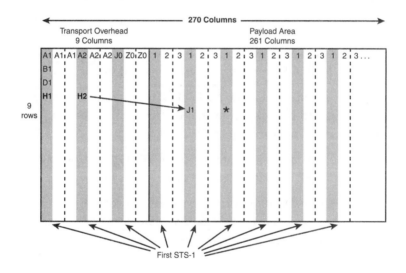

First STS-1

All of the STS-N formats follow the same pattern, as shown in Figure 4.18. The first 3N columns contain the interleaved transport overheads. The next 87N columns contain the interleaved payload areas. For each of the N interleaved STS-1 signals, there is a pointer in its transport overhead columns that shows where its SPE begins.

Concatenated STS-Nc Frames

The STS-1 format provides a convenient capacity for carrying a DS3 payload or several DS1, E1, or DS2 payload streams. However, frequently payloads will not be made up of these lower-rate streams.

Figure 4.18   STS-N format.

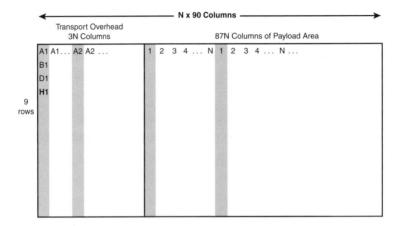

The *concatenated* STS-Nc format is designed to carry bigger payloads. The SPE in an STS-Nc payload area is a single item that is transported and switched as an integral unit.

Figure 4.19 shows the format of an STS-Nc frame. The transport overhead columns have the same format as the STS-N transport overhead. That is, each column is repeated N times. However, not all of the bytes need to be used.

As was the case for STS-N formats, pointer bytes identify the offset location of the SPE, which floats in the other 87N columns of the frame.

Because there is only one payload, only one path overhead column is needed. The remaining 87N-1 columns are filled with data. For example, an STS-3c contains 9 columns of transport overhead, 1 column of path overhead, and 260 columns of payload data.

The STS-3c format is used today to carry asynchronous transfer mode (ATM) traffic. ATM is described in Part III, "ATM."

STM Frame Formats

ITU-T defines two formats for an STM-1 signal. These match the STS-3 and the concatenated STS-3c formats.

STM payloads are made up of various types of *virtual containers (VCs)*:

- The payload area of a SONET STS-1 signal corresponds to an STM virtual container of type 3 (VC-3).

- The payload area of a SONET STS-3c signal corresponds to an STM virtual container of type 4 (VC-4).

Figure 4.19   An STS-Nc frame.

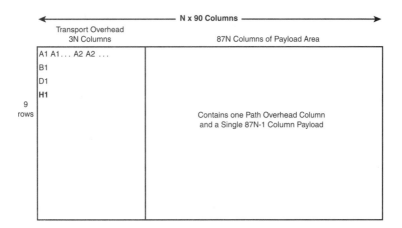

An STM-1 can contain three VC-3s, giving it the same format as an STS-3, or one VC-4, giving it the same format as an STS-3c. For example, the payload area of the STM-1 signal shown in Figure 4.20 contains a VC-4 container and the overall format matches that of an STS-3c signal.

The ITU-T uses different terminology for the overhead byte areas. The first three rows of overhead are called the *regenerator section overhead (RSOH)*. Rows 5 through 9 make up the *multiplex section overhead (MSOH)*. However, the SONET name, "path overhead," is used for the column of overhead bytes in the payload area.

The same matching of formats holds at higher levels. The format of an STM-N corresponds to the format of an STS-3N or an STS-3Nc.

Figure 4.20 STM-1 frame.

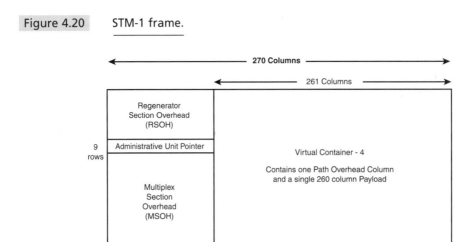

Signal Mappings

SONET needs to carry legacy payloads from the existing plesiochronous hierarchy as well as new, large payloads.

The basic unit of measurement in the SONET/SDH hierarchy is 155.52Mbps. The STS-1 size, which is 1/3 of the basic unit, was included as a convenient size to carry a DS3 signal. This permits easy interworking between legacy networks and SONET networks. An STS-1 also can be used to carry multiple DS1, E1, DS1C, or DS2 signals in convenient packaging.

Encapsulating a DS3 in an STS-1

The DS3 signal rate is 44.736Mbps, or 5,592 bits every 125 microseconds. This means that each STS-1 SPE needs to carry 5,592 bits of a DS3 signal. An STS-1 SPE has room for 6,192 bits, so there will be some extra, unused bandwidth.

An SPE contains 9 rows, with 688 bits in each row. 5,592 is not a multiple of 9. If exactly 621 DS3 payload bits were placed in each row, the SPE would hold 5,589 bits, 3 less than are needed. Hence, 3 more bits need to be inserted somewhere in the SPE. (One bit in every third row of the SPE suffices.)

The 621 payload bits that appear in every row are spread across the row. Figure 4.21 shows the pattern that is used.

The byte types in the figure are

I: Information

R: Reserved

X: Holds the bit pattern RRCIIIII

Y: Holds the bit pattern CCRRRRRR

Z: Holds the bit pattern CCRROORS

In the X, Y, and Z bit patterns

I is an information bit.

R is a reserved bit.

C is *stuff control.* The value in the five C bits determines whether the S bit contains DS3 payload.

O is an overhead bit.

S is the *stuff opportunity* bit. It contains a DS3 payload bit if CCCCC=00000. (CCCCC should be set to 11111 otherwise.)

Figure 4.21   Packaging 5,592 DS3 bits in an SPE.

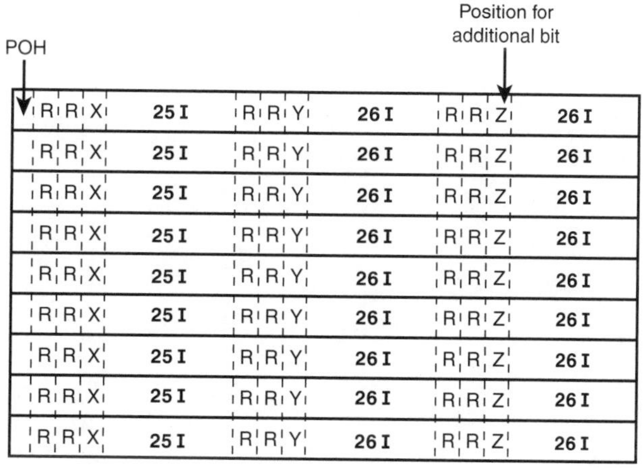

Virtual Tributaries and Virtual Tributary Groups

DS1, E1, DS1C, and DS2 signals are carried within an STS-1 as units called *virtual tributaries (VTs)*. Each virtual tributary is packaged within a *virtual tributary group*.

An STS-1 SPE that carries virtual tributaries contains 7 virtual tributary groups. Each virtual tributary group occupies 12 columns. The 7 groups occupy a total of 84 columns.

Two more columns remain in the payload area. These are reserved columns that do not carry data. Columns 30 and 59 are set aside as the reserved columns.

The format of an SPE carrying virtual tributaries is shown in Figure 4.22:

- Column 1 of the SPE contains the path overhead.

- Columns 30 and 59 are reserved.

- Columns 2–29, 31–58, and 60–87 contain the seven virtual tributary groups, which are byte-interleaved.

- The 12 columns 2, 9, 16, 23, 31, 38, 45, 52, 60, 67, 74, and 81 contain the bytes for the first virtual tributary.

- The 12 columns 8, 15, 22, 29, 37, 44, 51, 58, 66, 73, 80, and 87 contain the bytes for the last virtual tributary.

Figure 4.22   Interleaving virtual tributary groups.

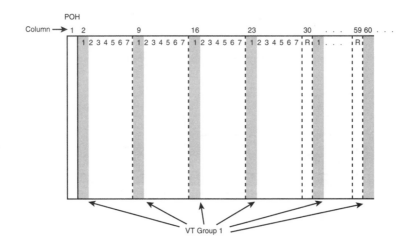

Figure 4.23 represents the multiplexing process. You can see that it is quite easy to multiplex virtual tributary groups into a signal at one node, and extract it at another. The position of each virtual tributary group is clearly established.

Figure 4.23   Multiplexing seven virtual tributary groups.

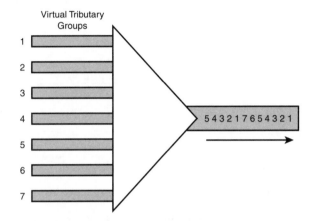

Types of Virtual Tributaries

Virtual tributary groups carry four types of low-speed virtual tributaries, which are listed in Table 4.2. A virtual tributary group can carry four DS1 signals, three E1s, two DS1Cs, or one DS2.

Only one type can be carried within a particular group, but different types can be carried within the seven groups in an SPE. For example, an SPE could contain three VT1.5 groups, two VT2 groups, a VT3, and a VT6.

Table 4.2   Types of Virtual Tributaries

VT Type	Signal Carried	Signal Bit Rate in Mbps	Number of Columns per Signal	Bandwidth of the Columns in Mbps	Number in VT Group
VT1.5	DS1	1.544	3	1.728	4
VT2	E1	2.048	4	2.304	3
VT3	DS1C	3.152	6	3.456	2
VT6	DS2	6.312	12	6.912	1

As shown in Table 4.2, each virtual tributary is allotted more bandwidth than is needed to carry its signal. Some extra bytes are used for path overhead bytes associated with the tributary. There are additional unused filler bits or bytes for some of the signals.

Virtual tributary payloads can be inserted into their allotted areas in either of two modes. In fixed mode, the payload is locked into a fixed position. For the more flexible floating mode, a signal payload is inserted into its allotted columns at a convenient point—much as an SPE floats in its payload area. A pointer located in the virtual tributary overhead bytes identifies the starting point of the signal payload.

For example, of the three columns (27 bytes) allotted to a floating VT1.5:

- The first two bytes are used for pointer and overhead bytes.

- The next 24 bytes carry bytes from a DS1 frame.

- The next byte contains the DS1 framing bit (and reserved bits).

Note

Pointer and path overhead bytes actually are defined across four consecutive 125 microsecond periods. A total of eight overhead bytes are identified for a VT1.5. Two bytes form a pointer and six others are assigned to various other VT1.5 path overhead functions.

SONET Ring Topology

Ring configurations are popular in SONET installations, because mechanisms for rapid recovery are easily implemented with a ring topology. There are two frequently used ring architectures: *unidirectional path switched ring (UPSR)* and *bidirectional line switched ring (BLSR)*.

Unidirectional Path Switched Rings

The nodes in a unidirectional path switched ring (UPSR) are connected by two rings of fiber. The same data is transmitted onto each fiber, but in opposite directions. Specifically, as shown in Figure 4.24, data is transmitted onto one fiber in the clockwise direction, and onto the other in the counterclockwise direction. A receiver examines both payloads, and keeps the "best" one.

Note that data sent from A to B will arrive once on the direct path from A to B, and again on the path that passes through C.

Figure 4.24   A unidirectional path switching ring.

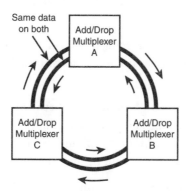

If there is a cable failure between node A and node B, then, as shown in Figure 4.25, data cannot flow from A to B or C on the clockwise circuit. However, data still is carried from A to C and B on the counterclockwise circuit.

Similarly, data cannot flow from B to A on the counterclockwise circuit, but still flows from B to C to A in the clockwise direction.

Note that there is no disruption of service with this configuration.

Figure 4.25   Recovery from a cable failure in a unidirectional path switching ring.

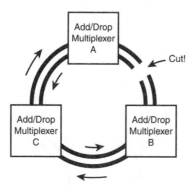

Bidirectional Line Switched Rings

Bidirectional line switched rings (BLSRs) are configured with either two or four rings of fiber.

For a two-fiber ring, different data is transmitted on each of the two fibers. However, only half of the capacity of each fiber is used as the normal *working* capacity. The remaining half is reserved for *protection*.

As shown in Figure 4.26, if there is a cable break between node A and node B, traffic that normally would be sent across the failed line is sent in the opposite direction using the protection capacity on each ring. More specifically, as the right side of Figure 4.26 shows, traffic is "wrapped around" from one ring to the other, which means

- Traffic traveling from node C to node A on the outer ring is processed at A. Some is siphoned off ("dropped") for delivery via lines attached to node A (not shown). Some is added via lines attached to node A (also not shown). The new multiplexed bundle is transmitted from A to C on the inner ring.

  After the add/drop process is performed at node C, a freshly multiplexed bundle is then forwarded to node B on the inner ring.

- Traffic traveling from node C to node B on the inner ring is processed at B. After the add/drop process, the freshly multiplexed bundle is transmitted from B to C on the outer ring.

  After the add/drop process is performed at node C, a freshly multiplexed bundle is then forwarded to node A on the outer ring.

Figure 4.26   A two fiber bidirectional line switched ring configuration.

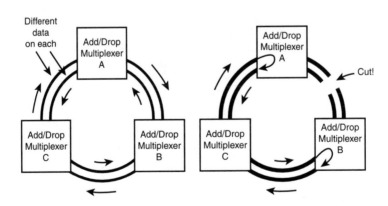

The full transmission capacity of two of the rings is used for a four-fiber ring. There is only one working fiber in each direction of transmission during normal operation. A protection fiber is assigned to each working fiber. If a working fiber fails, traffic is transmitted in the opposite direction on its protection fiber.

Packet Over SONET

Like any point-to-point line, a SONET carrier can be used to transport data link frames. The PPP frames mentioned in Chapter I-1 are favored because PPP can transport IP, NetWare IPX, DECnet, AppleTalk, and other types of layer 3 traffic, as well as bridged LAN frames. In addition, PPP is an efficient, low overhead protocol. The use of PPP over SONET is called *Packet Over SONET* or *POS*.

References

Additional information about SONET can be found in ANSI standards:

- T1.105-1995: *Synchronous Optical Network (SONET)—Basic Description Including Multiplex Structures, Rates, and Formats* (1995)

- T1.105.01: *Synchronous Optical Network (SONET)—Automatic Protection Switching* (1995)

- T1.105.02: *Synchronous Optical Network (SONET)—Payload Mappings* (1995)

- T1.105.03: *Synchronous Optical Network (SONET)—Jitter at Network Interfaces* (1994)

- T1.105.03a: *Synchronous Optical Network (SONET)—Jitter at Network Interfaces—DS1 Supplement* (1995)

- T1.105.03b: *Synchronous Optical Network (SONET)—Jitter at Network Interfaces— DS3 Wander Supplement* (1997)

- T1.105.04: *Synchronous Optical Network (SONET)—Data Communication Channel Protocols and Architectures* (1995)

- T1.105.05: *Synchronous Optical Network (SONET)—Tandem Connection Maintenance* (1994)

- T1.105.06: *Synchronous Optical Network (SONET)—Physical Layer Specifications* (1996)

- T1.105.07: *Synchronous Optical Network (SONET)—Sub STS-1 Interface Rates and Formats Specification* (1996)

- T1.105.07a: *Synchronous Optical Network (SONET)—Sub STS-1 Interface Rates and Formats Specification (Inclusion of N X VT Group Interfaces)* (1997)

- T1.105.09: *Synchronous Optical Network (SONET)×Network Element Timing and Synchronization* (1996)

A sampling of the ITU-T recommendations dealing with the synchronous digital hierarchy and STM formats includes

- G.707: *Network node interface for the synchronous digital hierarchy (SDH)* (1996, replaces older G.707, G.708, and G.709)

- G.774.02: *Synchronous digital hierarchy (SDH) configuration of the payload structure for the network element view* (1994, Corrigendum 1 added in 1996)

- G.780: *Vocabulary of terms for synchronous digital hierarchy (SDH) networks and equipment* (1994)

- G.781: *Structure of Recommendations on equipment for the synchronous digital hierarchy (SDH)* (1994)

- G.782: *Types and general characteristics of synchronous digital hierarchy (SDH) equipment* (1994)

See the list of ITU-T G Series documents for further references.

Several interworking drafts have been published by the SONET Interoperability Forum.

PART II

Frame Relay

Data Networks

In the early years of computer networking, organizations that needed robust wide area data transmission facilities had only one choice: They had to connect sites using costly point-to-point digital leased lines.

Point-to-point leased line technology is well understood and very reliable. Leased digital line speeds range from 9.6 kilobits per second (Kbps) to millions of bits per second (Mbps). An organization can count on steady, uninterrupted bandwidth and low, predictable delay between two sites when it installs a leased line.

However, leased lines have a number of disadvantages. They are costly to set up. Monthly charges are proportional to distance and are substantial. The cost of a fully meshed network (like the one shown in Figure 1.1) is very steep if the sites are far from one another.

Furthermore, a network like the one in Figure 1.1 is complicated to maintain. The 5-node network in the figure contains 10 lines and 20 CSU/DSU access devices. An organization that wants to connect N nodes with a fully meshed network of leased lines needs to support

$(N^2-N)/2$ lines

N^2-N access devices

For example, meshing 20 sites requires 190 lines and 380 access devices, and meshing 30 sites requires 435 lines and 870 access devices.

Figure 1.1 A fully meshed leased line network.

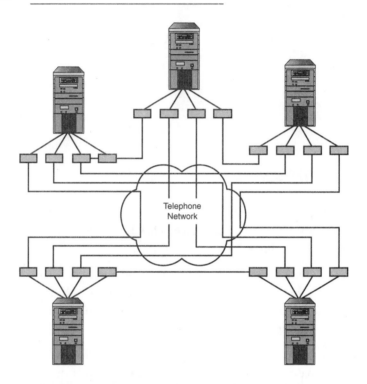

ITU-T Public Data Network Architecture

A more cost-effective option called a *public data network* was introduced in the early 1980s by the ITU-T, the ruling standards body for telephone networks. A company that operates a public data network is called a *public data network service provider* or, more succinctly, a *service provider*.

The data network architecture introduced by the ITU-T has a lot in common with the architecture of a telephone network. In a public telephone network

- There is a standard interface between an end-user device—a telephone—and the public network.

- Customers (also called *subscribers*) can set up switched circuits on demand or contract for permanent circuits.

- Telephone networks all over the world are linked into a global telephone system. This is possible because the ITU-T has defined a standard network-to-network interface.

- There is a standard interface between an organization's private telephone network (implemented by a PBX) and a public telephone network.

Similarly, for the ITU-T data network architecture

- There is a standard interface between an access device, such as a computer, router, bridge, or switch, and the network.

- Customers can set up switched circuits on demand or contract for permanent circuits.

- Public data networks all over the world can be linked into a global data network. This is possible because the ITU-T defined a standard data network-to-network interface.

- An organization's private data network (implemented by appropriate data network switches) can be connected to a public data network via a standard interface.

Some key features that make data networks very different from conventional telephone networks are

- The cost of a public data network circuit does not depend on the distance traversed across the data networks.

- A subscriber device can establish hundreds of concurrent circuits via one port on the device and one communications line that connects the port to the data network.

Figure 1.2 is a conceptual illustration of the way an organization plugs systems into a public data network and sets up circuits between systems. For example, in Figure 1.2, there are three circuits between System A and other systems attached to the data network. The three circuits share the single line that connects System A to the network.

Figure 1.3 shows a close-up view of a line that connects a system to a data network. The customer's system is called an *access device*. The line is called an *access line*. The black lines represent circuits that share the access line.

Virtual Circuits

A data network circuit is called a *virtual* circuit because, unlike a telephone call, a fixed bandwidth is not reserved for the exclusive use of the circuit. Instead, traffic for many circuits shares links within the network. This is a reasonable design to use for data transmissions, which are intermittent and bursty.

Figure 1.2   Systems accessing a public data network.

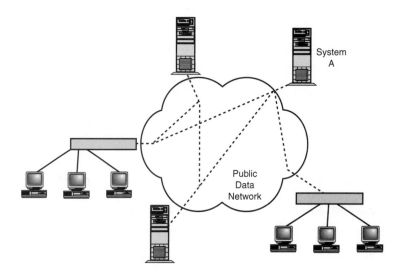

Figure 1.3   Circuits sharing an access line.

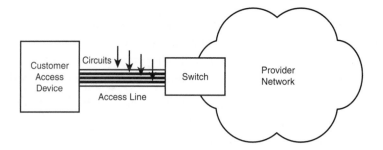

Internal Structure

Internally, a public data network is made up of a mesh of switches and high-bandwidth lines, as shown in Figure 1.4. A high-bandwidth line is a lot cheaper than many separate low-bandwidth lines that add up to the same total capacity. Bulk bandwidth is a bargain. Public data network customers enjoy cost savings because they *share* the bandwidth in the high-capacity lines within the provider's network.

A service provider places switches that interface to customer sites at strategically located sites called *points of presence (POPs)*. A subscriber accesses a service provider's network by connecting to the nearest POP. In most cases, this is a leased line connection.

| Figure 1.4 | Structure of a public data network. |

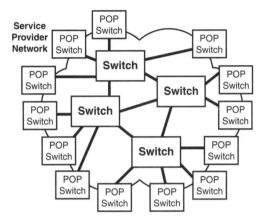

UNI

The precise *internal* structure of a public data network is not standardized. A data network service provider can use any technology it likes inside its network. Of course, the network has to be engineered to support the services the provider has promised to deliver.

However, standards are needed to define the *interface* between customer premise equipment and a switch that belongs to the provider network. A standard interface promotes open competition between vendors that build customer premise access devices. It enables customers to plug into the network easily. The interface between customer premise equipment and data network equipment is called a *user-network interface* or *UNI* (see Figure 1.5).

A customer needs four access devices and four lines at each site to build the fully meshed leased line network in Figure 1.1. A data network customer needs only one access device and one line at each site to build a network that has hundreds of circuits between remote sites. As shown in Figures 1.4 and 1.5, several virtual circuits share an access line.

Data Network Standards

The original ITU-T public data network architecture was defined in the related standards X.25 and X.75. Conforming networks are called *X.25 networks*. Unfortunately, X.25 interfaces are relatively complicated, and it is difficult to work with them. Furthermore, X.25 network throughput has been disappointingly low.

Figure 1.5   A user-network interface.

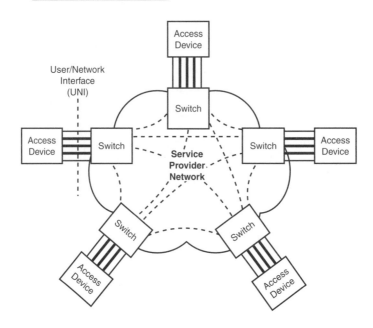

An improved *frame relay* public data network was defined in the early 1990s as part of the ITU-T narrowband *Integrated Services Digital Network (ISDN)* effort. A customer connects to one of these new networks via an extremely simple *frame relay* interface. Frame relay public data networks were engineered for very high throughput.

Note

Many sources refer to X.25 and frame relay as *connection-based* services. All this means is that a virtual circuit is set up between a source and destination for a period of time. Even though a precise bandwidth is not set aside for exclusive use by this circuit, network resources are reserved so that a contracted average bandwidth for the circuit is maintained, and the customer's data is delivered without too much delay.

This contrasts, for example, with communication across a traditional broadcast-style Ethernet LAN. A system attached to an Ethernet LAN can send a frame to another system at any time. Systems on a traditional Ethernet try to grab bandwidth whenever they need it. There is no way to guarantee that a system will get a specific amount of bandwidth or that there will not be long delays.

Initially, frame relay circuits were used for long-term LAN-to-LAN connections, replacing more costly leased lines. As confidence in the technology grew, IBM bisynchronous and SNA traffic was moved off leased lines and onto frame relay circuits. Today, voice, voice-band fax, and modem data also are carried on frame relay circuits.

Many communications companies have built frame relay service networks and have jumped into the public data network business. A customer can choose from an abundant number of competing offerings, especially if its sites are located in major urban centers.

Frame Relay Standards Organizations

Several organizations have participated in the frame relay standards effort, which still continues today.

As was mentioned earlier in this chapter, the ITU-T organization initiated work on frame relay standards. The *American National Standards Institute (ANSI)* contributed to the ITU-T effort and added features specific to the North American communications environment.

The *Internet Engineering Task Force (IETF)* has published several useful *Request for Comment (RFC)* documents relating to frame relay.

Without a doubt, the most influential frame relay standards organization is the Frame Relay Forum. *The Frame Relay Forum* is an international organization established by frame relay vendors and service providers.

The stated purpose of the Frame Relay Forum is to promote frame relay technology. Forum volunteers write and publish *implementation agreements* that define features vendors should support to build products that interwork with one another.

These implementation agreements were a key factor in the rapid deployment of frame relay. Continuing cooperation between vendors has speeded the addition of new capabilities.

The Forum got its start because four vendors became impatient with the slow pace of ITU-T and ANSI standards development. Digital Equipment Corporation, Northern Telecom, StrataCom, and Cisco joined together to work on a management protocol that would report on the status of permanent virtual circuits. An organization evolved from the efforts of these first four vendors, who were called the "Gang of Four."

The Frame Relay Forum has been very effective, and it now is common for vendors to cooperate on implementation agreements whenever any important new technology is introduced. For example, the ATM Forum has made significant contributions to the implementation of ATM products.

Extensive information on frame relay technology and copies of the frame relay implementation agreements are available at the Frame Relay Forum World Wide Web site: `http://www.frforum.com/`.

Outline of Part II

In this part of the book, after a brief look at X.25 technology in Chapter II-2, you are introduced to the expanding set of services offered by frame relay providers in Chapter II-3 and discover the significance of the fine print in *service level agreements (SLAs)* in Chapter II-4. You explore frame relay technology and protocols from the users' and the network service providers' points of view in Chapters II-5, II-6, II-8, and II-9. Several mechanisms that help a subscriber manage frame relay circuits are explained in Chapter II-7. And finally, solutions to special problems that arise when IP, IBM SNA, and voice traffic are carried across frame relay circuits are explored in Chapter II-10.

2

X.25 Data Networks

Note

This chapter describes X.25 networks, the first public data networks. If you read this chapter, you can gain insight into data network concepts and the evolution of data networks. However, this material is not required to understand frame relay; you can skip it if you do not have an interest in X.25.

The X.25 public data networks that appeared on the scene in the early 1980s offered a cost-effective alternative to leased lines. X.25 promised delivery of data from source to destination with a good level of reliability. Best of all, the distance traveled across a public data network was not a factor in the cost of the service.

X.25 originally was designed for host-to-host communications. The creators of X.25 believed that host applications would communicate directly via X.25 virtual circuits.

Throughout its early years, the bulk of the traffic carried by X.25 providers did not run between hosts but instead carried data between end-user ASCII terminal devices and hosts, and supported computer time-sharing services. To reach a remote host, an ASCII terminal user connected to a nearby server called a *Packet Assembler/Disassembler (PAD)* via an ordinary dialup modem. The PAD stuffed terminal data bytes into X.25 messages and forwarded them to destination hosts.

Eventually, X.25 also was used to connect IBM terminals and printers to mainframe hosts, and for IBM host-to-host communications.

By the end of the 1980s, organizations were moving away from host-to-host or terminal-to-host communications and toward bridged or routed LAN-to-LAN communications. X.25 interfaces were implemented in bridges and routers, although X.25 had not originally been designed for this purpose.

Unfortunately, X.25 is slow, complex, and often hard to configure. X.25 providers offer only low-bandwidth connections to their customers.

Time-sharing has been replaced by Internet surfing, and frame relay data networks have become the method of choice for LAN-to-LAN communications. However, X.25 still is used in IBM networks and interconnects LANs in areas where frame relay service is not available. X.25 also continues to be popular for applications such as bank Automatic Teller Machine connections and credit card validations. A version of X.25 operating across an ISDN Basic Rate Interface D channel is very cost effective for intermittent, low-bandwidth data communications.

X.25 Architecture

X.25 provides a digital data service that is structured like ordinary telephone service. X.25 defines a standard interface between a customer device and a data network, just as there is a standard interface between a telephone instrument and the telephone network.

In fact, X.25 standardizes only the user-network interface between a device and the data network. It does not deal with the internal implementation of the data network. However, X.25 networks normally are implemented as a mesh of switches, called *packet switches*.

One of the virtues of X.25 is that public networks around the world are interconnected, and destinations in just about any country can be reached via X.25 service. A second standard, X.75, defines the network-to-network interface between two X.25 data networks.

X.25 Circuit Services

X.25 provides virtual circuit services. There are two types of X.25 circuits. *Permanent virtual circuits (PVCs)* are preconfigured and set up for an extended period of time (usually months or years). *Switched virtual circuits (SVCs)* are set up on demand and are terminated at the convenience of the user, much like an ordinary telephone call.

X.25 is a mature technology and supports both PVC and SVC services to locations around the world.

X.25 Protocol Layering

X.25 describes how a customer *data terminal equipment (DTE)* device connects to a service provider *data circuit-terminating equipment (DCE)* device, which usually is a packet switch. As shown in Figure 2.1, a reliable link is set up between the DTE and DCE. Theoretically, up to 4,095 virtual circuits can be established within this link. Circuits are numbered, and the numbers usually are broken into two ranges: One range is used for PVCs, and the other is used for SVCs.

Figure 2.1   Virtual circuits within a reliable X.25 link.

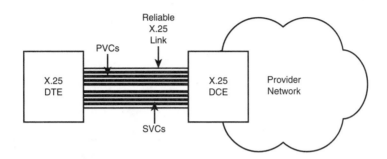

The X.25 protocol operates at three layers, shown in Figure 2.2. There are well-established physical layer standards for the cabling and connectors to be used at an X.25 interface.

A layer 2 data link protocol called *Link Access Protocol Balanced (LAPB)* is used between a customer DTE and a network DCE. The link layer protocol data unit is called a *frame*.

Like ISDN LAPD, LAPB belongs to the *High-level Data Link Control (HDLC)* family of protocols. Each LAPB frame that carries data is numbered and acknowledged, and LAPB is called a *reliable data link protocol*. However, like all HDLC-based link protocols, LAPB has a very limited capability to recover from errors and cannot guarantee delivery of all data frames.

The separate virtual circuits are defined at X.25 layer 3, the *packet layer*. Not surprisingly, the packet layer protocol data unit is called a *packet*. Each packet that carries data is numbered and acknowledged.

Figure 2.2   X.25 layers.

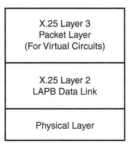

Figure 2.3 shows the X.25 protocol architecture and the location of an X.75 interface. The sections that follow present an overview of the protocols at the X.25 user-network interface.

Figure 2.3   X.25 protocol architecture.

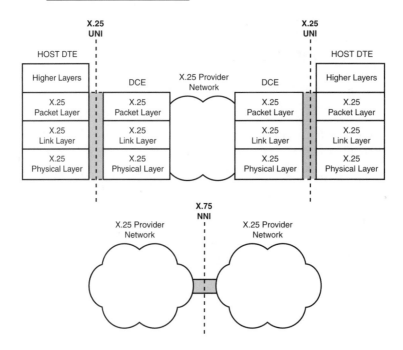

LAPB

The LAPB protocol, which is used between a customer DTE and a network DCE, belongs to the *High-level Data Link Control (HDLC)* family of data link protocols.

Just as was the case for LAPD (see Chapter I-3), one or more HDLC *flag* bytes separate each pair of transmitted LAPB frames, as shown in Figure 2.4. Contiguous flags are sent out by an interface during idle times, when there are no LAPB frames awaiting transmission. Recall that the HDLC flag pattern is the binary string, 01111110.

LAPB Information Frame Format

The overall format of a LAPB information frame follows the standard HDLC pattern, as shown in Figure 2.5. The LAPB *address field* indicates if the destination is the DCE or DTE. There are standard DTE and DCE address numbers.

Figure 2.4   LAPB frames separated by flags.

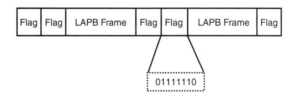

The *control field* contains send and receive sequence numbers. The receive sequence number acknowledges frames by identifying the number of the next expected information frame. Two numbering ranges are supported:

- Count from 0 to 7, and then roll back to 0 (modulo 8 counting)
- Count from 0 to 127, and then roll back to 0 (modulo 128 counting)

A 1-byte control field is used with modulo 8 counting, and a 2-byte control field is used with modulo 128 counting.

Like other HDLC frames, a LAPB frame ends with a frame check sequence field that is used to determine if data has been corrupted in transit.

Figure 2.5   LAPB information frame format.

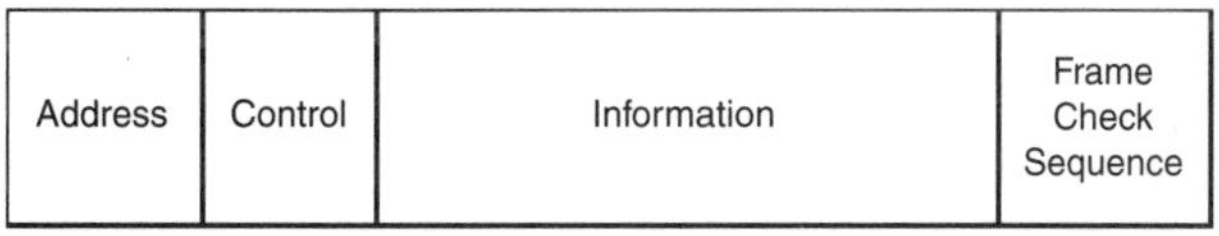

Address	Control	Information	Frame Check Sequence

LAPB Windowing

The maximum number of unacknowledged information frames that can be in transit at any time is limited. A preconfigured window size determines this number. The window size ranges from 1 to 7 when modulo 8 numbering is used and from 1 to 127 when modulo 128 numbering is used.

LAPB data transmission is easily bogged down. Frames must arrive in exact sequence order. If a frame is lost or corrupted in transmission, the receiver discards all subsequent frames until the missing frame arrives. Until this happens, no data can be received successfully. The receiver speeds the process of recovery by sending a *reject (REJ)* frame that announces the number of the next in-sequence frame that is expected.

This means that information transmission for all virtual circuits stops dead in its tracks in the direction for which a frame was lost. The lost frame and all its successors must be retransmitted.

Other LAPB Frames

Like other members of the HDLC family, in addition to information frames, there are two other categories of frames:

- Unnumbered frames used to set up and terminate a link and report a serious error

- Numbered supervisory frames used for acknowledgments and flow control, and to signal a missing frame

LAPB Link Startup

A DTE or DCE initiates a link by sending a startup request and receiving an acknowledgment. The startup request is either a *set asynchronous balanced mode (SABM)* frame or a *set asynchronous balanced mode extended (SABME)* frame.

SABM indicates that modulo 8 numbering will be used, while SABME indicates that modulo 128 numbering will be used. In either case, information frame numbering starts at 0. Modulo 128 numbering was introduced for satellite links, which have a long delay time.

The positive response to a SABM or SABME is an *unnumbered acknowledgment (UA)* frame. The partner can refuse to open the link by sending a *disconnected mode (DM)* response.

LAPB Flow Control, Acknowledgments, and Retransmission

A DTE or DCE sends a supervisory *receive not ready (RNR)* frame to indicate that it is busy and temporarily is unable to accept additional information frames.

The RNR also contains an acknowledgment of received frames. Several frames can be acknowledged at once. For example, ACK 5 means: "Frames up to and including 4 have been received. Number 5 is expected next."

A DTE or DCE sends a supervisory *receive ready (RR)* frame to indicate that it is not busy and is able to receive information frames. The RR also contains an acknowledgment of received frames.

Information frames also can be acknowledged by an information frame received from the partner, because each information frame header contains a receive number as well as a send number.

As mentioned earlier, the supervisory *reject (REJ)* frame is used to recover from lost or corrupted frames. A reject is effective when there is a flow of frames and it is evident that a frame is missing. If other frames do not follow a frame that is lost, the sender will retransmit after a timeout period during which an acknowledgment is not received.

Disconnecting a LAPB Link

A *disconnect (DISC)* frame requests termination of the link. The partner confirms the disconnect with a UA frame.

Sometimes an incoming frame passes the frame check sequence test but contains a serious protocol violation (such as an invalid acknowledgment number or an information field whose size is greater than the maximum size). This creates a non-recoverable error, which is signaled by a *frame reject (FRMR)* frame. The result is drastic. The link has to be reset—that is, reinitialized with a SABM or SABME. Numbering on the link—and on all enclosed virtual circuits—will restart at 0. This almost always results in some loss of data.

Note

X.25 often is called a reliable data service. However, X.25 does not guarantee that all data sent across a circuit will be delivered reliably. Resets lead to data loss, which has to be corrected by a higher layer protocol.

X.25 Packet Level

Multiple virtual circuits share a common underlying LAPB link. The behavior of each separate virtual circuit is defined by the X.25 packet layer protocol.

Each packet has a header that identifies the circuit to which it belongs. The header of a data packet also contains send and receive numbers. When a circuit is initiated, numbering starts at 0.

Figure 2.6 shows a data packet encapsulated inside a LAPB frame. When a DCE receives an encapsulated packet from the DTE, the DCE uses the LAPB frame check sequence to verify that the frame has not been corrupted. The DCE then checks the validity of the frame header, makes sure that the LAPB frame gets acknowledged, and strips away the LAPB frame header and trailer.

The payload is passed to the packet layer software in the DCE, which checks the validity of the packet header, makes sure that the packet gets acknowledged, and identifies the circuit on which the payload needs to be forwarded. The payload will be encapsulated in some manner before it is passed on through the data network. The encapsulation method depends on the switch technology that is used within the network.

Figure 2.6   A data packet encapsulated within a LAPB frame.

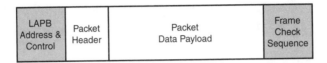

Logical Channel Numbers

Each circuit has a two-part numeric identifier that appears in the header of every packet sent across that circuit. The identifier is made up of

- A 4-bit logical channel group number

- An 8-bit logical channel number

These numbers have only local significance, which means that different numbers can be used at each end of a circuit. The network performs number translations so the appropriate pair of numbers appears at a packet's destination. For example, Figure 2.7 shows a virtual circuit between DTE A and DTE B. At DTE A, the circuit is identified by logical channel group number 5 and logical channel number 21. At DTE B, the circuit is identified by logical channel group number 7 and logical channel number 34.

Figure 2.7   Packet logical channel group numbers and logical channel numbers.

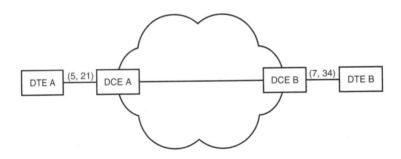

Packet Headers

Every packet header contains

- A 4-bit *general format identifier*. This field indicates whether modulo 8 or modulo 128 packet numbering is used. For data packets, bits in this field also are used to flag some special functions.

- A logical channel group number and logical channel number.

- Packet type identification.

Inclusion of additional fields in the packet header depends on the packet type.

Packet Windowing and Flow Control

The data transfer procedures for each virtual circuit at the packet layer are similar to the procedures for the entire link at the LAPB layer. Each data packet is numbered (modulo 8 or 128), and there is a preconfigured window size that determines the maximum number of unacknowledged packets that can be outstanding for an individual virtual circuit.

Outgoing data is acknowledged by receive numbers in incoming data, RR, or RNR packets.

There are two options for handling acknowledgments:

- An acknowledgment received by the DTE might mean that the local DCE has received the data.

- An acknowledgment received by the DTE might mean that the remote DTE has received the data.

A customer decides which option to use. The first option results in better throughput, while the second option indicates if end-to-end delivery has really been completed. The customer sets a "D-bit" flag in the general format identifier header field to 1 to indicate that remote acknowledgment is desired.

By default, there is no packet retransmission and no recovery from an out-of-sequence packet. After all, each packet is carried within a LAPB frame, and LAPB already should have retransmitted missing data. A customer can subscribe to an optional facility that supports packet retransmission for a virtual circuit. This allows a DTE to send a DTE reject packet that identifies the logical channel and the packet sequence number at which retransmission should start.

However, if the optional facility is not used, receipt of an out-of-sequence packet causes the circuit to be reset.

Packet Level Resets

A temporary network problem causes a DCE to reset an affected permanent virtual circuit. This means that the network discards all packets for that circuit that are in transit. The DTE and DCE must make a fresh beginning, numbering subsequent packets starting from 0. Note that an event as simple as an out-of-sequence packet can cause a circuit reset, and data is lost due to circuit resets.

A more drastic *restart* procedure simultaneously clears all switched virtual circuits and resets all permanent virtual circuits. The result is that all switched calls disappear, while the numbering on all permanent virtual circuits restarts at 0. A DTE or DCE sends a restart packet when it has detected serious errors in packet layer transmissions.

Switched Virtual Circuits

X.25 providers support switched virtual circuits, which, as you remember, are set up on demand.

As is the case for telephone calls, the ability to make data calls depends on having a global numbering plan in place. In addition, a user needs to exchange signaling information with the network to set up a call. The tones that represent dialed digits, the sound of ringing, and the click when the far end receiver is picked up are familiar telephone signals.

The X.25 world has its own numbering plan and signaling system:

- A destination is identified by a "DTE address" instead of a "telephone number."

- Formatted messages are used to request a call and receive notification that the call has been set up.

The following sections describe the DTE address numbering system and outline the steps followed to set up and end a switched X.25 data call.

X.121 Addresses

ITU-T standard X.121 defines the global addressing scheme for X.25 DTEs. X.121 addresses also are called *International Data Numbers (IDNs)*.

The length of an X.121 address is not fixed; however, the length is limited to a maximum of 14 decimal digits. The first three digits of the address identify a country. The fourth digit identifies a specific *packet-switched data network (PSN)*. When combined, the first four digits are called the *Data Network Identification Code (DNIC)*.

The remaining address digits identify a specific DTE attached to this network. The format of an X.121 address is shown in Figure 2.8.

Figure 2.8   X.121 address format.

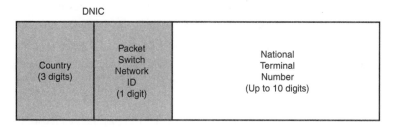

DNIC

| Country (3 digits) | Packet Switch Network ID (1 digit) | National Terminal Number (Up to 10 digits) |

Call Setup and Termination

To set up a telephone call, you dial a number, and the digits get sent to your local telephone switch. To set up a data call, a DTE sends a call request packet to its adjacent DCE. The call request includes

- The calling DTE number.

- The called DTE number.

- Optional parameters that define *facilities*, which are special services that are requested for the call, such as maximum packet size, window size, or a desired limit on transit delay. (Some parameters can have different values for each direction of the call.)

- An optional call user data field. This can be used for just about anything. For example, it sometimes is used to identify the type of higher layer protocol data (such as IP or SNA) that will be carried in the data payloads exchanged across this circuit.

Figure 2.9 illustrates the simple call setup procedure. The caller selects an unused channel group number and channel number, and creates a *call request* message that includes the addresses and parameters for the call. At the called end, the network selects an unused channel group number and channel number, and uses the call request information to create an *incoming call* message. The called party accepts the call via a *call accepted* message, which is reflected back to the caller as a *call connected* message.

Figure 2.9   X.25 call setup procedure.

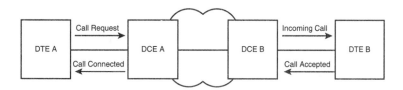

Figure 2.10 shows the sequence of messages used to clear a call. Either party can terminate the call. In the figure, the original caller takes the initiative. The caller sends a *clear request*. The DCE responds with a *DCE clear confirmation*. The DCE does not have to wait for clearing at the called end to complete before sending its confirmation.

Author Note

A clear request also is used to refuse an incoming call.

The far end DCE sends a *clear indication* to the called DTE. The called party sends a *DTE clear confirmation*.

If the network is unable to continue a call because of some problem, it can initiate a clearing procedure and send a *clear indication* to a circuit endpoint. The clear indication describes the nature of the problem. A DTE responds with a *DTE clear confirmation* message.

| Figure 2.10 | X.25 call clearance procedure. |

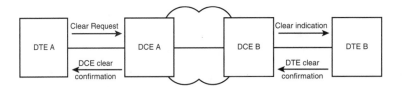

Note

When X.25 is offered as an ISDN service, DSS1 messages across a LAPD D-channel link are used to set up and terminate a virtual circuit.

X.25 Packet Types

The preceding sections present the main features of the X.25 packet layer protocol. Many details have not been covered. In fact, several packet types have not even been mentioned.

For your reference, brief descriptions of the packet types are presented in Tables 2.2 through 2.7. There are seven categories of packets:

- Call setup and clearing
- Data and interrupt
- Flow control
- Reset
- Restart
- Diagnostic
- Registration

Table 2.2   Call Setup and Clearing Packet Types

Name	Description
Call request	Initiates a call, identifying the called address, calling address, and other parameters.
Incoming call	DCE reports a call request to the called party.
Call accepted	The called party accepts the call.
Call connected	DCE reports call setup completion.
Clear request	Asks for termination of a call.
Clear indication	Indicates notification that the partner or the network is terminating the call.
DCE clear confirmation	Accepts the termination request.
DTE clear confirmation	Accepts the termination request.

Table 2.3   Data and Interrupt Packet Types

Name	Description
DTE data	Carries outgoing data payload from the DTE.
DCE data	Carries incoming data payload to the DTE.
DTE interrupt	Enables a DTE to transmit a small amount of unnumbered data across the circuit, even if the DCE has signaled RNR. Receipt of the interrupt packet must be confirmed by the DCE before another interrupt can be sent.
DCE interrupt confirmation	Confirms receipt of a DTE interrupt packet sent by the local DTE.
DCE interrupt	Indicates an incoming interrupt packet to the recipient DTE.
DTE interrupt confirmation	Confirms receipt of an interrupt packet.

Table 2.4	Flow Control Packet Types
Name	Description
RR	Receive ready. Indicates ready state and acknowledges data.
RNR	Receive not ready. Indicates busy state and acknowledges data.
REJ (optional)	Reject. An option that might not be available on all networks. Indicates that one or more frames need to be retransmitted.

Table 2.5	Reset Packet Types
Name	Description
DTE reset request	DTE requests reinitialization of a switched or permanent virtual circuit. Circuit data in transit through the network is discarded. New data is numbered starting at 0.
DCE reset confirmation	The DCE confirms the reset.
DCE reset indication	A DCE informs an endpoint that a reset is in progress.
DTE reset confirmation	The DTE confirms the reset indication.

Table 2.6	Restart Packet types
Name	Description
DTE restart request	A DTE can request a restart, which clears all switched virtual circuits and resets all permanent virtual circuits.
DCE restart confirmation	The DCE confirms the restart.
DCE restart indication	A DCE indicates a restart. This might result from a remote DTE restart, or might be sent by the network because of a network problem.
DTE restart confirmation	The DTE confirms the DCE's restart indication.

Table 2.7	Diagnostic and Registration Packet Types
Name	Description
Diagnostic	Issued by the DCE to report a network problem and provide diagnostic information.
Registration request	Enables the customer to use an interactive procedure for registering the facilities it would like to use.
Registration confirmation	Confirms the registration.

Comments on X.25 Layering

Note

The material in this section is intended as food for thought and indicates that layering is not always a clear-cut matter.

ISO standards view the X.25 packet layer as a layer 3 network protocol. When they defined the ISO model, ISO standards makers believed that X.25 virtual circuits would be used for all end-to-end data communications and that X.121 addresses would be used to identify the endpoints of every network communication.

The ISO model was created before the personal computer had established a beachhead in businesses, before local area networks had snaked their way across corporate premises, before routers started to connect network components, and before a legion of other wide area technologies had arrived on the scene.

A network protocol is supposed to take traffic from its source to its destination. Today, an X.25 circuit most often is just a convenient wide area hop in a longer path from a source to a destination. It simply replaces a leased line or dialup line. Although X.25 is complex internally, the service that an X.25 circuit provides is equivalent to a point-to-point layer 2 data link.

For example, Figure 2.11 shows IP traffic being routed across a wide area X.25 connection between a pair of routers. Each router connects to an Ethernet LAN. Traffic from a host on LAN A to a host on LAN B crosses three links:

- LAN A
- An X.25 virtual circuit
- LAN B

In this figure, IP addresses provide the end-to-end addressing, and IP network layer protocol data units (called *datagrams*) are carried inside X.25 packet payloads.

Figure 2.11   Carrying IP traffic across an X.25 link.

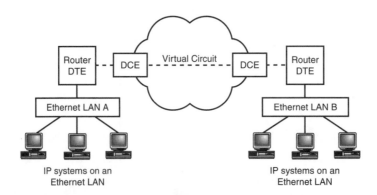

Figure 2.12 illustrates two LANs that are bridged across a wide area X.25 connection. In this figure, MAC addresses provide the end-to end addressing. The X.25 connection replaces a leased line that might otherwise connect the two bridges.

In Figure 2.12, MAC frames are carried inside X.25 packet payloads.

Figure 2.12   Bridging two LANs across an X.25 link.

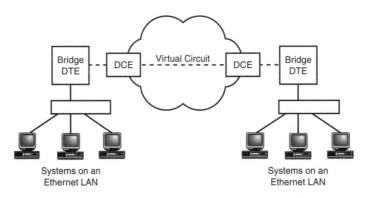

Now, we are ready to leave the complicated world of X.25 and examine a more modern service: frame relay.

References

The classic data network specification is ITU-T Recommendation X.25, *Interface between data terminal equipment (DTE) and data circuit-terminating equipment (DCE) for terminals operating in the packet mode on public data networks* (1984). An updated version was published in 1993.

The physical layer is described in ITU-T Recommendation X.21, *Interface between data terminal equipment (DTE) and data circuit-terminating equipment (DCE) for synchronous operation on public data networks* (1980).

Addresses for X.25 DTEs are described in ITU-T standard X.121, *International Numbering Plan for Public Data Networks* (1992).

Using Frame Relay

The streamlined frame relay data network service introduced in 1991 has the characteristic data network features outlined in Chapter II-1:

- A frame relay customer connects an access device to a service provider network using a single line.

- Sites communicate via virtual circuits.

- Multiple virtual circuits share the physical access line that connects a customer site to the network.

- Distance across the provider's network is not a factor in the cost of the virtual circuit.

- Frame relay standards focus on external interfaces: the *user-network interface (UNI)* between a user access device and the network, and the *network-to-network interface (NNI)* between two frame relay networks.

A frame relay service provider builds its network by positioning switches in strategic locations and connecting the switches via high-capacity (usually T3 or better) long haul lines. Customer traffic shares these lines. The service network can be built in any manner the provider wants.

You get a chance to dive into all the technology and protocol details in later chapters. This chapter describes the major characteristics of frame relay technology and discusses the nuts and bolts issues that arise when planning for frame relay and negotiating with service providers.

Basic Frame Relay Technology

Frame relay is bare-bones simple. It is a layer 2 networking service. Data is carried in frames that have a brief header containing a circuit number (and a few flag bits) and a trailer that contains a frame check sequence (see Figure 3.1). The *frame check sequence field* contains the result of a *Cyclic Redundancy Check (CRC)* that is performed by the sender on the remainder of the frame. The receiver performs the same calculation and compares the result with the value in the frame check sequence field. If the answer does not match, the frame must have been corrupted, and it is discarded.

Figure 3.1 shows the protocol layering for frame relay and sketches the overall format of a frame relay frame. You get a chance to examine the bits and bytes in Chapter II-5.

| Figure 3.1 | Frame relay layering and format of a frame relay frame. |

When a frame is sent from an access device to the adjacent network switch, the switch forwards the frame to the next switch based on the frame's virtual circuit number. All frames follow the same path, and they are delivered in order.

Note

After a path has been set up for a circuit, traffic follows that path as long as it is possible to do so. If a link or switch in a frame relay network fails, most frame relay equipment can create a new path and prevent a circuit connection from being lost—as long as a physical path between the source and destination still exists.

If at any point the frame check sequence indicates that a frame has been corrupted, it is discarded. It then is up to higher layer protocols to retransmit data that needs to be delivered reliably.

Mangled data is not the only cause of frame loss. If a switch in a service provider's network becomes congested, the switch discards some frames.

Structural Differences Between Frame Relay and X.25

There are major differences between frame relay and X.25 data networks. These differences are summarized in Table 3.1.

Table 3.1 Features of X.25 and Frame Relay

X.25	Frame Relay
X.25 has link and packet protocol levels.	Frame relay is a simple data link layer protocol.
The link level of X.25 consists of a reliable data link protocol called LAPB.	Frame relay provides a basic data transfer service that does not guarantee reliable delivery of data.
X.25 LAPB information frames are numbered and acknowledged.	Frame relay frames are not numbered or acknowledged.
Circuits are defined at the packet layer, which runs on top of the LAPB data link layer. Packets are numbered and acknowledged.	Circuits are identified by an address field in the frame header.
There are complex rules that govern the flow of data across an X.25 interface.	Data is packaged into simple frame relay frames and transmitted toward its destination.
These rules often interrupt and impede the flow of data.	Data can be sent across a frame relay network whenever there is bandwidth available to carry it.

The result of these differences is that X.25 behaves like a tractor while frame relay behaves like a sturdy, speedy van. Frame relay wins the race when it comes to hauling data down the information highway.

Frame Relay Benefits

When frame relay came on the scene, it was clear that it was an ideal technology for pumping data from one site to another:

- Frame relay can operate across a wide range of bandwidths.

- Frame relay is flexible. It usually is easy to adjust the bandwidth of a virtual circuit up (to handle increasing demand) or down (to save money by adjusting an oversized circuit to a more accurate level).

- Most providers allow customers to transmit bursts of data that temporarily exceed their contracted data rate (which is called the *committed information rate* or *CIR*). If the excess data does not encounter a congested switch, the provider delivers it.

- Frame relay customer premise equipment is cheap and easy to configure and run.

- Some providers offer management functions that enable users to view the status of their circuits within the provider's network. In some cases, a customer even can create new permanent virtual circuits and modify or delete existing circuits interactively.

Frame relay was adopted as soon as it became cost effective. The price/performance ratio has continued to drop as volume has built up. Companies that adopt frame relay often are able to improve network capacity and connectivity while realizing large cost savings.

The popularity of frame relay services has grown steadily. Service is available in countries around the world, and frame relay customers number in the tens of thousands. The reason for this popularity is that frame relay wide area connectivity has been implemented in service offerings that are flexible as well as cost-effective.

Frame relay continues to invade new markets, and some companies are compressing time-sensitive voice traffic and sending it across frame relay circuits.

Planning for Frame Relay

A number of issues need to be handled during the frame relay planning process. Before implementing frame relay, it is important to

- Know what you have

- Know what you want

You need to perform up-front network analysis to identify

- Existing and planned traffic flows between sites. These should be broken down by protocol because you often need to segregate traffic into different circuits by protocol. Some protocols can share a circuit satisfactorily, while others cannot.

- The average bandwidth required for each flow.

- Response time requirements. A breakdown by protocol or by application might be needed if there is much variation.

- Reliability requirements. Some protocols are very sensitive to frame loss.

- Availability requirements.

There are situations in which a lot of traffic flows in one direction, and relatively little flows back. Providers can set up asymmetric circuits that are less costly than circuits that have the same bandwidth in both directions.

The overall capacity needed for all the circuits terminating at the site's frame relay interface determines the minimum bandwidth that is needed for the short access line (typically a leased line) that connects a site to a provider's switch.

Allowing Extra Bandwidth for Growth

If you want to take advantage of the ability to burst data down the line at varying transmission rates, it pays to install a line with plenty of extra bandwidth. That extra bandwidth also enables you to add new circuits when they are needed. This can be done quickly and non-disruptively.

Plugging a site into a frame relay network is like plugging a building into the electrical distribution system. Within cost constraints, it might be useful to have excess capacity on tap, even though your normal planned usage is a lot less than the maximum.

For example, a customer connecting a site to a provider network via a T1 line might contract for five circuits whose contracted bandwidths are

64Kbps

64Kbps

64Kbps

128Kbps

256Kbps

Recall that the contracted bandwidth is called the committed information rate or CIR. The customer is charged according to the number of circuits and the CIR of each. In this configuration, the customer has contracted for five circuits with a total CIR of 576Kbps. Note that there is an extra 960Kbps of bandwidth on the T1 line that connects the site to the provider.

Checking Out the Provider's Network

Frame relay traffic is forwarded to its destination through a series of switches. When traffic is heavy, a frame might be delayed at each switch while it waits its turn to be transmitted. This stretches out the time that elapses before frames are delivered by unpredictable amounts. Furthermore, some frames are discarded if a switch gets overloaded. Figure 3.2 shows bursts of incoming frames arriving on two different transmission lines. Both bursts need to be transmitted out of the switch on the same line. A queue of frames has started to build up.

Figure 3.2   Frames waiting to be transmitted.

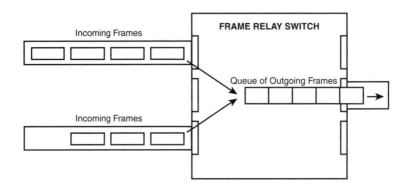

A subscriber needs to verify that delays and data losses will not cause an unacceptable degradation of service. Many providers offer several *quality of service levels.* It might be prudent to isolate traffic that is sensitive to delay onto a premium circuit that is given high priority.

When you consider connecting your network to a provider's network, you should keep in mind that the provider's links and switches will become part of the fabric of your network. It is important to check that

- The provider's network has sufficient bandwidth to carry its subscriber's traffic. Request a monthly report that shows network capacity and usage.

- State-of-the-art switching equipment and switch technology is used. Ask the provider which switch models it uses, and check the vendor's Web site for product timeliness. Up-to-date providers use internal ATM switches.

- Network availability can be maintained by using spare equipment and backup power supplies.

- A responsive network management center is staffed for 24 by 7 support. Call it on a Saturday night and see how long it takes to get to a staff member.

- Trouble ticket procedures are in place, and problems are handled within a predictable time period. Examine the forms used for problem reporting and resolution.

- The provider has implemented a disaster recovery plan. Get a copy of the plan.

It can be helpful to discuss the service with an existing reference customer. Most important of all, make sure that the provider's responsibilities in all these areas are explicitly covered in your service contract and that penalties and rebates are specified if the terms are not met.

Getting Ready to Connect

Any device that has a serial interface and appropriate software can act as a frame relay access device. Frequently, a router or bridge with frame relay interface software is used as an access device. Frame relay software is a standard feature of up-to-date bridge and router products. There also are special-purpose access devices that connect bisynchronous or SNA lines to frame relay networks.

Frame relay access devices are called *FRADs*. However, some vendors reserve the term *FRAD* for the special access devices that connect bisynchronous or SNA lines to frame relay networks.

From a customer's point of view, getting ready for frame relay is straightforward. The customer

- Connects a frame relay access device at each site to the provider's network via an access line. Many providers are willing to perform this chore for the customer and, for a fee, will take responsibility for monitoring the line.

- Selects the locations that need to be connected to one another by virtual circuits and selects the bandwidth for each virtual circuit.

Often, it is not even necessary to buy any new customer premise equipment. An available bridge or router with the right software and an unused serial interface can act as a frame relay access device. Frame relay software also is available for some host systems, which can be directly connected to a frame relay network.

Figure 3.3 shows the protocol layering for a bridge and a router connected to a frame relay network. Chapter II-6 describes how bridged or routed protocol data units are carried inside frame relay frames.

In the figure, a local Ethernet, Token Ring, or FDDI LAN is connected to a bridge or router via a physical medium such as twisted pair or fiber optic cable. The bridge or router connects to a frame relay switch via a wide area connection such as a 56Kbps, 64Kbps, or T1 leased line.

Figure 3.3   Bridge and router protocol layering.

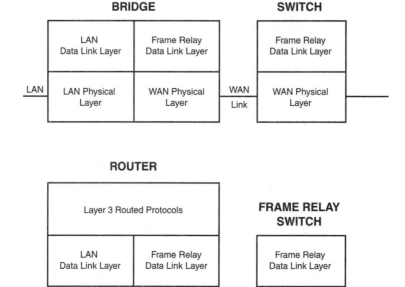

Installing the Access Line

For a typical installation, an end-user site connects to the provider's "cloud" by leasing a line between an access device at the customer's site and a nearby switch operated by the service provider. Popular access line speeds include

- 56Kbps or clear channel 64Kbps

- Fractional T1 (128, 256, 384, or 512Kbps access speeds)

- T1 (1.544Mbps)

- Fractional T3 or Full T3 (45Mbps)

In countries supporting the E-carrier hierarchy, connectivity is available at the E1 (up to 2Mbps) speed. E3 (up to 35Mbps) can be offered where demand is strong and the network infrastructure supports it.

Fee Structure

A customer pays a fixed monthly fee for the access line that attaches a customer device to the service provider's network. The cost of this line depends on the distance between the subscriber's site and the provider's network. A provider helps its customers keep this cost down by installing equipment at dozens—or hundreds—of *points of presence (POPs)*. As illustrated in Figure 3.4, these POPs are dotted across the region the provider supports.

The equipment at a point of presence is either a full-fledged switch that connects to subscribers and also is part of the provider's core network, or a multiplexer that combines traffic from several low-speed subscriber lines onto a high-speed line connecting back to the core network.

Figure 3.4   Points of presence for subscribers.

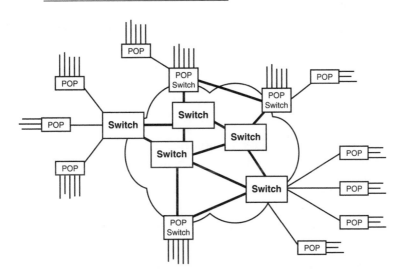

The cost of a circuit that crosses the frame relay provider's network normally does not depend on distance, although there might be a surcharge for a circuit that spans thousands of miles or crosses national boundaries. A circuit fee normally is calculated according to

- The bandwidth in each direction of each virtual circuit

- The degree to which you can burst extra traffic onto the circuit

- Special features, such as a high level of reliability or high-priority delivery

Zero Committed Information Rate

One of the options offered by some frame relay service providers is a *zero CIR*. Instead of promising to deliver a specific average bandwidth, the provider allows the customer to transmit frames onto the network at any rate up to some maximum. In some cases, the only limit is the capacity of the access line.

The features of a zero CIR service vary greatly from vendor to vendor. Sometimes, zero CIR is marketed as a low-cost, best-effort service. The provider does not promise that a specific throughput rate will be sustained, and a congested switch is likely to discard some zero CIR frames. This service is useful for applications (such as background file transfer) that are not sensitive to delay and occasional frame loss. A low-cost zero CIR service is ideal for nightly server backup to a disaster recovery site. Because the transfer occurs at off-peak hours, frame loss is very unlikely.

Some providers offer a high-quality zero CIR service that guarantees that almost all data (on the order of 99 percent) will be delivered. The advantage of this service is that you can burst data all the way up to the access line speed while still having good assurance of delivery.

Oversubscription

While allowing for lots of bandwidth is a prudent strategy for many subscribers, some benefit from the opposite philosophy. Let's examine a typical scenario.

A subscriber might want to connect several sites to one another in the most cost-effective manner possible. There are only brief, sporadic bursts of data between this subscriber's sites. Because of the location of the sites, fees for access lines between the sites and the provider's network are high.

In this case, the customer might decide to use a technique called *oversubscription*, which is illustrated in Figure 3.5. As shown in the figure, the customer has connected three sites to the provider's network. Each is connected via a 64Kbps leased line. The customer has asked the service provider to configure 64Kbps virtual circuits between each pair of sites.

How can the customer squeeze two 64Kbps circuits out of one 64Kbps access line? The customer is betting that it is unlikely that data will burst across both circuits at the same time. The benefit is that data is transmitted—with some risk—at 64Kbps instead of safely at 32Kbps.

Figure 3.5   Oversubscribed lines.

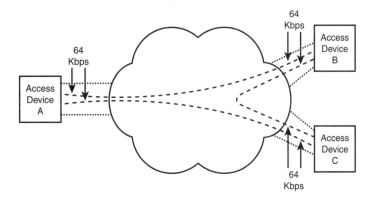

Building a Private Frame Relay Network

An organization can build its own private data network by buying frame relay switch equipment and connecting the switches via leased lines. Each site then connects to a switch via a local cable or a short point-to-point connection. Figure 3.6 portrays a private frame relay network.

> ### Note
>
> Building a private frame relay network is not a chore to be undertaken lightly. A public carrier offers alternate lines, industrial strength switches, backup equipment, and a trained and dedicated 24 by 7 staff that monitors and troubleshoots the network.
>
> The usual motive for "going it alone" is to save money; however, unless a company already has in place a substantial network infrastructure, creating the environment needed to support a reliable private frame relay network will be very expensive.

An organization with a private network might decide to expand the scope of its reachable sites by connecting its private network to a public provider network, as shown in Figure 3.7. The two networks communicate with one another across a network-to-network interface (NNI).

For simplicity, the discussion in most of this book focuses on issues that relate to connecting customer sites to a public service provider network; however, much of the discussion of public network technology applies equally well to private networks. Later, we also discuss network-to-network interface issues.

Figure 3.6   A private frame relay network.

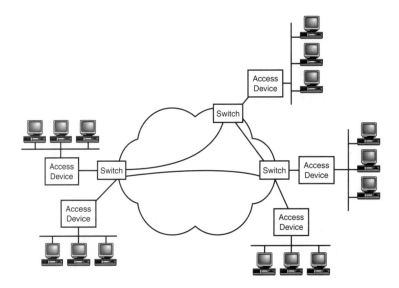

Figure 3.7   Connecting a private network to a public network.

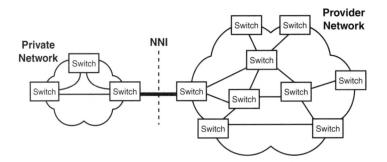

Frame Relay Circuit Services

As was the case for X.25, there are two types of frame relay circuits. *Permanent virtual circuits (PVCs)* are preconfigured and set up for an extended period of time (usually months or years). *Switched virtual circuits (SVCs)* are like telephone calls. They are set up by the user on demand and are terminated at the convenience of the user.

Currently, most providers offer only PVCs. However, some providers offer a very limited form of SVC service. The circuits for the limited SVC service must be preconfigured.

Then, they can be used for SVC-like calls on an as-needed basis. Perhaps *intermittent circuit* would be a better name for the current form of this service than *switched virtual circuit.*

An intermittent circuit service can be beneficial because a lower cost is associated with this type of circuit. Furthermore, as shown in Figure 3.8, if all the circuits were activated all the time, only a small amount of bandwidth would be available for each. But if only a few circuits are active at the same time, each circuit can be configured to use an ample bandwidth when it is activated.

Figure 3.8   Circuits preconfigured for on-demand use.

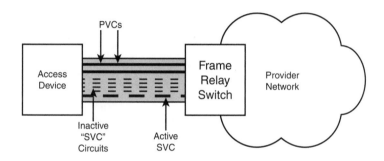

Intermittently used switched virtual circuits also offer a convenient way to have extra bandwidth on tap and ready to turn on under peak load conditions.

One-Way Circuits

Frame relay is very flexible. Some applications require only a one-way flow of data. The technology can support this easily, and the customer benefits by getting a cut-rate cost for the one-way circuit.

Multicasts

For most of today's applications, data flows to one receiver; however, the frame relay architecture is flexible enough to support multicast communications.

Possibilities include

- A *lecturing* mode where there is one sender and many receivers. Formally, this is called a *one-way* multicast. This could be used for corporate announcements or simultaneous distribution of stock market information.

- An interactive lecture mode, where all frames from a sender are delivered to many receivers, and any receiver can communicate back to that sender. Formally, this is called a *two-way* multicast. This could be used for distance learning.

- A *conferencing* mode for which all participants are peers. Data sent by any participant is received by all the other participants. Formally, this is called an *N-way* multicast. This mode supports multimedia conferencing.

Closing Comments

This chapter has focused on planning for frame relay: selecting the services needed, plotting out a diagram of the sites that need to be interconnected, and selecting a reliable provider network. Now, it is time to focus on the details, such as circuit bandwidths, acceptable delays, and network reliability and availability. Chapter II-4 deals with these issues.

4

Frame Relay Parameters and Service Level Agreements

A leased line service offers a precise level of bandwidth and promises a consistent, predictable level of delay. Frame relay measurements are expressed in terms of averages and probabilities. This does not make these measurements less important. A subscriber needs to negotiate frame relay service quantities and qualities in concrete terms.

This chapter explains the parameters that define your frame relay service, clarifies the fine print issues in a service contract, and highlights some key features to look for when you shop around for a frame relay service provider.

Measuring Circuit Traffic Levels

Figure 4.1 illustrates some important features of a frame relay circuit. The access device in the figure is connected to a frame relay provider's switch by a T1 line. Several virtual circuits have been configured for this line.

The figure shows outgoing traffic for one 256Kbps virtual circuit. Data traffic is bursty, and the instantaneous transmission rate for the circuit varies. Sometimes the rate exceeds 256Kbps, and sometimes the rate is far below 256Kbps. The big T1 "pipe" easily carries the bursts of data. The frame relay switch forwards the data as long as it stays within some measurable limit. In fact, the switch even forwards some amount of excess data. However, if the circuit data passes through a congested switch, some of the excess frames may be discarded.

Figure 4.1   Traffic levels on a virtual circuit.

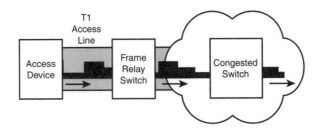

Figure 4.1 provides an intuitive picture of the behavior of a frame relay circuit. However, a subscriber needs to define circuit characteristics in measurable terms. There are four parameters that establish the basic behavior of a frame relay circuit:

- **Committed information rate and committed burst size**—Establish the average transmission level.

- **Excess burst and excess information rate**—Measure a legitimate amount of additional data that can be passed to the network for transmission.

Committed Information Rate

As Figure 4.1 illustrates, there is an important difference between a 64Kbps leased line and a virtual circuit with a 64Kbps committed information rate occupying part of the bandwidth on a T1 access line.

On a leased line, you cannot transmit data at a rate higher than 64Kbps. But data transmission is bursty; that is, during some periods, you will have little or no data to send, while at other times you might want to blast data down a line at a rate higher than 64Kbps. There is plenty of extra bandwidth on a T1 line that can support up and down variations in the rate of data transfer.

When you contract for a 64Kbps virtual frame relay circuit, 64Kbps represents an average rate called the *committed information rate (CIR)*. Each service provider interprets the meaning of the committed information rate of a circuit slightly differently. The formal definition is the average rate (in bits per second) at which the network commits to deliver data under normal conditions. The average is measured for a specified time interval (called Tc).

Note

Providers might differ in the ways they measure Tc and CIR. The Frame Relay Forum glossary states that Tc is not a periodic interval. Incoming data triggers a fresh Tc interval. If there is no incoming data when time Tc has elapsed, a new interval will not start until some new data is sent to the network.

Figure 4.2 shows traffic on a 64Kbps frame relay circuit during a time interval Tc. Sometimes the instantaneous rate is higher than the CIR, and sometimes it is lower. The average rate for the interval is

(Number of bits sent during the interval)/Tc

Clearly, the capability to burst above the committed rate is very convenient.

Figure 4.2   Traffic variations during a time interval.

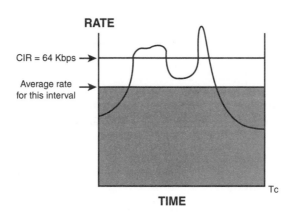

Note that the overall average rate for the data transferred interval in Figure 4.2 turns out to be smaller than the committed information rate. It is a good idea to monitor circuits to find out if this happens consistently across most intervals and if you are paying for bandwidth you are not using.

Committed Burst Size

The *committed burst size (Bc)* of a circuit is just another way of measuring the amount of data a provider agrees to carry for a customer. Bc is the maximum number of bits a provider contracts to deliver during a measurement interval, Tc.

There is a simple relationship between the committed burst and the committed information rate:

$$CIR = (\text{Committed burst size Bc})/Tc$$

or

$$Bc = CIR \times Tc$$

For example, if Tc is 60 seconds and the CIR is 64Kbps, the corresponding Bc is 3,840 Kbits.

It is easy for an administrator to estimate the committed burst size (Bc) a site will need by monitoring the average frame size (in bits) and the average number of frames sent per second. Then, a simple calculation transforms Bc into the CIR.

Excess Burst

The frame relay marketplace is competitive, and many providers allow customers to exceed the committed burst size, as long as the provider's network has the capacity to handle the extra traffic.

Often, the provider sets a limit on how much excess data can be transmitted during a time interval. The *excess burst size (Be)* for a circuit is the number of excess bits the network attempts to deliver during a measurement interval. The light gray area in Figure 4.3 represents the Bc bits for the interval, and the dark gray area represents the Be bits.

Often, the switch adjacent to a customer's access device immediately discards frame traffic that exceeds the Bc + Be level.

Figure 4.3   The committed burst size and the excess burst size.

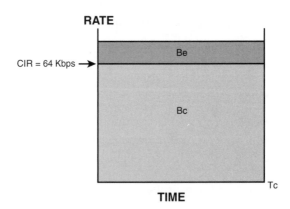

Excess Information Rate

The excess burst can be expressed as a rate called the *Excess Information Rate (EIR)*:

$$EIR = Be/Tc$$

Having extra bandwidth on the line that connects the site to the provider makes it possible to send excess burst traffic on several circuits at the same time.

Discard-Eligible Traffic

A provider might be willing to attempt delivery of Bc + Be bits across a circuit during time interval, but if the network is busy, it might not be possible to deliver all the frames.

Figure 4.4 shows the usual way that frame relay providers handle this problem. If the provider's network switch already has received Bc bits on a virtual circuit during the current time interval, additional frames received during the interval are marked as *eligible for discard*. These additional frames might be thrown away if they reach a switch that is overloaded.

A switch that is flooded with more traffic than it can handle is said to be *congested*. When a switch becomes congested, it needs to discard some of its traffic. A congested switch throws away frames that are marked as eligible for discard in preference to frames that have not been marked.

| Figure 4.4 | Discard-eligible traffic. |

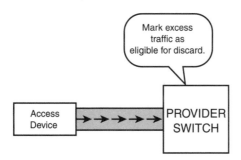

This turns excess data bursting into a gamble. However, some customer access equipment can take the sting out of the gamble. The customer can take control of what is discarded by identifying types of traffic that have lower priority. If the customer's flow of data exceeds the committed information rate, the customer's access device can mark selected low priority outgoing frames as discard-eligible.

A customer might occasionally transmit data that exceeds even the excess burst level. It is up to the provider to decide how this is handled. The extra data might be discarded by the entry switch, or the switch might mark it discard-eligible and forward it if the network currently has a large amount of unused capacity.

When planning for frame relay, it is a good idea to find out how your provider handles excess bursts and congestion, and check if you will be able to control the discard policy for your data.

Service Level Agreements

When you use frame relay, you will share network resources with many other customers. Traffic that belongs to other customers might pile up at switches internal to the frame relay network and cause unpredictable delays. How can you assure that you receive an appropriate quantity and quality of service?

The solution is to negotiate a *service level agreement (SLA)* with the provider. An SLA includes verifiable, quantitative thresholds that define the provider's deliverables, and sets penalties (such as customer credits) that will be imposed when the provider does not meet its target thresholds. These agreements can be very complex, and it is important to read the fine print!

Vendors and providers that participate in the frame relay industry have recognized the need to define standard measurements that can be used as the basis of SLAs. SLA parameters are defined in Frame Relay Forum document FRF.13. Four parameters have been identified:

- Frame transfer delay

- Frame delivery ratio

- Data delivery ratio

- Service availability

Standardizing these quantities is important. It has enabled vendors to create test equipment that measures the degree to which the provider has met service level agreement targets. For example, as shown in Figure 4.5, a provider or customer can obtain "smart" CSU/DSU units that monitor lines and report the values of many performance variables, including service level parameters. These devices generally can be accessed via the *Simple Network Management Protocol (SNMP)*. SNMP is used to configure the devices and obtain information that the devices have accumulated by monitoring the access lines.

Alternatively, the provider's switches can be the source of network monitoring information.

Figure 4.5 Monitoring frame relay interfaces.

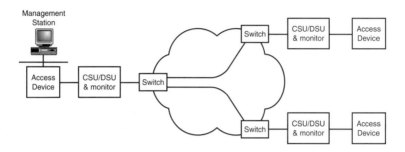

Customer Influence on Service Levels

Before focusing on the mechanisms you can use to measure and track the service level your provider delivers, it is worth noting that your own actions can have a significant impact on your quality of service.

For example, excessive bursting of TCP traffic often leads to slow response time. This happens if some of the TCP traffic needs to be discarded, because TCP automatically slows down drastically following data loss.

Figure 4.6 illustrates another way a customer could hurt the performance of some of its own circuits. The virtual circuits connecting Router B and Router C to Router A are supposed to support the same CIR. However, the customer consistently bursts excess traffic from Router B to Router A, and the provider tries to be "nice" and attempts to deliver all the frames.

Figure 4.6 Excess traffic from Router B to Router A.

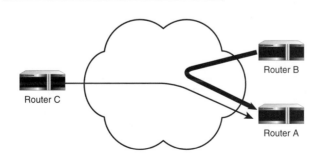

Figure 4.7 shows a close-up view of what happens. The provider switch adjacent to Router A maintains a queue of frames to be sent down the line to Router A. The source of each frame is indicated in the figure. Excess traffic from Router B causes the frames from C to get backed up and delayed.

Figure 4.7   Congestion at an exit switch.

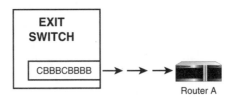

Service Level Parameters

The sections that follow describe the service level framework established in FRF.13. The framework establishes the scope across which measurements are made and the quantities that are measured.

Real measurements that are applied to real networks are based on averages computed across extended time periods. Note that some of the definitions that follow appear to measure the behavior of a single frame. These definitions are purely conceptual. They are needed to clarify the meaning of the useful real-world average quantities.

Measurement Scopes

There are three different ways a provider can compute the parameters in an SLA, and the method that is used can make a big difference to the customer. The methods are illustrated in Figure 4.8.

If a provider wants to protect itself from problems caused by the user, the provider uses an *edge-to-edge egress queue measurement*. This means that the scope for a measurement extends from the point of entry into the network up to the point at which a frame enters its exit queue. The provider will not take responsibility for output queue delays or line problems.

An *edge-to-edge parameter* is measured based on what happens between the entry and exit points for the provider's network. This means that exit queue delays are wrapped into the measurements.

Figure 4.8   Scope alternatives for provider measurements.

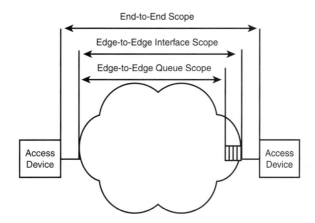

Finally, *end-to-end measurements* are calculated all the way from the customer's source access device to the destination access device. These measurements are the most meaningful for a customer. The providers most likely to commit to end-to-end performance are those that contract to install and monitor the lines between the network and the customer site as part of their service.

The sections that follow describe the four service level parameters.

Frame Transfer Delay

Frame Relay Forum document FRF.13 includes a precise definition of the way the delay between a source and destination point should be measured:

The delay is the difference (in milliseconds) between the time that the first bit of the frame's address field passes the source boundary point and the last bit of the closing flag of the frame crosses the destination boundary point.

The *frame transfer delay (FTD)* is the time required to transport a frame between the entry and exit points, measured according to this definition of delay time. (Keep in mind that there are three different specifications for the location of the entry and exit points, depending on the agreed measurement scope.)

Figure 4.9 illustrates this definition when the scope is networked edge-to-edge.

Figure 4.9 Measuring frame transfer delay.

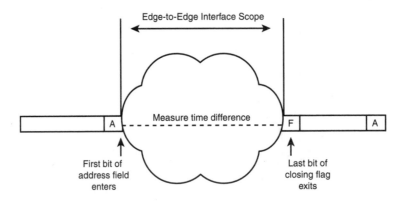

It takes more time to deliver large frames than small frames. To ensure accurate measurements, FRF.13 states that measurements should be made relative to frames containing a 128-byte payload (although a different size could be specified in the SLA).

To get a precise measurement, a provider might generate its own test traffic on a special control connection. The frame transfer delay is the only measurement that requires a fixed frame size and might be based on test traffic. The remaining quantities are based on real and complete customer traffic flows.

Frame Delivery Ratio

The *frame delivery ratio* measures the proportion of frames successfully delivered. To get a meaningful result, this is measured for one direction of traffic on one virtual circuit. To compute the frame delivery ratio

- A measurement interval is established.

- The number of frames sent during this interval is counted.

- Of these, the number successfully delivered is counted.

Then, the following quotient is calculated:

$$FDR = \frac{\text{Total frames delivered}}{\text{Total frames offered}}$$

Two other quotients round out the picture of what actually occurred:

- FDRc measures the ratio for frames within the committed information rate.

- FDRe measures the ratio for all frames sent in excess of the committed information rate.

The precise formulas are:

$$FDRc = \frac{\text{Total frames within CIR delivered}}{\text{Total frames within CIR offered}}$$

and

$$FDRe = \frac{\text{Total excess frames delivered}}{\text{Total excess frames offered}}$$

These raw quotients are not entirely fair to the provider. The subscriber might have sent many more frames onto a circuit than were stipulated in the service contract. There might be loss at a subscriber's egress queue because of oversubscription. There might be loss because the customer premise equipment at the subscriber's end is down. A provider removes frames that fall into these categories from the count of offered frames.

Data Delivery Ratio

The *data delivery ratio (DDR)* is similar to the frame delivery ratio, except it measures the quotient for delivered payload bytes:

$$DDR = \frac{\text{Total payload bytes delivered}}{\text{Total payload bytes offered}}$$

This gives a customer a measure of the proportion of its data that is getting through. This ratio should be close to the frame delivery ratio.

A data delivery ratio is measured over a specified time interval for one direction of one virtual circuit. The offered payload bytes that are counted would correspond to those within frames that were not excluded from the frame delivery ratio count.

Ratios also are defined for the data bytes transmitted within the committed information rate and those sent in excess of the committed information rate. These are called *DDRc* and *DDRe*.

Good application performance depends on having high data delivery ratios in both directions. For example, in Figure 4.10, Host A is transferring a file to Host B. The raw DDR in the direction from A to B is excellent. However, for some reason, the network is congested in the opposite direction, and many of the frames sent from B to A are being lost.

The result is that the file transfer performance is poor. Although the data flow is from A to B, the loss of acknowledgements flowing in the opposite direction causes retransmissions and a slowdown in the actual rate at which application data is delivered from A to B.

| **Figure 4.10** | Poor performance due to congestion in one direction. |

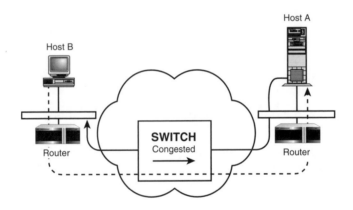

Service Availability

Currently, *service availability* measurements are applied to individual virtual circuits. There are three criteria of service availability:

- The percentage of time a virtual circuit is available

- The average time to repair a broken virtual circuit

- The average time between fault outages for a virtual circuit

Before signing on the dotted line, a subscriber should check the provider's definition of what constitutes an outage. Providers justifiably exclude outages that result from failed customer premise equipment. They might also exclude a weekly or monthly scheduled maintenance period. If the provider is not supporting end-to-end service, failures in an access line or in a network under the control of a different provider would be excluded. Some providers do not count transient outages whose duration falls below a minimum threshold.

The outage time that is left after all the exclusions have been subtracted is the period of service loss that is admittedly the fault of the provider.

There are three parameters that correspond to the three availability criteria listed earlier. These parameters measure availability over some pre-established time period. Times are measured in minutes.

The *frame relay virtual connection availability (FRVCA)* is the percentage of the time when there is no fault caused by the provider:

$$FRVCA = \frac{(\text{Interval - time Excluded outage time - Outage time})*100}{\text{Interval time - Excluded outage time}}$$

Note that if the only outages that occur are excluded ones, the provider will report that 100 percent availability was attained.

When provider outages do occur, customers will be concerned about the mean time to repair. The *frame relay mean time to repair (FRMTTR)* is measured as the outage time (not counting excluded time) divided by the number of outages:

$$FRMTTR = \frac{\text{Outage time}}{\text{Outage count}}$$

It would be nice to know how often outages happen, so the *frame relay mean time between service outages (FRMTBSO)* also is of interest:

$$FRMTBSO = \frac{\text{Interval time - Excluded outage time - Outage time}}{\text{Outage count}}$$

Reporting Service Level Measurements

After contracting to meet specified service levels, a provider should issue periodic reports that describe measurement results to the customer. For example, a report could be included with each monthly bill.

There are many different ways to sample and aggregate service measurements. The weakest information is obtained from sporadic test traffic samples.

A delay, delivery ratio, or outage measurement for real customer traffic can be reported as an average across all devices or broken out by individual interface or circuit. The customer might be given a single average across a long time period, or a set of averages for a recurring short interval.

A truly comprehensive report presents statistics

- By site, interface, and circuit

- By hour, day, business week, and full seven-day week

Instead of basing a service level report directly on the parameter measurements, a provider might specify its commitment in terms of thresholds. For example, the provider might

- Promise that some percentage of the customer's traffic will be delivered within a given time; for example, "99 percent of all frames will be delivered within 200 ms."

- Stipulate that some percentage (for example, 99 percent) of offered data that is within the CIR will be delivered.

Before signing up with a provider, be sure that your reports contain the level of detail you need. It is hard to get something fixed if you can't prove that it is broken!

References

Frame relay SLAs are discussed in the Frame Relay Forum *Service Level Definitions Implementation Agreement, FRF.13 (1998)*.

Remote monitoring variables are described in the IETF documents

- RFC 1757. *Remote Network Monitoring Management Information Base* (1995).

- RFC 2021. *Remote Network Monitoring Management Information Base Version 2 Using SMIv2* (1997).

There are many IETF RFC documents that deal with the SNMP. Among the important ones are RFCs 2274, 2271, 2011, 2012, 2013, 1907, 1905, 1902, 1215, 1213, and 1157. The author's book, *SNMP: A Guide to Network Management*, contains a detailed description of version 1 of SNMP.

CHAPTER 5

Basic Frame Relay Protocol Elements

As you will see in this chapter, the main protocol mechanisms that underlie a frame relay service are straightforward. They include

- Numeric identifiers, called *Data Link Connection Identifiers (DLCIs)*, for virtual circuits

- An uncomplicated frame format

- Methods of indicating that a network is congested

Recall that a frame relay network is made up of a set of interconnected switches. In some cases, an organization buys switches and builds its own private frame relay network. More often, an organization subscribes to a frame relay service offered by a public provider. An access device at a customer site connects the site to the public frame relay network.

We'll call any private or public frame relay network a *provider network*.

Frame Relay Protocol Layer

Frame relay is a layer 2 (data link) level protocol. Figure 5.1 shows the protocol layering when a router is used as a frame relay access device. Traffic for one or more layer 3 protocols, such as IP, NetWare IPX, DecNET, and so on, is packaged in frame relay frames and is exchanged across the layer 2 frame relay link.

From the point of view of the router endpoints, the frame relay virtual circuit acts as a replacement for a point-to-point line.

Figure 5.1   Frame relay protocol layering.

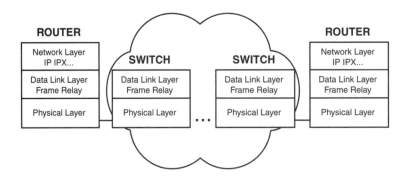

Data Link Connection Identifiers

A single physical connection between a customer access device and a provider network switch can carry several virtual circuits. For example, in Figure 5.2, a site in New York is connected to sites in Boston and Philadelphia by frame relay circuits that share the access line that connects Router A to a network switch.

When Router A in New York launches a frame toward Boston, the frame header must include a circuit identifier so the network switch can forward the frame along the appropriate circuit.

Figure 5.2   Sending a frame on a virtual circuit.

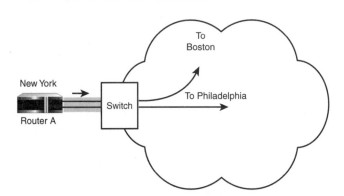

Each frame relay virtual circuit at a site is assigned a circuit number called a *Data Link Connection Identifier (DLCI)*. A DLCI has local significance; that is, the DLCI numbers at the endpoints of the virtual circuit do not have to be, and usually are not, the same.

Figure 5.3 shows three routers connected by frame relay circuits. The circuit that is tagged with DLCI 21 at Router A is identified by DLCI 34 at Router B.

Figure 5.3   Data link connection identifiers.

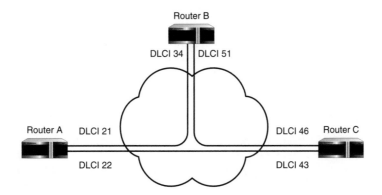

This is a convenient arrangement. You do not need to worry about administering circuit numbers, even if you have a large number of sites and many virtual circuits between them. The fact that the DLCI number assignment is local also reflects the nature of the frame relay service. A customer's frame relay interface enables the customer to interact with a provider network. Data is transferred via a series of separate interactions:

• Source customer premise equipment to provider switch

• Provider switch to provider switch (repeated as many times as necessary)

• Provider switch to recipient customer premise equipment

Figure 5.4 shows frames being transmitted from a router to a provider's frame relay switch. The DLCI in each frame header identifies its virtual circuit. The method that the provider uses to implement these virtual circuits is completely up to the provider. The switch maintains a table that can map the incoming DLCI value to a value that might be based on a completely independent addressing scheme.

The technology used inside the provider's "cloud" is totally unrestricted. The provider just has to make sure that the frame will pop out of the network and onto a connection that leads to the correct destination, and that the frame is labeled with the DLCI that has been assigned to the far end of the circuit.

Figure 5.4 A switch translating DLCI numbers.

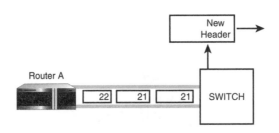

> **Note**
>
> Several vendors offer custom frame relay switches that can be used inside a frame relay network "cloud." Each frame relay switch contains a table that translates an (incoming port number, incoming DLCI number) pairing to a corresponding (outgoing port number, outgoing DLCI number) pairing. The DLCI value can change at every switch that is traversed between a frame's source and its destination.
>
> However, note that the major frame relay service providers use ATM switches inside their networks rather than frame relay switches. Chapter III-5 describes the way frame relay interworks with ATM.

DLCI Values

DLCIs can be 10, 16, or 23 bits in length. Some early implementations used 11- or 13-bit DLCIs. These are now obsolete, and, today, a 10-bit DLCI is the norm. This means that local circuit numbers can range from 0 to 1023. Some of the numbers are reserved for special purposes.

Table 5.1 shows 10-bit DLCI assignments that initially were recommended by the Frame Relay Forum. When the Forum wrote its *Local Management Interface (LMI)* specification, ANSI and ITU-T committees had not yet decided which channel should carry the LMI status messages. The Forum selected DLCI 1023 for this purpose. However, ANSI and ITU-T committees later decided to use DLCI 0 for both call setup signaling and management status messages.

Table 5.1	Original Frame Relay Forum 10-bit DLCI Usage
DLCI Value	**Function**
0	Reserved for in-channel signaling
1–15	Reserved
16–1007	Can be assigned to a circuit endpoint
1008–1022	Reserved
1023	Used for the Local Management Interface (LMI)

Table 5.2 shows the ANSI (T1.618) and ITU-T (Q.922) breakdown for 10-bit DLCI values. (Because the standards groups had an ISDN orientation, they specified that the values shown in Table 5.2 were to be used within an ISDN B or H channel.)

Table 5.2	ANSI/ITU-T 10-bit DLCIs
DLCI Value	**Function**
0	In-channel signaling and management
1–15	Reserved
16–991	Can be assigned to a circuit endpoint
992–1007	Layer 2 management of the frame relay bearer service
1008–1022	Reserved
1023	Reserved for in-channel layer management

Frame relay service could be provided on an ISDN D channel (although it rarely is). ANSI and the ITU-T have defined address usage ranges for 10-bit DLCIs used on the ISDN D channel; Table 5.3 lists these ranges.

Table 5.3	ANSI/ITU-T 10-bit DLCI Values for the ISDN D Channel
DLCI Value	**Function**
512–991	Can be assigned to a circuit endpoint

ANSI and ITU-T also specify how 16-bit and 23-bit DLCIs should be used. Tables 5.4 and 5.5 present these values. 16-bit DLCIs are contained in 3-byte address fields. 23-bit DLCIs are contained in 4-byte address fields. (Here again, because of their ISDN orientation, ANSI and ITU-T specified that the values included in these tables were to be used within an ISDN B or H channel.)

Table 5.4	16-bit DLCI Values
DLCI Value	**Function**
0	Reserved for in-channel signaling
1–1,023	Reserved
1,024–63,487	Can be assigned to a circuit endpoint
63,488–64,511	Layer 2 management of the frame relay bearer service
64,512–65,534	Reserved
65,535	In-channel layer management

Table 5.5	23-bit DLCI Values
DLCI Value	**Function**
0	Reserved for in-channel signaling
1–131,071	Reserved
131,072–8,126,463	Can be assigned to a circuit endpoint
8,126,464–8,257,535	Layer 2 management of the frame relay bearer service
8,257,536–8,388,606	Reserved
8,388,607	In-channel layer management

Frame Format

The data traveling across a frame relay network is packaged in *frames*. Frame relay is a layer 2 (data link) level protocol. The frame format is shown in Figure 5.5. Each frame starts with an address field that contains a DLCI and a few *flag bits*. The payload follows the address field. A frame ends with a two-byte *frame check sequence field*. This contains the result of a function (called a *cyclic redundancy check*) computed on the 0s and 1s of the address and payload fields.

Figure 5.5   Frame format.

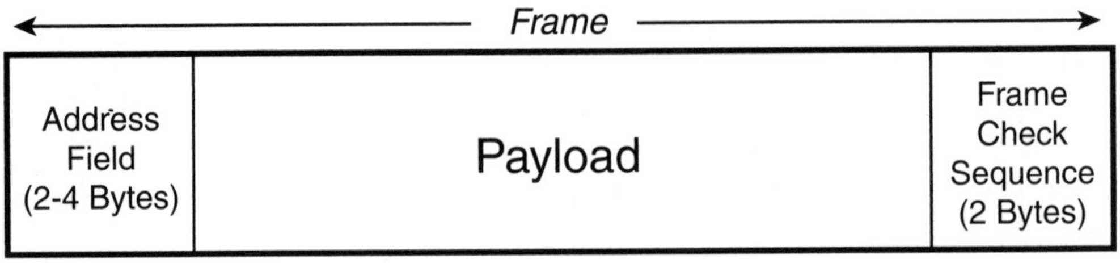

The simple frame format shown in Figure 5.5 was defined in ITU-T Recommendation Q.922. Q.922 describes *link access procedures to frame-mode bearer (LAPF) services.* The frames sometimes are referred to as LAPF or LAPF-CORE frames.

Maximum Payload Size

The frame relay standards did not mandate a specific maximum size for the payload within a frame. However, an engineer designing a device has to make a firm decision on a cutoff size.

It is a good idea to set a level to be supported by all vendors of customer and network equipment so devices can interwork. The Frame Relay Forum implementation agreements require vendors and service providers to support frames that carry up to 1600 bytes of payload. (This is the size of the information field and does not include the address field or frame check sequence bytes.) The 1600-byte value is a common denominator chosen to promote interoperating.

A vendor can build equipment that supports bigger payloads. However, a customer using this equipment has to be careful to configure a maximum value that is supported by all the other devices that process the frames.

Treatment of Frame Check Sequence

Because the value in the DLCI field usually changes as the frame traverses the provider's network, the frame check sequence value also usually changes. Depending on the internal implementation, the frame check sequence value may be recalculated at every switch along the way as well as at the destination. At any point, if the calculated value of the check function does not match the value in the frame check sequence field, the frame will be discarded.

Flag Bytes

Network devices need a way to recognize where each incoming frame begins and ends. The method that is used was borrowed from the venerable *High-level Data Link Control (HDLC)* layer 2 transmission protocol. One or more flag bytes separate each pair of frames that is transmitted, as shown in Figure 5.6. Contiguous flags are sent out by an interface during idle times, when the interface has no data to transmit. The flag pattern 01111110 was defined in the HDLC protocol standard.

Figure 5.6   Flag delimiters.

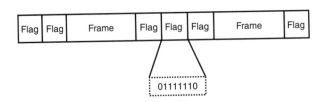

As you saw in Chapter II-2, using HDLC flags as delimiters causes a standard data transmission problem, which has a standard solution. A frame's data might contain a bit-pattern that is identical to the flag bit pattern. A transmitting communications interface guards against this by transforming the bits in the frame before sending them onto the medium. The sender inserts a 0 after any sequence of five contiguous 1s in the frame. The receiving communications interface restores the frame to its original state by removing a 0 that follows five 1s. Chapter II-2 contains an example that illustrates this procedure.

Address Field

An address field can be 2, 3, or 4 bytes in length. Current access devices use the 2-byte format, shown in Figure 5.7. Figure 5.8 displays the 3-byte format, and Figure 5.9 shows the 4-byte format.

All the components of the address field are explained in the sections that follow.

Figure 5.7   Format of a 2-byte address field.

Figure 5.8   Format of a 3-byte address field.

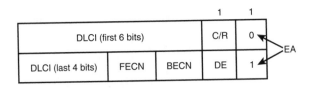

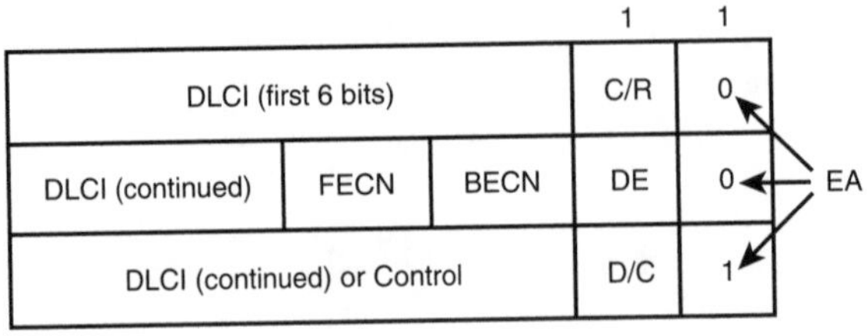

Figure 5.9   Format of a 4-byte address field.

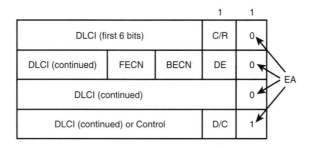

DLCI Subfields

The DLCI in an address field is broken into two or more pieces. It is translated into a decimal number after concatenating the pieces. The high-order bits come first.

Thus, a 10-bit DLCI in a 2-byte address field that is packaged as

0 0 0 0 1 0

0 1 1 1

can be rewritten as the binary number 0000100111, which translates to the decimal number

32 + 4 + 2 + 1 = 39

Command/Response (C/R) Bit

The *Command/Response flag bit* is not used for the frame relay data transfer protocol. It is available for use for any convenient purpose by higher layer protocols.

Extended Address (EA) Bits

The last bit of each byte in an address field is an extended address (also called an *address extension*) flag. The bit is set to 0 in all the bytes except for the last one. Thus, address extension flag bits are used to indicate if the length of an address field is 2, 3, or 4 bytes.

Discard Eligibility (DE) Bit

Given the bursty nature of data traffic and the fact that many users temporarily exceed their committed rates, it is not surprising that, occasionally, a network switch gets congested and is not able to handle all of its traffic. Some of the traffic has to be discarded. The question is, which traffic?

The fairest solution is to discard frames that were sent in excess of the committed rate. These excess frames are marked by setting their DE flags to 1. The marking is done either at the customer access device or by the adjacent network switch. Configuring the access device to set the DE bit to 1 on lower priority traffic can be beneficial to the customer. It can prevent the network from randomly choosing frames to be marked for discard.

Note that a severely congested switch might have to discard additional frames whose DE value is 0.

Backward and Forward Explicit Congestion Notification

Figure 5.10 depicts a flow of frames on a virtual circuit between access device A and access device B. Device A is sending a heavy load of traffic to B on the circuit. The flow from B to A is light. The link between provider switch 2 and switch 3 is overloaded with other traffic, and a backlog of frame traffic is piling up at switch 2, which is congested. Switch 2 signals this situation by

- Setting the *Forward Explicit Congestion Notification (FECN)* flag to 1 in frames sent onto the congested link

- Setting the *Backward Explicit Congestion Notification (BECN)* flag to 1 in frames sent back to the source of the traffic

In Figure 5.10, the arrow from switch 2 to switch 3 is thinner than the arrow from switch 1 to switch 2. This is intended to reflect the fact that switch 2 has discarded some of the traffic sent on the virtual circuit.

Figure 5.10   Using FECN and BECN bits to signal congestion.

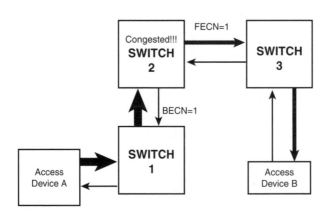

Note that the BECN bit is the one that can get results. When an access device receives frames whose BECN is set to 1, the device should throttle back its outgoing flow of frames so it does not exceed the CIR for the circuit. This will help to relieve the pressure on the congested switch and make discards less likely.

Most types of data communication involve a two-way flow of frames. During a download of data from one host to another, normally we expect the recipient to send frames that acknowledge the receipt of incoming data. This back-traffic provides a flow of frames that can carry the BECN warnings.

In contrast, there is no standard mechanism that the recipient of an FECN can use to warn its partner to throttle back. The treatment of incoming FECN bits is left unspecified, but some vendors implement features that support useful feedback.

Address Field Trace

Listing 4.1 is a trace of a 2-byte frame relay address field. The frame relay access device plays the DTE role, and the adjacent frame relay switch is the DCE. The frame in the trace was sent from the DCE to the DTE.

Each bit in the 2-byte address field is displayed. The DLCI value is 27 (0000011011 in binary). The Discard Eligible flag and the congestion notification flags are set to 0.

Listing 5.1	2-byte Frame Relay Address Field

```
Decode from WinPharoah
----------Frame Relay Q.931 Format (ANSI T1.607)-----
Direction =  DCE->DTE
Address Field (2 octets) = 04B1
DLCI = 27 (Assigned using frame relay connection procedures)
Address Octet 1
    0000 01..          DLCI (High-order)
    .... ..0.          C/R  - Command/Response indicator
    .... ...0          EA   - Address field extension bit
Address Octet 2
    1011 ....          DLCI - (Low-order)
    .... 0...          FECN - Forward Explicit Congestion Notification
    .... .0..          BECN - Backward Explicit Congestion Notification
    .... ..0.          DE   - Discard Eligibility
    .... ...1          EA   - Address Field Extension
```

Consolidated Link Layer Management

There are some applications that do not involve a backflow of frames, such as real-time voice or video multicasts. Although rare today, use of one-way data flows is expected to increase in the future.

Without a backflow of frames, the data transmitter will not receive frames that signal congestion via BECN flags.

The frame relay standards define a special *Consolidated Link Layer Management (CLLM)* message that can be used in this situation. CLLM messages also can report problems other than congestion, such as a facility or equipment failure.

CLLM messages are sent on the reserved circuit with DLCI 1007. A CLLM message contains

- A code that indicates the cause and expected duration of the problem

- A list of DLCIs affected by the problem

The Frame Relay Forum implementation agreements do not require vendors and providers to support CLLM messages. However, an increasing number of vendors and providers support this useful feature.

Other Congestion Control Mechanisms

Frame relay standards and implementation agreements focus on external interactions. They define user-to-network and network-to-network interfaces. They do not deal with the internal operations of a provider network.

Frame relay service is very popular, and huge amounts of traffic speed across today's frame relay networks. Routine variations in traffic can lead to congestion within the service network.

Many frame relay service providers compete for subscriber business, and subscribers can shop around for services that can meet their quality of service requirements. Controlling congestion has become essential. In the absence of standards, vendors and providers have implemented proprietary methods of damping down congestion and meeting their contracted service levels. The process often is called *closed-loop congestion control*.

The way that closed-loop congestion control is implemented differs for each vendor, but the basic idea stays the same: Notify the entry point switches that are causing the congestion to throttle back on the incoming traffic. *Closed loop* refers to the fact that there is feedback to an entry switch that tells it what is happening inside the network.

To accomplish this, network switches exchange information about the state of internal links, reporting on their level of congestion. When traffic begins to pile up along a path traversed by one or more virtual circuits, the entry switches will know about it.

An entry switch responds to congestion by cutting back on the amount of traffic it forwards into the network.

The goal is to preserve each customer's committed information rate, so cutbacks are made in the excess burst traffic. The action taken by the entry switch can be minor or drastic, depending on the level of congestion. For example, options might include

- For congested circuits, reduce the acceptable excess burst traffic by a preset percentage. For example, 60 percent of the usual excess burst traffic rate might be acceptable. Traffic above this threshold would be discarded.

- For all circuits, reduce the acceptable excess burst traffic by a preset percentage.

- For congested circuits, discard all excess burst traffic.

- For all circuits, discard all excess burst traffic.

Some products allow the network provider to define several congestion levels. The amount by which the excess burst traffic must be reduced is determined by the congestion level that has been experienced.

If the provider network has enough resources to cover all its contracted committed information rates, the closed loop strategy ensures that committed traffic can get through.

Multicast Technology and Protocols

The discussion so far has focused on conventional point-to-point virtual circuits. However, frame relay networks also can support point-to-multipoint multicast circuits. Recall that multicasts can be used for lectures, conferences, and other applications that require the distribution of identical information to multiple recipients; for example, an instantaneous stock market quote service.

Multicasting is not currently a widely used service but might become popular in the future. Multicast service conventions are described in Frame Relay Forum implementation agreement FRF.7. The service described in the agreement is implemented by preconfiguring permanent virtual circuits (PVCs) that are used for multicasts.

The fact that DLCIs have only local significance makes it fairly easy for frame relay switch vendors to implement a multicast capability. In Figure 5.11, a network switch has been configured to act as a network *multicast server*. The multicast server delivers copies of every frame whose incoming DLCI is 50 to DLCIs 61, 62, and 63. The access devices in the figure are said to be members of a *multicast group*.

Figure 5.11   A multicast group and a multicast server.

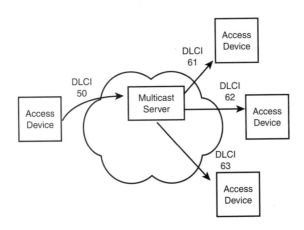

Frame relay multicasting is still an immature technology. Vendors and service providers have a lot of latitude in the ways they can design and implement a multicast service. The Frame Relay Forum has tried to expedite the development of the service by outlining models that indicate how three types of services might be implemented.

One-Way Multicast Service

The one-way multicast service has one sender and multiple receivers. The sender is called the *root*. The receivers are called *leaves*. The Forum suggests the following implementation model:

• An ordinary two-way PVC should be set up between the sender and each receiver.

• An additional one-way PVC should be set up between the sender and a multicast server that resides in the network. The multicast server forwards frames sent on this one-way PVC to the receivers in the group. The frames arrive as if they have been delivered on the ordinary PVC that exists between the sender and each receiver.

This model is illustrated in Figure 5.12. There are ordinary two-way permanent virtual circuits between the sender and the other three devices. These three circuits can be used for ordinary two-way traffic.

The sender passes multicast frames to the network's multicast server via the circuit with DLCI 50. The server adds these frames to the flows that are delivered to the receivers via DLCIs 61, 62, and 63.

Figure 5.12   An implementation of a one-way multicast service.

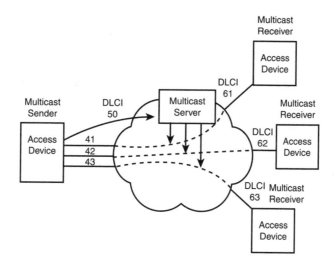

Although this model has been labeled "one-way," note that the root can exchange private data with any leaf. This data is separate from the multicast data that is sent to all the leaves.

Two-Way Multicast Service

A two-way multicast is similar to an interactive lecture. Frames from the root are forwarded to all receivers. Frames from any leaf member are forwarded to the root. Figure 5.13 illustrates this model. The virtual circuit that has DLCI number 41 at the sender's end is simultaneously connected to the three remote endpoints with DLCIs 61, 62, and 63. Traffic can be sent and received on all three circuits.

This model is useful when there are a lot of receivers or when there is no need for separate, non-multicast data exchange between the root and the receivers.

Figure 5.13   Model for a two-way multicast service.

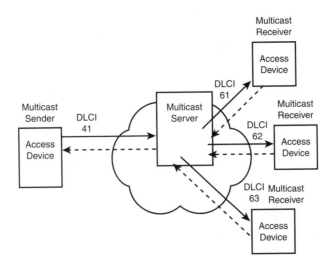

N-Way Multicast Service

An N-way multicast service supports conferencing applications. All participants act as senders and receivers.

Each participant has a virtual circuit that connects it to a network server for the specific multicast. Any datagram that is transmitted by a participant on this circuit is delivered to all the other participants. Figure 5.14 illustrates this model.

Figure 5.14   Model for an N-way multicast service.

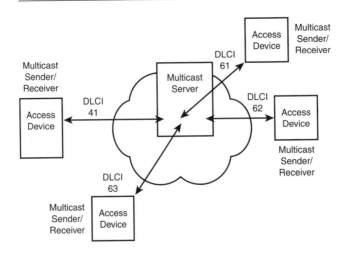

Moving on to Other Frame Relay Protocol Elements

Frame relay is based on a small set of protocol mechanisms that have been described within a few pages. However, the original protocol definition was a little too sparse. It omitted an ingredient that is needed by many real-world users.

Chapter II-6 adds this ingredient: a method of identifying the type of protocol data that is carried inside a frame relay payload field.

References

There are many ITU-T documents that relate to frame relay. The basic protocol features are described in

- Recommendation Q.921, *ISDN User-Network Interface—Data Link Layer Specification* (1997).

- Recommendation Q.922, *ISDN Data Link Layer Specification for Frame Mode Bearer Services* (1993).

ANSI described the basic protocol features in T1.618, *Telecommunications—Integrated Services Digital Network (ISDN)—Core Aspects of Frame Protocol for Use with Frame Relay Bearer Service*, 1991, revised 1997.

The Frame Relay Forum selected features of ITU-T and ANSI standards that should be implemented in its *User-to-Network (UNI) Implementation Agreement*, 1995 (FRF.1.1). Models for multicast service are described in the forum's *Frame Relay PVC Multicast Service and Protocol Description*, 1994 (FRF.7).

There are many ANSI and ITU-T standards that describe the physical interfaces that can be used with frame relay equipment. See FRF1.1 for a list.

IETF Encapsulation

Today's enterprise networks carry a diverse array of protocols. IP, NetWare, DECnet, and other protocol traffic share LAN and wide area links. The LANs and wide area circuits that make up these networks are glued together by multiprotocol routers that process the traffic mix. These routers need to sort out the incoming frames and pass each to an appropriate protocol handler.

Incoming LAN and Point-to-Point Protocol (PPP) frames are not a problem. The headers of Ethernet, Token Ring, FDDI, and PPP frames include a field that identifies the protocol being carried. This enables a router (or other networking device) to process each frame appropriately.

Unfortunately, the frame relay standards did not define a header field that identifies the type of protocol data that is carried in a frame relay payload. This is not a problem when a virtual circuit carries only a single protocol. In this case, the protocol type is identified when the circuit is configured.

However, using separate circuits for each protocol usually is more costly than combining traffic on a shared circuit. In addition, a subscriber might be able to use throughput more effectively by merging bursty traffic onto a shared circuit. For example, if IP and NetWare traffic is sent between two sites on separate 128Kbps circuits, many of the frames in a short IP burst at 256Kbps are likely to be discarded. If both types of traffic share a 256Kbps circuit and there is a lull in the NetWare transmission, the IP burst would be within the CIR.

An Internet Engineering Task Force (IETF) working group defined frame relay encapsulation formats that include a field identifying the protocol being carried. By supporting IETF encapsulations, providers give their customers the opportunity to choose if they want to merge traffic for multiple protocols on one circuit.

Note that you cannot tell whether or not a frame contains an IETF header simply by examining the frame. The frame relay address field provides no clue to what follows. An end system will know that IETF headers are included in frames arriving on a circuit because the circuit explicitly was configured to use IETF headers.

IETF Multiprotocol Interconnect

IETF header information is described in a Request for Comments (RFC) document entitled *Multiprotocol Interconnect over Frame Relay*. The version of this document currently referenced by vendors is RFC 1490. Vendor configuration manuals refer to the use of the additional header information as RFC 1490 or IETF encapsulation. However, the specification has been clarified and updated in RFC 2427, which makes the RFC 1490 version obsolete.

RFC 1490/2427 outlines a general format for the extra header information and provides details on how to encapsulate several layer 3 protocols (such as IP, IPX, and DECnet) as well as layer 2 bridged traffic. Details on how to encapsulate IBM System Network Architecture (SNA) and NetBIOS traffic were spelled out separately in the Frame Relay Forum document entitled *Multiprotocol Encapsulation Implementation Agreement* (FRF.3.1). This document actually was written by IBM staff.

Frames with Unique NLPIDs

Figure 6.1 presents the simplest format for a frame containing IETF protocol header information. The first byte is a control field with the value X'03, which means *unnumbered information*. The next byte is a *Network Layer Protocol Identifier (NLPID)* code. NLPIDs are administered by the International Standards Organization (ISO) and the ITU-T. For example, IP version 4 has been assigned the NLPID value X'CC, and the ISO Connectionless Network Protocol (CLNP) has been assigned X'81. (These codes are assigned in ISO TR 9577.)

| Figure 6.1 | A simple IETF encapsulation with an NLPID code. |

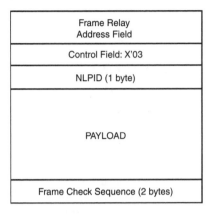

Table 6.1 lists NLPIDs that identify specific protocols and can be used with frame relay.

| Table 6.1 | Specific NLPIDs |

NLPID	Protocol
X'81	ISO Connectionless Network Protocol (CLNP)
X'82	ISO End System to End System (ES-IS)
X'83	ISO Intermediate System to Intermediate System (IS-IS)
X'8E	IP version 6
X'B0	FRF.9 Data Compression Protocol frames
X'B1	FRF.12 Fragmented frames
X'CC	IP version 4
X'CF	Point-to-Point Protocol (PPP) in Frame Relay

An IETF-encapsulated IP protocol data unit is displayed in the trace that follows.

Note

An IP protocol data unit is called an *IP datagram*.

The frame was delivered on DLCI 27. The Network Layer Protocol ID value of X'CC indicates that an IP datagram is shown in Listing 6.1.

Listing 6.1   Network Layer Protocol ID Value

```
Decode from WinPharoah
-----Frame Relay Q.931 Format (ANSI T1.607)-----
Direction =  DCE->DTE
Address Field (2 octets) = 04B1
DLCI = 27 (Assigned using frame relay connection procedures)
Address Octet 1
    0000 01..          DLCI (High-order)
    .... ..0.          C/R  - Command/Response indicator
    .... ...0          EA   - Address field extension bit
Address Octet 2
    1011 ....          DLCI - (Low-order)
    .... 0...          FECN - Forward Explicit Congestion Notification
    .... .0..          BECN - Backward Explicit Congestion Notification
    .... ..0.          DE   - Discard Eligibility
    .... ...1          EA   - Address Field Extension
Control field = 03 Unnumbered(UI)
    .... 0... - Poll/Final
-------Multiprotocol over Frame Relay-------
Network Level Protocol ID = CC (Internet IP)
---------Internet Protocol (IP)---------
```

Frames with SNAP Header Fields

As you can see from Table 6.1, very few protocols have been given specific ISO/ITU NLPIDs. However, many protocols have been assigned identifiers by other organizations. An NLPID value of X'80 introduces a *Sub-Network Access Protocol (SNAP)* field that contains a protocol identifier assigned by an organization other than ISO or ITU.

Figure 6.2 shows the layout of a frame with a SNAP field. A padding byte (X'00) has to be inserted after the X'03 control field in order to align the end of the header on a 2-byte boundary. The first 3 bytes of a SNAP subheader identify the organization that is responsible for the 2-byte protocol identifier that follows. The 3-byte code is called the *Organizationally Unique Identifier (OUI)*.

two FCS fields at the end of the frame. The first is part of the enclosed LAN frame and is inside the payload area. The second is the frame relay FCS and is calculated on the entire frame relay frame.

Figure 6.4   A bridged LAN frame.

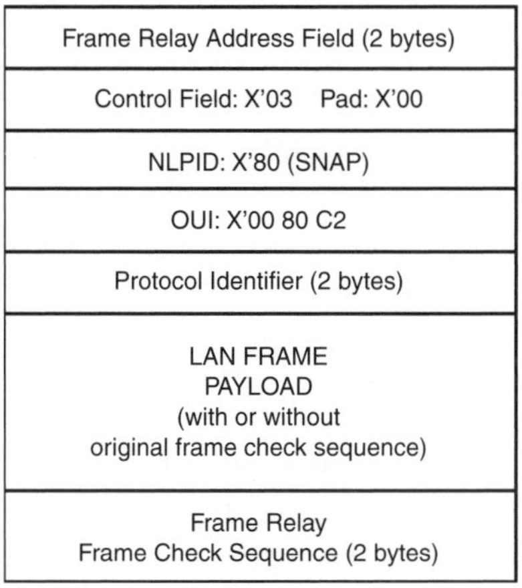

Frame Relay Address Field (2 bytes)
Control Field: X'03   Pad: X'00
NLPID: X'80 (SNAP)
OUI: X'00 80 C2
Protocol Identifier (2 bytes)
LAN FRAME PAYLOAD (with or without original frame check sequence)
Frame Relay Frame Check Sequence (2 bytes)

In Figure 6.4, note that the frame relay address field is followed by

- A control field with value X'03 (meaning unnumbered information) and a pad byte

- A Network Layer Protocol ID field with value X'80, which indicates that a SNAP subheader follows

- The Organizationally Unique Identifier, whose value is the IEEE 802.1 code X'00 80 C2—this indicates that the payload contains a bridged LAN frame

The protocol identifier field indicates

- The type of LAN frame that follows

- If an entire frame, including its original frame check sequence, is contained in the payload

The IEEE 802.1 committee has assigned the protocol identifier values listed in Table 6.2 for bridged frames.

Table 6.2   Protocol Identifiers for Bridged Frames

Type of Frame	Protocol ID When Original FCS Is Enclosed	Protocol ID When Original FCS Is Not Enclosed
802.3 (Ethernet)	00 01	00 07
802.4 (obsolete Token Bus)	00 02	00 08
802.5 (Token-Ring)	00 03	00 09
FDDI	00 04	00 0A

Sorting Out the Traffic

Like sharing an apartment, sharing a circuit can be cost effective and efficient—if the partners are compatible. IP and DECnet protocols operate on similar principles and usually get along well together. SNA traffic (which is described in Chapter II-10) is sensitive to delay and works best on separate, high-priority circuits. NetBIOS traffic is chatty and can hog resources needed by others.

Local usage levels of each protocol also make a difference in how well a particular mix works. Initial experimentation and ongoing monitoring are needed to make sure that circuits deliver the best performance possible.

The chapter that follows discusses frame relay network management. The latter part of Chapter II-7 shows how network management tools can be used to track circuit performance.

References

The current version of the Internet Engineering Task Force document, *Multiprotocol Interconnect over Frame Relay,* is in RFC 2427 (1998).

IBM SNA and NetBIOS encapsulations are described in FRF.3.1, *Multiprotocol Encapsulation Implementation Agreement* (1995).

The ISO document that defines NLPIDs is ISO/IEC TR 9577, *Information Technology— Telecommunications and Information Exchange between Systems—Protocol Identification in the Network Layer* (1992).

Managing Frame Relay

Up to this point, we have focused on presenting the services that frame relay permanent virtual circuits can support and outlining how these services are implemented.

There is one important factor that has not yet been discussed. Customers need the ability to monitor and manage their permanent virtual circuits.

At minimum, an administrator at a site connected to a frame relay network needs some very basic local information—whether the link to the provider network is up and running and whether the permanent virtual circuits are alive. This information is obtained by means of an exchange of management messages across the user-network interface; that is, between the customer's access device and the adjacent provider switch.

Administrators also need a global view of their circuits to gather baseline statistics, analyze traffic behavior, and troubleshoot problems. Some providers give customers a network management window into the network that enables a customer to view information specific to its own circuits.

Both the local and the global network management facilities are discussed in the sections that follow.

Local Network Management

Local management across the user-network interface is implemented by an exchange of messages across a special virtual circuit that connects the customer's access device to the adjacent provider switch. Figure 7.1 illustrates this arrangement. In the figure, an access device at a customer site interfaces to three virtual circuits that lead to remote locations. An additional special virtual circuit between the access device and the switch is reserved for local management messages.

Figure 7.1   The local management circuit.

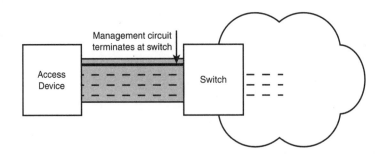

The access device and the switch exchange periodic keep alive messages. After a configured number of keep alive intervals, the access device asks for a report on the status of all PVCs.

Local Management Standards

ANSI and ITU went to work on the details of how this message exchange should be done, but progress was slow because of disagreements on some of the details. This caused the "Gang of Four" founders of the Frame Relay Forum to band together to produce their own specification.

In the end, several local management message formats were defined:

- LMI, created by the Gang of Four in 1990
- ANSI T1.617 Annex D (1991)
- ITU-T Q.933 Annex A (1992)
- ANSI T1.617 Annex B (1997)

The ITU-T version is the one currently required by the Frame Relay Forum implementation agreements. However, all the PVC local management interface specifications have been implemented. To add to the confusion, the messages used to implement any of these standards often are referred to as *LMI messages*. This makes the term *LMI* ambiguous. It might convey the fact that Gang of Four LMI messages are being used, or it might refer to messages for one of the other protocols.

An access device needs to be configured to use the version of the local management protocol that is supported by the network. Some customer equipment can monitor the line leading to the network and automatically discover the local management protocol used by the service provider. If a device cannot do this, the customer has to ask the provider which version has been selected, and manually configure its devices to use the correct version.

Local Management Protocols

For the Gang of Four LMI, management messages are exchanged across the special virtual circuit with DLCI 1023. ANSI and ITU messages are exchanged across the virtual circuit with DLCI 0. All versions of the local management interface enable a customer to

- Check that the connection to the provider's switch is working

- Request and receive full status reports that list all current virtual circuits

The basic idea behind all three versions is the same. The customer device periodically sends a *status enquiry* keep alive message that contains

- Its own current sequence number

- The last sequence number received from the network switch

The network switch responds with a *status* message that contains

- Its own current sequence number

- The last sequence number received from the customer

After a preconfigured number of keep alive status enquiries, the customer's access device will send a *full status enquiry* message. The network responds with a *full status response* that contains a series of entries. Each entry

- Identifies a virtual circuit DLCI

- Indicates if the circuit is new

- Indicates if the circuit is active

The ITU-T Q.933 Annex A specification requires a full status response to include an entry for *every* PVC that terminates at the user interface. If the maximum frame relay information field is 1600 bytes in length, then at most 317 PVC information elements can fit into an ITU full status response message. This acts as a limit on the number of concurrent PVCs at the interface!

Keep Alive Status Message Exchanges

Listing 7.1 shows summary information from a trace of keep alive messages. Each partner numbers its messages independently. A message states the sender's own current sequence number and the last number received from the partner.

In the first status enquiry message, the sender announces that its current number is 143 and that the last sequence number received from the partner was 122. The partner responds by increasing its sequence number to 123 and acknowledging that it received 143. Each party continues to increase its own number and acknowledge receipt of the partner's number.

Listing 7.1   Summary Information of Keep Alive Messages

```
Status Enquiry (Sequence verification only)
Keep alive sequence number = 143
Last received sequence number = 122

Status (Sequence verification only)
Keep alive sequence number = 123
Last received sequence number = 143

Status Enquiry (Sequence verification only)
Keep alive sequence number = 144
Last received sequence number = 123

Status (Sequence verification only)
Keep alive sequence number = 124
Last received sequence number = 144
```

LMI Status Enquiry and Response Message Formats

Figure 7.2 shows the format of a Gang of Four LMI status enquiry message, which is identified by a message type code of X'75. The status response has the same format, except the message type is X'7D.

Figure 7.2   Gang of Four LMI status message.

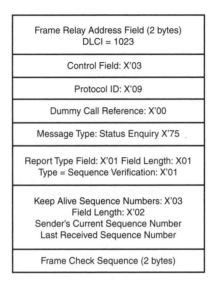

Recall that these LMI messages are sent on the circuit with DLCI 1023. Like all frame relay management and signaling messages, a status enquiry message consists of a few introductory header fields followed by a set of *information elements (IEs)* that carry the data that is of interest.

Each LMI message is introduced by an X'03 control field (meaning unnumbered information). The introductory header fields that follow are

- A protocol discriminator (X'09).

- A dummy call reference byte (X'00).

- A message type (X'75).

Several information elements follow the message type. Each information element is coded in the form

Element ID, Length, Value

The first information element in an LMI message identifies the message report type. Report type 1 indicates that these are sequence verification (keep alive) messages. The next element contains the sender's current sequence number and echoes the partner's sequence number.

ANSI Status Enquiry and Response Message Formats

The format of the ANSI status enquiry message is shown in Figure 7.3. Like the LMI version, an ANSI status enquiry has message type X'75, and the status response has message type X'7D.

Figure 7.3   Format of an ANSI status enquiry message.

Frame Relay Address Field (2 bytes) DLCI = 0
Control Field: X'03
Protocol ID: X'08
Dummy Call Reference: X'00
Message Type: Status Enquiry X'75
Locking Shift: ANSI Code Set: X'95
Report Type Field: X'01 Field Length: X01 Type = Sequence Verification: X'01
Keep Alive Sequence Numbers: X'03 Field Length: X'02 Sender's Current Sequence Number Last Received Sequence Number
Frame Check Sequence (2 bytes)

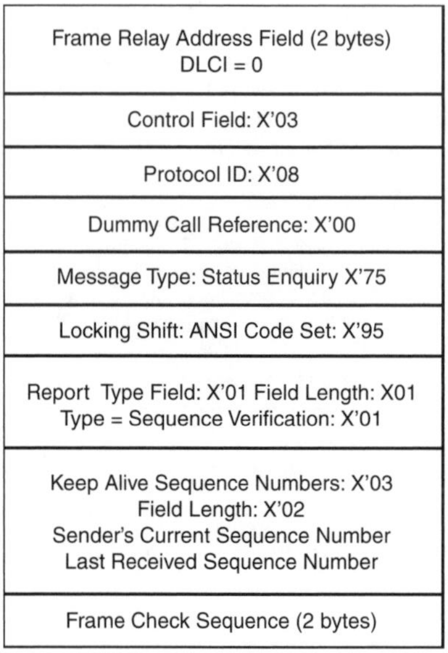

Note that the ANSI format is very similar to the LMI format. The differences between them are

- The ANSI messages are sent on the virtual circuit with DLCI 0.

- A protocol discriminator of X'08 is used for ITU-T or ANSI messages.

- A *locking shift* field value, X'95, indicates that the remaining information elements are defined using an ANSI code set (rather than in LMI or ITU-T format).

ANSI documents use the term *link integrity verification* instead of *keep alive*.

ANSI Status Enquiry and Response Trace

Listing 7.2 presents an ANSI status enquiry message and the status response.

Listing 7.2   ANSI Status Enquiry Message and Status Response

```
Decode from WinPharoah
------------Frame Relay Q.931 Format (ANSI T1.607)-------------
Direction =  DTE->DCE
Address Field (2 octets) = 0001
DLCI = 0 (In-channel signalling)
Address Octet 1
     0000 00..          DLCI (High-order)
     .... ..0.          C/R  - Command/Response indicator
     .... ...0          EA   - Address field extension bit
Address Octet 2
     0000 ....          DLCI - (Low-order)
     .... 0...          FECN - Forward Explicit Congestion Notification
     .... .0..          BECN - Backward Explicit Congestion Notification
     .... ..0.          DE   - Discard Eligibility
     .... ...1          EA   - Address Field Extension
----------Frame Relay Local Management Interface Layer (LMI)----------
Control = 03  (UI)
Protocol discriminator = 08  Network Call Control
Call reference = 00  (Dummy)
Message type = 75  Status Enquiry
Information element = 95  Locking shift
Information element = 01  Report type
     Length = 1
     Report type = 01  Sequence verification only
Information element = 03  Keep alive sequence
     Length = 2
     Current sequence number = 143
     Last received sequence number = 122


------------Frame Relay Q.931 Format (ANSI T1.607)-------------
Direction =  DCE->DTE
Address Field (2 octets) = 0001
DLCI = 0 (In-channel signalling)
Address Octet 1
     0000 00..          DLCI (High-order)
     .... ..0.          C/R  - Command/Response indicator
     .... ...0          EA   - Address field extension bit
```

continues

Listing 7.2   Continued

```
Address Octet 2
     0000 ....              DLCI - (Low-order)
     .... 0...              FECN - Forward Explicit Congestion Notification
     .... .0..              BECN - Backward Explicit Congestion Notification
     .... ..0.              DE   - Discard Eligibility
     .... ...1              EA   - Address Field Extension
----------Frame Relay Local Management Interface Layer (LMI)----------
Control = 03  (UI)
Protocol discriminator = 08  Network Call Control
Call reference = 00  (Dummy)
Message type = 7D  Status
Information element = 95  Locking shift
Information element = 01  Report type
    Length = 1
    Report type = 01  Sequence verification only
Information element = 03  Keep alive sequence
    Length = 2
    Current sequence number = 123
    Last received sequence number = 143
```

ANSI Full Status Enquiry Message Format

The format of the message used for an ANSI full status enquiry is the same as the status enquiry format, except that the value in the report type field is X'00.

ANSI Full Status Enquiry Trace

Listing 7.3 presents an ANSI full status enquiry message.

Listing 7.3   ANSI Full Status Enquiry Message

```
Decode from WinPharoah
-------------Frame Relay Q.931 Format (ANSI T1.607)-------------
Direction =  DTE->DCE
Address Field (2 octets) = 0001
DLCI = 0 (In-channel signalling)
Address Octet 1
     0000 00..              DLCI (High-order)
     .... ..0.              C/R  - Command/Response indicator
     .... ...0              EA   - Address field extension bit
```

```
Address Octet 2
     0000 ....            DLCI - (Low-order)
     .... 0...            FECN - Forward Explicit Congestion Notification
     .... .0..            BECN - Backward Explicit Congestion Notification
     .... ..0.            DE   - Discard Eligibility
     .... ...1            EA   - Address Field Extension
----------Frame Relay Local Management Interface Layer (LMI)----------
Control = 03  (UI)
Protocol discriminator = 08  Network Call Control
Call reference = 00  (Dummy)
Message type = 75  Status Enquiry
Information element = 95  Locking shift
Information element = 01  Report type
     Length = 1
     Report type = 00  Full status message
Information element = 03  Keep alive sequence
     Length = 2
     Current sequence number = 145
     Last received sequence number = 124
```

ANSI Full Status Response Message Format

Figure 7.4 outlines the format of an ANSI full status response, which contains

- A report type field whose value is X'00.

- A link integrity verification (keep alive) sequence number field containing current and received sequence numbers.

- A series of PVC status information elements introduced by identifier X'07. For each DLCI, flags indicate if it is new and if it currently is active or inactive.

ANSI Full Status Response Trace

Listing 7.4 shows the format of an ANSI full status response message. It contains a series of PVC status information elements (introduced with identifier X'07) for DLCIs 16–22. For each DLCI, flags indicate whether it is new, and whether the circuit currently is active or inactive.

Figure 7.4 ANSI full status response message.

```
┌─────────────────────────────────────────────┐
│     Frame Relay Address Field (2 bytes)       │
│                 DLCI = 0                       │
├─────────────────────────────────────────────┤
│              Control Field: X'03               │
├─────────────────────────────────────────────┤
│              Protocol ID: X'08                 │
├─────────────────────────────────────────────┤
│          Dummy Call Reference: X'00            │
├─────────────────────────────────────────────┤
│          Message Type: Status X'7D             │
├─────────────────────────────────────────────┤
│      Locking Shift: ANSI Code Set: X'95        │
├─────────────────────────────────────────────┤
│  Report Type Field: X'01 Field Length: X01     │
│      Type = Full Status Message: X'00          │
├─────────────────────────────────────────────┤
│    Keep Alive Sequence Numbers (4 bytes)       │
├─────────────────────────────────────────────┤
│                 PVC Status                     │
├─────────────────────────────────────────────┤
│                 PVC Status                     │
├─────────────────────────────────────────────┤
│                    ...                         │
├─────────────────────────────────────────────┤
│        Frame Check Sequence (2 bytes)          │
└─────────────────────────────────────────────┘
```

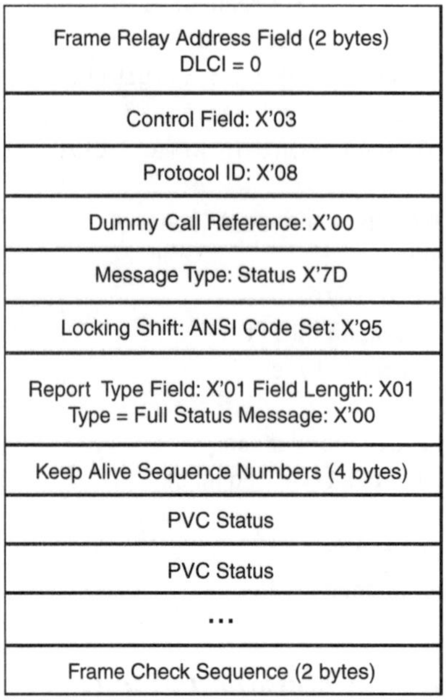

Listing 7.4 ANSI Full Status Response Message

```
Decode from WinPharoah
------------Frame Relay Q.931 Format (ANSI T1.607)------------
Direction =  DCE->DTE
Address Field (2 octets) = 0001
DLCI = 0 (In-channel signalling)
Address Octet 1
    0000 00..           DLCI (High-order)
    .... ..0.           C/R  - Command/Response indicator
    .... ...0           EA   - Address field extension bit
Address Octet 2
    0000 ....           DLCI - (Low-order)
    .... 0...           FECN - Forward Explicit Congestion Notification
    .... .0..           BECN - Backward Explicit Congestion Notification
    .... ..0.           DE   - Discard Eligibility
    .... ...1           EA   - Address Field Extension
```

```
----------Frame Relay Local Management Interface Layer (LMI)----------
Control = 03  (UI)
Protocol discriminator = 08  Network Call Control
Call reference = 00  (Dummy)
Message type = 7D  Status
Information element = 95  Locking shift
Information element = 01  Report type
    Length = 1
    Report type = 00  Full status message
Information element = 03  Keep alive sequence
    Length = 2
    Current sequence number = 125
    Last received sequence number = 145
Information element = 07  PVC status
    Length = 3
    PVC DLCI = 16
        ..00 0001  PVC DLCI (msb)
        .000 0...  PVC DLCI (lsb)
    PVC status = 82
        .... 0...  New PVC
        .... ..1.  Active PVC
Information element = 07  PVC status
    Length = 3
    PVC DLCI = 17
        ..00 0001  PVC DLCI (msb)
        .000 1...  PVC DLCI (lsb)
    PVC status = 82
        .... 0...  New PVC
        .... ..1.  Active PVC
Information element = 07  PVC status
    Length = 3
    PVC DLCI = 18
        ..00 0001  PVC DLCI (msb)
        .001 0...  PVC DLCI (lsb)
    PVC status = 82
        .... 0...  New PVC
        .... ..1.  Active PVC
Information element = 07  PVC status
    Length = 3
    PVC DLCI = 19
        ..00 0001  PVC DLCI (msb)
        .001 1...  PVC DLCI (lsb)
```

continues

Listing 7.4   Continued

```
    PVC status = 82
         .... 0...  New PVC
         .... ..1.  Active PVC
Information element = 07  PVC status
    Length = 3
    PVC DLCI = 20
         ..00 0001  PVC DLCI (msb)
         .010 0...  PVC DLCI (lsb)
    PVC status = 82
         .... 0...  New PVC
         .... ..1.  Active PVC
Information element = 07  PVC status
    Length = 3
    PVC DLCI = 21
         ..00 0001  PVC DLCI (msb)
         .010 1...  PVC DLCI (lsb)
    PVC status = 82
         .... 0...  New PVC
         .... ..1.  Active PVC
Information element = 07  PVC status
    Length = 3
    PVC DLCI = 22
         ..00 0001  PVC DLCI (msb)
         .011 0...  PVC DLCI (lsb)
    PVC status = 80
         .... 0...  New PVC
         .... ..0.  Active PVC
```

ITU-T Message Formats

The ITU-T formats are very similar to the ANSI formats. However, ITU-T messages do not include a locking shift field. They also differ in the codes used to identify information elements in the message, as shown in Table 7.1.

Table 7.1   ANSI and ITU-T Encoding of Information Elements

Information Element	ANSI Code	ITU-T Code
Report Type	X'01	X'51
Link Integrity Verification (keepalive)	X'03	X'53
PVC Status	X'07	X'57

Configuring the Local Management Interface

A number of variables need to be configured for a management interface. The definitions, ranges, and defaults listed in Table 7.2 are defined in RFC 2115, which defines the *Simple Network Management Protocol (SNMP) Management Information Base (MIB)* variables for a frame relay access device. Vendors usually are guided by SNMP specifications and align their configuration values with SNMP definitions. However, some equipment might provide different default values.

The polling interval timer and the counters (N391, N392, and N393) in Table 7.2 originally were defined in ANSI and ITU standards documents.

Table 7.2 Local Management Configuration Variables

Configuration Variable	Description
Polling Interval Timer T391	The number of seconds between status enquiry messages. Range: 5–30 Default: 10
Full Enquiry Interval Counter N391	The number of status enquiry intervals that pass before issuing a full status enquiry message. Range: 1–255 Default: 6
Error Threshold Counter N392	The maximum number of unanswered status enquiries allowed before declaring that the interface is down. Range: 1–10 Default: 3
Monitored Events Counter N393	The number of status polling intervals over which the number of errors is accumulated and compared to the error threshold. Range: 1–10 Default: 4
Maximum Supported Virtual Circuits	The maximum number allowed for the interface.
Multicast	Indicates whether the interface uses a multicast service.

Global Network Management

The local management interface described previously is useful, but it provides very limited information about a customer's PVCs. All that a customer can do is check if an adjacent switch believes that its local PVCs are active.

To perform serious management and troubleshooting, customers need a global view of all their PVCs. A network administrator wants to gather overall performance and error statistics, detect faults, check what the current configuration is, and even activate and terminate PVCs.

One way to gather statistical and error information is for the customer to attach monitor devices to each line between its access devices and the service provider. As noted in Chapter II-4, there are products that bundle powerful monitoring capabilities into CSU/DSU devices. Figure 7.5 illustrates this approach.

Figure 7.5   Monitoring frame relay interfaces.

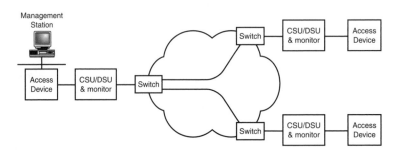

The information gathered by these devices is then accessed via an SNMP network management station and enables the customer to

• Detect line and circuit problems quickly

• Gather data used to determine if service level agreement levels are being met

Although setting up a complete monitoring system can be costly, it provides complete and instantaneous access to status and performance information.

Customer Network Management

However, there is an attractive alternative that is available from some providers. These providers offer *Customer Network Management (CNM)* as part of their service. In this case, the provider opens up its internal network management information database so a customer can access all network configuration, performance, and error data that relates to the customer's own circuits. A customer might even be able to create new circuits between sites as they are needed. This option can be very helpful.

The Frame Relay Forum published an implementation agreement (FRF.6) that specifies that providers should offer CNM service via SNMP. Figure 7.6 shows one way that this can be set up. The path from a customer's network management station goes through an

Ethernet switch into an access device and then crosses a permanent frame relay circuit that has been set up for this purpose. This circuit terminates at the provider's management center.

Some providers offer Internet access to CNM. The customer connects to the provider's management center with an ordinary browser using an encrypted secure sockets layer (SSL) session. The customer's IP address, a password, and some other customer-specific data are used for authentication.

| Figure 7.6 | A management station accessing CNM information. |

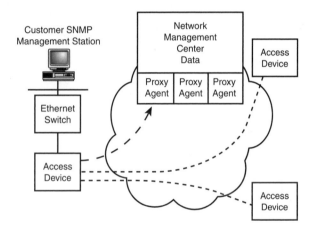

The customer's management station interacts with an application called a *proxy agent* that relays requests and responses between the customer's management station and the provider's management information. The proxy agent controls the customer's access to the provider network's management data so the customer sees only information relating to its own circuits. The proxy agent isolates the customer from data that relates to other customers.

Role of RFC 1604

The Frame Relay Forum CNM implementation agreement is based on IETF document RFC 1604, *Definitions of Managed Objects for Frame Relay Service*. RFC 1604 defines the frame relay PVC variables whose values can be extracted via SNMP. If allowed by the provider, the customer will be able to add or modify his or her own configuration information via SNMP.

PVC Segments

The management information described in RFC 1604 is presented from the provider's point of view. For example, the endpoints of a PVC are the points at which a circuit enters and exits the provider's network. This chunk of the circuit is called a *PVC segment*.

A number of providers have inter-connected their networks, and some PVCs span multiple networks. In this case, a PVC is made up of several separate segments—one for each network that is traversed. Some of the segment endpoints will be located at network-to-network interfaces (NNIs). NNIs are discussed in Chapter II-8.

To manage a PVC that spans multiple networks, a customer needs an SNMP view into each provider network that contains a segment of the PVC.

Overview of RFC 1604 Tables

The global management variables defined in RFC 1604 are organized into a set of tables:

- **Logical Port Information table**—Includes general configuration information about a frame relay interface. The variables are displayed in Table 7.3.

- **Virtual Circuit Signaling Parameters and Errors table**—Devoted to local management interface information. It lists local management configuration and error parameters. The variables are displayed in Table 7.4.

- **PVC End-Point table**—Contains configuration variables and statistics for PVC segment endpoints. The variables are listed in Table 7.5. Some providers allow a customer to create new PVC endpoints or change the characteristics of an existing PVC by updating this table. If so, the subscriber can use SNMP to

  - Identify and reserve traffic resources for the endpoints of a new circuit

  - Modify parameters of an existing endpoint

  - Delete PVC endpoints

- **Frame Relay PVC Connection table**—Indicates which PVC endpoints need to be connected to form PVC segments. Point-to-point, point-to-multipoint, and multipoint-to-multipoint circuits can be defined. The PVC connection variables are shown in Table 7.6.

RFC 1604 includes two more tables. These contain information that can be used for accounting. The information consists of counts of PVC segments and logical ports. Details will not be presented here.

The sections that follow tabulate and describe variables that belong to the RFC 1604 tables. Each of these variables has a formal SNMP MIB variable name. Unfortunately, these names (for example, `frLportVCSigProtocol`) tend to cause eyes to glaze over. In each table, the formal names have been replaced by ordinary words that are easier to read. See RFC 1604 for the original variable names.

Logical Port Information

Many SNMP variables describe characteristics of communications interfaces. Anyone who uses a networked computer is familiar with an Ethernet or Token Ring LAN interface. Just as an Ethernet interface connects a device to an Ethernet LAN, a frame relay interface connects a device to a frame relay network. However, MIB documents and vendor manuals often use the term *logical port* instead of the term *frame relay interface.*

To some extent, this is just a language convention that grew up inside the vendor community. However, the terminology also reflects the fact that a frame relay interface differs from a LAN interface in some important ways.

A LAN interface corresponds to a single identifiable hardware connector and cable that transmits data onto a single LAN. In contrast, the wide area serial interfaces that are used to connect a device to a frame relay network can be channelized in various ways, and different networks can be accessed via the separate channels. For example, Figure 7.7 shows a channelized T1 interface at a frame relay switch. The T1 interface has been split into two subinterfaces. Each supports a fractional T1 connection to a customer access device. Each of these fractional T1s can be viewed as a separate logical port. Both logical ports share the same physical connector and cable. Table 7.3 shows basic logical port information.

Figure 7.7   Logical ports sharing a serial interface.

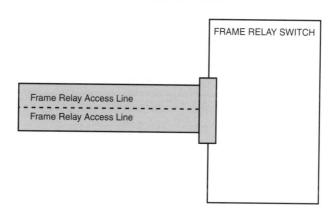

Table 7.3	Logical Port Information Table
Variable	**Description**
Logical port numbering plan	Numbering plan (if any). If SVCs are supported, then ports probably would be numbered via E.164 or X.121 addresses.
Logical port contact person	Network contact person.
Logical port location	Port location.
Type of logical port	Type: UNI or NNI.
DLCI address length	DLCI address length (10, 16, 17, or 23 bits).
Local signaling protocol	Type of management signaling protocol: Gang of Four LMI, ANSI T1.617 Annex D, ANSI T1.617 Annex B, or ITU-T Q.933A.
Signaling pointer	A pointer to a table that contains signaling parameters and error counts for this interface. (See Table 7.4.)

Local Management Interface Information

The first part of this chapter described the local management interface signaling messages that are exchanged across a user-network interface. Local management messages also are exchanged across a network-to-network interface, as you will see in Chapter II-8. Table 7.4 lists local management interface configuration parameters and error counts for a logical port.

If the logical port plays a user-side role, only the user-side table variables will have meaningful values. If the logical port plays a network-side role, only the network-side table variables will have meaningful values.

Table 7.4	Virtual Circuit Signaling Parameters and Errors
Variable	**Description**
Signaling procedure	Whether polling is user-to-network (normal for UNI) or bidirectional (the usual setup for NNI).
User-side N391 variable	The number of status enquiry intervals that pass before the user side issues a full status enquiry message (N391).
User-side N392 variable	The maximum number of unanswered user-side status enquiries allowed before the user-side declares that the interface is down (N392).

Variable	Description
User-side N393 variable	The number of user-side status polling intervals over which the number of errors is accumulated and compared to the error threshold (N393).
User-side T391 timer	The number of seconds between user-side status enquiry messages (T391).
Network-side N392 variable	The maximum number of unanswered network side status enquiries allowed before the network side declares that the interface is down (N392 for ANSI/ ITU, nN2 for LMI).
Network-side N393 variable	The number of network-side status polling intervals over which the number of errors is accumulated and compared to the error threshold (N393 for ANSI/ ITU, nN3 for Gang of Four LMI).
Network-side T392 timer	The number of seconds between network-side status enquiry messages (T392 for ANSI/ITU, nT2 for Gang of Four LMI).
LMI nN4 variable	The Gang of Four LMI network-side maximum status enquiries received value (nN4).
LMI nT3 timer	The Gang of Four LMI network-side timer over which nN4 status enquiries received is counted (nT3).
User link reliability errors	The number of user-side link reliability errors; that is, missing status or status enquiry messages or invalid sequence numbers.
User-side signaling protocol errors	The number of messages that contained an incorrect protocol identifier, message type, call reference, or mandatory information element.
User-side channel inactive	The number of times the user-side channel was declared inactive (because of N392 unanswered status enquiries in N393 polling intervals).
Network-side link reliability errors	The number of network-side link reliability errors; that is, missing status or status enquiry messages or invalid sequence numbers.
Network-side protocol errors	The number of network-side protocol errors; that is, incorrect protocol identifier, message type, call reference, or mandatory information elements.
Network-side channel inactive	The number of times the network-side channel was declared inactive (because of N392 unanswered status enquiries in N393 polling intervals).

Segment Endpoint Configuration and Statistics

For the purposes of CNM, a provider's network is seen as a single big black box that has numbered endpoints situated at convenient locations. Figure 7.8 shows how a segment, endpoints, incoming traffic, and outgoing traffic look from this point of view.

Table 7.5, the PVC endpoint table, contains information about one customer's PVC endpoints. Each entry corresponds to a single endpoint, which is identified by a unique interface index assigned by the network provider and the customer's DLCI.

Keep in mind that the variables in Table 7.5 are described from the point of view of the network. As shown in Figure 7.8, an *incoming frame* is a frame that enters the provider's network at a segment endpoint. An *outgoing frame* is a frame that is exiting the provider's network at the segment endpoint.

Figure 7.8   Network view of a PVC segment.

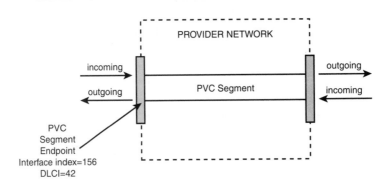

Table 7.5   The PVC Endpoint Table

Variable	Description
Interface index	A number that uniquely identifies the logical port (frame relay interface) at which this PVC endpoint is located.
DLCI index	The DLCI to which the remaining variables apply.
Incoming maximum frame size	The maximum information field size for frames sent into the frame relay network at this PVC endpoint.
Incoming Bc	The committed burst size (Bc) measured in bits, for traffic sent into the network at this PVC endpoint.
Incoming Be	The excess burst size (Be) measured in bits, for traffic sent into the network at this PVC endpoint.

Variable	Description
Incoming CIR	The committed information rate (measured in bits per second) for traffic sent into the network at this PVC endpoint.
Outgoing maximum frame size	The maximum information field size for frames exiting the frame relay network at this PVC endpoint.
Outgoing Bc	The committed burst size (Bc), measured in bits, for traffic exiting the network at this PVC endpoint.
Outgoing Be	The excess burst size (Be), measured in bits, for traffic exiting the network at this PVC endpoint.
Outgoing CIR	The committed information rate (measured in bits per second) for traffic exiting the network at this PVC endpoint.
Endpoint connection identifier	A unique identifier assigned to a PVC. Entries that have the same value for this identifier are endpoints of the same PVC. This value is the PVC Connection Index in Table 7.6.
PVC status received via local management interface	The PVC status (active, inactive, or deleted) received by this endpoint. This is defined only for network-to-network interfaces.
Incoming frames	The number of incoming frames received by this endpoint (including frames that the network may have discarded immediately).
Outgoing frames	The number of outgoing frames sent by the network at this endpoint.
Incoming DE frames	The number of incoming frames with DE bit set to one received by this endpoint.
Incoming excess frames	The number of incoming frames received at this endpoint that were treated as excess traffic.
Outgoing excess frames	The number of outgoing frames sent by this endpoint that were treated as excess traffic.
Incoming frames discarded	The number of incoming frames received by this endpoint that were discarded due to traffic enforcement.
Incoming bytes	The number of incoming bytes received by the network for this PVC.
Outgoing bytes	The number of outgoing bytes sent by the network for this PVC.

Configuring PVC Segments

Single endpoints are married to one another to form PVC segments using Table 7.6, the PVC connection table.

Each PVC segment that is created needs to be assigned a unique identifier (index number). This is implemented by means of a special variable (whose formal name is frPVCConnectIndexValue) that acts like a take-a-number in a delicatessen.

An administrator defining a new circuit segment reads this variable to get a unique identifier and then writes that identifier into the first variable of a new connection table entry. The entry also must include a pair of segment endpoints. The segment endpoints are identified by their interface numbers and DLCIs. The table is organized so that the smaller interface number always is listed first.

Table 7.6   The PVC Connection Table

Variable	Description
PVC connection index	The unique identifier for this PVC segment.
Low interface index	The smaller of the two UNI/NNI endpoint interface index numbers.
DLCI for the low index	The DLCI number associated with the interface that has the lower index.
High interface index	The larger of the two UNI/NNI endpoint interface index numbers.
DLCI for the high index	The DLCI number associated with the interface that has the higher index.
Desired administrative status of segment	The desired status—active, inactive, or testing—of this segment. An administrator updates this variable to activate or deactivate the PVC segment.
Operational low to high status of segment	The actual current status of the segment in the low-to-high direction. It can be reported as active, inactive, testing, or unknown.
Operational high to low operational status	The actual current status of the segment in the high-to-low direction. It can be reported as active, inactive, testing, or unknown.
Time of the last operational change for the low to high direction	A time value indicating when this segment entered the current operational state for the low-to-high direction. (The value is relative to the time that the provider's proxy agent last initialized.)
Time of the last operational change for the high to low	A time value indicating when this segment entered the current operational state for the high-to-low direction. (The direction value is relative to the time that the provider's proxy agent last initialized.)

References

The Frame Relay Forum document, *Frame Relay Service Customer Network Management Implementation Agreement*, FRF.6 (1994), outlines the use of SNMP to obtain frame relay performance monitoring, fault detection, and configuration information from a service provider.

FRF.6 references IETF document RFC 1604, *Definitions of Managed Objects for Frame Relay Service* (1994), for specifications of the management variables to be implemented in network equipment.

IETF RFC 2115, *Management Information Base for Frame Relay DTEs Using SMIv2* (1997), describes management variables for frame relay access devices.

Annex D to ANSI T1.617 (1991, revised 1997) describes local management messages. ANSI T1.617 deals with signaling, which includes both call setup messages and management messages. The full title of the specification is *Telecommunications— Integrated Services Digital Network (ISDN)—Signaling Specification for Frame Relay Bearer Service for Digital Subscriber Signaling System Number 1 (DSS1)*.

Annex A to ITU-T Q.933 (1991, revised 1995) describes management messages. Q.933 also deals with both call setup and management messages. The title of the Q.933 specification is *DSS1 Signalling Specification for Frame Mode Basic Call Control*.

CHAPTER 8

Network-to-Network Interface

So far, we have concentrated on the user-network interface (UNI), the interface between a customer access device and a provider switch. However, there also is a need to connect frame relay networks.

As is the case for telephone service, increasing the number of locations that can be reached increases the value of the service. Network-to-network interconnections are especially useful when providers want to deliver data across national boundaries.

Standards organizations have defined a formal frame relay network-to-network interface (NNI) that enables circuits to be set up across a chain of provider networks. Currently, only PVCs are supported across multiple networks. Switched virtual circuits are difficult to implement, even for a single provider network. At the time of this writing, providers were not yet ready to tackle multi-network switched circuit projects.

Types of Network-to-Network Interfaces

Some organizations have built their own frame relay networks by buying a set of switches and connecting them with leased lines. At a later time, a company might need to add circuits to distant locations. The company might discover that the most cost-effective way to do this is to connect the private network to a provider network. The result is shown in Figure 8.1. The private network is connected to the provider's network via an NNI. In this case, it is a private network to provider network interface.

Figure 8.1   An NNI between a private and public network.

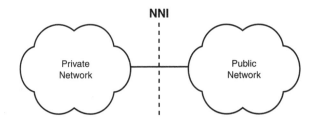

There also are NNIs between providers. Although providers compete ferociously, sometimes cooperation is mutually beneficial. The popularity of frame relay has led to increasing scope for its use and, inevitably, a need for customers to link sites that have been connected to different frame relay providers.

Providers have started to make bilateral agreements with peers to create PVCs that span networks. Their customers benefit from the coverage of a larger range of destinations. Figure 8.2 illustrates a PVC connection that crosses two public networks.

A multi-network PVC contains two or more PVC segments. In Figure 8.2, one segment crosses Network 1, and the other crosses Network 2. Frames for the circuit also must pass across the link that connects the two networks.

The number of networks that can be connected is not limited to two. A PVC could cross a chain of networks and consist of several segments.

Figure 8.2   Segments of a multi-network PVC.

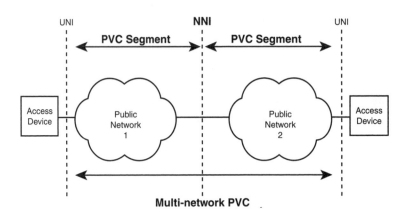

NNI *Provider Issues*

The interconnected telephone system is mature, and services are very well defined. For example, the service provided by a leased T1 line is fixed and straightforward. Access equipment and switching equipment is built to tight standards and interoperates.

Interconnected telephone service companies have set up cooperative network management procedures. Customer service responsibilities are well defined. The telephone networks have established settlement procedures for sharing revenues. Billing software has had many years to evolve.

Even so, when a T1 line crosses multiple carriers, customers sometimes experience frustration in getting problems resolved in a timely manner.

In contrast to telephone service, frame relay is relatively young, and network-to-network relationships still are immature. Even when only PVC support is involved, linking two or more frame relay networks is not a trivial task. Providers differ greatly in the way they structure their services. For example, one provider might stress end-to-end service level guarantees and promise to deliver at least 99.9 percent of all frames that are within a circuit's CIR. Another provider might not make any delivery guarantees but might offer low-cost and best-effort delivery of all frames presented to the network.

These policies cannot be altered with a simple change of a few configuration parameters. The providers have customized their networks to fit their business strategies. It just might not be worthwhile for providers to make the effort to connect public networks that have been designed to meet very different needs.

In spite of interoperability agreements, there are significant differences between the switches produced by different vendors. Each vendor adds special features or takes a technical approach it hopes will make its product attractive. Problems can arise when vendors who use different types of switches attempt to lock their networks together.

But technical problems might not be the biggest hurdle. Fulfilling an order for PVCs that span two or more provider networks requires cooperation and coordination. Order fulfillment procedures vary. The average order fulfillment times for each network might be very different.

While each partner might be willing to supervise its segment of a PVC, a customer needs to communicate with someone who is responsible for fault detection and troubleshooting for the whole circuit—especially when there are unresolved, recurring problems. The partners have to come up with a uniform fee structure, decide on what information will be included in bills, establish who will send them and collect the revenues, and how revenues will be divided. The partners need to share and coordinate billing information. A customer who has experienced outages and is entitled to a large rebate could experience weeks of frustration in trying to get a bill corrected, while each provider blames its partner's computer for the failure to get the bill right.

NNI Customer Issues

Before signing a three-year contract for multi-network PVCs, it is a good idea to check that issues that might impact customer service have been resolved! Specific items that need to be verified include

- All the providers are willing and able to sustain a common service level agreement.

- The maximum frame size is compatible across all networks.

- Each network-to-network connection has enough bandwidth to cover the sum of all of the CIRs for the PVCs that span the networks.

- There is a reasonable amount of bandwidth available to accommodate excess burst rate.

- Traffic discard policies are consistent.

- There is a well-defined point-of-contact person who is responsible for resolving your circuit problems—no matter which segment is involved.

- Billing errors will be corrected on the next bill that is issued.

NNI Standards

ITU-T and ANSI standards exist that describe the NNI. The standards address many aspects of the interface, including the physical connection, the data link layer, DLCI addressing, and management interface status messages.

As usually is the case with ITU-T and ANSI standards, there are many options and many fuzzy points. Implementations that interwork require a more focused approach. The Frame Relay Forum published a PVC NNI agreement in FRF.2, which appropriately is entitled *Frame Relay Network-to-Network Interface Implementation Agreement*.

Making the Network-to-Network Connection

There are many ways to create the physical connection between two frame relay networks. The providers might install switches at a common location and connect the switches with a high-bandwidth cable. Alternatively, they might use a long-distance connection such as fractional T3 or T3 line.

DLCIs at the Network-to-Network Interface

Each virtual circuit that spans more than one network must be assigned a DLCI at each network-to-network boundary crossed by the virtual circuit. Figure 8.3 shows the DLCIs at the UNIs and NNIs of a PVC that spans two networks:

- DLCI 25 identifies the circuit at the interface between User Access Device A and Network 1.

- DLCI 132,145 is the identifier used for the same PVC across the interface between Network 1 and Network 2.

- DLCI 29 identifies the circuit at the interface between Network 2 and User Access Device B.

The Frame Relay Forum agreement specifies that two- or four-byte address fields can be used at the NNI. Four byte address fields are recommended; a pool of almost 1,000 10-bit addresses is more than adequate for a UNI, but a network-to-network link is likely to be a very high-capacity link and might carry thousands of virtual circuits.

| Figure 8.3 | DLCIs for multi-network PVCs. |

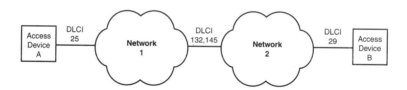

Multi-Network Virtual Circuit Management

A customer's access device expects to receive periodic reports on the status of its PVCs. If a PVC spans two or more networks, its status must be based on the condition of all the segments that make up the circuit.

To get this information, networks exchange segment status information across the NNI. The overall PVC status then is reported to customer access devices.

Figure 8.4 illustrates this point. A virtual circuit between Access Devices A and B spans two frame relay networks. The segment within Network 1 is functioning correctly, but a broken link in Network 2 has disrupted several virtual circuits, including the one joining A and B. The news that the link is broken is forwarded to all the switches in Network 2. Standard NNI management messages transmitted to Network 1 will include the list of disrupted circuits.

> **Note**
>
> The method that switches within a frame relay network used to exchange information about network topology or link status has not been standardized. Vendors are free to develop proprietary protocols. However, the most popular option is to use a protocol based on Open Shortest Path First (OSPF), whose original purpose was to enable IP routers to discover network topology and link status.

Figure 8.4   Discovering the status of a complete circuit.

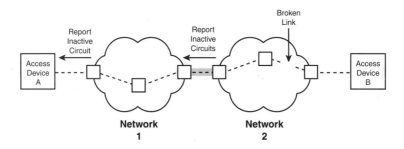

The Frame Relay Forum has defined two methods that can be used for exchanging status information across the NNI. The first, called bidirectional procedures, is based on the status reporting protocol already defined for the UNI local management interface. The second, called event driven procedures, keeps partners informed of changes to circuits and adds diagnostic information that is not included in the UNI local management interface reports.

Bidirectional Management Procedures at the NNI

The bidirectional procedures method is simple. Instead of designing a new protocol, the existing UNI procedure is used across the NNI interface—but it is used in both directions. Each network must play both a user (polling) role and network (polled) role. Each partner sends both status enquiries and status reports.

In Figure 8.5, Network 1 plays the user role in the upper set of message exchanges. That is, Network 1 sends status enquiries to Network 2. Network 1 plays the network role in the lower set of message exchanges in Figure 8.5 and responds to status enquiries from Network 2. All these messages are passed between the networks in frames whose DLCI is 0.

A network connected to a PVC endpoint must report the status of the whole PVC to its endpoints. The same principle holds whether a PVC crosses two networks or several networks. For example, when all is well, a series of reports like the following will flow toward an endpoint:

active —> active —> active —> active

If the second segment is damaged, the reports would be

active —> inactive —> inactive —> inactive

Reports flowing in the opposite direction would carry the news that the PVC is down to the other endpoint.

Figure 8.5   Bidirectional management procedures.

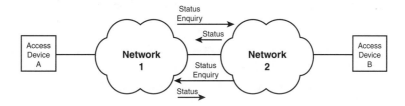

It is important for a network to report new PVCs, deleted PVCs, PVC breakages, and PVC repairs as quickly as possible across an NNI. Major events in the life of a PVC include

- Creating a PVC by adding a segment to each network it crosses.
- Deleting a PVC by removing a segment from each network it crosses.
- A broken segment. The segment (and PVC) becomes inactive.
- A repaired segment. It is active again.
- Loss of connectivity at one of the UNIs.
- Repair of the connectivity at one of the UNIs.
- Failure of an NNI.
- Repair of an NNI.

To get the news out to its partner network, a network on which a change occurs will either respond to the next incoming poll with a full status response or it will send an asynchronous (unpolled) full status report without waiting to be polled.

The timing and counter parameters, the parameter ranges, and the defaults used for the management interface across the NNI are the same as those introduced in Table 7.1 (Chapter II-7).

Event Driven Procedures at the NNI

A different approach is taken for the second alternative: *event driven procedures.* Messages still are exchanged across DLCI 0 at the NNI. However, a reliable data link protocol (reliable LAPF, which is similar to LAPB) is used. This means that frames are numbered and acknowledged, and are retransmitted if an acknowledgment is not received within a timeout interval. Chapter II-9 includes a discussion of reliable LAPF.

There is no need for keepalive polling messages because the reliable data link protocol keeps track of whether the partners are connected. (Specifically, if an inactivity timeout period elapses, the LAPF data link protocol automatically sends a supervisory frame that elicits a response.) ITU-T Q.921 and Q.922 contain a detailed description of the data link protocol.

Neither side polls for status information. After the link has been set up, each partner sends status reports that list its PVC segments and indicate whether each segment is active. Thereafter, update reports are sent as needed to notify a partner of a change.

An update report does not list all PVCs. It only contains information about new or deleted PVCs, or PVCs whose active/inactive state has changed. These reports have an expanded format that includes extra parameters:

- An *inactive reason* field that indicates the type of event or problem. For example, a PVC might have been added or deleted, a PVC might have failed or been restored, or a UNI or NNI (other than this one) might have failed.

- A *country code* and *national network identifier* that pinpoint the network in which an event occurred.

There is a significant advantage to using event-driven procedures over bidirectional procedures. Recall that for a UNI, a full status report had to include status information for every PVC. Because there is always some limit on message size, there was an artificial limit on the number of PVCs at a UNI.

An NNI between two public networks might need to carry a very large number of circuits. However, the update PVC status messages used for event-driven procedures report only changes. If needed, updates can be spread across several messages.

References

Two standards that apply to the network-to-network interface are CCITT Recommendation I.372: *Frame Relaying Bearer Service Network-to-Network Interface Requirements* (1992), and ITU-T *Recommendation Draft Q.frnni 1: Frame Relay Services Network-to-Network Signalling Protocol For PVC Monitoring* (1994).

Annex A to ITU standard Q.933 spells out bidirectional procedures in detail.

The Frame Relay Forum published the *Frame Relay Network-to-Network (NNI) Implementation Agreement* (1995) as FRF.2.1.

Annex 1 to FRF.2.1 describes the event-driven procedures. This Annex has been submitted to the ITU for standardization. ITU-T Q.921 describes the reliable data link protocol that is used.

CHAPTER 9

Frame Relay Switched Virtual Circuits

Initially, frame relay providers concentrated on permanent virtual circuit offerings. PVC service is straightforward: Circuits are statically configured, and a provider can focus on keeping its network healthy and keeping a fairly predictable and controlled load of frames rolling.

PVCs are a flat-rate service. Once a contract has been hammered out with the customer, the provider prints a monthly bill based on the number of circuits, the CIR of each, and the class of service that the customer has ordered.

It is relatively easy for a provider to maintain its network when its customers use PVCs. Network usage is reasonably stable. A customer might keep its circuits active for a period of months or years.

At the time of writing, some equipment vendors have included switched virtual circuit (SVC) capabilities in their frame relay switches and access devices. However, several considerations have caused frame relay network providers to put switched service on the back burner. The technology required to support SVCs is fairly complicated. New call accounting software and billing practices need to be put in place for SVC customers. And, opening up a network to dynamic calling makes it difficult to estimate the capacity that will be needed to satisfy customer needs.

Benefits of Switched Circuits

Real SVCs can be useful to customers in a number of situations:

- Configuring and managing a fully meshed PVC network between a large number of sites is a daunting task.

- There may be sites within a business that only need to communicate occasionally.

- SVCs can provide a useful backup for leased lines or frame relay PVCs.

- SVCs can be activated to add bandwidth on an as-needed basis for heavy traffic loads.

- Two businesses may need to share information for a joint project over a limited period of time.

- SVCs provide an attractive way to conduct business-to-business transactions when stability and predictable response time are important.

If frame relay service survives far into the future, then users eventually will demand the any-to-any connectivity that the voice network supports through the use of switched circuits. Whether frame relay will provide universal switched service or be bypassed in favor of ATM circuits remains an open question.

The sections that follow sketch the features of the user-network interface (UNI) for a switched service, as outlined by the Frame Relay Forum in implementation agreement FRF.4. This is a scaled-down version of the original ITU SVC signaling specification, *DSS1 Signaling Specification for Frame Mode Basic Call Control*, published as recommendation Q.933. (DSS1 stands for Digital Subscriber Signaling System number 1.) In fact, the FRF.4 implementation agreement cuts DSS1 to the bone, restricting the parameters within the messages to an essential subset.

Switched Service Technology Requirements

SVCs are set up much like ordinary telephone calls. First and foremost, this means that a global numbering scheme must be in place so that each participating access device interface can be assigned a fixed, unique number.

An access device has to signal across the UNI to identify the called number and other call parameters. Additional signaling messages are generated to notify the called device that there is an incoming call and to complete the call setup.

Up to this point, setting up a data call does not seem very different from setting up a voice call. However, when you set up a voice call, you do not need to specify traffic parameters. A long-distance telephone call always occupies 64Kbps and is supposed to satisfy some well-established quality requirements. (Otherwise, you can call an operator and complain.) In contrast, several traffic attributes need to be established for a frame relay call:

- Throughput

- Maximum size of the information payload

- Committed burst size

- Excess burst size

The values need to be negotiated between the calling device, the network, and the called device. All three must agree on values that they can support.

SVC User-Network Connection Procedures

Instead of the old analog pulses or more modern Dual-tone Multi-frequency (DTMF) touch-tone signals that are used between a Plain Old Telephone Service (POTS) telephone set and the telephone network, a frame relay SVC is set up by exchanging formatted messages.

The exchange of messages is referred to as *signaling*; this term has been used for call setup and control processes since the dawn of telephone service. There are two distinct signaling categories:

- Signaling between an access device and the network across a UNI

- Signaling internal to the network, between network devices across a network-to-network interface (NNI)

We discuss only user-network signaling here.

Digital Subscriber Signaling System Messages

The user-network signaling protocol for frame relay is *Digital Subscriber Signaling System number 1* or *DSS1*. DSS1 was designed for ISDN call setup and termination and then was adapted for frame relay SVC call setup and termination.

The Frame Relay Signaling Circuit

In the ISDN world, DSS1 call setup and termination messages are exchanged between a user access device and a network switch across a separate D, signaling channel.

The ITU-T and ANSI originally designed frame relay service to be an integral part of ISDN. In their view, a switched frame relay call was just one of many standard ISDN call types; it needed to be set up via DSS1 signaling messages exchanged across an ISDN D channel.

Frame relay vendors and providers redefined frame relay to operate independently of ISDN. Although they adopted DSS1 messages to set up switched frame relay circuits, the messages are not sent across a D channel. They are exchanged across whatever type of physical link has been set up between an access device and its adjacent frame relay network switch. The messages are transmitted across the special virtual circuit with DLCI 0.

Figure 9.1 shows a leased line used as the physical link between an access device and a frame relay switch can be a leased line. This might originally have been installed to carry some PVCs. However, SVC service does not have to be restricted to leased line subscribers. The provider may allow an access device to connect to its network via a switched 56Kbps link or via an ISDN call to a frame relay network switch. A DLCI 0 circuit automatically would be established between the access device and the switch, across the switched 56Kbps line or the ISDN bearer channel.

Ironically, the only configuration that is *not* supported by current Forum implementation agreements is the one originally envisioned by the ITU-T and ANSI—namely, signaling across a D channel to a frame relay service that is an integral part of an ISDN service.

A frame relay service that is integrated with ISDN and whose calls are set up using ISDN D channel signaling is called a *Case B service*. Figure 9.1 describes *Case A service*, which is not integrated with ISDN.

Figure 9.1   Case A configuration for setting up SVCs.

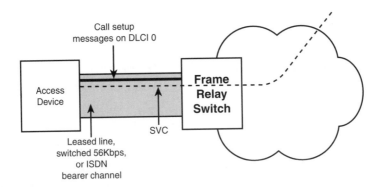

The Signaling Data Link

Signaling messages are important and need to be delivered dependably. A reliable layer 2 data link is established between the user endpoint device and the adjacent network switch to carry the call setup (and termination) signaling messages. The information frames on this link are numbered and acknowledged. The frames that are used are called *LAPF-CONTROL* (or just *LAPF*) *frames*, in contrast to the simple *LAPF-CORE frames* that carry data across customer circuits.

Note
ITU-T Q.921 and Q.922 describe the LAPF reliable link procedures, and ITU-T Q.933 describes the call control messages.

LAPF belongs to the family of reliable data link protocols that includes LAPB and LAPD. Figure 9.2 shows that unlike a LAPF-CORE frame, a LAPF frame includes a control field.

Figure 9.2   LAPF-CORE and LAPF frames.

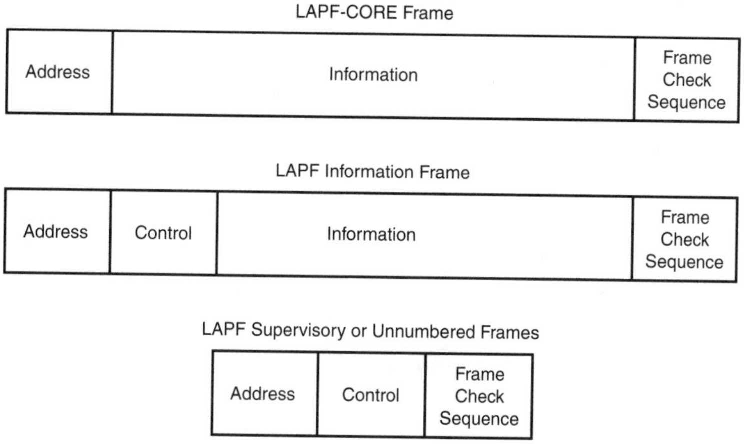

LAPF-CORE Frame

Address	Information	Frame Check Sequence

LAPF Information Frame

Address	Control	Information	Frame Check Sequence

LAPF Supervisory or Unnumbered Frames

Address	Control	Frame Check Sequence

As was the case for LAPB, a reliable LAPF data link is opened via a SABME request followed by a UA response. Supervisory RR and RNR frames impose flow control and acknowledge received data. A link is terminated by a DISC request and UA response. See Chapter II-2 for details. The biggest difference between LAPB and LAPF is the fact that the LAPF address field contains a DLCI and DE, FECN, and BECN flag bits.

SVC Numbering Plans

Before a frame relay interface can initiate or receive a switched call, it must be assigned a number. There are two numbering plans that can be used for frame relay data calls: the X.121 data numbering plan, and the E.164 ISDN/Telephony numbering plan. E.164 is preferred for the long run.

X.121

The *X.121* numbering plan originally was designed to number X.25 data terminal endpoints (DTEs). It is a hierarchical plan. X.121 addresses are up to 14 digits long, and have the structure:

    Country-Code   Provider   DTE-Number

The first digit of the country code is a zone number that identifies a part of the world. For example, Zone 2 covers Europe and Zone 3 includes the United States, Canada, Mexico, the Caribbean, and Central American countries.

More details are shown in Table 9.1. This plan is convenient for the short run, because frame relay is a provider-based service today, rather than a global service.

Table 9.1   Components of the X.121 Address

Address Component	Number of Digits	Description
Country Code	3	More than one country code may be assigned to a country.
Provider	1	Assigned by a national administrative agency.
Terminal Number	Up to 10	Assigned by the customer's service provider.

E.164

E.164 is a hierarchical global telecommunications numbering plan. E.164 addresses have the form

Country-Code   National-Destination-Code   Subscriber-Number   Subaddress

Details are shown in Table 9.2. The combined lengths of the Country Code, National Destination Code, and Subscriber Number can add up to as much as 15 digits. However, a country can choose to use fewer digits. Note that adding subaddresses can lead to very lengthy addresses.

Table 9.2   Components of the E.164 Address

Address Component	Number of Digits	Description
Country Code	1, 2, or 3	Based on the international telephony numbering plan. (See your telephone book for these numbers.)
National Destination Code and Subscriber Number	Maximum is 14, 13, or 12	A country can design its internal hierarchy according to its needs.
Subaddress	Up to 40	Used to select a PBX extension or identify a data network address (for example, an IP address).

Switched Call Setup and Termination

Figure 9.3 illustrates the messages used to set up and terminate a switched frame relay call:

1. The access device sends a SETUP message to the network. This message includes the called party address (and optionally the calling party address) and parameters such as the committed burst size (Bc), the excess burst size (Be), the quality of service, and the maximum information field size. Both the network and the called device may decrease these values if they cannot support the requested values.

2. The network processes the SETUP message.

3. The network sends a CALL PROCEEDING message to the caller. This message contains the DLCI to be used by the calling end of the connection.

4. The network also sends a SETUP message to the called device. This message contains the DLCI to be used by the called end of the connection.

5. If the called device accepts the call, it sends a CONNECT message to the network.

6. The network processes the CONNECT message and sends a CONNECT to the caller.

After the call setup is complete, the partners can exchange data across the circuit. Either party can choose to close the circuit.

Figure 9.3   Setting up a frame relay SVC.

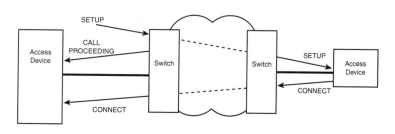

Figure 9.4 illustrates the messages used to end a frame relay switched call. Either party can terminate the call. In the figure, the original caller terminates the call. The steps are

1. The closer sends a DISCONNECT message to the network.

2. The network disconnects the circuit and sends a RELEASE message to each partner.

3. Each partner releases the DLCI and sends a RELEASE COMPLETE message back to the network.

4. The network releases the DLCI and the circuit's resources are reclaimed.

Figure 9.4 Terminating a frame relay SVC.

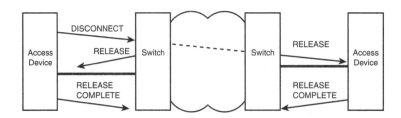

Signaling Messages

The messages used to set up and terminate calls are part of the larger family of DSS1 signaling messages. This family includes the local management interface messages already described in Chapter II-7.

The DSS1 signaling messages originally were defined in ITU-T Q.933. The Frame Relay Forum has restricted the set of signaling messages that need to be supported to the list shown in Table 9.3. A hexadecimal code that identifies each type of message also is shown.

Table 9.3 Signaling Message Types

Hex Code	Message Type
01	SETUP
02	CALL PROCEEDING
07	CONNECT
45	DISCONNECT
4D	RELEASE
5A	RELEASE COMPLETE
75	STATUS ENQUIRY
7D	STATUS

Like the local management interface status messages described in Chapter II-7, the format of the other messages consists of a few introductory header fields followed by a set of information elements (IEs) that are relevant to the type of message. Figure 9.5 shows the overall format of a signaling message.

The control field in a call setup or termination message contains sequence and acknowledgment numbers, because these messages are sent reliably.

The call reference number is local to an endpoint and its adjacent switch. It enables the endpoint and switch to identify the call to which a message applies.

For example, when an endpoint wants to set up a new call, it chooses an unused call reference number and includes it in its SETUP request message. When the endpoint receives a CONNECT message that has the same call reference, the endpoint knows that its call has gone through.

| Figure 9.5 | Format of a signaling message. |

```
+--------------------------------+
|   Frame Relay Address Field    |
|           DLCI = 0             |
+--------------------------------+
|         Control Field          |
+--------------------------------+
|  Protocol Discriminator: X'08  |
+--------------------------------+
|      Call Reference Value       |
+--------------------------------+
|          Message Type          |
+--------------------------------+
|            Other               |
|         Information            |
|          Elements              |
+--------------------------------+
|  Frame Check Sequence (2 bytes) |
+--------------------------------+
```

In addition to cutting back on the number of messages, the Frame Relay Forum also has cut down on the number of information elements to be supported in each message. To provide an idea of the type of information elements that may appear, a SETUP message can include:

- Bearer capability (requests a frame mode data call)

- Data link connection identifier (to be used for the call)

- Link layer core parameters (includes outgoing and incoming maximum frame information field sizes, outgoing and incoming CIR, committed burst size, and excess burst sizes)

- Calling party number

- Calling party subaddress

- Called party number

- Called party subaddress

- Transit network selection (identifies a transit network to be used, when such a choice is available)

- Low layer compatibility

- User-user data (content is not interpreted by the network, but is delivered to the remote endpoint device)

A called or calling party number information element includes parameters that indicate whether a call is international, and what type of numbering plan applies. Recall that a called or calling party subaddress can be used to identify a specific device at a destination— for example, by an IP address or MAC address.

SVC Service Features

Vendors and providers still are working out the features that SVC service subscribers will need. Several features that have been identified and implemented are discussed in the sections that follow.

Quality of Service

No industry-wide standard quality of service (QoS) levels have been defined for frame relay at this time. However, it is clear that at least three service levels are needed:

- A service that limits overall delay and delay variation (also called *jitter*), for applications such as voice or video.

- A service that has a low data loss rate, for applications that require high reliability. This is implemented by reserving buffer space in network switches. Data may occasionally need to be held in a buffer briefly until outgoing bandwidth is available.

- A low-cost service that can tolerate moderate data loss and variable delay times.

A customer can request a different QoS for each direction of a call, if this makes sense for the type of data that is carried on the circuit.

The most common situation that leads to different QoS settings in each direction is a one-way circuit. The opposite direction still needs to be configured, but it is given a 0 CIR and a minimal QoS rating.

A more interesting example is a circuit that carries real-time telemetry data in one direction, while the other direction carries configuration commands to the equipment. The telemetry data must be delivered with minimal delay. The commands need to be transmitted as reliably as possible, but are not sensitive to minor delays.

Security and Access Limitations

Few network security administrators would be happy to allow one of their routers to place data calls to anywhere and accept incoming calls from anywhere. Outgoing frame relay calls need to be limited and incoming calls need to be screened.

There are many ways to do this. The simplest method is to configure each SVC access device with the numbers or number prefixes of the devices that may be called, and whose calls will be accepted.

A customer desiring fuller insulation from outside contact can ask its provider to define a *virtual private network (VPN)*. A frame relay VPN is described by listing the X.121 or E.164 numbers of the devices that may communicate with one another. The provider then automatically restricts all of the customer's switched calls to destinations on the list. Outsiders are prevented from reaching these destinations.

If more flexibility is needed, call privileges can be based on *closed user group (CUG) membership*. Members of a CUG are identified by their X.121 or E.164 numbers or number prefixes. After one or more groups have been defined, an organization can configure communication rules for the groups, such as:

- Members of CUG A may only place calls to, and receive calls from, other members of CUG A.

- Members of CUG B can place calls to members of CUG C, but can receive no calls.

- Members of CUG C can accept calls from members of CUG B, but may not place calls.

- Members of CUG D can receive calls from anywhere, but cannot place calls.

Clearly, a wide variety of privileges can be defined using CUGs. Many organizations are familiar with CUGs, since CUGs have been a popular feature of X.25 service for many years.

Opening up a site to switched access can be a security hazard. CUGs provide controls that can plug security gaps. For example, engineers from two companies may need to cooperate in a joint development project for a period of months. A switched frame relay service could give them the temporary low cost, high bandwidth connectivity that they need. CUG restraints could be used to block out unwelcome outsiders.

References

ITU-T Recommendation Q.922, *ISDN Data Link Layer Specification for Frame Mode Bearer Services* (1992), describes the LAPF reliable link procedures.

ITU-T Recommendation Q.933, *Signaling specifications for frame mode switched and permanent virtual connection control and status monitoring* (1995), describes SVC call control messages.

The prevalent standard for telecommunications numbering is ITU-T Recommendation E.164/I.331, *The International Public Telecommunication Numbering Plan* (1997).

ANSI has published its own versions of the standards relating to DSS1:

- ANSI T1.617: *Signaling Specification for Frame Relay Bearer Service for Digital Subscriber Signaling System Number 1 (DSS1)*, (1991).

- ANSI T1.618: *Core Aspects of Frame Protocol for Use with Frame Relay Bearer Service* (1991, revised 1997).

Frame Relay Forum document FRF.4 contains the *Frame Relay UNI SVC Implementation Agreement* (1994).

10

Applications of Frame Relay

After looking at frame relay architecture, technology, and protocols, you'd think you would be all ready to implement a frame relay network. In the real world, however, getting frame relay to work is not as simple as it sounds in a technology discussion.

This chapter presents some of the special problems IP, IBM SNA, and voice traffic pose for frame relay and describes the solutions that have been developed.

Frame Relay and IP

The TCP/IP protocol suite has become a widely accepted standard for network communications. IP, the Internet Protocol, is the component of the TCP/IP suite that is responsible for routing data to its destination. IP operates at layer 3, the network layer. (TCP operates at layer 4.)

IP is a best-effort delivery service that carries layer 3 protocol data units called *IP datagrams* from source systems to destination systems. Frame relay is very well-suited to carrying IP datagram traffic, which typically is bursty in nature. Frame relay and IP are a well-matched team—they work well together to make efficient use of wide area bandwidth.

Figure 10.1 shows the relationship between the IP and frame relay protocols.

The sections that follow present some of the ways that frame relay circuits are used within IP networks and explain *inverse ARP*, which is a shortcut that automates a key step in configuring IP to work with frame relay.

Figure 10.1 IP and frame relay layering.

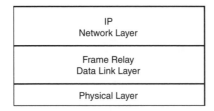

Using Frame Relay in an IP Network

A frame relay circuit can simply be used as a replacement for a point-to-point leased line in an IP network. For example, Site A and Site B in Figure 10.2 are connected by a frame relay circuit instead of a more costly leased line. 199.17.28.200 and 199.17.28.201 are the IP addresses assigned to the router interfaces that connect to the frame relay virtual circuit.

Figure 10.2 Replacing a leased line with a frame relay circuit.

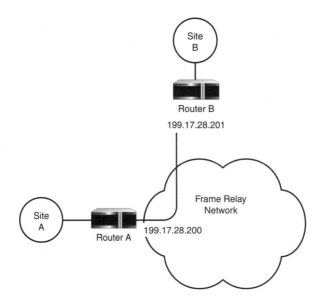

Virtual IP Subnets

Multiple IP routers can be connected into a frame relay configuration that behaves like a virtual LAN—or in IP terminology, a virtual IP *subnet*. An IP subnet is a set of systems (usually located on a LAN) that have some special characteristics:

- Their IP addresses start with the same network and subnet numbers.

- Any system can communicate *directly* with any other system in the subnet. Data will not flow through an intermediate router.

Figure 10.3 shows three routers that are connected by frame relay circuits. This is a *fully meshed* set of connections—that is, each system has direct connections to the other systems and hence can communicate directly with the other systems.

A set of fully meshed systems can be treated as a virtual IP subnet. In Figure 10.3, each interface is given an IP address that starts with the same network and subnet numbers. Note that even though there are two separate frame relay virtual circuits at each interface, each interface has been assigned a single IP address.

Figure 10.3   A virtual IP subnet.

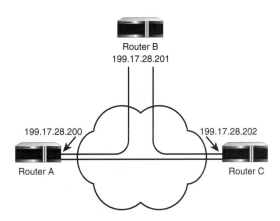

In Figure 10.4, a new circuit has been set up between Router A and Router D. Router D is not fully meshed with the other routers, and the connection between Routers A and D is treated as a separate subnet. New IP addresses are assigned at each endpoint of the connection.

Thus:

- Sometimes, a single IP address can be assigned to an entire frame relay interface.

- In other cases, one or more DLCIs form a subinterface. Each subinterface is assigned an IP address. (It also is possible to leave the endpoint of a point-to-point connection unnumbered. However, this is not relevant to the present discussion.)

Figure 10.4   Adding a new IP subnet.

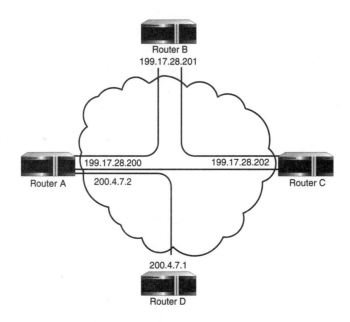

Packaging IP Datagrams

Figure 10.5 shows the simple IETF encapsulation that is used to carry IP datagrams. Recall that ISO has assigned the NLPID value X'CC to IP. The frame relay address field is followed by a 1-byte X'03 control field and the IP NLPID.

Figure 10.5   IETF encapsulation for IP.

Frame Relay Address Field (2 bytes)
Control Field: X'03
NLPID = X'CC
IP PAYLOAD
Frame Check Sequence (2 bytes)

The section in Chapter II-6 titled "Frames with Unique NLPIDs" contains a listing of an encapsulated IP datagram (see Listing 6.1, "Network Layer Protocol ID Value").

Address Resolution Protocol (ARP)

Systems on a LAN transmit data to one another by wrapping the payload in a LAN frame whose header contains the layer 2 Media Access Control (MAC) address of the destination's LAN interface card. A system cannot communicate with a neighbor until it has discovered the neighbor's MAC address. This discovery step is carried out by means of a procedure called the *Address Resolution Protocol (ARP)*.

Figure 10.6 shows how ARP operates for IP systems on an Ethernet LAN. Host A, which has IP address 172.16.1.40, wants to connect to Server B, which has IP address 172.16.1.1. Host A broadcasts an ARP query message asking the system that has IP address 172.16.1.1 to respond. Server B replies, providing its Ethernet MAC address.

| Figure 10.6 | Using ARP to discover a system's MAC address. |

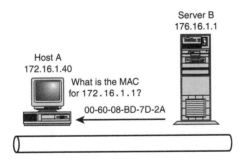

Host A maintains an Ethernet ARP table that records layer 3 IP address to layer 2 MAC address translations. Host A uses the server's response to add a new row to this table:

IP Address	MAC Address
172.16.1.1	00-60-08-BD-7D-2A

Server B also has benefited from the exchange of messages. The ARP request contained Host A's IP address and hardware address, so Server B also can add an entry to its ARP table.

ARP is not confined to IP and Ethernet. It is used to translate many different layer 3 network address types to many different layer 2 interface address types. The fields in an ARP message are shown in Table 10.1. Note that an ARP request has operation code 1 and the response has operation code 2. The desired (target) hardware address is set to X'000000000000 in the outgoing request.

The example shown in Table 10.1 relates to Ethernet and Ethernet hardware addresses. But note how flexible the ARP message format is. It was designed to be used with any type of hardware.

Table 10.1   Fields in an ARP Message

Field	Field Size	Ethernet Example
Type of hardware	2 bytes	Ethernet = 1
Type of layer 3 protocol	2 bytes	IP = X'0800
Length of each hardware address	1 byte	6 for Ethernet
Length of each protocol address	1 byte	4 for IP
Operation code	2 bytes	ARP request = 1; ARP response = 2
Source hardware address	As indicated	006008A124D1
Source protocol address	As indicated	172.16.1.40
Target hardware address	As indicated	In a request, 000000000000
Target protocol address	As indicated	172.16.1.1

Inverse ARP

ARP allows a system to build a table that maps the IP addresses of systems on a LAN to the layer 2 MAC addresses of the systems. *Inverse ARP*, however, makes it even easier to build a table that maps the IP addresses of systems connected by a frame relay virtual LAN to the layer 2 DLCIs of the circuits that connect to the systems.

The routers in Figure 10.7 are interconnected by frame relay circuits and form a virtual LAN.

Router A needs to find out the IP addresses of its neighbors before it can forward traffic to them using the IP protocol. Router A also needs to match each neighbor's IP address to the DLCI that is used to reach the neighbor. That is, Router A needs a table of the form:

IP Address	DLCI Number
199.17.28.201	21
199.17.28.202	22

The left column holds the IP address of a neighbor that Router A wants to reach. The right column identifies the circuit that leads to that neighbor.

Figure 10.7   IP addresses and DLCIs for a virtual subnet.

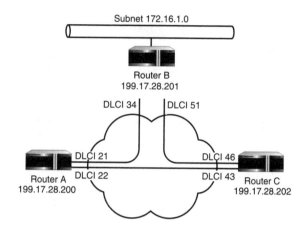

An administrator could configure a table like this into each router manually, but it is a lot easier to let the routers build their tables automatically. The most efficient way to build this table is for each router to follow the procedure:

1.   Send a message across each virtual circuit asking for the value of the IP address at the remote end.

2.   Record the IP address and the corresponding virtual circuit DLCI in the table.

The ARP message format is reused for this purpose along with a modified procedure that is called inverse ARP. New operation codes have been defined to identify the inverse ARP request and response messages:

8	Inverse ARP request message
9	Inverse ARP response

Figure 10.8 illustrates an inverse ARP conversation.

Inverse ARP Encapsulation and Trace

Figure 10.9 shows how an inverse ARP message is encapsulated when it is sent across a frame relay network.

Figure 10.8   Inverse ARP request and response.

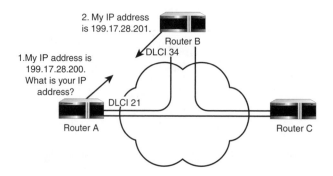

Figure 10.9   Inverse ARP message encapsulation for frame relay.

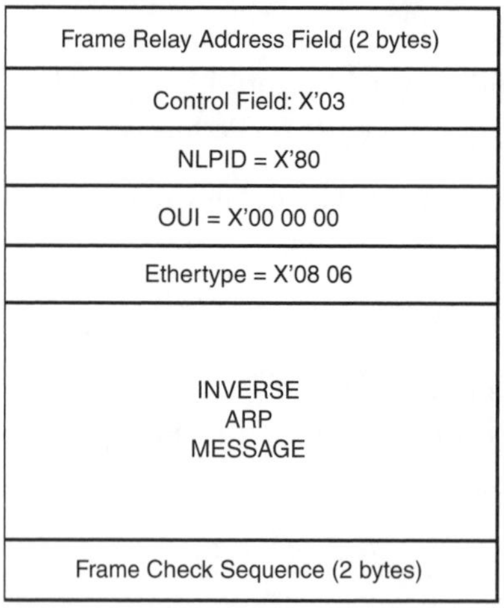

Frame Relay Address Field (2 bytes)
Control Field: X'03
NLPID = X'80
OUI = X'00 00 00
Ethertype = X'08 06
INVERSE ARP MESSAGE
Frame Check Sequence (2 bytes)

Listing 10.1 shows an inverse ARP request message.

Listing 10.   Inverse ARP Request Message

```
Decode from WinPharoah
-------------Frame Relay Q.931 Format (ANSI T1.607)-------------
Direction =  DTE->DCE
Address Field (2 octets) = 0451
DLCI = 21 (Assigned using frame relay connection procedures)
Address Octet 1
    0000 01..              DLCI (High-order)
```

```
    .... ..0.              C/R  - Command/Response indicator
    .... ...0              EA   - Address field extension bit
Address Octet 2
    0101 ....              DLCI - (Low-order)
    .... 0...              FECN - Forward Explicit Congestion Notification
    .... .0..              BECN - Backward Explicit Congestion Notification
    .... ..0.              DE   - Discard Eligibility
    .... ...1              EA   - Address Field Extension
Control field = 03 Unnumbered(UI)
--------------Multiprotocol over Frame Relay---------------
Network Level Protocol ID = 80 (SNAP)
-------------Sub-Network Access Protocol (SNAP)--------------
Organizationally Unique ID = 000000  Ethertype
PID = 0806  ARP
-------------Address Resolution Protocol(ARP)--------------
Hardware type = 15 (Frame Relay)
Protocol = 0800 (Internet IP(IPv4))
Hardware address length = 2 byte(s)
Protocol address length = 4 byte(s)
Operation = 8 (InARP-Request)
Sender hardware address = 0000
Sender protocol address = 199.17.28.200
Target hardware address = 0451
Target protocol address = 0.0.0.0
```

This frame was sent on a virtual circuit with DLCI 21. The frame's header information includes

- The frame relay address field containing DLCI 21

- A control field with value X'03, meaning unnumbered information

- A Network Layer Protocol ID field with value X'80, which indicates that a SNAP subheader follows

- An Organizationally Unique Identifier value of X'00 00 00, which indicates that an Ethertype protocol identifier follows

- And at last, the identifier X'08 06, which indicates that the payload contains an ARP message

The ARP message

- Identifies the "hardware type" as 15, meaning frame relay.

- Indicates that the purpose of the ARP message is to discover the translation between an IP address and a frame relay address. Here, the IP Version 4 protocol is identified by its Ethertype code, which is X'08 00.

- Includes the frame relay "hardware" address: the 2-byte address field (X'04 51) which contains DLCI value 21.

- States that IP addresses are 4 bytes long.

- Carries an operation code of 8, which indicates that this is an inverse ARP request.

- Provides the sender's own IP address, 199.17.28.200.

- Shows a frame address field containing the DLCI at the sender's end of the circuit.

Filling in the target hardware address field does not actually serve a purpose, because the enclosed DLCI is a local value and would be meaningless to the receiver. Neither hardware address field is useful—they could be set to 0 in both requests and responses.

When the target, Router B, receives this message, it takes note of the DLCI value in the incoming frame's address field. The frame relay network has changed this value from 21 to 34. Router B extracts the sender's IP protocol address from the message and can create the table entry:

IP Address	DLCI Number
199.17.28.200	34

Router B sends back an inverse ARP response that contains its own IP address in the source protocol address field and Router A's IP address in the target protocol address field. Here again, the values in the hardware address fields are not relevant. Some implementations will fill them with zeros, while others will fill in frame relay address field values in a manner that looks rather odd. Consider Listing 10.2, for example.

Listing 10.2   An Inverse ARP Response

```
Hardware type = 15 (Frame Relay)
Protocol = 0800 (Internet IP(IPv4))
Hardware address length = 2 byte(s)
Protocol address length = 4 byte(s)
Operation = 9 (InARP-Response)
Sender hardware address = 0451
```

```
Sender protocol address = 199.17.28.201
Target hardware address = 0821
Target protocol address = 199.17.28.200
```

Router A will receive the response from Router B on DLCI 21. Router A can then add an entry to its frame relay ARP table. Router A also can send an inverse ARP request on DLCI 22, and will receive a response from Router C. This enables Router A to create the table entries:

IP Address	DLCI Number
199.17.28.201	21
199.17.28.202	22

There is a price for the convenience of using inverse ARP. A device only can identify that a frame contains an inverse ARP message if IETF encapsulation is used on the circuit.

Inverse ARP and IP Routing

The information that is learned via inverse ARP is very useful to IP routers. An IP router forwards data by looking up the data destination in a routing table. Suppose Router A in Figures 10.7 and 10.8 has a routing table that includes the information of the form

Destination	Forward via Router
172.16.1.0	199.17.28.201

To move an IP datagram toward destination 172.16.1.x, Router A looks in its routing table and discovers that the datagram should be passed to the router with IP address 199.17.28.201. Router A then can check the frame relay inverse ARP table to find the DLCI number (21) of the circuit that leads to the router whose IP address is 199.17.28.201.

Using Inverse ARP with Other Protocols

The preceding sections showed how inverse ARP is used for IP address discovery. However, inverse ARP does just as good a job at discovering the AppleTalk, Banyan VINES, DECnet, Novell IPX, and XNS addresses at the remote end of a frame relay circuit.

This is the benefit of the flexible ARP message format, which enables the sender to identify the protocol of interest and the length of the protocol address.

Frame Relay and SNA

For many years, IBM mainframes ruled the world of computers and IBM's Systems Network Architecture (SNA) ruled the networks. SNA no longer is the dominant architecture that it once was, but still remains very important.

Frame relay is attractive for use in IBM SNA networks because of its favorable pricing and its clean architecture, which replaces a clutter of lines and many separate, slow interface devices with a single wide area high speed interface.

However, some problems arise when SNA traffic is transmitted across frame relay circuits. SNA was engineered to run on top of reliable links and support predictable response time. Some extra effort is needed in order to mate SNA equipment with frame relay service, which tends to have variable, unpredictable response times.

Traditional SNA Network

Figure 10.10 depicts a traditional SNA network.

Figure 10.10   A traditional SNA network.

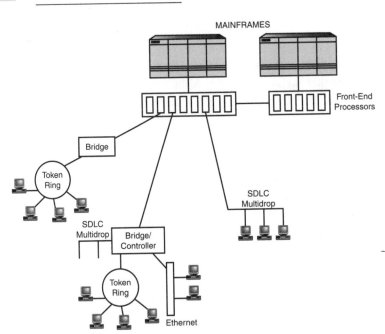

Components of a traditional SNA network include

- **Front-end processors**—Offload the work of coordinating the communications between IBM hosts and thousands of remote devices.

- **Remote controllers**—Located at remote locations, and connect to LANs and low bandwidth leased lines. They concentrate several sources of remote traffic onto one high bandwidth connection to a front-end processor.

Figure 10.10 includes some *multidrop* lines. IBM's multidrop technology makes frugal use of leased lines. Several devices are attached to the same leased line. A front-end processor or remote controller polls devices so they take turns in communicating across the line.

In fact, IBM's entire traditional wide area communications architecture is based on polling. A front-end processor controls when each of its connected remote devices can send and receive data.

When a front-end processor or other communication controller polls, it expects to receive a response within a preconfigured timeout. The timeout threshold usually is fairly low—a few seconds. If the timeout expires, the poll is retransmitted. Frame discards and late frame arrivals can disrupt SNA communications.

SNA Data Link Protocols

A reliable data link protocol is used on the links joining front-end processors to one another or connecting a front-end processor to a device on a multidrop line or on a LAN. Two reliable link protocols are used in an SNA network: *Synchronous Data Link Control (SDLC)* and *Logical Link Control type 2 (LLC2)*.

Modern SNA networks also support end-to-end sessions that are set up using *Advanced Peer-to-Peer Networking (APPN)*. APPN also relies on reliable LLC2 links. Figure 10.11 illustrates a network in which a mainframe, AS/400 hosts, and LAN systems are communicating via APPN.

Finally, IBM offers a *High Performance Routing (HPR) extension* to APPN that optionally can run without LLC2. That is, it can run without an underlying reliable link protocol. Retransmission and flow control are performed end-to-end by a higher layer protocol. HPR traffic that does not run on top of an LLC2 link can be transmitted across frame relay lines without encountering the problems that arise when a reliable link is used.

Figure 10.11   APPN communications.

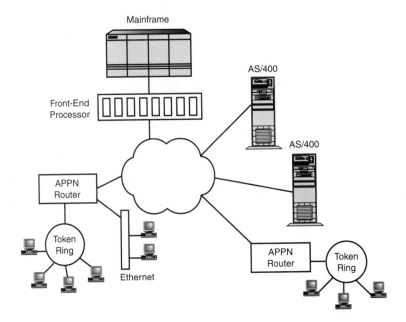

SDLC and LLC2 Features

The IBM SDLC link layer protocol was designed for SNA leased line communications. SDLC has a number of features that cause problems when a leased line is replaced by a frame relay circuit:

- **SDLC is a master/slave polling protocol**—A front-end processor or controller polls devices in turn to find out whether they have data to send and to deliver data to them. Polling traffic is heavy. Poll messages use up valuable bandwidth, and responses must be sent back within a strictly predictable time limit.

- **SDLC makes liberal use of control frames for flow control**—A frame relay circuit that carries raw SDLC traffic will be cluttered with polls and control traffic.

- **Each SDLC information frame is numbered in sequence and contains a number that acknowledges received frames**—After a preset number of frames has been sent, data transmission cannot proceed unless an acknowledgment from the partner is received.

SDLC is not used for peer-to-peer LAN communications. An SNA LAN frame contains an LLC2 header that holds the frame sequence number and the acknowledgment number.

LLC2 does not have SDLC's polling overhead, but still has the overhead associated with reliable, ordered, flow-controlled delivery of data across a link.

Using Frame Relay Circuits in an SNA Network

In Figure 10.12, frame relay virtual circuits have replaced leased line connections.

| Figure 10.12 | Connecting SNA devices using frame relay circuits. |

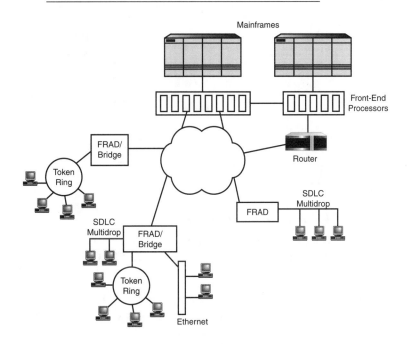

Treatment of SDLC over Frame Relay

Because of the heavy polling data and the problems that can be caused by intermittent delays in the frame relay network, sometimes SDLC does not perform well across a frame relay circuit.

Figure 10.13 shows a popular way to handle this. It requires replacing one link with three consecutive links.

The SDLC multidrop line is terminated at the FRAD, which polls the SDLC devices locally. The devices believe that they are talking to a remote front-end processor.

The data is repackaged using a format (defined in FRF3.1) that wraps LLC2 frames inside frame relay frames. The LLC2 link terminates at a remote router. This LLC2 link is totally under the control of network administrators, and its parameters can be set to match the delay characteristics of the frame relay circuit.

The far-end router can pass data to a front-end processor or host using a fresh LLC2 link.

Figure 10.13   Replacing one link with three more efficient ones.

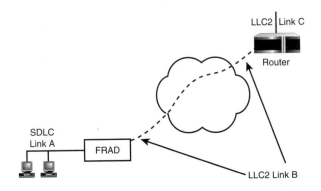

Treatment of LLC2 over Frame Relay

IBM has defined a format for encapsulating LAN MAC frames that contain LLC2 headers within frame relay frames. This enables a single end-to-end LLC2 link to connect two computers that communicate across a frame relay network, as shown in Figure 10.14.

But, even though LLC2 is not as demanding a protocol as SDLC, frame relay delays still could cause trouble. Breaking one LLC2 link into three links, as shown in Figure 10.15, helps. Once again, this gives network managers the opportunity to customize the middle link to take wide area communication delays into account.

Figure 10.14   Encapsulating LLC2 frames.

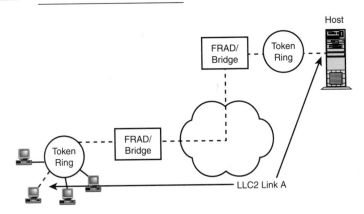

Figure 10.15 Segmenting an LLC2 link.

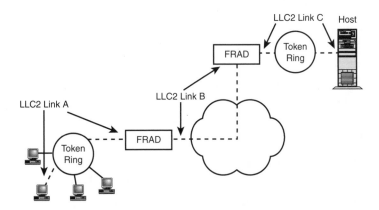

Data Link Switching

When a frame relay circuit carries reliable link traffic, there is a substantial amount of extra overhead. One circuit may carry dozens of separate reliable links. Each is burdened with acknowledgment and flow control messages.

Figure 10.16 illustrates *Data Link Switching (DLSw)*, which is one way to avoid carrying LLC2 links across a frame relay circuit. The LLC2 links are terminated at each router. Incoming data is sent across the wide area frame relay network via a TCP session. It then is forwarded across a fresh LLC2 link. DLSw actually works for any type of wide area connection. Its use is not restricted to frame relay.

TCP sessions support reliable data transfer, so the SNA traffic will not be lost. TCP adjusts well to sporadic delays, manages acknowledgments efficiently, and carries out flow control without using extra messages.

The disadvantage is the extra overhead caused by adding TCP/IP headers to the data.

Figure 10.16 Data link switching.

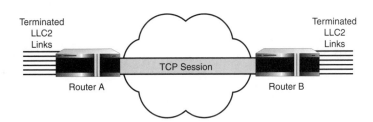

SNA, Frame Relay, and Standards

The only aspect of SNA transmission that has been standardized is the packaging of SNA data. The header formats that are used are described in the Frame Relay Forum document FRF.3.

The mechanisms used to manage delay, cut down on overhead traffic, and improve efficiency are left to vendor ingenuity. As a result, implementations differ greatly, and you usually need to have the same vendor's equipment at both ends of an SNA circuit.

Types of SNA Traffic

IBM's SNA protocol family is large and complex, and there are several different types of SNA traffic. We will start by examining some sample configurations.

Figure 10.10 displayed a traditional hierarchical SNA network with two mainframe hosts. The hosts are connected to IBM front-end processors that handle all of the communications with remote dependent devices (such as workstations and printers). Some of the remote devices are attached to a Token-Ring or Ethernet. Others are multi-dropped off a serial line.

Two different SNA protocol formats are used in hierarchical SNA. Mainframe data is sent between front-end processors using *subarea Format Identification 4 (FID4) messages*. Front-end processors exchange data with dependent devices using *peripheral Format Identification 2 (FID2) messages*.

IBM's APPN provides an alternative to the old hierarchical topology. APPN supports direct host-to-host communication. There are three types of SNA APPN messages. The original APPN used APPN FID2 messages across reliable links. A newer version of APPN supports IBM's High Performance Routing (HPR) protocol, which can run on top of an LLC2 link or without an underlying reliable link protocol.

Encapsulating SNA Traffic

Two different methods are used to encapsulate SNA data sent across a frame relay circuit. IBM has called these methods *Boundary Network Node (BNN)* and *Boundary Access Node (BAN)*.

• The BNN method uses SNA formats that are defined in Frame Relay Forum document FRF.3.1.

• The BAN method encloses bridged LAN frames inside frame relay frames.

There is nothing new about the BAN encapsulation format. It simply is the SNAP format used to bridge frames that was described in Chapter II-6.

Boundary Network Node Formats

The general format for the extra header information added to a BNN frame that carries SNA data across a frame relay circuit was described in Chapter II-6. The encapsulation follows the pattern shown in Figure 2.4 of Chapter II-6, which describes the format when there is no assigned NLPID or SNAP. It consists of

X'03 + X'08 NLPID + layer 2 and 3 header types + protocol-specific data

The exact encapsulation format depends on the type of SNA message that is enclosed.

Figure 10.17 displays the BNN format that is used for SNA Subarea FID4, peripheral FID2, APPN FID2 traffic, and APPN HPR frames that include an LLC2 header.

Figure 10.17 SNA formats for BNN.

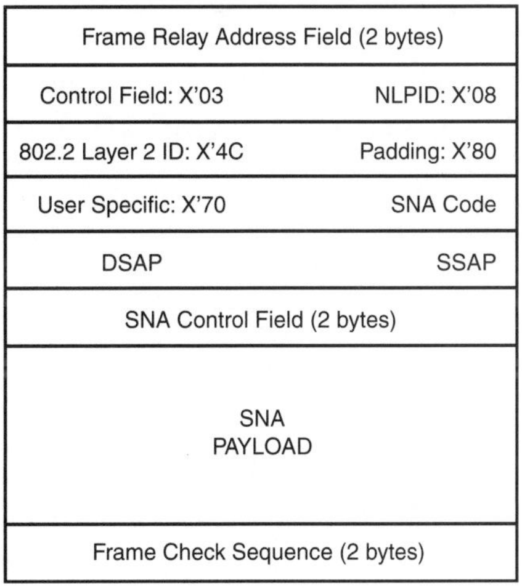

Frame Relay Address Field (2 bytes)	
Control Field: X'03	NLPID: X'08
802.2 Layer 2 ID: X'4C	Padding: X'80
User Specific: X'70	SNA Code
DSAP	SSAP
SNA Control Field (2 bytes)	
SNA PAYLOAD	
Frame Check Sequence (2 bytes)	

The fields include

- A control field value of X'03

- An NLPID value of X'08, which means that this protocol (SNA) does not have an official NLPID or SNAP value assigned to it

- A layer 2 protocol identifier of X'4C, which means that an IEEE 802.2 LLC2 header will appear after the SNA code

- A pad field with value X'80

- A layer 3 protocol identifier of X'70, which means *user specified* (proprietary)

- An SNA code that identifies the type of SNA data enclosed

- The LLC2 header, which consists of a Destination Service Access Point (DSAP), Source Service Access Point (SSAP), and a 2-byte control field

Table 10.2 contains the list of the SNA codes that identify the various types of traffic.

Table 10.2   Codes Used with SNA Encapsulations

Code Point	SNA Usage
X'81	Subarea (FID4 SNA Headers)
X'82	Peripheral (FID2 SNA Headers)
X'83	APPN (FID2 SNA Headers)
X'84	Network Basic Input Output System (NetBIOS)
X'85	APPN with High Performance Routing (HPR)

The format in Figure 10.18 is used when HPR does not run over LLC2. Note that a user specific layer 2 ID of X'50 replaces the 802.2 layer 2 ID, X'4C, and there are no DSAP and SSAP fields.

Figure 10.18   Format for HPR without LLC2.

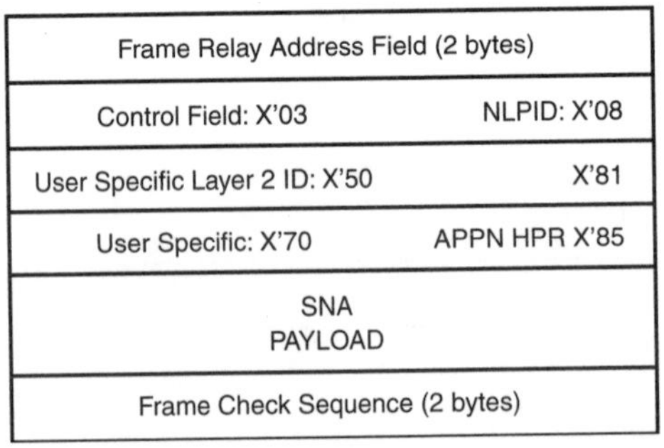

Frame Relay Address Field (2 bytes)	
Control Field: X'03	NLPID: X'08
User Specific Layer 2 ID: X'50	X'81
User Specific: X'70	APPN HPR X'85
SNA PAYLOAD	
Frame Check Sequence (2 bytes)	

Note

Because much of today's NetBIOS traffic runs over TCP/IP, the NetBIOS encapsulation format has been omitted.

An encapsulated SNA FID2 protocol data unit is displayed in Listing 10.3. The frame was transmitted on DLCI 19. The NLPID value, X'08, announces that this is a frame for which there is no assigned NLPID or SNAP. The layer 2 ID, X'4C, indicates that an LLC2 header is enclosed, and the user (IBM) specified code X'83 indicates that the payload carries an SNA FID2 message.

Listing 10.3   Encapsulated SNA FID2 Protocol Data Unit

```
Decode from WinPharoah
-------Frame Relay Q.931 Format (ANSI T1.607)-------
Direction =  DCE->DTE
Address Field (2 octets) = 0431
DLCI = 19 (Assigned using frame relay connection procedures)
Address Octet 1
    0000 01..           DLCI (High-order)
    .... ..0.           C/R  - Command/Response indicator
    .... ...0           EA   - Address field extension bit
Address Octet 2
    0011 ....           DLCI - (Low-order)
    .... 0...           FECN - Forward Explicit Congestion Notification
    .... .0..           BECN - Backward Explicit Congestion Notification
    .... ..0.           DE   - Discard Eligibility
    .... ...1           EA   - Address Field Extension
Control field = 03 Unnumbered(UI)
    .... 0... - Poll/Final
--------Multiprotocol over Frame Relay---------
Network Level Protocol ID = 08 (Q.933)
Layer 2 ID = 4C (802.2)
Padding byte = 80
Layer 3 ID = 70  User specified layer 3 protocol
User specified layer 3 protocol information = 83
-------Logical Link Control Protocol 802.2 (LLC)------
DSAP = 12 Individual,
SSAP = 4 SNA
Control = 0A Information N(S)=5, N(R)=5, P/F=0
    0000 101. - N(S)
    0000 101. - N(R)
    .... ...0 - Poll/Final
---------SNA Transmission Header (TH)---------
Byte   Bit   Content
  0    0-3   Format ID                 = 0010   FID2
  0    4-5   Mapping field             = 10     First segment
  0    7     Expedited flow indicator  = 0      Normal
  1          Reserved                  = x'00'
  2          Destination address field = x'02'
  3          Origin address field      = x'00'
  4-5        Sequence number field     = 2
--------SNA Request/Response Header (RH)---------
(Remainder of SNA message)
```

BNN SAP Multiplexing

When a host needs to communicate across a frame relay network with systems attached to a remote LAN, the BNN header lacks an important piece of information. When the access device that connects the LAN to the frame relay network receives an incoming BNN LAN, there is no field in the header that identifies which LAN device is the frame's destination.

The SAP fields in the LLC2 part of the header usually contain fixed dummy values. Since they normally perform no useful function for data frames, these fields can be used to identify source and destination devices. This use of the SSAP and DSAP fields is called *SAP multiplexing.*

A SAP field is 1 byte long. However, some SAP values are reserved and there are only 127 numbers that can be used to distinguish sources and destinations within one virtual circuit. This means that many separate virtual circuits might have to be set up in order to reach systems on a large LAN.

Furthermore, the SAP numbers need to be configured manually, and this can turn into a big job. The BAN format discussed in the next section is a lot easier to work with.

Boundary Access Node Format

Recall that the BAN format is simply the SNAP bridged format shown in Figure 4 of Chapter II-6. BAN solves the problem of identifying LAN systems because the system's LAN MAC address is in the encapsulated LAN frame.

This solution is straightforward, but adds more overhead bytes to each frame than BNN does.

Vendor Contributions

Although frame relay and SNA are far from a perfect blend, vendors have implemented innovative solutions that prioritize SNA traffic and smooth over delay problems. The use of frame relay for wide area SNA connectivity is growing steadily.

Voice Over Frame Relay (VoFR)

Like other applications of frame relay, adoption of *voice over frame relay (VoFR)* has been driven by efficiencies that lead to cost reductions.

In the classic telephone network, a conventional digital voice call is encoded according to the ITU Pulse Code Modulation (PCM) standard and occupies a 64Kbps channel. A very simple alternative, *Adaptive Delta Pulse Code Modulation (ADPCM)*, reduces the required bandwidth to 32Kbps. However, a variety of recently developed compression methods can drastically reduce the bandwidth required for a voice call to 16, 8, or 4Kbps—or even less.

It is highly efficient to send compressed voice over data circuits, and very natural to try to add voice to the frame relay service offering.

VFRADs

Adding voice to the mix of frame relay traffic has resulted in a new type of device—the *voice frame relay access device* or *VFRAD*. The name suggests that the device is devoted exclusively to voice traffic, but this is misleading. VFRADs can multiplex voice, fax, voice-band modem data, and ordinary data across frame relay circuits.

Figure 10.19 shows a very simple application of VoFR. An organization that has built a private leased line network between three sites to carry its telephone traffic (using multiple conventional T1 lines) can replace the leased lines with connections to a frame relay network. Using compression, the same number of calls can be transmitted with much less bandwidth.

Figure 10.19   Voice and fax over a frame relay network.

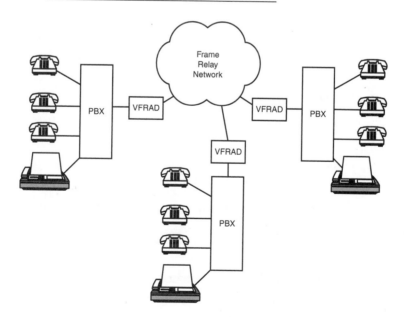

Alternatively, the organization can maintain the same bandwidth level that it originally had while increasing the number of calls that can be carried between the sites (via compression) or adding data traffic. In Figure 10.20, the sites are exchanging a mix of voice, fax, and data traffic.

Figure 10.20   Voice, fax, and data traffic across a frame relay network.

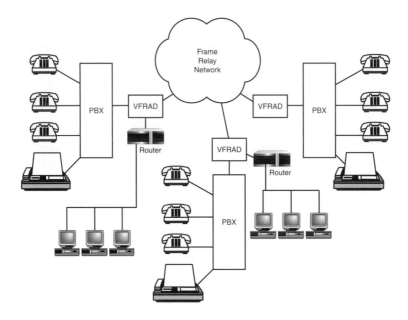

VoFR Relay Quality Issues

Time is a very important factor in delivering voice. Very long delays are intolerable, and variations in delivery time (*jitter*) cause distortions in the voice signal.

Unfortunately, occasional long delays and variability in delivery time are common characteristics of frame relay. Vendors overcome these problems using several mechanisms:

- Voice traffic is placed in a high-priority transmission queue at the sending VFRAD.

- The VFRAD fragments long data frames so voice traffic can be interleaved between chunks of data.

- The receiving VFRAD stores incoming voice traffic in a buffer briefly and allows a few payloads to accumulate. This enables the VFRAD to deliver the voice in a smooth, undistorted stream.

These mechanisms are illustrated in Figure 10.21.

Figure 10.21 Controlling voice delivery delays and smoothing voice delivery time.

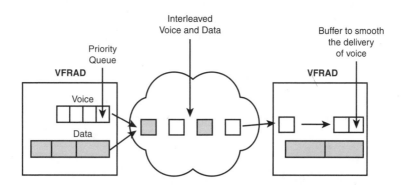

Frame Relay networks deliver the frames on a virtual circuit in the same order in which they are submitted to the network. A service provider cannot give special priority to voice frames that share a virtual circuit with data frames once the frames have entered the network. However, the provider may be able to offer a superior class of service to a selected virtual circuit. In this case, it makes sense to isolate the voice traffic onto a separate, high-priority circuit.

These mechanisms are very helpful. However, there is no guarantee that a customer will be satisfied with the quality of the voice traffic. The only way to find out is to thoroughly test a product across the frame relay network that will be used to carry voice calls.

VoFR Administrative and Maintenance Issues

Call quality is not the only issue to be considered when switching to VoFR. The effect of the change on current billing and accounting procedures needs to be considered.

The format of billing data may be very different, and current software used for accounting and charge-back might have to be replaced. The VFRAD product that is used needs to be chosen carefully, to make sure that it will be possible to gather the detailed information that an organization needs for charge-back.

A hidden cost of the switchover is that maintenance and troubleshooting will require an entirely new set of skills and equipment.

VoFR Technology and Protocols

The Frame Relay Forum deals with VoFR technology issues in implementation agreement FRF.11. A related implementation agreement, FRF.12, enables a sender to fragment big data frames into pieces that are reassembled by the receiver. Fragmenting big data frames allows voice and data traffic to be interleaved and avoids big delays in voice delivery. Currently, the agreements apply only to implementations on permanent virtual circuits (PVCs).

The sections that follow present an overview of VoFR technology, and describe the mechanisms introduced in FRF.11.

Subframes

Voice traffic normally is compressed into small chunks. These chunks need to be sent out promptly. However, the overhead involved in switching a huge number of tiny frames between locations would cut down on throughput. Since there may be many concurrent voice calls between a pair of sites, it makes sense to bundle payloads from several different voice calls into one frame. Each payload is packaged in a *subframe*.

Voice and data traffic can be carried between sites on separate virtual circuits, or multiplexed onto a single circuit. Although it may be easier to prioritize and control voice when it is isolated onto its own circuit, if data traffic peaks at a different time of day than voice traffic, a shared circuit may be very efficient. Furthermore, a single circuit with a merged CIR costs less than separate circuits.

If data and voice are sent on a single circuit, fragments of data can be packaged into subframes, too. Figure 10.22 displays several subframes that have been packed into a single frame.

Figure 10.22   Packing subframes into a frame.

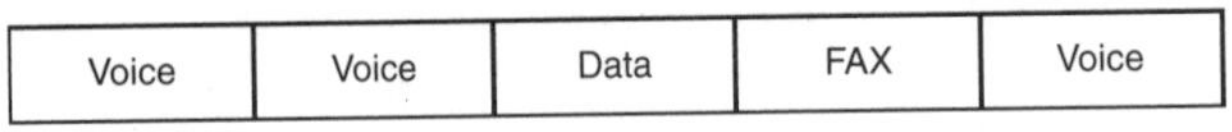

Voice	Voice	Data	FAX	Voice

Subchannels

Each voice or fax subframe in Figure 10.22 needs to be associated with a specific call. The receiving endpoint also needs to know where one subframe ends and the next begins.

The solution is simple. In order to make sense of the various streams of data that share a virtual circuit, the streams are organized into numbered *subchannels*. Up to 255 subchannels can be multiplexed onto a single frame relay circuit. Each subframe has a short header that identifies its subchannel. If a frame contains multiple subframes, then the headers of all but the last subframe also will contain a payload length field.

Subchannel Payload Types

Each subchannel carries a *primary payload* that is one of the following:

- Encoded voice for a call

- Encoded fax for a fax transmission

- Ordinary data

In addition to its primary payload, a subchannel can carry auxiliary *signaled payload* information needed to support the subchannel. There are several types of signaled payload information, and each has been assigned a *payload type number*. Payload types and type numbers are listed in Table 10.3.

Table 10.3   Payload Types and Payload Type Numbers

Type Numbers	Payload Types
0	The primary payload for the subchannel. (Encoded voice, encoded fax, or data.)
1	Dialed digits.
2	Signaling information.
3	Fax data, when the primary payload already is being used for encoded voice.
4	A Silence Information Descriptor, which indicates the end of a talk spurt.

The numbers to the left are the *payload type numbers*. Note that a primary payload always has type number 0. This is the default payload type.

Subframe Format

The header of a subframe that contains a non-primary (and therefore non-default) type must include an extra field that indicates the type number. Figure 10.23 shows voice and dialed digits subframes within a frame, and indicates the fields that are included in each subframe header.

Figure 10.23 Subframes with headers.

Subchannel number	Length	Voice Payload	Subchannel number	Length	Type	Dial Digits	Subchannel number	Voice Payload

The detailed subframe format is shown in Figure 10.24. Subchannel headers add extra overhead to every frame. Furthermore, every byte counts when sending real-time voice. The second or third byte is omitted when it is not absolutely needed:

- If a subframe is the last (or only) subframe within a frame, then the length indication (LI) flag is set to 0, and the payload length byte (the third byte) is omitted.

- The second byte in Figure 10.24 is needed only if the subchannel identification number is bigger than 64, or if the subframe does not contain a primary payload. If the subchannel identification (CID) number is less than 64 and the subframe contains a primary payload (which is the default type), then the extension indication (EI) flag is set to 0 and the second byte in Figure 10.24 is omitted.

Figure 10.24 VoFR subframe format.

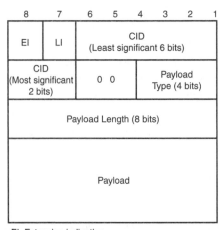

EI=Extension indication
LI=Length indication
CID=Subchannel identification

Transfer Syntax

There are several commonly used voice compression methods, and each works differently. It is impossible to package all of them in the same way. This has been solved by defining a different packaging—called a *transfer syntax*—for each. Appendixes to FRF.11 contain transfer syntax definitions for voice encoding methods, including

- Pulse Code Modulation (PCM) and Adaptive PCM

- Conjugate Structure—Algebraic Code Excited Linear Predictive (CS-ACELP)

- G.727 Discard-Eligible Embedded Adaptive Differential Pulse Code Modulation (E-ADPCM)

- G.728 Low Delay—Code Excited Linear Prediction (LD-CELP Transfer Syntax)

- G.723.1 Multi Pulse Maximum Likelihood Quantizer (MP-MLQ) Dual Rate Speech Coder

Note

The G.xxx identifiers are ITU standards numbers.

Formats for carrying dialed digits, alarm indications and channel-associated signaling bits (such as ringing or release of a circuit), fax, and fragments of ordinary data frames also are defined in Annex sections of FRF.11.

References

For more information about TCP/IP, see my earlier book, *TCP/IP: Architecture, Protocols, and Implementation with IPv6 and IP Security*, Signature Edition (McGraw-Hill, 1998).

Inverse ARP is described in IETF Request for Comments document 2390 (RFC 2930), *Inverse Address Resolution Protocol.*

IBM BNN encapsulations are described in the Frame Relay Forum document, *Multiprotocol Encapsulation Implementation Agreement*, 1995 (FRF.3.1).

An expository document titled *SNA over Frame Relay* was published by the APPN Implementers Workshop and is available at the Frame Relay Forum Web site.

Voice implementation issues are dealt with in the *Voice over Frame Relay Implementation Agreement*, 1997 (FRF.11) and in annexes to that agreement.

PART III

ATM

The Converged Voice/Data Network

The pattern for the digital telephone network was set in the 1960s. The telephone network backbone was built out of T1 and T3 lines and was based on *time division multiplexing (TDM)*.

The 64Kbps channel was the basic building block of the system. However, during transmission, bits in a channel were interleaved with bits from many other channels. Each bit was carried in a reserved time slot.

Transmission technologies have advanced by great leaps in recent years. Fiber optic lines provide transmission rates that are orders of magnitude greater than the old T3 rate. Even copper transmission rates have hit levels that no one thought were possible a few years ago.

But it is not just the capacity of telecommunications networks that has changed; the nature of the traffic these networks carry also has changed significantly. A few years ago, data accounted for a small fraction of the traffic transmitted across the telecommunications infrastructure. Today, that trickle of data traffic has grown to a flood.

Not only is data now overtaking voice, but voice—and video—are being viewed as specific types of data to be carried across a converged, multi-application network. Voice and video compression methods have become very sophisticated, and faster, cheaper *digital signal processors (DSPs)* make real-time compression feasible. Therefore, voice and video services that formerly required large, fixed amounts of bandwidth now can be sent in compressed form as variable-bandwidth data.

Near the end of the 1980s, anticipating a new, converged, bandwidth-rich environment, standards bodies started to search for an entirely fresh approach to building the global transmission network.

Broadband ISDN

Broadband ISDN (B-ISDN) was the name given to the new framework the standards bodies agreed on, and *asynchronous transfer mode (ATM)* was the technology chosen to implement B-ISDN.

The title is somewhat misleading because B-ISDN is not merely an extension of the old standard. ISDN (now called *narrowband ISDN* or *N-ISDN*) replaced the analog telephone local loop with a digital service. N-ISDN did not change the old time division telecommunications architecture. In contrast, B-ISDN is the blueprint for a completely new telecommunications infrastructure.

B-ISDN Services

The designers of B-ISDN wanted to build networks that would meet customer needs for many years into the future. They compiled a wish list of capabilities. The new networks should

- Be capable of operating across a broad range of media and bandwidths
- Be scalable so they can support higher bandwidths as they are made available by improvements in fiber optic technology
- Support permanent and switched virtual circuit services
- Provide efficient and cost-effective voice, video, and data circuits
- Make it possible to offer special services, such as multicasting, virtual private networks, and virtual LANs
- Interwork with existing voice and data networks
- Enable traffic to share transmission lines efficiently
- Be capable of delivering the quality of service associated with traditional time division multiplexing telecommunications networks

B-ISDN Requirements

The old time division architecture that was the basis of the traditional, plesiosynchronous telephone network could not be adapted to the broadband ISDN requirements.

A new architecture that could be implemented in fast, scalable switches was needed; otherwise, it would not be possible to construct networks that actually could take advantage of new, high-speed fiber optic transmission techniques.

An additional, highly demanding requirement was set for B-ISDN. The potential for a massive transmission capability was mated with a desire for total flexibility. In other words, a user placing a call should be able to obtain the bandwidth and quality of service that meets the specific needs of that call. For example, by choosing different parameters, a B-ISDN call should efficiently support

- Time-sensitive real-time voice and video

- Time-sensitive but bursty compressed voice and video

- Interactive computer sessions

- Bulk data transfer

Furthermore, a user should be able to select different service levels in each direction on a circuit. For example, an application such as bulk data transfer from Computer A to Computer B requires a lot of bandwidth in one direction and very little in the opposite direction. The user must be able to request—and pay for—precisely the service that is needed.

B-ISDN Technology: Asynchronous Transfer Mode

Asynchronous transfer mode (ATM), the technology chosen to implement B-ISDN, is a great departure from the classic, tightly structured, time division, multiplexed telecommunications network. In a time division multiplexed system, data must be sent in a reserved time slot. This means that, whether you are making a telephone call at 64Kbps or leasing a data line at 1.544Mbps, your bandwidth is locked in place for the duration of your call or lease. Resources you do not use because of silence during a call or a lack of data to send are not available to anyone else.

In contrast, ATM users send and receive data using *statistical multiplexing*, rather than time division multiplexing. However, ATM multiplexing differs from traditional multiplexing. In traditional statistical multiplexing

- Several data streams (circuits) share one physical link.

- No time slots are reserved, but the multiplexer makes sure that each circuit gets roughly its preconfigured share of the bandwidth.

- Each chunk of data needs to be tagged with a header so the receiving multiplexer (MUX) can sort out the data streams.

This behavior is illustrated in Figure 1.1. If the MUX in the figure has started to send a big chunk of data (such as a 4K Token Ring frame) for data stream b, data for the other streams is held up until the entire chunk has been transmitted. If the data for stream a is especially time-sensitive, nothing can be done about it; it simply is delayed.

ATM avoids this problem by breaking data frames into small pieces.

Figure 1.1   A conventional (non-ATM) statistical multiplexer.

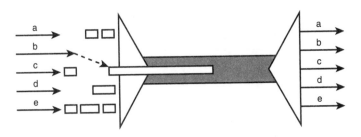

Use of Cells

Like a frame relay subscriber, an ATM subscriber connects a device to an ATM network via an access line. The device communicates with remote sites via virtual circuits. However, for an ATM network, data is segmented into small, fixed-size cells before it is transmitted.

Cells for the various virtual circuits are multiplexed onto the access line. Each cell has a header that identifies the circuit to which it belongs.

Figure 1.2 illustrates the use of cells to transmit data for virtual circuits labeled a–e. Each cell carries data for one of the circuits, and the cells for the various circuits are interleaved on the access line. (This process often is called *cell relay*.)

If (as was the case for Figure 1.1) a big 4 K Token Ring frame had to be transmitted for virtual circuit b, the frame would be broken into cell payloads, and these payloads would be interleaved with data for the other virtual circuits. If the data for virtual circuit a is time-sensitive, it can be packaged in cells and transmitted promptly.

Note that the outgoing bandwidth on the access line shown in Figure 1.2 is viewed as a steady stream of cells. One of the cells is "empty" because no outgoing data was available when it was time to fill the cell and send it. (The header of an empty cell indicates that it is unused, and its payload is filled with a dummy bit pattern.)

Incoming data is delivered via a similar stream of incoming cells.

Figure 1.2	Sending data in cells.

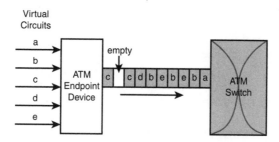

Asynchronous Service

The service is called *asynchronous* because a flexible cell mechanism is used instead of a strict, synchronous time slot. Data is placed into cells and is transmitted at a rate that, *on average*, matches a specified bandwidth. Because most information transfer (including compressed voice and compressed video) is bursty rather than steady, the ability to send at a variable rate rather than a steady rate is an advantage.

The underlying ATM cell technology can be adapted to many different services. For example, digitized voice transmission is time-sensitive. When a voice connection is requested, the network makes sure that an adequate number of cell slots is made available to carry the voice traffic across the network in a timely manner. At the other extreme, an organization might be happy to transmit bursts of data when bandwidth is available and accept fairly large variations in delay time, as long as the price is low.

ATM Universality

So far, we have discussed ATM in the context of public telecommunications networks. But ATM switches can be used to build private wide area networks—and private local area networks as well.

Frame relay is a wide area technology used to connect distant sites. Often a single access device at a site interfaces to a frame relay network.

In contrast, ATM interface cards are available for PCs and hosts, as well as for bridges, routers, LAN switches, and other networking devices. Some day, there might be ATM interface chips in PBX switches, telephones, and television sets. Any of these systems can act as an *ATM endpoint device.*

In the world of telephony, telephone switches in public networks provide wide area connectivity, while PBX switches within a premise offer local connectivity. Local and wide area telephony communications share a common architecture. Some proponents of ATM technology have an ambitious vision, which is nothing less than a world of voice, video, and data communications that has been converted to one universal technology: ATM.

ATM has gained rapid acceptance as a wide area technology. Its role in local networking will be determined by the usual criteria applied by network planners: price, performance, ease of use, reliability, availability, and ease of servicing.

ATM Network Architecture

ATM combines features of voice networking with data networking. A public or private ATM network is made up of a set of ATM switches controlled by the same administration. Devices connected to ATM network switches can communicate with one another across the network.

The devices connected to the frame relay networks studied earlier normally were routers, bridges, IBM front end processors, or IBM SNA FRADs. These devices also can connect to an ATM network, but so can computers and workstations. For this reason, the term *user device* or *endpoint device* commonly is used when discussing ATM networks, instead of the term *access device*. ATM networks can be interconnected to expand the range of endpoints that can communicate with one another.

Figure 1.3 shows routers, server hosts, and PBX switches connected to an ATM network.

Figure 1.3   Devices connected to an ATM network.

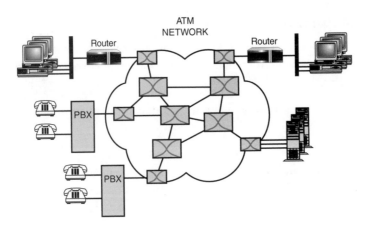

ATM Connections

ATM is connection-oriented, which means that a communications pipeline must be set up between endpoints before they can start to exchange information. In this respect, ATM is similar to the conventional telephone network and to the X.25 and frame relay networks discussed earlier.

Emulating Connectionless Service

ATM documents sometimes refer to the provision of connectionless services on top of ATM. A *connectionless service* delivers data to an endpoint without setting up a prior communications pipeline.

ATM always requires that a prior connection be set up before two systems can communicate. However, it is possible to *emulate* connectionless data delivery over ATM. But special servers and extra, hidden connections always are used to implement the emulation.

For example, a provider could set up a virtual IP subnet using the simple method shown in Figure 1.4. As shown in the figure, the customer has several sites it wants to connect via IP routers, and the customer wants those routers to behave as if they belong to an ordinary LAN.

Figure 1.4 also shows that the provider implements the virtual LAN by setting up a special VLAN switch within the network and by creating permanent virtual circuits between each site and the VLAN switch. The VLAN switch assembles incoming cell payloads into LAN frames. It examines the MAC address in each LAN frame to determine its destination. Then it resegments the frame into cells and forwards it to its destination across the appropriate ATM virtual circuit.

Figure 1.4   Supporting a virtual LAN service for an ATM customer.

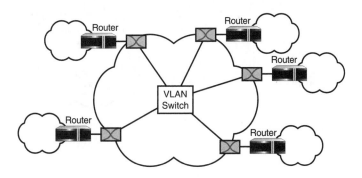

The *LAN Emulation (LANE)* standard discussed in Chapter III-10 describes a far more complex—but also more efficient—method of emulating a LAN at the layer 2 (MAC) level. Three special servers are required to support LANE.

ATM Interfaces

If you want to plug devices and switches together and create a real, multivendor network, you need standard, well-defined interfaces. Figure 1.5 illustrates the ATM user-network and network-to-network interfaces, which include

- Public and private user-network interfaces (UNIs)

- A simple Data eXchange Interface (DXI) user-network interface that enables an endpoint device to communicate with an ATM network via a simple serial interface

- A private network-to-network (switch-to-switch) interface (PNNI)

- A public network-to-network broadband intercarrier interface designed to connect B-ISDN carriers (B-ICI)

Figure 1.5   ATM interfaces.

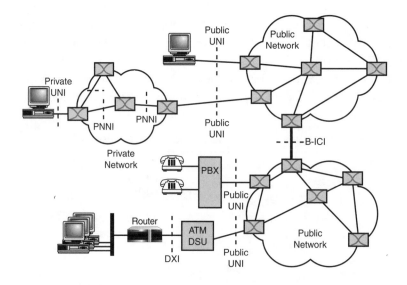

ATM UNI

In an ATM network, a standard *user-network interface* defines the interactions between

- An endpoint device and a private network switch
- An endpoint device and a public network switch
- A private network switch and a public network switch

Fortunately, the main difference between these three UNIs is in the type of physical connection used across the interface.

ATM DXI

The *Data eXchange Interface (DXI)* enables a router that has DXI software to communicate with an ATM network via an ordinary serial interface.

A special smart ATM DSU is required to do this. The router connects to the DSU across a serial line using a simple layer 2 frame-based link protocol. The smart DSU segments the frames into cells and connects to an ATM switch via a conventional ATM user-network interface.

ATM PNNI

Communication between internal switches was not standardized for X.25 and frame relay networks. Proprietary methods of communication could be used. On the other hand, there are strict national and international standards that enable telephone switches to cooperate with one another.

The ATM Forum is evolving a standard ATM private switch-to-switch interface. The same interface can be used to connect two private networks. This interface is called *PNNI*, which stands for both *private network node interface* and *private network-to-network interface*. PNNI enables switches built by different vendors to cooperate. Of course, vendors also can choose to build proprietary interfaces for use between their own switches.

PNNI is receiving good initial support from the vendor community. Some public carriers are considering using PNNI inside their networks.

ATM B-ICI

Public ATM networks must be interconnected to create a global telecommunications network. The *B-ISDN intercarrier interface (B-ICI)* describes public network-to-network interface points.

ATM Interface Functions

Standards for each type of interface describe

- Acceptable types of physical connections

- Data transfer mechanisms

- Methods of managing traffic flow

- Signaling messages used to set up switched calls

- The exchange of operations, administration, and maintenance information

- The exchange of network management information

The PNNI specification also deals with the routing of circuit paths, while the B-ICI specs include usage measurement functions that provide input to accounting and billing functions.

Interworking with Other Services

You will not wake up one morning next week and discover that the conventional telephone network, the existing frame relay data networks, or even the X.25 data networks are gone, magically replaced overnight by ATM networks. These networks will live far into the future. Change will be evolutionary, which means that legacy networks and ATM networks need to be interconnected and cooperate to provide services to users.

There are several interworking standards that describe the interfaces between an ATM network and legacy voice and data networks.

ATM Standards Groups

Several standards bodies have contributed to the B-ISDN and ATM efforts. The Telecommunication Standardization Sector of the International Telecommunications Union (ITU-T) is the preeminent standards body for B-ISDN and has published dozens of documents on the many facets of B-ISDN. The first set of documents was published in 1988. Working groups under the American National Standards Institute (ANSI) and the European Telecommunications Standards Institute (ETSI) have made important contributions to the ITU-T effort as well.

The ATM Forum, which was established in 1991, enables equipment vendors and service providers to cooperate in developing interworking ATM products and services. The goal of the ATM Forum is to promote the use of ATM. In addition to creating interoperability specifications, the ATM Forum has made substantial contributions to ATM technology. In

1993, a User Committee made up of end-user organizations was formed. This committee provides input on real end-user needs.

In the early days of ATM, the technology evolved quickly, and new versions of standards were not compatible with old versions. In 1996, the ATM Forum Technical Committee published an agreement called the *Anchorage Accord* that identified 60 foundation ATM specifications and pledged that future standards upgrades would be backward-compatible with these specifications.

As was the case for frame relay, the Internet Engineering Task Force (IETF) has defined encapsulations for multi-protocol traffic and standards for network management. The IETF also contributes detailed specifications that describe how IP operates in an ATM environment.

Outline of Part III

In Part III, you'll find out about the broad range of services that are delivered by an ATM network. Chapter III-2 introduces basic ATM concepts and describes ATM protocol sublayering. Chapter III-3 presents ATM network internals and shows exactly how traffic speeds to its destination packaged in a series of cells. Chapter III-4 describes the many types of physical connections that can carry ATM traffic, while Chapter III-5 presents the data link layer frame formats used with ATM.

ATM supports flows of traffic ranging from real-time voice to best-effort background data transfer. Chapter III-6 analyzes the complex traffic contracts that nail down the performance and quality of service of each permanent or switched virtual circuit. The signaling protocols used to set up switched ATM circuits are described in Chapter III-7.

The broad and varied set of network management mechanisms that have been incorporated into ATM are described in Chapter III-8. These mechanisms include global management via SNMP, automatic configuration via the *Integrated Local Management Interface (ILMI)*, and the clever use of special operations, administration, and maintenance (OAM) cells that automatically report network problems, track data loss, and signal congestion.

Unlike the other networks that have been studied, ATM standards define private network node interface protocols that operate *inside* a network. These protocols, which can generate routes for both permanent and switched virtual circuits, are studied in Chapter III-9.

Finally, in Chapter III-10, the *LAN Emulation (LANE)* protocol is described. LANE enables current applications to run on top of ATM and enables the fundamentally connection-oriented ATM service to emulate a connectionless virtual LAN service.

ATM Concepts

Like frame relay and X.25, ATM provides a *virtual circuit* service to its users. This simply means that the bandwidth available in the network is statistically shared by users. ATM supports

- Permanent virtual circuits (PVCs), created by preconfiguration

- Switched virtual circuits (SVCs), created via signaling

ATM also has other similarities with the older data network technologies:

- An ATM customer can connect an access device to a service provider network using a single line.

- Multiple virtual circuits share the access line that connects a customer site to the network.

However, ATM differs from the old data network services in offering an integrated bundle of voice and data services, and in the fact that it can support a very wide variety of service classes. Furthermore, ATM technology extends into the enterprise via ATM local area network switches.

For many years to come, ATM will need to interwork with the legacy global telephone network and with existing frame relay data network services. ATM also supports and interworks with *Switched Multi-megabit Data Service (SMDS)*. SMDS is a high-speed public data network service originally offered by Regional Bell Operating Companies (RBOCs) and is described in Chapter III-5. In addition, ATM can be tightly integrated with local area networks and interworks with Ethernet and Token Ring LANs.

Types of ATM Connections

ATM is *connection-oriented*, which means that a communications pipeline must be set up between two endpoints before they can start to transfer data.

ATM supports both point-to-point and point-to-multipoint connections. In either case, data sent across an ATM connection is delivered in the same order in which it was sent.

ATM does not guarantee delivery, and data might be lost due to transmission errors or congestion. Loss rates due to transmission errors are expected to be low in public ATM networks, which largely are based on fiber optic media. However, data might be discarded by a congested switch in a network. The way a congested switch handles excess data for a particular ATM connection depends on the type of service that has been contracted for that connection.

Bidirectional Point-to-Point Virtual Circuits

Like frame relay and X.25 circuits, ATM offers a bidirectional point-to-point virtual circuit service. Figure 2.1 depicts a virtual circuit between two endpoints. The circuit in the figure passes through three switches.

Figure 2.1   An ATM virtual circuit.

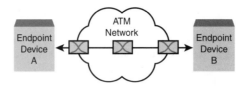

Virtual Channel Connections

A point-to-point circuit actually is made up of a pair of connections—one for each direction. Formally, each of these connections is called a *virtual channel connection (VCC)*.

For example, the virtual circuit in Figure 2.2 is made up of a VCC from endpoint A to endpoint B and a VCC from endpoint B to endpoint A. The bandwidth and delay characteristics can be different for each channel—that is, for each direction of the circuit.

Both channels use the same path through the network. In other words, cells flowing from endpoint B to endpoint A pass through the same set of switches as cells flowing from A to B (but in the reverse order).

Figure 2.2   Virtual channel connections for a virtual circuit.

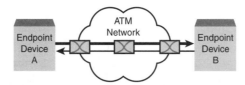

A connection's route normally remains fixed throughout its existence—or at least for long periods of time—because changing routes can cause data to be delivered out of order.

> **Note**
>
> ATM network robustness has been enhanced by the introduction of *soft permanent virtual connections (SPVCs)*, also sometimes called *Smart PVCs*. The endpoints of an SPVC are configured manually. The route then will be generated automatically, and also can change automatically if there is a network failure.
>
> The *private network-to-network interface (PNNI)* standard discussed in Chapter III-10 defines how this can be done in a standard way and enables a network built from switches acquired from different vendors to support Smart PVCs.

End-to-End Virtual Path Connections

A conventional telecommunications subscriber can order a T1 line between a pair of sites and use the channels within the T1 in any desired manner.

Similarly, an ATM subscriber can order an end-to-end *virtual path connection service*, which is illustrated in Figure 2.3. A virtual path connection is made up of a bundle of virtual channel connections. In the figure, several virtual channel connections extending from endpoint A to endpoint B are packed into a single virtual path connection.

Bundling virtual channels that have the same endpoints into a virtual path connection simplifies the job of configuring a large number of channels that have common endpoints. It also simplifies the job of switching the data from its source to its destination. All the channels are switched as a single virtual path unit.

Figure 2.3   Virtual channels within an end-to-end virtual path connection.

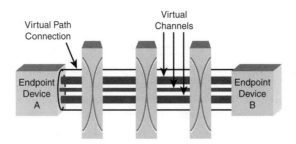

Unlike a T1 line, a virtual path connection is a logical entity rather than a physical entity. The access line between an endpoint and the adjacent network switch can carry many separate virtual paths. Figure 2.4 illustrates the relationship between the access line, virtual paths, and virtual channels.

Figure 2.4   Access line, virtual paths, and virtual channels.

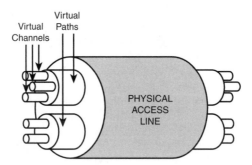

There is one important rule for an end-to-end virtual path connection: All of the channels within an end-to-end path are carried with the same quality of service. The quality of service is associated with the entire path.

A channel (or path's) quality of service determines how an ATM switch processes its data. For example, priority, buffering, and discard strategies depend on the quality of service. It would not make sense to bundle a time-sensitive voice channel into the same end-to-end virtual path as data channels that are being used for low-priority background data transfer.

Other Virtual Paths

A channel always is bundled inside some virtual path, even when the customer is not using an end-to-end virtual path connection service.

To understand the concept, suppose that a telephone service subscriber has a PBX that is connected to a telephone central office via a T1 line. Every channel within the T1 line carries a different telephone call. At the central office, each channel is switched into different T1s that lead to the call destinations.

As a call is carried across the telephone network, there might be several intermediate switching points at which the call's T1 bundle is demultiplexed and the call is routed into a different T1 bundle.

Figure 2.5 shows one telephone call being switched through a series of T1s. The first T1 bundle connects PBX A with switch S1. The next T1 bundle passes through switch S2 without change; however, its channels are demultiplexed and routed at switch S3. The next T1 extends from switch S3 to S4, and the final T1 connects to PBX B. Note that the time slot used by the channel changed each time the call was switched.

| Figure 2.5 | A call switched through a series of T1s. |

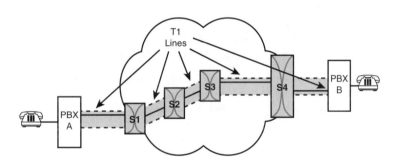

A virtual path is similar to a T1 bundle. Figure 2.6 shows a virtual channel connection that is being switched through a series of virtual paths. A new virtual path is formed whenever the enclosed channels are broken out and rerouted.

Four virtual path connections are shown in the figure, including the following:

- The path connecting endpoint A to switch S1.

- The path between switches S1 and S3. This path passes through switch S2 unchanged; that is, its channels are not broken out and rerouted.

- The path between switches S3 and S4.

- The path connecting switch S4 to endpoint B.

There is one additional term used in discussions of virtual paths. Each switch-to-switch hop is called a *virtual path link (VPL)*. Figure 2.6 shows five virtual path links.

Figure 2.6   A virtual channel connection switched through a series of virtual paths.

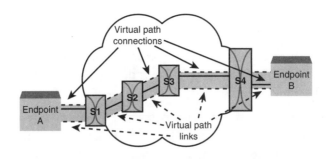

> ### Note
>
> Virtual paths are used to simplify network configuration. For example, suppose that a provider needs to set up 100 virtual channel connections with the same quality of service between sites on the east coast and sites on the west coast. These channels terminate in different endpoints, but they can be routed through the same set of network switches. It is a lot easier to configure the route and quality of service for a virtual path connection and then toss in the channels than it is to configure each virtual channel separately.
>
> Also, if the route that is followed between the east and west coasts needs to change, it is a lot easier to update the route for a single virtual path connection than update 100 separate virtual channel connections. If the channels are part of a virtual path connection, they will go wherever the virtual path connection goes.

The difference between a multiplexed telephony bundle (such as a T1) and an ATM virtual path is that

- An ATM virtual path can carry one channel or thousands of channels. The bandwidth for each channel can be set at whatever level is needed by its user, as long as it is within a capacity limit that has been set for the path.

- An ATM virtual path can emulate the behavior of a conventional T1 or E1 telephony service and carry data at a constant bit rate, or it can be configured to carry bursty data at a variable throughput rate.

Point-to-Multipoint Connections

ATM supports unidirectional point-to-multipoint connections like the one depicted in Figure 2.7. The characteristics of an ATM point-to-multipoint connection are

- One "root" node initiates the call.

- Data sent by the root is received by all the other nodes, which are called *leaves*.

- Leaves cannot use the connection to communicate with the root or with one another. Traffic flows only from the root to the leaves.

In the future, a service might be defined that enables leaves to send information to the root.

Figure 2.7   ATM point-to-multipoint connection.

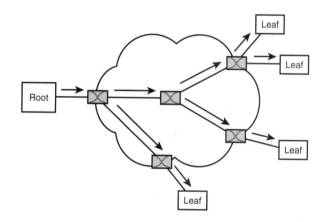

Auxiliary Connections

In addition to the end-to-end connections that carry user data between endpoint devices, an ATM network also supports *auxiliary connections* that are used for:

- Signaling to set up switched calls.

- Exchange of network topology information between switches.

- Exchange of network configuration information.

- Exchange of network operations, administration, and maintenance (OAM) information. OAM connections are used for functions such as reporting that a path has been disrupted, performing a loopback test, or gathering performance data.

Some auxiliary connections join an endpoint device to a network switch, while others join pairs of network switches. For example, in Figure 2.8 an endpoint exchanges messages with its adjacent switch in order to set up a switched virtual circuit. Chapters III-7 and III-9 discuss signaling.

Figure 2.8   Signaling in an ATM network.

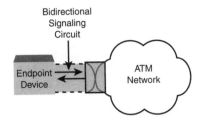

Figure 2.9 displays an end-to-end OAM connection and a switch-to-switch OAM connection.

Figure 2.9   Operations, administration, and maintenance connections.

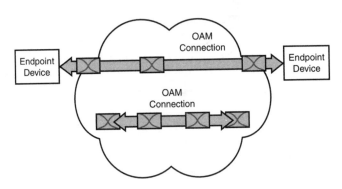

Cell Relay

The most remarkable difference between ATM and conventional telephony or data networks is the fact that ATM is based on cell relay. One of the attractive features of cell relay is that cells are used for both:

- The interface between an endpoint device and a switch

- The interface between two switches

This builds great uniformity into the technology. The physical interface for an endpoint device looks a lot like the physical interface for a switch. The data stream format between an endpoint device and a switch looks a lot like the data stream format between a pair of switches. This cuts back on data reformatting which is costly in terms of both implementation complexity and run-time delays.

Overall ATM Cell Format

Figure 2.10 shows the overall format of an ATM cell. A cell consists of a 5-byte header followed by 48 bytes of payload.

> **Note**
>
> The 48-byte payload size was a compromise between groups that wanted a 32-byte size and a 64-byte size.

The header contains numeric identifiers that indicate the path and channel to which the cell belongs.

The fact that each cell has fixed size and carries its own path and channel information means that cells can be processed by ATM chip hardware, and the processing can be done very quickly.

Note that the cell format includes a fairly hefty overhead burden—more than 10%. Balanced against this is the ability to utilize bandwidth that currently is wasted, and the prospect of the huge bandwidth bonanza that fiber optic technology offers for the future.

Figure 2.10   ATM cell format.

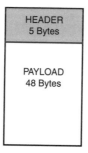

Transmitting and Switching Cells

Before data transfer onto a channel starts, an end-to-end route for the channel is established through a series of switches. Then, the following occurs:

1. At the source endpoint device, data is broken into small, fixed-sized cell payloads before it is transmitted. Each cell has a header that identifies the path and channel to which it belongs.

2. Each switch examines the header and determines the appropriate output line.

3. The cell payloads are extracted at the destination endpoint.

Cells belonging to several virtual channels are interleaved when they are sent across a transmission line. Figure 2.11 illustrates this process. Endpoint A is transmitting interleaved cells for two channels. The cells for one of the channels are shaded while cells for the other channel are vertically striped. Some cell slots are unused. In the figure, unused cell slots are white. The switch routes the shaded cells onto output line 1 and the vertically striped cells onto output line 2.

Endpoint B is transmitting cells for a single channel. Its cells are indicated by slots with horizontal stripes. The other cell slots are unused. The switch routes the horizontally striped cells onto output line 1.

One feature that the figure does not represent accurately is the fact that switch-to-switch lines usually have a far greater capacity than the access lines that connect a switch to endpoints. Hence, cells for many incoming channels can be interleaved onto a switch output line.

Figure 2.11   Switching cells.

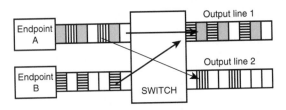

> **Note**
>
> Like frame relay DLCIs, ATM path and channel numbers are local. A cell's path and channel numbers may change several times as the cell is forwarded toward its destination. This process will be described in detail in Chapter III-3.

Although the reverse flow of data is not shown in Figure 2.11, the same procedure is used for ATM cells flowing from right to left. The fact that each channel is made up of a unidirectional flow of cells explains why a bidirectional virtual circuit must be implemented as a pair of unidirectional virtual channels.

ATM Layering

ATM protocols span the physical and data link layers. However, as shown in Figure 2.12, there are three lower layer components instead of the two shown in the OSI layering model on the left.

Payload data is encapsulated within frames at the *ATM Adaptation Layer (AAL)*, which corresponds to the data link layer. Frames larger than a cell payload are sliced up before transmission and reassembled at the receiving end.

Because ATM has to support diverse services, several different service-specific standard ATM Adaptation Layer protocols have been defined:

- **AAL5**—The choice for most circuits that perform data transfer. AAL5 behaves like an ordinary data link protocol. Data is encapsulated into frames (which are sliced into cells before they are transmitted).

- **AAL3/4**—Designed with the connectionless Switched Multimegabit Data Service (SMDS) in mind, but also can be used for connection-oriented service. Data also is encapsulated into frames for AAL3/4. However, AAL3/4 includes some special formatting and protocol mechanisms modeled on SMDS. AAL3/4 rarely is used.

- **AAL2**—Designed to carry compressed voice traffic efficiently. At the time of this writing, chips that support AAL2 still are under development.

- **AAL1**—Used on virtual circuits that emulate conventional telecommunications circuits (such as DS1, fractional DS1, E1, or fractional E1 circuits). AAL1 includes several unusual formats and protocol elements.

- **AAL0**—A non-standard extension that enables experimental methods of packaging data to be tried. AAL0 currently is used as a null data link layer. Raw data is loaded into cells without any framing being added.

AAL service characteristics and formats will be described in Chapter III-5.

The physical layer for ATM communications is broken into two sublayers. The *ATM Layer* is at the heart of ATM technology. It is responsible for creating cell headers and managing the cell stream. The *ATM Physical Layer* performs a number of housekeeping chores and transmits cells onto a physical medium.

Figure 2.13 shows the layered components found within ATM endpoints and switches. The ATM Adaptation Layer and higher layers are found only at circuit endpoints. The ATM Layer and the ATM Physical Layer are implemented in both switches and endpoints.

Figure 2.12 ATM layers.

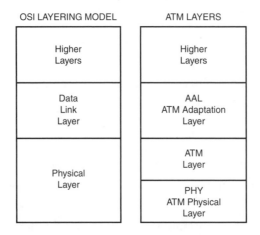

Figure 2.13 ATM layering within endpoints and switches.

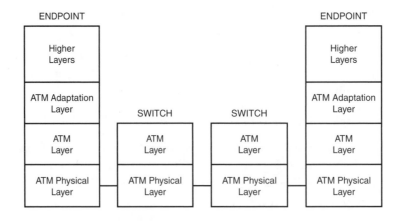

Table 2.1 outlines some of the specific functions that are performed at each layer. Chapters III-3, III-4, and III-5 will fill in the details and subdivide this structure into some further sublayers.

Table 2.1	Overview of ATM sublayer functions
Layer	**Description**
AAL ATM Adaptation Layer	OUT: Encapsulate outgoing data in frames. Segment frames into cell payloads and pass these to the ATM layer for transmission on a specified connection. IN: Reassemble cell payloads arriving on a connection into frames. Pass frame payloads up to the higher layer.
ATM Layer	OUT: Attach a cell header to a cell payload and fill in the path and channel identifiers. Use traffic parameters and the quality of service levels to create an appropriate multiplexed cell stream. IN: Deliver incoming cell payloads to the AAL layer.
PHY ATM Physical Layer	OUT: Compute and insert a checksum into each cell header. Package the cell stream into a physical layer format. Transmit onto a specific medium. IN: Receive incoming cells and validate the header checksums. Pass the incoming cells to the ATM layer.

Traffic Contracts

The characteristics of an ATM connection are specified in a *Traffic Contract*. A Traffic Contract spells out three things:

- A description of the traffic. For example:

  The long-term average rate of cell transmission for the circuit.

  The peak rate at which cells may be transmitted onto the circuit.

  A measure of how long a switch can continue to receive cells at or near the peak rate.

- The Quality of Service. Parameters that are relevant to quality of service include:

  The percentage of cells that are lost or corrupted.

  Estimates of delay time, such as the maximum and average time to transfer a cell between endpoints.

  The biggest expected variation in delay time.

- A description of the *usage parameter control (UPC)* function, which applies an algorithm at the traffic entry point to determine whether a channel is compliant to its contract, and takes actions when non-compliant traffic is detected.

Bearer Classes and Service Categories

The parameters listed previously are just a subset of the Traffic Contract parameters that have been defined. Engineering a network that can support arbitrary combinations of parameter values would be both difficult and foolish. Relatively few parameter combinations would correspond to the needs of real applications.

What is needed is a small set of application characteristics that can be used to determine the list of parameters to be specified. The ITU-T made the first step towards solving this problem in its initial Bearer Class definitions, shown in Figure 2.14.

Figure 2.14   The original ITU-T Bearer Classes.

A	B	C	D
Connection-oriented			Connectionless
Constant Bit Rate	Variable Bit Rate		
Timing Required		Timing Not Required	

Applications were classified according to whether they

• Were connection-oriented or connectionless

• Required a constant bit-rate circuit that behaved like a conventional leased line, or worked well with a virtual circuit that could carry bursty data

• Were sensitive to delay and delay variability (as voice traffic is) or could tolerate delay and delay variability

Over time, the role of Classes A and C changed, Classes B and D were set aside, and an additional catch-all class, *Class X*, was defined.

At some stage in the evolution of Bearer Classes, the ATM Forum indicated that Classes A, C, and X referred only to virtual channel connections. A new *Transparent VP Service Class* was associated with virtual path connections. The current Bearer Class definitions are:

• **Class A**—A connection-oriented, constant bit rate (CBR) virtual channel service. The network may perform internetworking. For example, the ATM circuit may connect to a DS1 or N-ISDN circuit.

• **Class C**—A connection-oriented variable bit rate (VBR) ATM virtual channel service. The network may perform internetworking. For example, the channel may connect to a frame relay circuit.

• **Class X**—A connection-oriented virtual channel service. It provides end-to-end ATM service.

• **Transparent VP**—A connection-oriented end-to-end virtual path service.

The ATM Forum created an improved, sharper division of connection characteristics by defining standard *Service Categories*. Current Service Categories are described in Table 2.2. Today, connections are described by both a Bearer Class and Service Category. Bearer Classes and Service Categories will be examined in more detail in Chapters III-6 and III-7.

Table 2.2   ATM Service Categories

Service Category	Description/Examples
CBR: Constant Bit Rate	A real-time service that provides a constant bandwidth. CBR supports applications such as constant bit-rate voice, constant bit-rate video, or a data connection that behaves like a leased line.

continues

Table 2.2	Continued
Service Category	**Description/Examples**
rt-VBR: Real-Time Variable Bit Rate	A real-time service that delivers a specified average bandwidth and supports applications that are sensitive to delay and to variations in delay, such as compressed voice or video.
nrt-VBR: Non-Real-Time Variable Bit Rate	A service that delivers a specified average bandwidth and supports applications that are not sensitive to delay. The service is suitable for bursty traffic that is not highly sensitive to delay, and can be used for applications such as LAN-to-LAN connectivity.
UBR: Unspecified Bit Rate	A service that is suitable for the delivery of non-time-critical bursty data. Traffic is delivered on a best-effort basis. Neither an average bandwidth nor a quality of service level are specified.
ABR: Available Bit Rate	A service that delivers varying amounts of bandwidth, depending on the availability of network resources. It is suitable for bursty data transfer. The sender must alter its transmission rate according to whether the network is congested. Flow control feedback information is passed back to the data origin in order to control the transmission rate.

ATM Benefits

ATM is capable of supplying levels of bandwidth to a customer's sites that are far beyond the range of a conventional telecommunications network.

ATM also is far more flexible than conventional telecommunications technologies:

- A customer can choose channel bandwidths that match the needs of each application. A channel's bandwidth is determined by the number of cells per second that it is allowed to use.

- Since every cell contains a header that identifies its channel, cells from many different channels can be freely interleaved.

- Cells are small. Unlike frame relay, time-sensitive data—such as a small chunk of digitized voice—is not delayed waiting in line behind one or more big frames that need to be transmitted. The chunk of digitized voice can be interleaved into the traffic flow in a timely manner.

- A customer can match a circuit's quality of service to the needs of the application.

- In the conventional telecommunications network, extra bandwidth is unusable. With ATM cell relay, a provider can offer a cheap, low-priority service based on available bandwidth. A customer's data is dropped into unused cells and delivered on a best-effort basis.

- The use of fixed-size cells with a simple, formatted header makes it easy to perform switching functions quickly, using a hardware implementation. Simplicity also results in less costly switching equipment.

Although originally conceived as a public wide area architecture, ATM has been adapted for use in private wide area networks and for local area networks. ATM boosters hope that someday one common interconnection technology will be used for voice and data, integrating local and wide area networks, and connecting private networks to public networks.

The challenge to switch vendors and providers is to support smart networks that can deliver the contracted amount of bandwidth to each customer, and meet the quality of service requirements of each traffic contract.

Now, it is time to focus on the details. The chapter that follows describes the internal operations of the ATM Layer.

The ATM Layer

ATM interface hardware manufactured by many different vendors is available for a great variety of endpoint devices. Setting standards for the interface between an endpoint device and a network switch is critical to the success of ATM technology.

Furthermore, ATM cannot succeed unless private LAN switches and private and public wide area switches built by different vendors are able to communicate with one another. Switch products need to cooperate to route calls and support requested levels of service; hence, standards are equally important for switch-to-switch interfaces.

The interface between an ATM endpoint device and an ATM switch is called the *user-network interface (UNI)*. The interface between a pair of ATM network switches is called a *network-to-network interface (NNI)*. Figure 3.1 shows ATM UNI and NNI interface points.

Figure 3.1 also indicates how ATM components are layered. The combined ATM Layer and ATM Physical Layer take the place of a conventional physical layer. The *ATM Adaptation Layer (AAL)* corresponds to a data link layer.

Both endpoint systems and network switches perform ATM Layer functions. The ATM Layer is at the heart of ATM's cell relay technology. This chapter presents ATM Layer concepts and mechanisms and describes the operation of the user-network and network-to-network interfaces at the ATM Layer.

Figure 3.1   User-network and network-to-network interfaces.

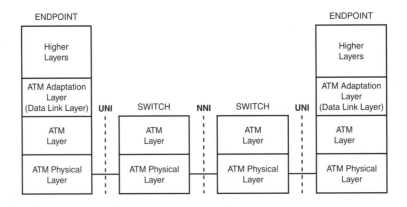

The ATM User-Network Interface

An ATM endpoint and adjacent ATM switch exchange cells across the user-network interface. The ATM Layer in the endpoint or switch has the job of creating the outgoing multiplexed cell stream, and of receiving and demultiplexing the incoming cell stream.

> **Note**
>
> Early ATM products were based on UNI specification 3.0. This version became obsolete when UNI 3.1, which is not backward-compatible, was released. UNI 3.1 subsequently was enhanced by version 4.0, which updates the user-network signaling portion of version 3.1.
>
> Equipment with UNI 3.0 software cannot interoperate with UNI 3.1/4.0 equipment.

Endpoint Device Functions

An ATM endpoint device needs to generate cell traffic that is within the limits of the ATM traffic contract for each channel. If not, a network switch can discard the overload. This might have severe consequences for the overall performance of the affected channels.

Specific tasks performed by the ATM layer at an endpoint system include

- Adding cell headers that have appropriate path and channel numbers to outgoing cell payloads

- Applying traffic and quality of service parameters to control the queuing of cells and schedule their transmission

- Passing the outgoing cells to the ATM Physical Layer for transmission

- Accepting incoming cells from the ATM Physical Layer and processing them, passing their payloads to the ATM Adaptation Layer

UNI Switch Functions

The ATM layer at the network switch adjacent to an endpoint transmits cells to the endpoint and processes cells received from the endpoint. The switch examines each incoming cell header to multiplex the cell onto an appropriate output line.

The switch can be configured to analyze traffic received from an endpoint to determine if it conforms to the circuit's traffic contract. The switch can take specific actions (such as marking traffic eligible for discard or actually discarding cells). This process is called *Usage Parameter Control (UPC)*.

Format of the UNI Cell Header

The header format for cells sent across the user-network interface is shown in Figure 3.2. There are six fields in the UNI cell header:

- Generic flow control (GFC)—4 bits

- Virtual path identifier (VPI)—8 bits

- Virtual channel identifier (VCI)—16 bits

- Payload type (PT)—3 bits

- Cell loss priority (CLP)—1 bit

- Header error control (HEC)—8 bits

Figure 3.2   ATM user-network interface cell header format.

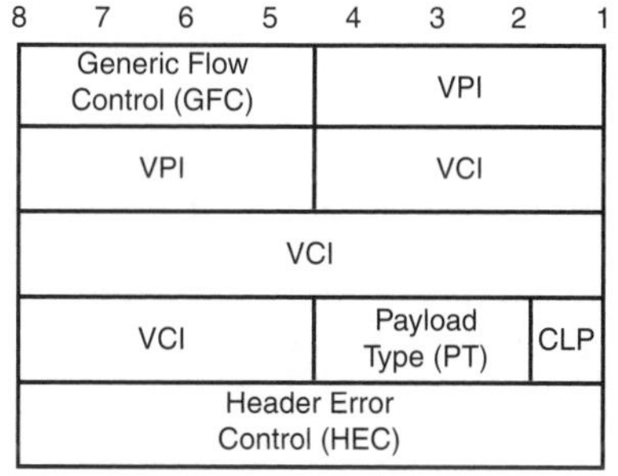

CLP = Cell loss priority
VPI = Virtual path identifier
VCI = Virtual channel identifier

GFC: Generic Flow Control

The Generic Flow Control field has been set aside for use by equipment within a customer site. As the title suggests, the intended use is to monitor local flow control. The GFC field must be set to 0 in cells that cross a user-network interface.

VPI and VCI: Virtual Path and Channel Identifiers

As Figure 3.3 shows, every cell belongs to a virtual channel, and every virtual channel is bundled inside a virtual path. You could view a virtual path as a highway and the virtual channels as lanes in the highway.

Figure 3.3   Virtual paths and virtual channels.

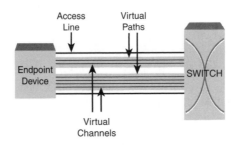

This path and channel structure is reflected in the two-tiered ATM cell address scheme. An ATM channel connection is identified by the combination of a *virtual path identifier (VPI)* and a *virtual channel identifier (VCI)*.

The UNI cell header contains an 8-bit virtual path identifier and a 16-bit virtual channel identifier. This means that

- VPI numbers can range from 0 to 255.

- VCI numbers can range from 0 to 65,535.

Altogether, there are $256 \times 65,536$ VPI/VCI combinations, allowing 16,777,216 separate connections to be identified across the UNI. It is not surprising that the set of numbers that actually is used at a particular UNI often is restricted to less than the full scope. To do this, several of the VPI or VCI bits are not used and are set to 0.

The bits in the VPI and VCI fields are ordered so the most significant bit appears first. For example, if the VPI bits are 01000011, the decimal value of the virtual path identifier is 67.

Network managers typically write a circuit's VPI and VCI in a form such as VPI/VCI or VPI-VCI. For example, channel 30 in path 2 could be written as 2/30 or 2–30.

Assignment of VPIs and VCIs

VPI and VCI values are either preconfigured for permanent virtual circuits or are assigned dynamically by network switches for switched virtual circuits. Like frame relay DLCI values, VPI/VCI assignments are purely local.

Figure 3.4 shows VPI and VCI assignments at the endpoints of an ATM connection.

Figure 3.4   VPI and VCI assignments at endpoints.

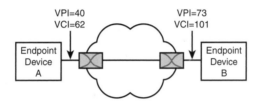

PT: Payload Type

As the name suggests, the main purpose of the 3-bit *payload type (PT)* field is to identify the type of information that is being carried in a cell. This information can be

- User data for a channel

- Operations, administration, and management (OAM) data relating to a given channel

Table 3.1 presents the list of PT values defined at the time of writing. As shown in the table, the leftmost bit (labeled U in the table) is the one that indicates if the payload is user data (0) or OAM data (1).

The use of the remaining PT bits depends on if the cell contains user data or OAM data.

For user data

- The network sets the middle bit (labeled C in the table) to 1 to indicate that the network was congested in the direction of delivery. This bit is called the *Explicit Forward Congestion Indication (EFCI) flag*.

> **Note**
>
> Reporting congestion in the forward direction might not seem like a very useful function, because the node receiving the traffic—rather than the node that sent the traffic—is notified. However, there are both standard and proprietary feedback mechanisms implemented in ATM networks that enable nodes to report the congestion back to the source. One of these mechanisms is described in Chapter III-6.

- The rightmost bit (bit 1) can be used for a higher layer protocol mechanism. It sometimes is called the *ATM-user-to-ATM-user indication flag*. It plays a very important role for circuits that carry the most popular type of frame, AAL5. In this case, the flag is set to 1 in a cell header to indicate that the cell contains the final piece of an AAL5 frame.

Table 3.1   Payload Type Field Values

PT Bits: U C X 3 2 1	Description
0 0 x	User cell, congestion not experienced
0 1 x	User cell, congestion experienced
1 0 0	OAM data for a channel segment
1 0 1	OAM data for an end-to-end channel
1 1 0	Identifies a resource management cell; used for a feedback mechanism that controls a sender's transmission rate
1 1 1	Reserved for future functions

Currently, two payload type codes are used for OAM data. In both cases, they carry OAM data that is associated with a specific channel—the channel identified by the VPI and VCI in the cell header.

For payload type 101, the OAM cell flow is end-to-end. For payload type 100, the OAM cell flow occurs between two devices that are endpoints of a segment of the full channel route. (A *segment* consists of one or more consecutive links along the route.) Chapter III-8 contains a detailed description of these OAM cells.

CLP: Cell Loss Priority

The ATM *cell loss priority (CLP)* bit is used like the frame relay discard eligibility bit. The cell loss priority flag in the ATM header indicates which traffic is more eligible for discard.

A CLP flag value of 1 indicates that the cell has low priority and should be discarded in preference to cells with CLP=0.

An originating device can set the CLP value to 1 for cells that have been selected according to preconfigured criteria. A switch will set the CLP to 1 in some cells when a customer's endpoint device transmits cells with CLP=0 at too high a rate.

HEC: Header Error Control

The 8-bit header error control field contains the result of a *cyclic redundancy check (CRC)* function calculated on the first 4 bytes of the cell header. The HEC can detect header errors and optionally can be used to correct single-bit errors.

> **Note**
>
> Correction of single-bit errors does not work for some media because of the way data is encoded onto the media.

The header error control field is recalculated at channel switching points and at the destination endpoint device. If a cell has a corrupted header and correction is not possible, the cell is discarded.

HEC calculation and checking actually is a physical layer function. It is not performed at the ATM layer.

UNI Cell Headers

Listing 3.1 displays header information for two cells sent across a user-network interface on VPI=90, VCI=91. These cells carried data that was part of an AAL5 frame. The payload type field of the first cell indicates that it carries user data. The cell has just been transmitted from the endpoint, so no congestion is reported. The cell loss priority is set to 0.

The ATM-user-to-ATM-user indication is 0 for the first cell but is 1 for the second cell, which means that the second cell contains the last segment of the AAL5 frame.

Listing 3.1   Header Information for Cells Sent on VPI=90, VCI=91

```
********************* Cell Number 1 *********************

SUMMARY:

  Number:        000001
  Status:        Good
```

continues

```
AAL:           AAL 5
VPI:           90
VCI:           91
Type:          RAW
Summary:       ATM Layer

DETAIL:

------------------Asynchronous Transfer Mode (ATM)------------------
Cell type = user-network interface (UNI)
Generic flow control (GFC) = 0
Virtual path identifier = 90
Virtual channel identifier = 91
Payload type identifier (PTI) = 0
     .... 0...    User data cell
     .... .0..    No congestion experienced
     .... ..0.    ATM-user-to-ATM-user indication = 0
Cell loss priority = 0
     .... ...0

********************* Cell Number 2 *********************

SUMMARY:

Number:        000002
Status:        Good
AAL:           AAL 5
VPI:           90
VCI:           91
Type:          RAW
Summary:       ATM Layer

DETAIL:

------------------Asynchronous Transfer Mode (ATM)------------------

Cell type = user-network interface (UNI)
 Generic flow control (GFC) = 0
 Virtual path identifier = 90
 Virtual channel identifier = 91
 Payload type identifier (PTI) = 1
      .... 0...    User data cell
```

```
    .... .0..    No congestion experienced
    .... ..1.    ATM-user-to-ATM-user indication = 1
Cell loss priority = 0
    .... ...0
```

The summary sections in Listing 3.1 announced that the cells belonged to an AAL5 virtual circuit. However, note that there is no field in the cell header (shown in the cell detail sections of the trace) that identifies the AAL type of the data that is carried.

> ### Note
> A circuit's AAL type only is known because it is configured when the circuit is set up. A virtual circuit can carry frames for only one AAL type.

Cell Rate Decoupling

ATM operates over a large number of different physical interfaces. Several of these physical interfaces are described in Chapter III-4. Almost all of these physical interfaces have been designed to carry a steady flow of cells. If the outgoing link provides more bandwidth than is being used, some cells that do not contain data need to be inserted into the flow. The ATM Layer inserts extra cells called *unassigned cells*. Unassigned cells fill in the blank spaces in the cell flow.

An ATM Layer receiver can recognize an unassigned cell by its header and discards any unassigned cell. Figure 3.5 shows the header format used for unassigned cells. The payload type (PT) bits (xxx in the figure) are ignored (and can be anything), and the cell payload does not matter.

The process of creating a steady stream of cells by inserting cells at the sender and discarding them at the receiver is called *cell rate decoupling*. The name reflects the fact that the ATM layer can mediate between the rate at which data is being submitted and the rate at which the underlying medium transmits cells.

Figure 3.5   Format of an unassigned cell header.

> **Note**
>
> The physical layer also can insert extra cells to maintain a steady cell flow. In this case, the extra cells are called *idle cells*. Idle cells are described in Chapter III-4.

Usage Parameter Control

Recall that *Usage Parameter Control (UPC)* is the process of examining incoming traffic to check if it conforms to the traffic contract, and then taking configured actions. The UPC function is applied to traffic entering the network by the entry switch at the user-network interface.

Now that you have a good idea of what happens across the user-network interface, it is time to look inside an ATM network and examine switch-to-switch interactions.

ATM Network-to-Network Interface

At an ATM network-to-network (switch-to-switch) interface, cells for many different channels are multiplexed across the physical link connecting the switches.

The primary job of the ATM Layer at a switch-to-switch interface is to process each incoming cell and route it to the appropriate output line. A switch examines the headers of incoming cells to route the cells to the appropriate output lines.

NNI Cell Header Format

The ATM cell header format for ATM cells transferred between network switches is slightly different from the header used for cells transferred across the user-network interface. As shown in Figure 3.6, the header for an NNI has no GFC field. Instead, the VPI field is enlarged from 8 bits to 12 bits, allowing for VPIs that range from 0 to 4,095.

Apart from the fact that there is no GFC field, the fields in an NNI cell header are the same as the fields in a UNI cell header.

VPIs and VCIs in the Network

When a connection is set up, VPI and VCI numbers are assigned to the connection at every node that it traverses.

Figure 3.6   ATM NNI cell header format.

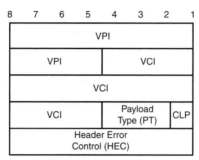

CLP = Cell loss priority
VPI = Virtual path identifier
VCI = Virtual channel identifier

We have seen that different pairs of VPI and VCI numbers can be used at each virtual channel endpoint. In fact, it is not unusual for VPI and VCI numbers for a channel to change at every switch that lies on the route through the network. The VPI and VCI numbers are different for each link along the way to the destination for the channel in Figure 3.7. The values are

VPI=1, VCI=62 for the link between endpoint A and switch S1.

VPI=21, VCI=44 for the link between switch S1 and switch S2.

VPI=11, VCI=39 for the link between switch S2 and switch S3.

VPI=3, VCI=101 for the link between switch S3 and endpoint B.

Figure 3.7   Network VPIs and VCIs for a connection.

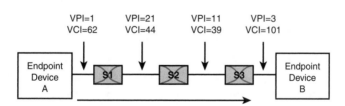

As a cell travels from endpoint A to endpoint B of the channel in Figure 3.7, each switch translates the incoming VPI and VCI values to the appropriate outgoing VPI and VCI values for the channel. Note that the HEC field in a cell header has to be revised every time the channel's VPI and VCI values change.

Note

A bidirectional virtual circuit is made up of two unidirectional virtual channel connections. Theoretically, the VPI/VCI numbers for the channel from B to A could be different from the VPI/VCI numbers for the channel from A to B.

As a practical matter, the same VPI/VCI selections are made in both directions. For example, in Figure 3.7, VPI=11 and VCI=39 would be used between switch S2 and switch S3 in both directions.

Switching Tables

Cells are forwarded at a switch by looking up VPI and VCI information in a switching table. For example, a cell for the channel shown in Figure 3.7 would be routed at switch S2 using a table entry like the one here:

Switch S2 Incoming Physical Interface	VPI	VCI	Switch S2 Outgoing Physical Interface	VPI	VCI
From Switch S1	21	44	To Switch S3	11	39

In a real switching table, each physical interface for a switch (also called a *switch port*) is assigned a numeric identifier. These numeric identifiers would appear in real switch tables, instead of phrases like "From Switch S1" and "To Switch S2."

A table entry is added to a switch table when a PVC is configured or during the signaling process when an SVC is created. For some products, an administrator has to create table entries manually every time a new PVC is set up. Other products automate this chore.

Table Entries for a Virtual Path Connection

As you might recall from Chapter III-2, a subscriber can order an end-to-end virtual path connection service that carries a bundle of customer circuits between endpoints. The end-to-end virtual path connection in Figure 3.8 carries three channels.

Figure 3.8   An end-to-end virtual path connection.

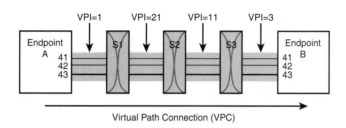

The VCIs of channels within a virtual path connection do not change along the way, and an intermediate switch does not have to examine the channel numbers. Each switch examines and translates only the path numbers. The following table entry shows how this is done at switch S2. The entry says, "Change the VPI field from 21 to 11 and forward the cell on the interface that leads to switch S3."

Switch S2 Incoming Physical Interface	VPI	VCI	Switch S2 Outgoing Physical Interface	VPI	VCI
From Switch S1	21	*	To Switch S3	11	*

The VCI numbers will remain 41, 42, and 43 from endpoint to endpoint. Individual VCI numbers do not have to be inspected until the end of the virtual path connection is reached.

Also, recall that sometimes it is convenient to bundle a group of permanent virtual channels that follow a common path through a series of network switches within a network, but do not originate and end at the same endpoint devices. In general, a virtual path connection can extend

- End-to-end, between a pair of endpoints

- Between a pair of network switches

- Between an endpoint and a network switch

Chapter III-2 describes a switch-to-switch virtual path connection that carries 100 virtual channel connections from the east coast to the west coast.

Note how easy it is, using switching table entries like the one shown earlier, to route or reroute a virtual path across a network. Apart from generating table entries at a few switches, the sole job that needs to be done is to identify the channels to be carried within the virtual path. This only needs to be done at the originating and terminating points of the path.

Cell Buffering

A switch sometimes must temporarily store incoming cells for a channel in a queue before transmitting them. This might be done for a number of reasons. For example:

- The outgoing link to be used for the channel's traffic is busy. To avoid having to discard incoming cells, the switch stores incoming cells in a queue until they can be transmitted. This keeps the cell loss rate at an acceptable level.

- A short burst of traffic for a channel has arrived at a high bit rate. The switch queues the cells so they can be transmitted onto the output line at a steady, controlled rate. This is called *traffic shaping*.

Cell Discard Strategies

A switch has a limited amount of memory for its output queues. A switch is said to be congested when too many cells pile up in a queue and memory starts to run out. A congested switch has to discard some of its cells. An administrator sets the threshold congestion level (based on the percentage of the queue memory that still is available) at which a switch will start to discard cells from a queue.

Discarding cells at random can be very wasteful. When one cell that is part of a large data frame is discarded, all the other cells for the frame become useless. (Because there is a missing piece, at the destination, the reconstructed frame will have a bad frame check sequence and will be thrown away.) ATM supports data frame sizes of up to 65,535 bytes, so this can add up to a lot of squandered cells.

An ATM switch vendor can improve the efficiency of a customer's AAL5 circuits by implementing smart cell discard strategies for AAL5 traffic.

When a cell is discarded, the remaining cells for that frame are of no use. A smart switch can discard these and salvage wasted bandwidth. This practice is called *partial packet discard (PPD)*.

However, partial packet discard still is somewhat wasteful, because the initial part of the frame already has been transmitted. This initial part might be quite large! An even smarter switch will deliver the cells that complete the current frame but discard the next frame for that channel in its entirety. This procedure is called *early packet discard (EPD)*.

It is easy to implement PPD and EPD for AAL5 channels, because the payload type field in cells that carry AAL5 frames contains a flag that is set to 1 at the end of an AAL5 frame; thus, the switch can easily detect where frames begin and end.

Special Cells

A number of special types of cells that do not carry user data have been mentioned in this chapter. For example, there are unassigned cells that are used as filler in the cell stream. These are recognizable by the fact that their VPI and VCI both are 0.

Other special cells carry OAM data that relates to a specific channel. They have the same VPI and VCI as the data cells for the channel but are recognizable as OAM cells because the payload type bits are 101 (when the OAM data travels end-to-end) or 100 (when the OAM data is associated with a segment of a channel).

These channel OAM cells are called end-to-end and segment *F5 flow* cells. The label "F5" comes from the definition of a hierarchy of OAM information that helps operators run a network. F1 information relates to the simplest devices in a network while F5 information relates to the highest level communications entity: a virtual channel.

One step down the hierarchy, *F4 flow* OAM cells are associated with either a segment of a virtual path or an entire end-to-end virtual path. OAM data relevant to an end-to-end virtual path is sent across channel 4 within the path. OAM data associated with a segment of a virtual path is sent across channel 3 within the path. Thus, cells with VPI=(anything), VCI=3 or VPI=(anything), VCI=4 always are special OAM cells and do not carry user data.

In fact, the ITU-T and the ATM Forum have set aside all the VCI numbers from 0–31 for special purposes, and these numbers cannot be used for end-user channels. For example, some of the special channels reserved for auxiliary network functions include

- **VPI=0, VCI=5**—Used for the signaling messages that set up SVCs.

- **VPI=0, VCI=16**—Reserved for the integrated local management interface (ILMI) protocol. ILMI enables adjacent devices to exchange configuration information.

- **VPI=0, VCI=18**—Reserved for private network-to-network interface (PNNI) messages; used to discover network topology.

Table 3.2 presents a list of channels used for special purposes. The table also includes entries for OAM F5 cells, so payload type fields are included. Bits labeled with "a" in the payload type field have a use that depends on specific procedures defined for the channel.

Table 3.2   Reserved Channels and Special Cells

VPI	VCI	PT	Description of Use
0	0	any	Unassigned cell.
0	1	0a0	Metasignaling. Default channel for metasignaling, used by a protocol that establishes and terminates non-default signaling channels.
any	1	0a0	Non-default channel for metasignaling.
0	2	0aa	Default channel for general broadcast signaling, used to broadcast signaling messages.
any	2	0aa	Non-default channel for general broadcast signaling.
any	3	0a0	Channel for OAM F4 data relating to a virtual path segment.
any	4	0a0	Channel for OAM F4 data relating to an end-to-end virtual path.
0	5	0aa	Default channel for signaling messages used to set up switched virtual circuits.
any	5	0aa	Non-default channel for signaling messages.
any	6	110	Channel for resource management cells relating to a virtual path connection.
0	16	aaa	Channel for Integrated Local Management Interface (ILMI) SNMP messages.
0	17	aaa	Channel that connects a LAN Emulation client to a LAN Emulation Configuration Server.
0	18	aaa	Channel for private network-to-network interface messages exchanged across a physical link, used to discover network topology.
any	18	aaa	Channel for private network-to-network interface messages exchanged across a virtual path connection, used to discover network topology.
any	any	100	Cells carry OAM F5 data relating to a virtual channel segment.
any	any	101	Cells carry OAM F5 data relating to an end-to-end virtual channel.
any	any	110	Cells carry resource management messages for a virtual channel connection.

A few of the entries in Table 3.2 use terminology that is unfamiliar. The ITU standards define some signaling mechanisms that are not covered in current implementation agreements. These include

- **Metasignaling cells**—Used to set up and release a channel that will subsequently be used for signaling. As shown in Table 3.2, these cells are sent on VPI=(anything), VCI=1, and the default VPI is 0.

- **Broadcast signaling cells**—Carry signaling messages that need to be delivered to a set of endpoints across a UNI. As shown in Table 3.2, these cells are sent on VPI=(anything), VCI=2, and the default VPI is 0.

References

ATM Layer behavior at the user-network interface is described in Chapter 3 of the ATM Forum *ATM User-Network Interface Specification*, Version 3.1 (1994).

The ATM Forum *Private Network-Network Interface Specification* Version 1.0 (1996) describes switch-to-switch behavior.

CHAPTER 4

The ATM Physical Layer

If there is any doubt that ATM boosters want to enable ATM everywhere, a look at the list of user-network physical layer implementations dispels it. The ATM Forum has defined many different physical layer implementations. Some are suitable for both public and private user-network interfaces, while others are appropriate for private user-network interfaces only. A sampling of supported interfaces includes

- A 155.52Mbps SONET/STS-3c public fiber optic interface

- Private 155.52Mbps unshielded twisted pair and shielded twisted pair interfaces

- DS1 and E1 user-network interfaces

- A 100Mbps private multimode fiber interface

- A 25.6Mbps private twisted-pair interface

- A simple, direct DS3 interface

- A DS3 interface with extra framing (PLCP interface)

- A frame-based data exchange interface (DXI)

- E1 and E3 interfaces

- A 622.08Mbps SONET STS-12c or SDH STM-4 interface

The first eight interfaces are described in this chapter to give you a good basis for understanding the major features of physical interface definitions.

The reference section at the end of this chapter lists the ATM Forum physical interface specifications that have been defined at the time of this writing.

The list of physical interface types is quite daunting, but, fortunately, a network administrator needs to deal with only a common, limited set of features.

The first step in understanding the ATM physical layer is to understand its breakdown into sublayers.

Physical Sublayers

The ATM physical layer is broken into two sublayers, shown in Figure 4.1. The lower sublayer is called the *physical medium dependent (PMD)* sublayer. This sublayer has the job of impressing 0s and 1s on a specific medium (such as twisted pair or fiber optic) and extracting the 0s and 1s at the receiving end.

The upper sublayer is called the *transmission convergence (TC)* sublayer. Several chores that prepare outgoing cells for transmission and process incoming cells are performed within this sublayer.

Figure 4.1   ATM physical layer sublayering.

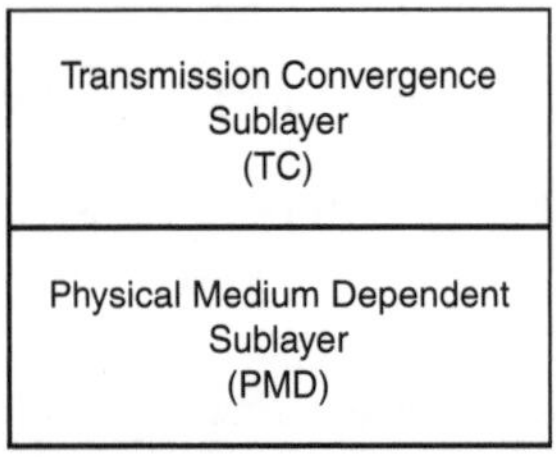

Transmission Convergence
Sublayer
(TC)

Physical Medium Dependent
Sublayer
(PMD)

Physical Medium Dependent Sublayer Functions

All the functions that depend on a choice of a specific physical technology are isolated in the PMD sublayer. Standards documents for this sublayer describe

- The medium
- Cables and connectors
- Encoding of 0s and 1s
- Clock recovery and bit timing

For some media, the PMD sublayer scrambles cells before placing them on the line and descrambles them at the receiving end. Scrambling gets rid of repeating patterns (such as 00000000... and 0101010101...) that can cause transmission problems or that might be mistaken for alarms on some telecommunications transmission lines.

Transmission Convergence Sublayer Functions

The transmission convergence sublayer performs some final processing on outgoing cells just before they are transmitted onto a medium. The TC sublayer also is responsible for recognizing cell boundaries in the stream of 0s and 1s that is received from the medium.

Some transmission convergence functions are performed for all physical interfaces, while others are specific to one medium or only a few types of media. The general functions are examined first. At any sending end, the transmission convergence sublayer generates the ATM header error control (HEC) field. At any receiving end, the TC sublayer

- Determines where each cell begins. This is called *cell delineation*.

- Uses the HEC field checksum value to determine if the cell header has been corrupted.

The remaining TC functions are performed only for selected interface types. At the sending end, a transmission sublayer might

- Add extra framing around bundles of cells.

- Perform physical layer cell rate decoupling; that is, insert a filler cell into the stream when a cell must be transmitted onto the medium, but the ATM layer has not submitted a cell to be sent.

- Scramble cells to prevent repeated bit patterns. (This is done in addition to, or instead of, the scrambling that is performed at the lower PMD sublayer.)

At the receiving end, the transmission sublayer for some selected interfaces might

- Use the HEC value to correct single-bit errors.

- Discard incoming idle filler cells. These cells must not be passed up to the ATM layer.

- Descramble cells if they have been scrambled.

Now it's time to examine some of these TC functions more closely.

Cell Delineation

Life would be easier if cell delineation always was done the same way. In fact, there are several methods, as you will see in the detailed discussions of specific interfaces later in this chapter.

The simplest method of determining where a cell starts is the one used with the 100Mbps private multimode fiber interface. A special signal placed on the fiber announces that a cell follows immediately.

The most frequently used method is more complicated. The receiver pins down the position of a cell header by searching for a byte that looks like it might be the header error control (HEC) value for the previous four bytes. More specifically

1. A receiver in *hunt state* checks if a byte contains the correct checksum of the previous four bytes. The receiver moves forward one bit at a time until a match is found. After a match is found, the receiver changes to *pre-sync state*.

2. The receiver moves from pre-sync state to *sync state* after a configured number (less than six) of consecutive valid HEC matches. If a match fails during this period, the receiver returns to hunt state.

3. A receiver in sync state switches to hunt state if more than a threshold number of HEC failures occur within a selected period (which must be configured as less than seven cell times).

Error Correction and Detection

Interfaces that support single-bit error correction usually provide it as an option. Thus, when configuring such an interface, an administrator has a choice between two modes:

- *Detection mode*—If the HEC field value does not match the recalculated value, the cell is discarded.

- *Correction mode*—The HEC value also can be used to correct a single-bit error. If the HEC value indicates that there are multiple errors, the cell is discarded.

Note

After an interface in correction mode has detected and corrected an error, it switches to detection mode for a while. This prevents the interface from performing a series of spurious "corrections."

Cell Rate Decoupling

For many interface types, a steady stream of cells must be transmitted through the interface. Recall that the job of interpolating cells when there is no data to be sent is called *cell rate decoupling*. When the ATM layer performs cell rate decoupling, it inserts *unassigned* cells into the stream. An unassigned cell has VPI=0, VCI=0, and CLP=0. (Refer to Figure 3.5 in Chapter III-3 to see the header of an unassigned cell.) At the receiver, the physical layer passes incoming unassigned cells to the ATM layer.

In some cases, the TC sublayer has to perform cell rate decoupling to ensure that the flow of cells is not interrupted. When a cell must be sent and none has been provided by the ATM layer, the TC sublayer inserts an *idle cell* into the stream. Incoming idle cells are not passed up to the ATM layer but are discarded immediately. An idle cell has the format shown in Figure 4.2.

Figure 4.2   Format of an idle cell.

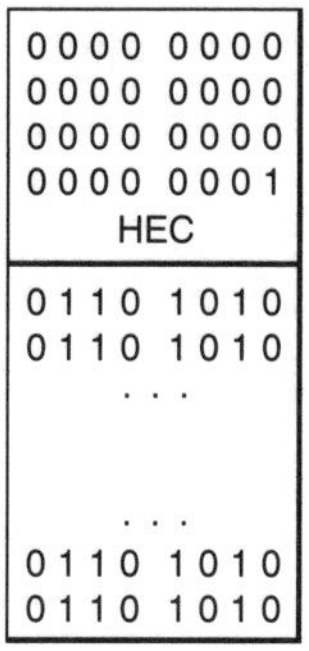

```
0000 0000
0000 0000
0000 0000
0000 0001
   HEC
0110 1010
0110 1010
   . . .

   . . .
0110 1010
0110 1010
```

Framing Groups of Cells

For some interfaces, batches of cells are packaged within framing that has been defined specifically for ATM interfaces. This packaging

- Might include bit patterns that are used to align cells

- In some cases, carries information that supports ATM operations, administration, and maintenance (OAM) functions

Keep in mind that this is *physical layer* framing.

The Physical Interfaces

With a firm understanding of physical sublayer functions, we're now ready to tackle some of the interfaces the ATM physical layer supports. SONET hierarchy-based interfaces are expected to be the long-term public and private ATM user-network standards. In the meantime, ATM interfaces are being defined for every commonly used medium.

The 155.52Mbps SONET/STS-3c public network interface is described later in this chapter. This interface is very important, but it also is very complicated. We'll describe four simpler interfaces first:

- The DS1 public/private interface

- A 100Mbps private multimode fiber interface

- Two DS3 public/private interfaces

After examining these examples, others based on the STS-3c format should be easier to master.

DS1 Public Interface

The DS1 interface is straightforward. Cells simply are dropped into a T1 payload. However, there are a few details worth mentioning. The DS1 ATM interface must run over a clear channel T1 line operating at 1.544Mbps:

- The clear channel is obtained using Bipolar 8 Zero Substitution (B8ZS).

- The 24-multiframe Extended Superframe Format (ESF) is used.

Recall that some ESF framing bits are used to align the payload, while others provide operations, administration, and maintenance (OAM) functions.

After subtracting the ESF framing bits, the remaining 1.536Mbps bandwidth is available for ATM cells. A steady flow of ATM cells is packed into the DS1 payload. A cell can start at any byte-aligned position relative to the DS1 framing. Cells wrap from one payload row to the next, as shown in Figure 4.3.

Figure 4.3   Dropping ATM cells into a DS1 payload.

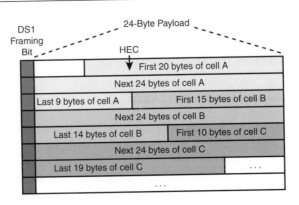

DS1 Cell Delineation

The receiver has to figure out where cells begin. Recall that the process of locating cell boundaries is called *cell delineation*.

The HEC field is used for determining cell boundaries. This method of cell delineation was described earlier in this chapter. Basically, the receiver has to find a series of candidate HEC fields whose values match checksums calculated on the previous four bytes.

DS1 Error Detection and Correction

Although the main function of the HEC field is to detect header errors, the HEC field also can be used to correct single-bit header errors for a DS1 interface.

DS1 Cell Rate Decoupling

The TC sublayer has to make sure that a steady stream of cells is transmitted. Hence, if the ATM layer has not provided a cell when one must be sent, the DS1 TC sublayer will inject an idle cell into the stream.

100Mbps Private Multimode Fiber Interface

The next interface we will examine—a private user-network interface over 100Mbps multimode fiber—is equally straightforward. This interface connects an ATM-enabled computer, bridge, or router to an ATM switch.

The lower sublayer physical components (the cable, connectors, and signal encoding) are borrowed from the components used for *Fiber Distributed Data Interface (FDDI)* LANs. Just as for an FDDI LAN interface, full duplex service is provided by two simplex (one-way) 62.5/125 multimode fiber links. Connections that are up to 2km long are supported.

Data is transmitted via a *4-bit/5-bit* (4B/5B) signal encoding that maps each 4-bit *nibble* (half-byte) into a 5-bit pattern. This encoding has two useful features:

- The 5-bit patterns used to represent four bits of data are chosen to reduce the likelihood of an undetected bit error.

- There are many unused patterns, and some of these can be used for control codes.

The technology is known as the *Transparent Asynchronous Transmitter/Receiver Interface (TAXI)*. The term "TAXI" is the name of an interface chip set that is a trademark of Advanced Micro Devices.

100Mbps Multimode Fiber Cell Delineation

Special 5-bit codes have been defined to represent an *idle (JK)* symbol and a *start of cell (TT)* symbol. These codes are

JK: 11000 10001

TT: 01101 01101

As a result, the implementation is extremely simple (as shown in Figure 4.4). Idle codes are placed on the line when there is no data to be sent. A cell can be placed on an idle line at any time by transmitting a start of cell TT code followed by the 53 cell bytes. Because the cell boundary is clearly marked, there is no need to use the HEC field for cell delineation.

Figure 4.4   Dropping cells onto a 100Mbps multimode fiber line.

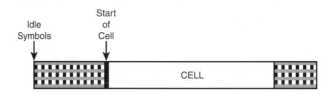

100Mbps Multimode Fiber Error Detection

Of course, the HEC field still is used for error detection. However, it cannot be used for single-bit header error correction because the process does not work with 4B/5B encoded data, because a single-bit line error in a transmitted 5-bit code can produce a pattern with no 4-bit equivalent or a 4-bit code with two errors.

Cell Rate Decoupling for 100Mbps Multimode Fiber

An ATM cell can be dropped onto the line at any time because it is announced by a symbol that says "Here it comes." Thus, no cell rate decoupling function is needed; it is not necessary to transmit a continuous stream of cells. An individual cell is sent as needed, and idle symbols fill the unused bandwidth. This is referred to as *asynchronous transmission*.

25.6Mbps Private Twisted-Pair Interface

The relatively slow 25.6Mbps interface is designed to operate over Category 3 (or better) unshielded twisted pair or on several types of shielded twisted pair. Its most likely use is to connect computers to a local ATM LAN switch. Connections of up to 100 meters are supported.

25.6Mbps Twisted-Pair Cell Delineation

Like the previous fiber interface, data is transmitted via a 4-bit/5-bit (4B/5B) signal encoding that maps each 4-bit nibble into a 5-bit pattern. A special command pattern is used to signal the start of a cell. Fill data is sent between cells.

25.6Mbps Twisted-Pair Error Detection

The HEC field is used for error detection. It is not used for single-bit error correction.

Cell Rate Decoupling for 25.6Mbps Twisted Pair

Just as for the 100Mbps multimode fiber interface described earlier, no cell rate decoupling function is needed because it is not necessary to transmit a continuous stream of cells.

DS3 Interfaces

A fairly complex DS3 format was defined early in the ATM standards process. It was a subset of the *Physical Layer Convergence Protocol (PLCP)* originally defined in IEEE 802.6.

Later, a far simpler direct mapping of cells into the DS3 payload was defined, and this became the preferred version. Both interfaces will be described in the sections that follow, but first we will briefly examine the underlying DS3 features both mappings share.

The physical medium for a DS3 interface consists of two coaxial cables. B3ZS line coding is used.

A DS3 interface operates at 44.736Mbps. There are several different DS3 physical framing formats. The C-Bit Parity Application format has been chosen to carry ATM cells. The format, which was described in chapter I-2, is shown in Figure 4.5.

To review briefly, as shown in the figure, the payload area is broken into 84-bit fields. Each 84-bit field is introduced by an overhead bit. A grouping called an M-Subframe is made up of eight of these 85-bit elements. Each of the overhead bits in an M-Subframe has a different title and function. An M-Subframe contains 680 bits.

Seven M-Subframes are concatenated to form a 4760-bit M-Frame. Note that the initial overhead bit in each M-Subframe has a different label. For example, the first M-Subframe in an M-Frame starts with an X1 bit, and the second M-Subframe starts with an X2 bit.

To summarize:

- The M and F bits are used for framing and alignment.

- Alarms, error indications, and parity checks are transmitted via the X and C bits.

Figure 4.5 DS3 C-bit Parity format.

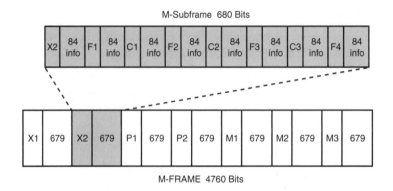

Optionally, the transmission convergence sublayer can perform cell scrambling for either DS3 interface.

Direct Mapped DS3 Interface

The cell mapping for the direct transmission convergence sublayer is as simple as the methods used in the two examples already described. A continuous stream of cells is dropped into the payload. The only restriction is that the cell stream must be aligned on a nibble boundary relative to the starting point of an 84-bit information field. That is, if the information bits are numbered from 0 to 83, a cell can start at bit 0, 4, 8, 16, ..., 76, or 80.

Because the flow of cells is continuous, some cells will start in one M-Frame and be completed in the next M-Frame. Using this mapping, the cell payload is transmitted at roughly 44.21Mbps.

Direct Mapped DS3 Cell Delineation

The HEC field is used for cell delineation.

Direct Mapped DS3 Error Detection

As usual, the TC sublayer generates and checks the HEC field. Error correction might be provided as an option.

Direct Mapped DS3 Cell Rate Decoupling

The implementer is free to use the ATM layer or the TC physical sublayer to perform cell rate decoupling. If the ATM layer executes this function, it inserts unassigned cells into the cell stream. If the physical layer performs the function, the TC sublayer inserts idle cells into the DS3 payload. Recall that incoming idle cells are not passed up to the ATM layer. Of course, unassigned cells, which belong to the ATM layer, are passed up.

PLCP-Based DS3 Interface

The more complex (and less preferred) PLCP-based interface wraps an additional layer of framing bytes around a cell payload. Keep in mind that the extra bytes that make up the PLCP wrapper are inside the DS3 payload.

The PLCP packaging enables 12 ATM cells to be transmitted each 125 microseconds. In other words, the bit rate for ATM cell transfer is

$$12 \times 53 \times 8 \text{ (bits per byte)} \times 8000 \text{ (per second)} = 40.70 \text{Mbps}$$

In contrast, the direct DS3 encapsulation provides a transmission rate of roughly 44.21Mbps.

PLCP-Based DS3 Format

A PLCP framed bundle can start anywhere within the DS3 payload, as long as it is nibble (4-bit) aligned with the DS3 payload. (That is, nibbles begin after a DS3 F, X, P, C, or M control bit.)

Figure 4.6 shows the format of a framed PLCP bundle. Each cell is introduced by two bytes, A1 and A2, that contain a framing pattern. A1 is X'F6 and A2 is X'28. Synchronizing on this pattern enables a receiver to determine where rows begin.

The *Path Overhead Identifier (POI)* bytes provide additional alignment, making it possible to identify the individual rows in the bundle. The POI patterns are shown in Table 4.1. Note that the patterns in each pair of adjacent rows differ in at least two positions.

Figure 4.6   Format of PLCP framed ATM cells in a DS3 payload.

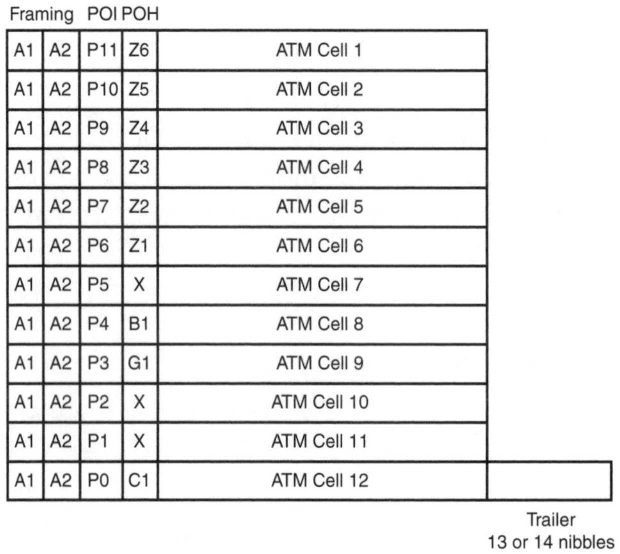

Framing POI POH

A1	A2	P11	Z6	ATM Cell 1
A1	A2	P10	Z5	ATM Cell 2
A1	A2	P9	Z4	ATM Cell 3
A1	A2	P8	Z3	ATM Cell 4
A1	A2	P7	Z2	ATM Cell 5
A1	A2	P6	Z1	ATM Cell 6
A1	A2	P5	X	ATM Cell 7
A1	A2	P4	B1	ATM Cell 8
A1	A2	P3	G1	ATM Cell 9
A1	A2	P2	X	ATM Cell 10
A1	A2	P1	X	ATM Cell 11
A1	A2	P0	C1	ATM Cell 12

Trailer
13 or 14 nibbles

Table 4.1   Path Overhead Identifier Codes

POI	POI Code
P11	0010 1100
P10	0010 1001
P9	0010 0101
P8	0010 0000
P7	0001 1100
P6	0001 1001
P5	0001 0101
P4	0001 0000
P3	0000 1101
P2	0000 1000
P1	0000 0100
P0	0000 0001

The Trailer and the C1 POH Byte

The nibbles in the trailer fill out the PLCP frame so that, on average, a PLCP frame is transmitted each 125 microseconds. The amount of fill varies across three PLCP frames. The first PLCP frame contains 13 nibbles, the second contains 14, and the third contains 13 or 14. The C1 Path Overhead byte identifies what is going on:

C1=X'FF flags the first frame in a series, which has a 13-nibble trailer.

C1=X'00 flags the second frame, which has a 14-nibble trailer.

C1=X'66 flags a third frame with a 13-nibble trailer.

C1=X'99 flags a third frame with a 14-nibble trailer.

The trailer repeats the nibble pattern 1100.

Other Path Overhead Bytes

The byte labeled B1 contains an even parity check byte. It is calculated over the bytes in the 12×54 array made up of the Path Overhead and ATM cells of the previous PLCP frame. The G1 byte contains subfields that report errors and alarms. The Z1–Z6 bytes are called *growth octets*. They are reserved for future use and currently are set to 0. The X fields are unassigned and are ignored by the receiver.

PLCP-Based DS3 Cell Delineation

The PLCP format enables the starting point of each ATM cell to be delineated correctly, so the HEC field is not used to determine where cells begin.

PLCP-Based DS3 Error Detection and Correction

The HEC field is, of course, still used for error detection and also must be used for single-bit error correction.

PLCP-Based Cell Rate Decoupling

The implementer is free to use the ATM layer or the TC physical sublayer to perform cell rate decoupling. If the ATM layer executes this function, it inserts unassigned cells into the cell stream. If the physical layer performs the function, the TC sublayer inserts idle cells into the DS3 payload.

SONET/STS-3c Public Fiber Optic Physical Interface

ATM was designed as the transport of choice for the new SONET/SDH digital communications hierarchy. Hence, the public interface encapsulation at 155.52Mbps is based on a Synchronous Transport Signal level 3 concatenated frame (STS-3c) format. Recall that an STS-3c signal is identical to an STM-1 signal, except for the use of some of the overhead bytes.

The use of STS-3c is defined for both public and private interfaces. For this framing, 2,430 bytes are transferred every 125 microseconds (that is, 8,000 times per second). Although the total bit rate is 155.52Mbps, 5.76Mbps is devoted to overhead, leaving 149.76Mbps for payload.

The STS-3c payload consists of a series of *synchronous payload envelopes (SPEs)*. As shown in Figure 4.7, each SPE is an array of bytes made up of nine rows and 261 columns. The first column contains path overhead bytes. The remaining 260 columns (2,340 bytes) contain user data.

Figure 4.7   An STS-3c synchronous payload envelope.

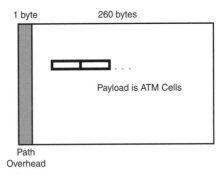

Cells in a Synchronous Payload Envelope

ATM cells are packed into the data portion of an SPE. The bytes are filled in across each row, wrapping onto the next row as needed. Cells start on a byte boundary but are not aligned with SPE boundaries. Note that 2,340 is not a multiple of 53, and the bytes of an initial or final ATM cell might be split across two SPEs.

Relationship of Transport Overhead to SPE

Figure 4.8 shows a more detailed layout, including the transport overhead block that is made up of section and line overhead bytes. Recall that the SPE is not aligned squarely with the transport overhead. It is chunked in starting from a convenient position indicated by a pointer in the line overhead area. A 261-byte row in the SPE wraps around, as shown in Figure 4.8.

Figure 4.8   Positioning the SPE within the payload area.

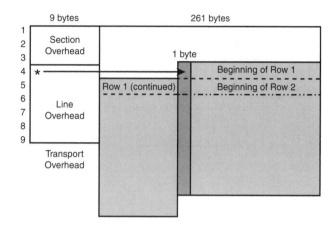

SONET/STS-3c Cell Delineation

The HEC field is used for cell delineation. A scrambling function is applied to each cell to avoid repeated bit patterns and improve the effectiveness of cell delineation. The receiver unscrambles incoming cells.

SONET/STS-3c Error Detection and Correction

The HEC field is used for error detection and optionally also can be used for single-bit error correction.

SONET/STS-3c Overhead Bytes and OAM

Figure 4.9 shows the transport and path overhead bytes used at the ATM user-network interface. Note that some of the bytes are repeated three times. The A1 and A2 bytes are used for overall frame alignment. H1 and H2 contain the pointer to the SPE. H3 can be used to carry an SPE byte when an adjustment is needed. The B1 and B2 bytes contain parity codes used to detect errors over a regenerator section or line.

J1 bytes carry a string that identifies the originator of the SPEs. Eight J1 bytes (from eight consecutive SPEs) are used for the identifier, which is repeated over and over.

The C2 byte in the path overhead column is set to X'13 to indicate that the payload contains ATM cells.

Other bytes are used to signal problems.

Figure 4.9   Transport and path overhead bytes used at the ATM STS-3c UNI.

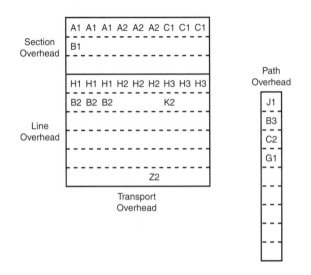

Private Twisted-Pair 155Mbps Interfaces

The ATM forum has defined private 155Mbps interfaces that connect computers, bridges, and routers to a private ATM switch. Physical media that can be used include

- Category 5 or category 3 unshielded twisted pair. Distances up to 100 meters are supported.

- 150 ohm shielded twisted-pair cable. Distances up to 100 meters are supported.

The transmission convergence sublayer for these interfaces is based on the SONET/ STS-3c TC sublayer. This makes it easy to interface a private switch with a public switch.

Data Exchange Interface

One of the attractive features of frame relay is that it is extremely easy for router and bridge vendors to turn their products into frame relay access devices. An ordinary serial interface can be enabled for frame relay via a straightforward software update that supports

- DLCIs for virtual circuits

- Encapsulating outgoing data in frame relay frames

- Processing incoming frames

- A standard local management interface

As shown in Figure 4.10, typically a cable connects a serial port on an access device to a telecommunications DSU/CSU that interfaces to a 56Kbps, 64Kbps, or T1 telecommunications line.

Figure 4.10   Serial router interface use for frame relay.

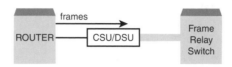

It makes very good sense for promoters of ATM to provide a frame-based interface for routers, bridges, switches, or hosts that also could be implemented via a simple software upgrade.

The *Data eXchange Interface (DXI)* serves this purpose. However, to make it work, a DSU/CSU must be replaced with a device that can exchange DXI frames with the router, while providing a UNI interface to an ATM switch. Such a device is called an *ATM DSU*. Figure 4.11 illustrates the role of an ATM DSU. The endpoint device is connected to the DXI DSU by a V.35, EIA/TIA 449/530, or HSSI physical interface.

Figure 4.11   ATM DSU relaying data to and from an ATM network.

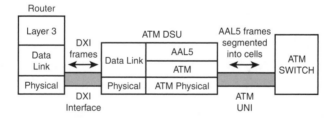

ATM DSU Modes of Operation

There are three operating modes for the Data eXchange Interface: mode 1a, mode 1b, and mode 2. Table 4.2 displays their characteristics. Recall that AAL5 and AAL3/4 are two different data link layers that have been defined for the ATM protocol stack. The frame formats used for AAL5 and AAL3/4 are different.

Table 4.2	DXI Modes
Mode	Properties
1a	AAL5 only AAL5 payload up to 9,232 bytes 2-byte DXI frame header 2-byte DXI frame check sequence Up to 1,023 virtual connections
1b	AAL5 supported AAL5 payload up to 9,232 bytes At least one AAL3/4 connection AAL3/4 payload up to 9,224 bytes 2-byte DXI frame header 2-byte DXI frame check sequence Up to 1,023 virtual connections
2	AAL5 and AAL3/4 supported Double encapsulation of AAL5 frames Payload up to 65,535 bytes 4-byte DXI frame header 4-byte DXI frame check sequence Up to 16,777,215 virtual connections

Mode 1 AAL5 Operation

AAL5 connections are handled in exactly the same way for mode 1a and mode 1b. Figure 4.12 illustrates how this works. For outgoing data,

- The endpoint device on the left (a router, in this case) bundles outgoing payload data into a DXI frame and transmits it to the ATM CSU/DSU.

- The ATM DSU strips off the DXI frame header and trailer and repackages the data in an AAL5 frame.

- The ATM DSU then segments the AAL5 frame into cells and transmits the cells across the user-network interface to an ATM switch.

For incoming data,

- The ATM switch transmits cells to the ATM DSU. The ATM DSU reassembles cells into AAL5 frames.

- The ATM DSU processes each AAL5 frame trailer and discards it.

- The DSU then packages each payload in a DXI frame and forwards the frame to the endpoint device.

Figure 4.12 Relaying AAL5 data across a DXI interface.

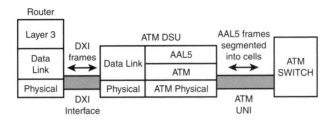

Mode 1b AAL3/4 Operation

Mode 1b can support AAL3/4 virtual circuits in addition to AAL5 virtual circuits. However, AAL3/4 frames are created at the source endpoint rather than at the ATM DSU. Figure 4.13 illustrates how this works. For outgoing data,

- The endpoint device bundles outgoing AAL3/4 frames within DXI frames and transmits them to the ATM CSU/DSU.

- The ATM DSU strips off the DXI frame header and trailer. It segments the enclosed AAL3/4 frame into cells and transmits the cells across the user-network interface to an ATM switch.

For incoming data,

- The ATM switch transmits cells to the ATM DSU. The ATM DSU reassembles cells into AAL3/4 frames.

- The ATM DSU packages each AAL3/4 frame within a DXI frame and forwards the frame to the endpoint device.

Figure 4.13 Relaying AAL3/4 data across a DXI interface.

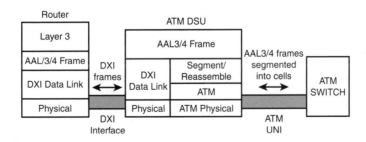

Mode 1 DXI Frames

Figure 4.14 shows the frame formats used for mode 1 DXI frames. Frames are delimited by HDLC flag bytes (X'7E), which are not shown. Recall that data for an AAL5 connection simply is encapsulated in a DXI header and trailer, while AAL3/4 frames are created at the source endpoint and are wrapped with a DXI frame header and trailer.

The maximum AAL3/4 payload size is 8 bytes less than the AAL5 size because of the extra 8 bytes of AAL3/4 header and trailer overhead.

Figure 4.14   Mode 1 DXI frame formats.

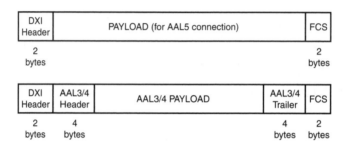

Mode 1 DXI Header

The source access device does not create cells, but it does have to tell the ATM DSU what it needs to know to convert a frame to cells—most notably, the VPI and VCI of the channel on which the frame should be transmitted. The DXI header carries this information.

Figure 4.15 displays the format of the 2-byte mode 1 DXI header. The header contains VPI and VCI values and flag bits used to announce discard eligibility for outgoing frames and report congestion for incoming frames. Two bits currently are unused and are set to 0. They are labeled as *reserve (RES) bits*.

The set of bits containing the VPI and VCI numbers is called the *DXI frame address*. An all-0s DXI frame address identifies a special channel used for communication between the endpoint system and the DXI DSU.

Figure 4.15   Mode 1 DXI header.

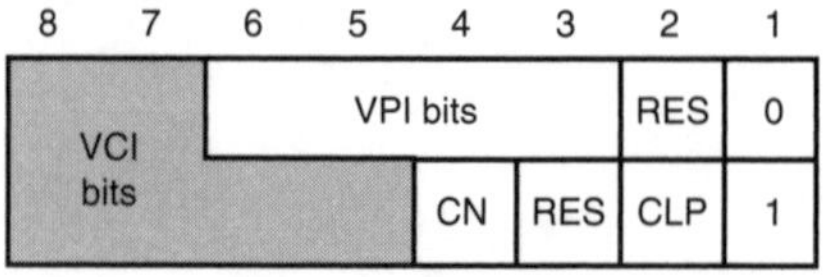

Note that the DXI frame address carries only four VPI bits and six VCI bits. The ATM DSU places these values into the low order (rightmost) bits of the VPI and VCI fields in the cell header, and fills in the rest of each field with zeros.

If the payload type field in the final cell of an incoming payload indicates that congestion was experienced, the DXI DSU sets the congestion notification (CN) flag to 1 in the DXI frame header before forwarding the frame to the endpoint device.

If the cell loss priority (CLP) flag is 1 in the header of a DXI frame sent by the endpoint device, the DXI DSU will set the cell loss priority flag to 1 in the cells produced by segmenting the frame.

Mode 2 DXI Frames

For mode 2, the endpoint device packages every payload into an AAL3/4 frame that then is placed inside a DXI frame. At the DXI DSU,

- If the data is to be sent on an AAL3/4 circuit, the enclosed AAL3/4 frame is appropriately segmented into cells and transmitted.

- If the data is to be sent on an AAL5 circuit, the enclosed AAL3/4 wrapper is removed, an AAL5 trailer is added to the data, and the AAL5 frame is segmented into cells and transmitted.

Mode 2 DXI Header and Trailer

As shown in Figure 4.16, the 4-byte mode 2 DXI header is large enough to include a full VPI/VCI address. There are eight bits that hold the VPI part and 16 bits that hold the VCI part.

Figure 4.16   Mode 2 DXI header.

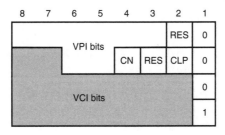

The mode 2 trailer also is larger and consists of a 4-byte frame check sequence field.

> **Note**
>
> Many vendors currently support the DXI interface. However, the Frame Relay Forum has published an improved and more functional frame-based user-network interface (FUNI). For example, the FUNI interface can send and receive operations, administration, and maintenance (OAM) information.

References

There is a sizable and growing list of ATM physical interface specifications. Check with the ATM Forum for the latest additions and updates.

- Physical Layer, issued as part of UNI 3.1 (1994).

- *Interface Specification for 155 Mb/s over Twisted Pair Cable*, Version 1.0 (1994).

- DS1 Physical Layer Specification Version 1.0 (1994).

- UTOPIA, *Universal Test & Operations PHY Interface for ATM* (1994).

- *Mid-range Physical Layer Specification for Category 3 Unshielded Twisted-Pair.* Version 1.0 (1994).

- *Physical Layer for 6,312Kbps Interface* (1995).

- *E3 Public UNI* (1995).

- *Utopia Level 2* (1995).

- *25.6 Mb/s over Twisted Pair Cable* (1995).

- *A Cell-Based Transmission Convergence Sublayer for Clear Channel Interfaces* (1995).

- *622.08Mbps Physical Layer Specification* (1996).

- *155.52Mb/s Physical Layer Specification for Category-3 Unshielded Twisted Pair* (1995).

- *Addendum to ATM Physical Medium Dependent Interface Specification for 155Mb/s Over Twisted Pair Cable* (1996).

- *DS3 Physical Layer Interface Specification* (1996).

- *155.52Mbps physical layer interface for short wavelength laser* (1996).

- *E1 Physical Interface Specification* (1996).

- *Inverse Multiplexing for ATM (IMA) Specification Version 1.0* (1997).

- *155Mbps Plastic Optical Fiber and Hard Polymer Clad Fiber PMD Specification* (1997).

- *Data Exchange Interface (DXI) Specification* (1993).

- *Frame-based User-to-Network Interface (FUNI) Specification V 2.0* (1997).

The ATM Adaptation Layer

The ATM adaptation layer provides data link layer services to a variety of upper-layer applications.

The designers of ATM wanted to support voice, video, and every type of data application. They realized that information would have to be packaged and handled differently, based on the requirements of various applications; for example:

- Ordinary data communications applications, such as LAN-to-LAN data transfer.

- Circuit Emulation Services that carry DS1 or E1 trunks across an ATM network. This service enables conventional network equipment to interwork with an ATM service network.

Few, if any, organizations would be willing to throw away all their current communications infrastructure and convert to ATM overnight. ATM needs to interwork with existing data communications technologies, such as frame relay and SMDS, and with traditional voice communications networks. In addition to supporting pure ATM service, the ATM adaptation layer also provides the foundation on which interworking functions (IWFs) are built.

ATM Adaptation Layer Protocols

The different needs of data, voice, and video applications have been accommodated by creating several distinct standard ATM Adaptation Layer (AAL) protocols:

- *ATM Adaptation Layer 5 (AAL5)*, also called the *Simple and Efficient Adaptation Layer (SEAL)*, is suitable for most data transfer applications. AAL5 was designed by the ATM Forum and subsequently adopted by the ITU-T.

- ITU-T groups worked on two other data transfer AALs. *ATM Adaptation Layer 3 (AAL3)* was targeted at connection-oriented data transfer, while *ATM Adaptation Layer 4 (AAL4)* was aimed at connectionless service. Both AAL3 and AAL4 borrowed formats and features from an existing data service as their model, namely the Bellcore Switched Multi-megabit Data Service (SMDS). The results were merged into a single AAL3/4. AAL3/4 is rarely used.

- *ATM Adaption Layer 2 (AAL2)* recently was redesigned, and enables voice to be carried over ATM efficiently.

- *ATM Adaptation Layer 1 (AAL1)* was designed to support applications that require a constant bit rate, such as DS1, E1, or fractional Nx64Kbps circuit emulation.

In addition, the ATM marketplace has added *ATM Adaptation Layer 0 (AAL0)*—which means none of the above! AAL0 currently is being used to simply load payload data into cells and deliver it without any additional processing.

An ATM circuit can be associated with only one type of ATM adaptation layer. The choice of AAL5, AAL3/4, or AAL1 (or AAL0) is established when a circuit is set up.

Figure 5.1 shows the relationship of the ATM adaptation layer to the ATM layer and the ATM physical layer. As shown in the figure, the ATM adaptation layer is broken into two sublayers:

- The *segmentation and reassembly (SAR) sublayer* stuffs payloads into cells at the sending end and extracts them at the receiving end.

- The *convergence sublayer* does anything else that needs to be done.

Figure 5.1   ATM adaptation layer and other ATM layers.

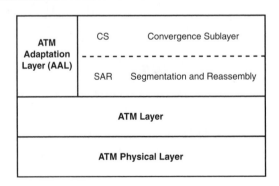

These definitions are vague because the processing is different for each AAL type. A better understanding is gained by looking at the sublayer activities for a specific ATM adaptation layer: AAL5. In this case

- The convergence sublayer packages outgoing data into AAL5 frames and processes incoming AAL5 frames.

- The SAR sublayer slices outgoing AAL5 frames into cell payloads and reassembles incoming cell payloads into AAL5 frames.

Figure 5.2 illustrates the processing of outgoing frames.

Figure 5.2   AAL5 sublayer functions.

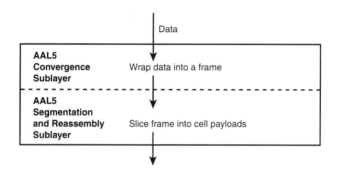

For each type of AAL, there are some special uses that require additional processing by the convergence sublayer. This is represented by a subdivision of the convergence sublayer, as shown in Figure 5.3. Functions common to all applications are carried out in the *common part convergence sublayer (CPCS)*. Special processing is carried out in the *service specific convergence sublayer (SSCS)*.

Note

In the world of ATM, no opportunity to define a new acronym ever is ignored.

Figure 5.3   Components of the convergence sublayer.

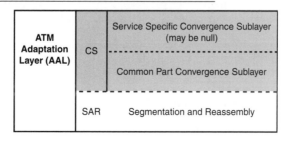

We'll start our discussion of the ATM adaptation layers by studying AAL5, which is the simplest of the standard AALs.

AAL5 Applications

ATM adaptation layer 5 is a workhorse that hauls data across ATM circuits. AAL5 is used to carry data between LANs and to connect remote sites to a mainframe. AAL5 was chosen as the vehicle for ATM LAN Emulation, which enables a user to design virtual LANs that include both ATM systems and systems connected to conventional LAN segments. AAL5 also has been chosen for some of the special jobs that need to be done within the network: carrying signaling messages and sharing network topology information.

To provide some of its services, AAL5 needs to be customized by adding extra functions to its convergence sublayer. But only the most elementary AAL5 components are needed in order to carry user data. The discussion of AAL5 starts with a description of the basic AAL5 data transfer service. The enhancements added when AAL5 carries signaling messages are described a little later.

Basic AAL5 Protocol

The basic AAL5 protocol packages data into a frame, chops the frame into pieces, and passes the pieces to the ATM layer. The AAL layer identifies the circuit on which the pieces should be transmitted.

Like frame relay frames, AAL5 frames are delivered on a best-effort basis. The AAL5 frame trailer contains a *Cyclic Redundancy Check (CRC)* code that is used to detect if the frame has been corrupted. A frame that has been corrupted is discarded.

AAL5 Frame Format

An AAL5 layer frame carries up to 65,535 bytes of data. A frame must be padded to a multiple of 48 bytes long so it can be evenly segmented into cell payloads.

The AAL5 frame format is shown in Figure 5.4. The frame is made up of data, a pad field (if needed), and a trailer. Unlike frames for LAN or frame relay communications, AAL5 frames have no header. No frame address is needed for ATM. Instead, the ATM adaptation layer identifies the virtual circuit on which the segments of the frame should be transmitted, and the ATM layer places the corresponding VPI/VCI number in the header of each cell.

The VPI/VCI value is preconfigured for a PVC. For an SVC, the VPI/VCI is established by call setup messages.

However, without a header, one field that might be useful is missing—namely, an identifier for the protocol being carried. When a protocol identification field is needed, it has to be placed at the beginning of the user data.

Figure 5.4	Format of an AAL5 frame.

Payload (Up to 65,535 bytes)	Pad 0-47 bytes	Trailer 8 bytes

AAL5 Trailer

As shown in Figure 5.5, an AAL5 trailer contains

- A 32-bit CRC, used to check that the frame has not been corrupted

- The length of the actual payload so pad bytes can be discarded

- A common part indicator (CPI) byte, currently used only to align the trailer on an 8-byte boundary

- A user-to-user (UU) byte that is available to special AAL5 applications or to higher layers

Figure 5.5	AAL5 trailer.

UU 1 byte	CPI 1 byte	Payload Length 2 bytes	CRC 4 bytes

Basic AAL5 Protocol Processing

Basic AAL5 protocol processing is straightforward. For outgoing data, the convergence sublayer

- Accepts higher-layer data for transmission

- Adds a pad at the end of the payload if the length of the payload field plus the 8-byte trailer is not a multiple of 48

- Adds the trailer and fills in the length, CPI, and UU bytes

- Computes the CRC on the rest of the frame and writes it into the CRC field

Then the SAR sublayer slices the AAL5 frame into 48-byte payloads and passes these to the ATM layer. Figure 5.6 shows how an AAL5 frame is segmented into cells.

Figure 5.6   Segmenting an AAL5 frame into cells.

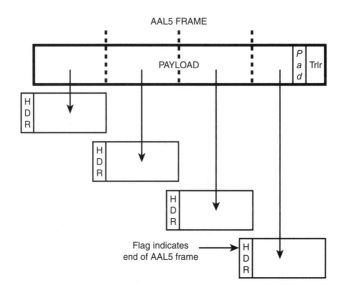

The last flag bit in the payload type field in each cell header now plays an important role. This *ATM-user-to-ATM-user bit* is set equal to 0 in each cell for a frame except for the last, when it is set to 1.

This bit makes it easy for a receiver to detect the end of a frame. It also makes it easy for a network switch to discard cells up to the end of the frame after one of the cells in the frame has been corrupted.

> ### Note
>
> The cells that make up a frame are sent across its channel in order. Cells for the next AAL5 frame waiting to be sent on the channel cannot be dispatched until the current frame has been completely transmitted. However, cells making up the frame are interleaved onto the physical link with cells for other channels.

For incoming data, the SAR sublayer concatenates cell payloads into a frame, using the ATM-user-to-ATM-user bit to recognize the end of the frame. The CRC is checked, and the length field is used to discard any pad bytes. The result is passed to a higher layer.

AAL5 Frames and Signaling

So far, the discussion has focused on the use of AAL5 to carry user data; however, AAL5 frames also are used to carry signaling information.

The special circuit with VPI=0 and VCI=5 is reserved for user-network signaling. The signaling channel is special. Because signaling messages are important, a special service-specific capability is added to the ATM adaptation layer that causes lost or corrupted frames to be retransmitted.

Service-specific enhancements to AAL5 are implemented by adding extra processing to the AAL convergence sublayer.

The enhanced AAL5 service that is used for signaling is called (appropriately) the *signaling AAL* or *SAAL.* Chapter III-7 contains further details.

AAL5 and Connectionless Service

AAL5 frames always are carried across ATM connections. However, the ATM Forum has defined how special servers can be used along with AAL5 circuit communications to create a virtual LAN that emulates connectionless service. The protocol is called *ATM LAN Emulation (LANE).*

AAL 3/4 Applications

ATM adaptation layer 3/4 (AAL3/4) was designed to be used for ordinary ATM connection-oriented data transfer or as part of a connectionless service. AAL3/4 is not used much today.

AAL3/4 frames are carried over connection-oriented ATM channels, and the standard form of AAL3/4 provides only connection-oriented service. Therefore, when AAL3/4 is used for connectionless service across an ATM network, special servers must be provided within the network in order to emulate connectionless behavior.

Two service modes are defined for AAL3/4:

- **Message mode**—An AAL3/4 frame payload contains a single ordinary service data unit.

- **Streaming mode**—An AAL3/4 payload can be made up of a sequence of smaller service data units. The format and handling rules for these subunits are application-specific endpoint issues, not ATM network issues.

AAL3/4 Frame Format

Like an AAL5 frame, an AAL3/4 frame can carry up to 65,535 bytes of payload data. The frame length must be a multiple of 4 bytes. As shown in Figure 5.7, an AAL3/4 frame is made up of a header, payload data, a pad field (if needed), and a trailer.

Figure 5.7   Format of an AAL3/4 frame.

CPI 1	BTAG 1	BASize 2	Payload (Up to 65,535 bytes)	*PAD* *0-3*	AL 1	Etag 1	Length 2

The fields in the frame are

- **CPI**—Common part indicator (1 byte)
  Indicates the counting units in which the buffer size (BASize) in the header and length in the trailer are counted. Currently sizes are given in bytes, which is indicated by CPI=X'00.

- **BTAG**—Beginning tag (1 byte)
  A numeric identifier that also is placed in the frame trailer, in the ETAG field. After segmentation and reassembly, the fact that these values match is used as a check that reassembly has been carried out correctly. The identifier is a counter that is incremented for each new frame that is prepared.

- **BASize**—Buffer allocation size (2 bytes)
  For ordinary message mode, this is just the length of the payload. (For streaming mode, the complete length might not be known at the time the frame header is being constructed. In this case, the buffer size is set to a value that will be at least the size of the payload.)

- **PAD**—Padding (0–3 bytes)
  Extra pad bytes are added if the length of the payload is not a multiple of 4.

- **AL**—Trailer alignment (1 byte)
  This byte is present to increase the trailer length to 4 bytes.

- **ETAG**—End tag (1 byte)
  The ETAG identifier has the same value as the BTAG for the frame.

- **Length**—(2 bytes)
  This field states the length of the payload in the selected units (bits or bytes). Once the length is known, pad bytes can be removed.

Note that something you might expect to see is not included in the trailer—namely, a CRC code.

Something else about this frame is mysterious. After an AAL3/4 frame has been sliced into cells and transmitted to a receiver, the receiver needs some way of knowing which cell contains the last part of an AAL3/4 frame. Unlike AAL5, the last bit in the cell payload type field is not used for this purpose. Because for streaming mode, the BASize in the header may be larger than the true length of an AAL3/4 frame, the BASize is not always a reliable way to identify the end of the frame.

To solve these riddles, we will have to examine the format of the cells that carry an AAL3/4 frame.

AAL3/4 SAR-PDU

An AAL3/4 frame gets sliced into 44-byte cell payloads instead of 48-byte cell payloads. The remaining 4 bytes are used to form a 2-byte header and 2-byte trailer that are wrapped around the 44 bytes. The result, which is shown in Figure 5.8, is called a *segmentation and reassembly protocol data unit*, or *SAR-PDU*.

Figure 5.8   An AAL3/4 SAR-PDU.

The fields in the SAR-PDU header are

- **ST**—Segment type (2 bits)
  The bit pattern identifies if this is the beginning of a message (BOM=10), continuation of a message (COM=00), end of a message (EOM=01), or an entire, single segment message (SSM=11).

- **SN**—Sequence number (4 bits)
  This counter is incremented for each segment of the frame and provides a check that all pieces are present.

- **MID**—Multiplex identification (10 bits)
  The multiplex identification counter is incremented for each AAL3/4 frame that is sent. The same multiplex identification number appears within every cell that holds part of the frame.

The segment type code provides a clear indication of where each frame begins and ends. The sequence number provides assurance that pieces of the frame are not missing.

The use of a multiplex identification field gives AAL3/4 a capability that AAL5 does not have. When an endpoint sends an AAL5 frame, no other data can be sent out on the *same* circuit until transmission of the original frame is complete. In contrast, several AAL3/4 frames can be interleaved on the same circuit. A receiver uses the multiplex identification number to sort out incoming SAR-PDUs and to reassemble several AAL3/4 frames arriving on a single circuit at the same time.

The fields in the AAL3/4 SAR-PDU trailer are

- **LI**—Length indicator (6 bits)
  Indicates the number of data bytes in the SAR-PDU payload. This is 44 for the beginning or continuation of a message, but may be less than 44 for an end of message cell or a single segment message.

- **CRC**—Cyclic redundancy check (10 bits)
  The CRC is computed against the rest of the AAL3/4 SAR-PDU. This solves the mystery of the lack of a CRC in the frame trailer. Separate CRCs are calculated on each segment of the frame.

AAL3/4 SAR-PDU Trace

Listing 5.1 was obtained by a Network Associates "Sniffer" network monitor. It consists of an AAL3/4 frame that has been broken into three pieces. Each piece is carried inside an AAL3/4 SAR-PDU. The trace shows the three SAR-PDUs, numbered 0, 1, and 2. Note that each SAR-PDU has its own CRC.

The first SAR-PDU is identified as the beginning of a message (BOM=10), the second is a continuation (COM=00), and the third is the end of the message (EOM=01).

Fields from the AAL3/4 frame header are displayed after the SAR PDU header in the first cell. The common part indicator is 0, meaning lengths are measured in bytes, and the begin tag is 1.

The buffer allocation size indicates that the AAL3/4 frame carries a 120-byte payload. Because 120 is a multiple of 4, no pad bytes need to be added to the end of the AAL3/4 payload. An AAL3/4 frame has a 4-byte header and a 4-byte trailer, so a total of 128 bytes need to be packed into the SAR-PDUs.

The first two SAR-PDUs each contain 44 bytes of the AAL3/4 frame. This leaves 40 bytes for the final SAR-PDU. The extra 4 bytes of space in the final SAR-PDU are filled with X'00 bytes.

Listing 5.1   An AAL3/4 Frame Divided into Three SAR-PDUs

```
Network Associates Sniffer Trace
- - - - - - - - - - - - - - - 1 - - - - - - - - - - - - - - -
AAL3/4: BOM seq#=0
AAL3/4: ----- AAL3/4 -----
      AAL3/4:
      AAL3/4: Segment Type      = 10.. ....(BOM)
      AAL3/4: Sequence Number   = ..00 00..(0)
      AAL3/4: Multiplex ID      = 1
      AAL3/4: CPI               = 0
      AAL3/4: Begin Tag         = 1
      AAL3/4: Buffer Allocation size = 120
      AAL3/4: Length Indicator  = 44
      AAL3/4: CRC               = 26C(correct)
      AAL3/4:

- - - - - - - - - - - - - - - 2 - - - - - - - - - - - - - - -
AAL3/4: COM seq#=1
AAL3/4: ----- AAL3/4 -----
      AAL3/4:
      AAL3/4: Segment Type      = 00.. ....(COM)
      AAL3/4: Sequence Number   = ..00 01..(1)
      AAL3/4: Multiplex ID      = 1
      AAL3/4: Length Indicator  = 44
      AAL3/4: CRC               = 097(correct)
      AAL3/4:

- - - - - - - - - - - - - - - 3 - - - - - - - - - - - - - - -
AAL3/4: EOM seq#=2
AAL3/4: ----- AAL3/4 -----
      AAL3/4:
      AAL3/4: Segment Type      = 01.. ....(EOM)
      AAL3/4: Sequence Number   = ..00 10..(2)
      AAL3/4: Multiplex ID      = 1
      AAL3/4: Length Indicator  = 40
      AAL3/4: CRC               = 2AE(correct)
      AAL3/4:
```

Figure 5.9 illustrates how the AAL3/4 frame is broken into SAR-PDUs.

Figure 5.9 Segmenting an AAL3/4 frame.

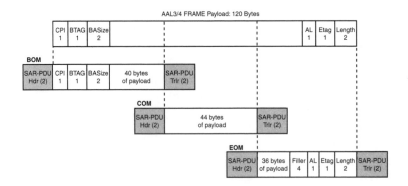

AAL3/4 SAR-PDU Inefficiency

Note that AAL3/4 is far less efficient than AAL5. An extra 4 bytes of overhead are added to each cell. Between them, the ATM cell header and SAR-PDU header and trailer add up to a throughput overhead that tops 20 percent. Creating and interpreting SAR-PDU headers and trailers—and computing a CRC for the SAR-PDU inside every cell—add a big processing burden.

AAL3/4 also makes it harder for a switch to implement a smart discard strategy at a congested switch. Recall that smart discard will either

- Throw away the remainder of a frame if a cell needs to be discarded. (This is called *partial* packet discard.)

- Deliver the remainder of the current frame but discard the entire next frame. (This is called *early* packet discard.)

The AAL3/4 SAR-PDU segment type and multiplex identification fields must be examined to locate cells that belong to a frame being discarded.

AAL3/4 was designed to be as compatible as possible with the already deployed *Switched Multi-megabit Data Service (SMDS)*. SMDS technology and its relation to AAL3/4 are discussed in the next sections.

SMDS

SMDS is a wide area service designed to support high-speed connectionless data transfer between sites. An SMDS provider can create a wide area virtual LAN operating at local LAN speeds and integrate it with a customer's enterprise network. Customers typically connect to an SMDS provider at access speeds ranging from 56Kbps to 34Mbps.

SMDS header overhead is the same as AAL3/4 header overhead. The result is that, at most, 1.2Mbps of payload throughput is available across a T1 access line, and at most 34Mbps is supported across a T3 access line.

Figure 5.10 shows how an SMDS service appears to a customer. Four routers and two servers are connected to a network that behaves like a high-speed backbone LAN. This configuration can support high-speed LAN-to-LAN connectivity as well as high-speed remote access to servers.

A system attached to the SMDS virtual LAN can send frames directly to other systems attached to the SMDS virtual LAN. An SMDS virtual LAN also supports the multicast and broadcast capabilities that are characteristic of real LANs. The user-network interface between subscriber equipment and an SMDS network is called the *subscriber-network interface (SNI).*

Figure 5.10   An SMDS virtual LAN.

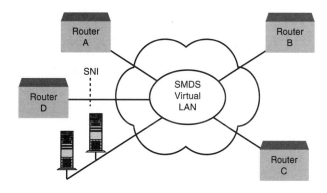

SMDS Subscriber-Network Interface Protocol

The SMDS subscriber-network access protocol is very different from the ATM user network interface. Several devices can share a common bus that connects a site to an SMDS provider network. For example, the two servers in Figure 5.10 share a high-speed bus connection to the SMDS network.

The official access protocol used at the interface is based on the IEEE 802.6 *Distributed Queue Dual Bus (DQDB)* protocol. This protocol prevents two systems from sending at the same time and guarantees that each system gets its fair share of the bandwidth. In reality, usually a single access device connects a site to an SMDS service network via an ordinary serial line, and the Distributed Queue Dual Bus protocol is not used.

There are striking (and not accidental) similarities between the data formats used for SMDS and AAL3/4. Like AAL3/4 frames, SMDS frames are segmented into cells before being sent across the subscriber-network interface. Each cell has a 5-byte header and a 48-byte payload.

AAL3/4 frame and cell formats were designed to be compatible with Switched Multimegabit Data Service (SMDS) frames and cells, but they are not identical. In the sections that follow, SMDS data formats are described and compared with AAL3/4 formats.

SMDS Frame Format

An SMDS frame is called an *SMDS Interface Protocol Level 3 Protocol Data Unit (SIP Level 3 PDU)*. As shown in Figure 5.11, an SMDS frame consists of a hefty 36-byte header, a payload of up to 9,188 bytes, padding, an optional CRC, and a 4-byte trailer.

Figure 5.11   Format of an SMDS frame.

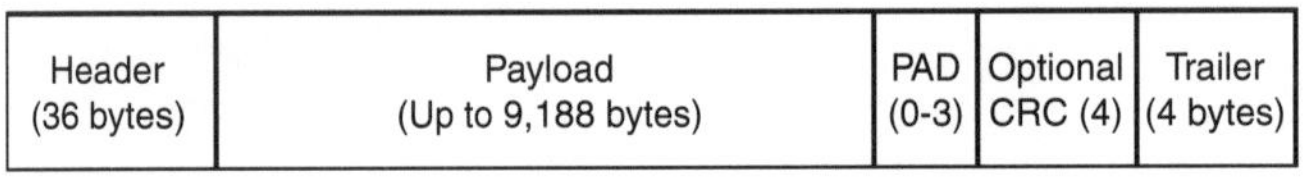

Header (36 bytes)	Payload (Up to 9,188 bytes)	PAD (0-3)	Optional CRC (4)	Trailer (4 bytes)

The PAD field is used to align the payload on a 4-byte boundary. The most important header and trailer fields are cited here:

- Like the AAL3/4 frame, the header contains beginning tag and buffer allocation size fields.

- The header also contains 8-byte global source and destination addresses. The SMDS numbering plan is based on the E.164 format.

- The trailer contains an end tag that equals the beginning tag.

- The trailer contains a length field whose value is equal to the buffer allocation size.

SMDS Addresses

The most notable difference between SMDS and AAL3/4 is that 8-byte source and destination addresses are included in an SMDS header. SMDS is a connectionless service, and a frame is directed to its destination based on its destination address.

As noted earlier, addresses follow the ITU-T E.164 format. In addition to unique destination addresses, a subscriber can set up group addresses that are used for multicasting. The first four bits of an address indicate if it is an individual or group address.

SMDS Subscriber-Network Cell Format

An SMDS frame is broken into cell payloads before being transported across the user network interface. An SMDS user-network cell is called a *SIP Level 2 PDU*. As shown in Figure 5.12, there are many similarities between a cell containing an AAL3/4 SAR-PDU and the SIP Level 2 PDU.

Figure 5.12   SIP Level 2 Protocol Data Unit.

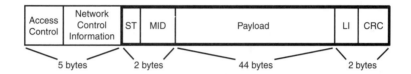

The first five bytes, which occupy the position of the cell header, contain access control and network control fields. These fields indicate if the cell contains data and flags used by the IEEE 802.6 DQDB SMDS access protocol.

The remaining 48 bytes contain

- **ST**—Segment type (2 bits)
  The bit pattern identifies if this is the beginning of a message (BOM), continuation of a message (COM), end of a message (EOM), or an entire, single segment message (SSM).

- **MID**—Message identifier (14 bits)
  The message identifier counter is incremented for each SMDS frame that is sent.

- **Payload:** (44 bytes)

- **LI**: Length indicator (6 bits)
  Enables the receiver to determine the number of payload bytes carried in the frame's final cell.

- **CRC**: Cyclic Redundancy Check (10 bits)

There only are small differences between the format of these 48 bytes and the format of the ATM SAR-PDU. For SMDS, there is no sequence number field, and the message ID occupies 14 bits instead of the 10 bits used for the AAL3/4 multiplex identification.

Message Identifiers: SMDS Versus AAL3/4

The role of the SMDS message identifier is somewhat different from the role of the AAL3/4 multiplex identification. For AAL3/4

- There is one endpoint device.

- The AAL3/4 multiplex identification enables cells for several frames sent by one endpoint device to be interleaved across a single virtual circuit.

The system at the remote end of the circuit uses the multiplex identification numbers to sort cells arriving on the same circuit into several distinct frames.

For SMDS, there is no concept of a virtual circuit at the SMDS subscriber-network interface. For SMDS,

- Several endpoint devices can share a logical bus connecting to the network. Each must use different message IDs for its frames.

- The SMDS message ID enables cells for frames sent by different devices to be interleaved across the subscriber-network interface.

Note that no addressing information is included in the SMDS cell header bytes. The destination address for the frame is located in the payload data of the first cell in a frame.

How are cells routed? That is up to the vendor of SMDS equipment. Because the first five bytes of the SIP Level 2 cell contain no useful information after the cell has reached the SMDS network, this area can be used for addressing information inside an SMDS network.

One option is shown in Figure 5.13. In the figure, an ATM network provides the SMDS service. There are virtual circuits between each switch that serves a particular customer and a central server. At a switch, SMDS cells are reformatted into AAL3/4 cells and sent to the server, which reads the SMDS destination address within each frame and forwards the cells to the appropriate destination switch. This is an example of an interworking function—in this case, enabling SMDS and ATM environments to connect and cooperate.

It is possible that two SMDS frames arriving at the destination site on different circuits might have the same message IDs. Message IDs for incoming frames need to be remapped so every frame interleaved across the bus to the customer site has a different MID.

Figure 5.13   SMDS service across an ATM network.

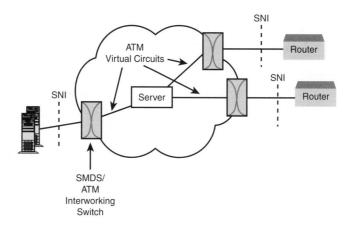

AAL1 and Circuit Emulation Service

ATM Adaptation Layer 1 (AAL1) is very different from AAL5 and AAL3/4. It is designed to carry time-sensitive, constant bit-rate traffic. Specifically, AAL1 is used to emulate conventional telecommunication circuits.

The ATM Forum has specified how AAL1 circuits can be used to emulate T1, E1, and fractional T1 or E1 services. Figure 5.14 illustrates how this might be used.

Figure 5.14   Using ATM to integrate services.

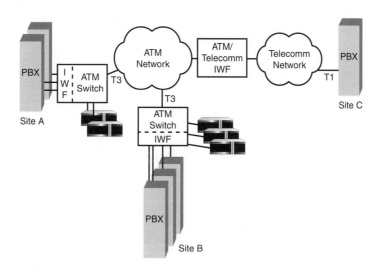

Many organizations have multiple T1, E1, or fractional T1/E1 lines connecting routers, PBXs, and other network equipment to a telecommunications network. In Figure 5.14, a subscriber has replaced many separate lines at two sites with ATM switches connected to T3 access lines. Because of its current high-bandwidth usage, the subscriber actually has been able to reduce its monthly bills while obtaining extra bandwidth in this arrangement.

The ATM switches at Sites A and B support an interworking function (IWF) that emulates an ordinary telecommunications network for its connection to the equipment—for example, providing a timing signal to conventional PBX units and CSU/DSU interface units.

The provider's ATM network is connected to a conventional telecommunications network by a device that supports ATM/telecommunications interworking. Users at Sites A and B can place and receive telephone calls across the global telephone network.

By connecting Sites A and B to an ATM network, the subscriber gains great flexibility in managing its bandwidth. For example, it is not necessary to install another access line if an additional wide area router needs to be installed. Bandwidth is assigned to a new permanent virtual circuit via a simple configuration operation. Temporary bandwidth needs can be satisfied via switched virtual circuits.

Site C in Figure 5.14 does not have sufficient bandwidth needs to justify a change of service. It has just one PBX, currently attached to a conventional telecommunications network. However, that network interfaces to the ATM network used by the other sites. The interworking function enables the PBX switch at Site C to communicate with the PBX switches at Sites A and B.

It is up to AAL1 to carry PBX traffic—or other traffic that requires a constant bit-rate circuit—across the ATM network in a manner that does not perturb the operation of the customer's conventional equipment. ATM *Circuit Emulation Service (CES)* provides the mechanisms to do this.

CES provides two types of service:

- Nx64Kbps (Fractional DS1/E1) Structured Data Transfer (SDT) Service
- DS1/E1 (1.544Mbps, 2.048Mbps) Unstructured Data Transfer (UDT) Service

AAL1 Cell Format

An AAL1 cell contains an AAL1 *segmentation and reassembly protocol data unit (SAR-PDU)* consisting of a 1-byte header and 47 bytes of data. The header contains a sequence number that enables the SAR sublayer to detect lost or misinserted cells.

Missing cells perturb the flow of bits across an emulated constant bit-rate circuit. The strategy used to fix this is to insert 1-bits in place of the missing cell data.

The format of the SAR-PDU is shown in Figure 5.15. The 5-byte ATM cell header that precedes a SAR-PDU is not shown in the figure. The only special feature of an AAL1 cell header is that its payload type field always is 000.

Figure 5.15   Format of an AAL1 SAR-PDU.

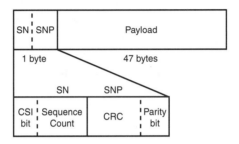

The 1-byte SAR-PDU header has two fields: a 4-bit sequence number (SN) field and a 4-bit sequence number protection field.

The sequence number field is made up of

- **CSI**—Convergence sublayer indication flag (1 bit)
  This flag is used differently depending on the specific service. Its roles for Nx64 and DS1/E1 are described later.

- **Sequence count field** (3 bits)
  The receiving AAL SAR sublayer uses the sequence count to detect lost or misinserted cells. The sequence numbers range from 0 to 7 and then wrap around to 0.

The sequence number protection (SNP) field lives up to its title. It is made up of

- A 3-bit CRC code computed on the previous 4-bit sequence number protection field

- A 1-bit even parity check computed on the preceding 7 bits

The receiver uses the CRC and the parity bit to detect whether the sequence number field has been corrupted and to perform the correction of a single-bit error.

> **Note**
>
> A receiver is not allowed to correct errors in consecutive cells. Specifically, the receiver starts out in *correction* mode. If a header with a single-bit error is received, it will be corrected. However, the receiver switches to *detection* mode after receiving a header with any error. Errors cannot be corrected until a header that is error free is received and the receiver is again placed in correction mode.

The sections that follow describe some of the ways that an AAL1 SAR-PDU carries constant bit-rate traffic. The main ideas are sketched. For details, see ITU-T I.363 and the ATM Forum document entitled *Circuit Emulation Service Interoperability Specification*.

Nx64Kbps Structured Data Transfer Service

The Nx64 Structured Data Transfer (SDT) service can carry up to twenty-four 64Kbps circuit timeslots for DS1, and up to thirty-one 64Kbps circuit timeslots for E1. There are two types of SDT service:

- Basic service

- Channel Associated Signaling (CAS) service, when DS1 robbed-bit signaling or E1 channel-associated signaling information is included

Nx64 SDT Basic Service

The data flow for the basic Nx64Kbps SDT service consists of repeating blocks of N bytes:

> Byte for circuit 1
>
> Byte for circuit 2
>
> . . .
>
> Byte for circuit N

Cell payload areas can simply be packed with these blocks of bytes.

If N is bigger than 1, some help is needed to keep track of where blocks begin. To do this, a byte in some cells is sacrificed to insert a pointer that indicates a start of block. A *pointer byte* is present if the CSI bit = 1. It can be placed only in an even-numbered cell (0, 2, 4, or 6). Figure 5.16 shows the format of an AAL1 payload containing a pointer byte. The pointer byte consists of one (currently) reserved bit followed by 7 bits containing the pointer value.

Figure 5.16 AAL1 SAR-PDU containing a pointer byte.

| SN | SNP | Pointer value 7 bits | Payload |
| 1 byte | | 1 byte | 46 bytes |

The pointer can indicate that a block starts in the payload of the current cell or of the cell that follows. Some sample pointer values and their meanings are

- **0**—The block starts right after the pointer.

- **12**—The block starts at the 13th byte after the pointer.

- **46**—The block starts at the first byte in the subsequent cell. Recall that there are only 46 payload bytes in the cell containing the pointer.

- **92**—The block starts at the last byte in the second cell.

- **93**—A special case. It means that the position 46+47 bytes away is the end of a structured block that did not start within the 93 bytes carried by this cell and the next.

Values larger than 93 are not allowed.

The AAL1 convergence sublayer carries out the job of creating and processing pointers.

Using Partially Filled Cells

Requiring cells to be full can cause delay. For example, if N = 2, only two time slots are being selected out of a T1 or E1 flow, and there would be a noticeable delay before a cell could be filled and forwarded.

For this reason, partially filled cells can optionally be used. The same number of data bytes must be placed in every cell. The number of bytes to be filled is preconfigured for PVCs or established during call setup for SVCs.

Just as for completely filled cells, a pointer can be used to identify the start of a block for partially filled cells.

Nx64 SDT CAS Service

A different packing format is used when *channel associated signaling (CAS)* is used with fractional DS1 or E1 circuits.

The block size used in this case is based on DS1 or E1 telephony multiframes. It consists of two portions. The first part of a block holds payload bytes, and the second holds signaling bits.

For a DS1 *Extended Superframe Format (ESF)*, the data portion consists of 24xN bytes. For Nx64 E1 using G.704 framing, the data portion consists of 16xN bytes.

The signaling part holds four signaling bits for each of the N circuits that is carried. If N is odd, the last 4 bits are filled with 0s to end this part on a byte boundary.

DS1 and E1 Unstructured Data Transfer Service

A DS1 or E1 circuit is carried across an ATM network using the AAL1 Unstructured Data Transfer service. For this service, bits from a 1.544Mbps DS1 or 2.048Mbps for E1 stream simply are packed into 47-byte payloads of an AAL1 cell. There is no attempt to align the signal with cell payload boundaries.

The loss of a cell is detected during reassembly of the stream via the AAL1 sequence number. The missing 47 bytes are replaced with 47 bytes consisting of 1 bit.

Timing

One of the issues that arises for circuit emulation service is the maintenance of timing at both ends of an AAL1 circuit. There are two timing modes for endpoints emulating DS1 or E1 service:

- **Synchronous mode**—The clocks at transmission sources are frequency locked to the ATM network clock.

- **Asynchronous mode**—The clocks at transmission sources are not frequency locked to the ATM network clock.

As an example of asynchronous mode, the telecommunications network connected to Site C in Figure 5.14 acts as the timing source for the bit stream that it transmits onto the ATM network.

Adaptive Clock Recovery

One of the methods used to handle timing for asynchronous mode circuits is called *adaptive clock recovery*. This method does not rely on network timing signals. Instead, timing is handled by buffer management at the ATM endpoint devices. The specific techniques to be used are left to the implementer.

Using SRTS to Fix the Clock

When a circuit is set up, the source data rate (1.544 or 2.048Mbps) is configured for a PVC or included in signaling information during SVC call setup. Thus, the expected rate of data transfer is known. However, for an asynchronous mode circuit, the source service clock is independent of the ATM network clock. Any clock has a certain degree of variance in its rate, and a service clock that is independent of the ATM network clock will not be perfectly synchronized with the ATM network clock.

The *Synchronous Residual Time Stamp (SRTS) method* enables a receiving ATM endpoint to recover a DS1 or E1 service clock frequency quite accurately. This is done by transmitting a *Residual Time Stamp (RTS)* measurement that reveals differences between the service clock and the ATM network clock.

The variation is measured across a period of 3,008 cycles (bit times) of the service clock. This is not a random choice. A sequence of 8 cells (numbered 0 to 7) carries 3,008 bits.

The residual time stamp is a 4-bit quantity. It is transported in the convergence sublayer indication (CSI) flag bits of an 8-cell block. Because only four of the eight CSI bits are needed, the CSI bits in cells with sequence numbers 1, 3, 5, and 7 are used.

Computing the RTS

To understand how the residual time stamp is measured, let's look at the example of an externally clocked 1.544Mbps circuit transported across an ATM network that provides an accurate 155.52MHz clock.

If the service clock were perfect, the source would transmit 3008 bits in T=0.001948 seconds. In this time, the 155.52MHz network clock would go through 302,982 cycles.

These two counting rates differ too widely. The first step is to define a scaled-down counter to be used at the ATM source and destination that is compatible with the network clock, but counts at a rate that is fairly close to the source rate.

Scaled rates that can be used with 155.52MHz are set at 155.52 divided by powers of two:

77.76, 38.88, 19.44, 9.72, 4.86, 2.43, 1.2, ...

The closest value larger than 1.544 must be chosen, namely 2.43 (which is 155.52/64).

Now, if the service clock could synchronize with the network clock perfectly, while the service clock counts 3,008 bit times, the time measured in scaled-down ATM network units would be a little over 4,734.09 counts.

The 3,008 counts are measured by 4,734 counts of the scaled ATM network clock, introducing a round-down error at the destination. A second source of disparity is that any network clock has a certain amount of variation in it, so the times do not map perfectly.

The source will measure the difference between the service and network clock counts and send the difference to the destination in the residual time stamp value. The difference will be small. In fact, the difference is expected to be within plus or minus 7 counts per 4,734 cycles, and a 4-bit RTS can report it.

Numbers from 0 to 15 can be written using 4 bits. An RTS of 1–7 indicates a positive value that needs to be added to 4,734 clock counts. An RTS of 9–15 indicates a negative correction: 15 corresponds to –1, 14 corresponds to –2, and so forth.

The method of measuring the RTS value is illustrated in Figure 5.17.

Figure 5.17   Computing the RTS value.

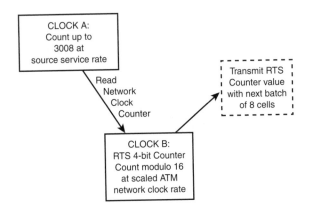

Two counters are used:

- Clock A counts modulo 3008 at the service clock rate (1.544MHz).

- At the same time, Clock B counts modulo 16 at the scaled network clock rate (2.43MHz).

When Clock A is ready to wrap, the RTS counter is read from Clock B and placed into the next 8-cell sequence that is sent.

A similar calculation can be performed for the E1 2.048MHz service clock rate.

Note

To translate the preceding explanation into the terminology used in the AAL1 standards:

fs is the original source service clock frequency.

fn is the ATM network clock frequency.

fnx is the scaled ATM network clock frequency.

$fnx = fn/x$. That is, x is the scaling factor. It must be a power of 2.

N = 3008. The service clock is sampled every N cycles. 3008 is used because it is the number of payload bits in 8 AAL1 SAR-PDU cells.

T = Time required to transmit 3008 bits at the source service clock frequency, fs.

y = The largest difference that can occur between a perfectly synchronized count and an actual count. This determines the number of bits that are needed for the residual time stamp.

AAL2

AAL2 supports flexible, efficient transmission of compressed voice, fax, and modem calls across an ATM network. See the AAL2 Addendum at the end of the chapter for more information.

AAL0

As was noted in the introduction, customer interest has caused an additional "none-of-the-above" AAL0 to be implemented. For AAL0, raw data is segmented into 48-byte payloads and packed into cells. At the receiving end, it is unpacked and delivered. There is absolutely minimal processing overhead. Product innovators can add extra AAL0 Convergence Sublayer functions if they wish. This might lead to the sprouting of many new varieties of AAL service.

Frame Relay Interworking

Earlier sections have discussed interworking between ATM and SMDS and between ATM and conventional telecommunications networks. ATM networks also need to interwork with existing frame relay equipment and frame relay networks.

The frame relay access devices in Figure 5.18 communicate with one another across an intermediate ATM network. Some of the frame relay access devices are connected to frame relay networks. Others connect directly to an ATM network via equipment that provides a frame relay/ATM interworking function.

The intervening ATM network is invisible to the frame relay endpoints. This type of connectivity is very common today.

Figure 5.18   Connecting frame relay devices across an ATM network.

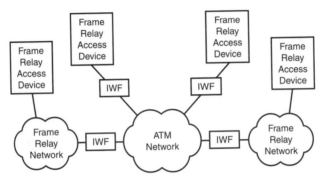

In Figure 5.19, the frame relay access devices also communicate with ATM endpoints that are directly connected to the ATM network. There is a frame relay virtual circuit at one end of the connection and an ATM AAL5 virtual circuit at the other end. Each endpoint is unaware that it is communicating with a device that is attached to a different type of network.

Figure 5.19   Connecting frame relay endpoints to ATM endpoints.

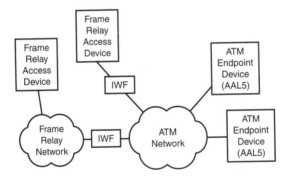

Location of the Interworking Function

Figures 5.18 and 5.19 are slightly misleading. In the figures, it appears that the interworking function is performed by devices that are not part of the networks they join together. In reality, interworking normally is performed by one of the following:

- A frame relay network switch with an ATM interface

- An ATM network switch with a frame relay interface

Figure 5.20 provides a more accurate layered picture that shows how the interworking function is implemented when two frame relay access devices communicate across an intervening ATM network. In the figure, the interworking function is performed by ATM switches that have a frame relay interface.

The ATM frame relay service specific convergence sublayer (FRCSS) performs the interworking chores.

Figure 5.20 The frame relay/ATM interworking function.

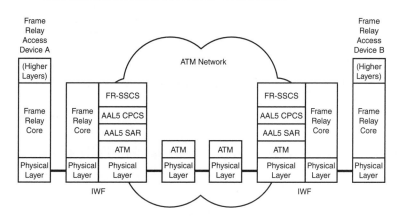

The Frame Relay Service Specific Convergence Sublayer

When a frame relay device transmits a frame across a virtual circuit, the frame relay service specific convergence sublayer at the interworking device

- Examines the incoming frame's DLCI and looks up the VPI and VCI of the ATM virtual circuit on which the frame needs to be transmitted.

- Places the frame relay address and payload fields into the payload of an AAL5 frame. Figure 5.21 displays this simple encapsulation.

Figure 5.21 An AAL5 frame carrying a frame relay frame.

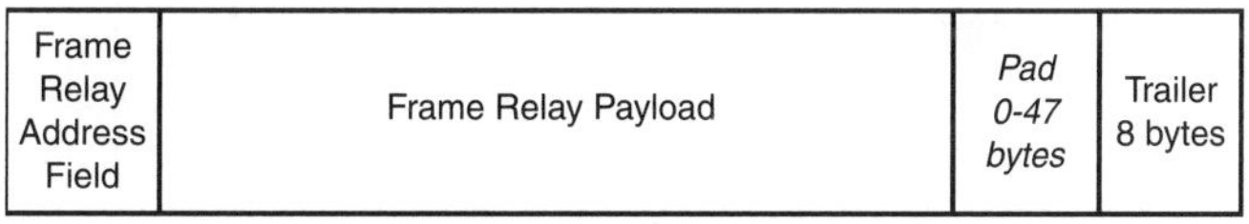

Frame Relay Address Field	Frame Relay Payload	Pad 0-47 bytes	Trailer 8 bytes

The ATM SAR sublayer segments the resulting AAL5 frame into cell payloads and passes these to the ATM layer, which transmits the cells across the network.

Incoming frames also are processed easily:

- An AAL5 frame is reassembled, its CRC is checked, and the PAD is removed.

- A fresh frame check sequence is appended to the address and payload fields.

- The frame relay frame is forwarded onto the virtual circuit identified by the DLCI in the address field.

The interworking function needs to perform appropriate mappings between

- Frame relay discard eligibility (DE) flags and ATM cell loss priority flags

- Frame relay and ATM congestion notification flags

See Frame Relay Forum document FRF.5 for details on how this can be done.

Multiplexing Frame Relay Circuits onto an ATM Connection

A separate ATM circuit could be set up for each frame relay virtual circuit. However, if several circuits have the same IWF endpoints, traffic for several frame relay circuits can be bundled across one ATM circuit that connects the two IWF endpoints. In Figure 5.22, five frame relay circuits are multiplexed across a single ATM virtual circuit that connects two interworking function nodes.

This is easy to do. For outgoing frame relay frames, multiple DLCIs can be translated to the same VPI/VCI. Because the payload of each incoming AAL5 frame starts with a frame relay address field, the DLCI of the incoming frame can be read from this field, and it can be transmitted onto the appropriate virtual circuit.

Figure 5.22   Multiplexing frame relay circuits across an ATM circuit.

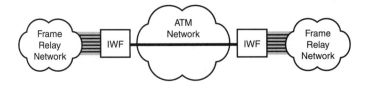

AAL5 Encapsulation

The data communications community has selected AAL5 as the preferred way to carry data payloads. AAL5 circuits are used to carry bridged LAN traffic and routed protocol data.

For reasons of cost or convenience, it sometimes is practical to carry several different protocols across a single virtual circuit. Just as was the case for frame relay, the ATM standards community did not include a field in AAL5 frames that identifies the protocol being carried. And, as was the case for frame relay, the *Internet Engineering Task Force (IETF)* defined headers that take care of this problem.

A header is not needed if only a single protocol is carried on a circuit. In this case, the protocol to be carried is a configuration parameter for permanent virtual circuits and a circuit setup parameter for switched virtual circuits. However, a header is needed when two or more protocols share a circuit.

Currently, header formats are defined in RFC 1483. An updated version of this document is in draft form. This draft has improved the description of the formats but does not change them.

Identifying Bridged LAN Frames

ATM circuits often are used to carry Ethernet, Token Ring, or FDDI frames between locations. Figure 5.23 shows the format of an encapsulated frame with a header that identifies the protocol being carried. The AAL5 payload is introduced by a Logical Link Control (LLC) header followed by a SNAP subheader. The LLC header consists of DSAP X'AA, SSAP X'AA, and a control field equal to X'03, which means unnumbered information.

The SNAP subheader starts with an organizationally unique identifier (OUI) field equal to X'00 80 C2, which indicates that bridged data will follow. The next two bytes indicate the type of LAN frame that is enclosed and if the frame check sequence (FCS) field is included. Because the AAL5 trailer contains a CRC value, some users choose to save some transmission bytes by omitting the FCS of the enclosed frame.

Protocol identifiers for bridged frames were defined in Table II-6.2. For example:

X'00 01 (Ethernet with FCS)

X'00 07 (Ethernet without FCS)

X'00 03 (Token Ring with FCS)

X'00 09 (Token Ring without FCS)

Figure 5.23   Format of an encapsulated LAN frame with a protocol identifier.

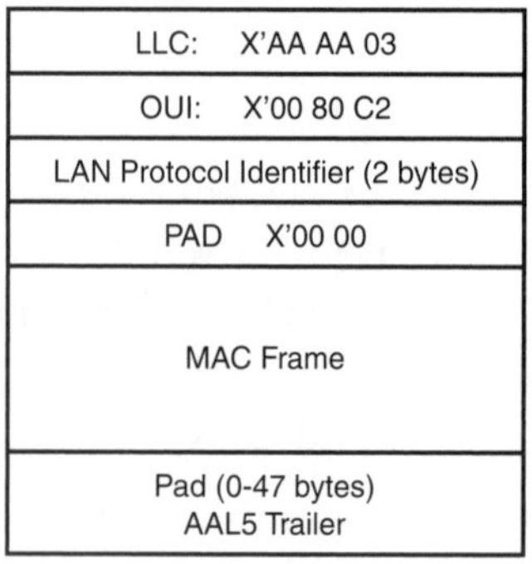

Listing 5.2, a WinPharoah trace, shows the introductory bytes of an AAL5 frame that contains a bridged MAC frame. The protocol identifier X'00 07 indicates that the content is an Ethernet MAC frame without an FCS field. An IP datagram is carried inside the payload of the Ethernet frame.

Listing 5.2   An AAL5 Frame that Contains a Bridged MAC Frame

```
Decode from WinPharoah
— — — — —·Logical Link Control Protocol 802.2 (LLC) — — — —·
 DSAP = AA Sub-Network Access Protocol (SNAP)
 SSAP = AA Sub-Network Access Protocol (SNAP)
 Control = 3 P/F=0, Unnumbered(UI command)
 — — — — — — — — —Sub-Network Access Protocol(SNAP) — — — — —
 Organization Code or Protocol ID = 0080C2
 Protocol ID = 0007 802.3/Ethernet w/o preserved FCS
 Pad = 00 00
 — — — — — — — — — —·Ethernet II — — — — — — — — — — — —·
 Destination address = 006008BC8105
 Source address = 006008BD4EA2
 Type = 0800  EthType IP
 — — — — — — — — — — — — — — — — — — — — — — — — — — — —·
(IP datagram follows)
```

Identifying Routed Protocol Payloads

A similar encapsulation is used when routed protocol data units are transmitted across a multiprotocol circuit. If the protocol can be identified by an Ethertype code, it is introduced by LLC and SNAP headers. Many routed protocols have been assigned Ethertype codes—for example, IP, DECnet, and VINES. As shown in Figure 5.24, the LLC header, X'AA AA 03, is followed by an OUI field equal to X'00 00 00, which introduces a 2-byte Ethertype identifier.

Format of an encapsulated routed PDU with an Ethertype identifier.

Listing 5.3, a Sniffer trace, shows an encapsulated IP datagram that was sent on VPI=0, VCI=33. The OUI value, X'00 00 00, is followed by the Ethertype code for IP, which is X'0800. The IP datagram starts immediately after this field.

Listing 5.3   An Encapsulated IP Datagram

```
Network Associates Sniffer Trace
- - - - - - - - - - - - - - - - - - - - - - - - - - - - - - - - - - -
LLC: C D=AA S=AA UI

SNAP: Ethernet Type=0800 (IP)
IP:  D=[161.69.113.95] S=[161.69.112.110] LEN=64 ID=41600

ICMP: Echo
ATM: ----- ATM Header -----
     ATM:
     ATM: Frame 1 arrived at  12:19:43.0000;
          frame size is 144 (0090 hex) bytes.
     ATM: Link = DTE
     ATM: Virtual path id = 0
     ATM: Virtual channel id = 33
     ATM:
LLC:  ----- LLC Header -----
     LLC:
     LLC: DSAP Address = AA, DSAP IG Bit = 00 (Individual Address)
     LLC: SSAP Address = AA, SSAP CR Bit = 00 (Command)
     LLC: Unnumbered frame: UI
     LLC:
          (OUI = X'00 00 00)
SNAP: ----- SNAP Header -----
     SNAP:
```

continues

Listing 5.3   Continued

```
        SNAP: Type = 0800 (IP)
        SNAP:
IP: ----- IP Header -----
        IP:
        IP: Version = 4, header length = 20 bytes
        . . . (Remainder of IP datagram)
ATM:
        ATM: ----- AAL5 Trailer -----
        ATM:
        ATM: 44 pad octets
        ATM: UU     = 0
        ATM: CPI    = 0
        ATM: Length = 92
        ATM: CRC    = 296AC7F8 (Correct)
```

Listing 5.4 shows an inverse ARP message that was sent on the same virtual channel. Inverse ARP is used to discover the IP address of the partner at the other end of the ATM connection. ATM addresses are used in the hardware address fields of an ATM inverse ARP message. See Chapter II-10 for an explanation of inverse ARP.

Note that protocol encapsulation headers are needed on an IP channel when inverse ARP is used, because IP and inverse ARP have different protocol identification types.

Listing 5.4   An Inverse ARP Message

```
Network Associates Sniffer Trace
- - - - - - - - - - - - - - - - - - - - - - - - - - - - - - - - - -
LLC: C D=AA S=AA UI

SNAP: Ethernet Type=0806 (ARP)

ARP:   S=[161.69.112.90]  D=[161.69.112.250] Op=InARP reply
ATM: ----- ATM Header -----
        ATM:
        ATM: Frame 42 arrived at  12:19:51.6468;
        frame size is 96 (0060 hex) bytes.
        ATM: Link = DTE
        ATM: Virtual path id = 0
        ATM: Virtual channel id = 33
        ATM:
LLC: ----- LLC Header -----
        LLC:
        LLC: DSAP Address = AA, DSAP IG Bit = 00 (Individual Address)
```

```
      LLC:  SSAP Address = AA, SSAP CR Bit = 00 (Command)
      LLC:  Unnumbered frame: UI
      LLC:
         (OUI = X'00 00 00)


SNAP: ----- SNAP Header -----
      SNAP:
      SNAP: Type = 0806 (ARP)
      SNAP:
ARP:  ----- ARP/RARP frame -----
      ARP:
      ARP: Hardware type = 19 (ATM Forum address family)
      ARP: Protocol type = 0800 (IP)
      ARP: Source ATM number
      ARP:      type   = ATM Forum NSAPA format
      ARP:      length = 20
      ARP: Source ATM subaddress
      ARP:      type   = ATM Forum NSAPA format
      ARP:      length = 0
      ARP: Opcode 9 (InARP reply)
      ARP: Length of source protocol address = 4
      ARP: Target ATM num
      ARP:      type   = ATM Forum NSAPA format
      ARP:      length = 20
      ARP: Target ATM subaddress
      ARP:      type   = ATM Forum NSAPA format
      ARP:      length = 0
      ARP: Length of target protocol address = 4
      ARP: Source ATM number       =
         39:0000:0000 0000 0000 0000 0000:0000A145705A:00
      ARP: Source protocol address  = [161.69.112.90]
      ARP: Target ATM number       =
         39:0000:0000 0000 0000 0000 0000:0000A14570FA:00
      ARP: Target protocol address  = [161.69.112.250]
      ARP:
ATM:
      ATM: ----- AAL5 Trailer -----
      ATM:
      ATM: 20 pad octets
      ATM: UU    = 0
      ATM: CPI   = 0
      ATM: Length = 68
      ATM: CRC   = C3605B5B (Correct)
```

Finally, a different encapsulation is used for ISO data sent across multiprotocol circuits. As shown in Figure 5.25, LLC field X'FE FE 03 is followed by a 1-byte Network Layer Protocol Identifier (NLPID).

Figure 5.25   Encapsulation for a routed ISO PDU.

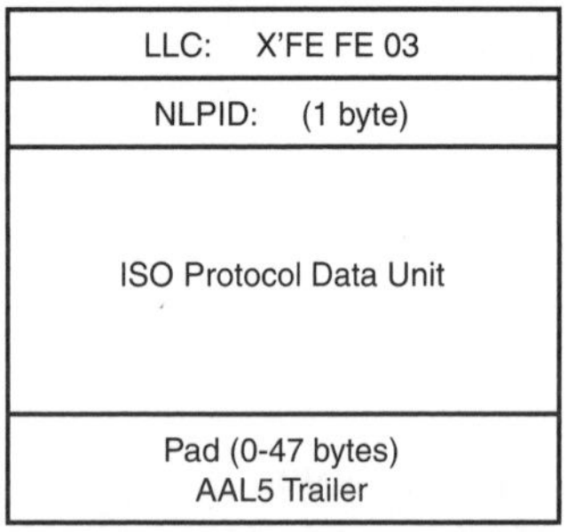

```
┌─────────────────────────────┐
│  LLC:    X'FE FE 03          │
├─────────────────────────────┤
│  NLPID:   (1 byte)           │
├─────────────────────────────┤
│                             │
│  ISO Protocol Data Unit     │
│                             │
├─────────────────────────────┤
│  Pad (0-47 bytes)           │
│  AAL5 Trailer               │
└─────────────────────────────┘
```

Note

Note that the folks who designed the ATM encapsulation for IP datagrams made a different choice from the folks who designed the frame relay encapsulation for IP. The ATM version introduces IP datagrams with LLC and SNAP fields instead of the IP NLPID value (X'CC) that is used for frame relay.

AAL2 Addendum

The evolving AAL2 service can be a significant step in breaking away from 64Kbps voice circuits. Compressed voice saves significant bandwidth, especially when intervals of silence are removed.

AAL2 enables several calls to be multiplexed onto a single ATM connection. For example, suppose that six concurrent compressed voice calls were assigned to one ATM connection. For each call, a few bytes at a time are packaged with a header that includes a call identifier. The packets are concatenated, and then are stuffed into cell payloads and transmitted across the ATM connection. When silence suppression is used, then even with modest 32Kbps Adaptive PCM compression, six calls can be carried on a 106Kbps circuit instead of six 64Kbps circuits.

References

Among the documents describing AAL functions are

- ITU-T I.362, *B-ISDN ATM Adaptation Layer (AAL) Functional Description* (1993).

- ITU-T I.363, *ATM Adaptation Layer (AAL) Specification* (1993).

- I.363.1, *B-ISDN ATM Adaptation Layer (AAL) Specification, Type 1 and 2* (1996).

- I.363.5, *B-ISDN ATM Adaptation Layer (AAL) Specification*, Type 5 (1996).

- ATM Forum *Circuit Emulation Service Interoperability Specification* (1995).

- ANSI T1.629, ATM Adaptation Layer 3/4 Common Part Functions and Specification (1993).

- ANSI T1.630, *B-ISDN ATM Adaptation Layer CBR Services* (1993).

See ITU-T, ANSI, and ATM catalogs for further listings.

Interworking between frame relay and ATM is described in the Frame Relay Forum document, *Frame Relay/ATM Network Interworking Implementation Agreement*, FRF.5 (1994).

The multiprotocol encapsulation described in this chapter was originally published as *RFC 1483, Multiprotocol Encapsulation over ATM Adaptation Layer 5 (1993)*. Check the RFC index for an updated version of this document.

ATM Traffic Contracts

An ATM network is not like the data networks that preceded it. ATM architects were inspired by the vision of a global network capable of providing a very wide range of services. A converged ATM voice/data network allows a subscriber to choose the way each of its connections behaves. A subscriber may request a reliable premium connection that emulates a leased line, and later ask for a low-cost connection that offers only a best-effort service. The ATM Forum has defined five different *service categories* that correspond to very different connection characteristics.

Every connection is described by its service category and a set of parameters that are called its *traffic contract*. Traffic contract parameters are preconfigured for permanent virtual circuits, and are negotiated during call setup for switched virtual circuits. Network switches use the traffic contract parameters to establish the resources that are needed for a connection.

It is a challenge to support a diverse set of services across one network. ATM architects have worked hard on the problem of designing mechanisms that

- Determine whether the network can provide the resources requested for a new switched virtual connection. This process is called *connection admission control (CAC)*.

- Enable a network to protect itself from excess traffic. Just as was the case for frame relay, many users connect to an ATM network via a physical link that has lots of extra bandwidth, so the potential for congestion is real. The process of monitoring and controlling traffic is called *usage parameter control (UPC)*.

- Adjust the traffic flow as it passes through the network in order to smooth out burstiness. This process is called *traffic shaping*.

This chapter will review the standard service categories, describe the parameters that make up traffic contracts, and briefly discuss connection admission control, usage parameter control, and traffic shaping.

ATM Forum Service Categories

There are over a dozen parameters that can be used to describe the behavior of a connection. It is impossible to design a network that supports arbitrary combinations of these values. The ATM Forum defined its five service categories to reduce the number of possibilities to a manageable level.

The service categories were introduced in Chapter III-2. To refresh your memory, they are listed again in Table 6.1, which also identifies the ATM Adaptation Layer types used for each category.

Table 6.1   Service Categories and Their AALs

Service Category	Usual AAL	Description/Examples
CBR, Constant Bit Rate	AAL1	A real-time service that provides a constant bandwidth. In addition to other fixed rate applications, CBR supports the DS1, E1, and Nx64Kbps services described in Chapter III-5.
rt-VBR, Real-Time Variable Bit Rate	AAL3/4 or AAL5	A real-time service that delivers a specified average bandwidth and supports applications that are sensitive to delay and to variations in delay, such as compressed voice or video.
nrt-VBR, Non-Real-Time Variable Bit Rate	AAL3/4 or AAL5	A non-real-time service that delivers a specified average bandwidth and supports applications that are not sensitive to delay. The service is suitable for applications such as LAN to LAN connectivity.
ABR, Available Bit Rate	AAL5	A service that delivers varying amounts of bandwidth, depending on the availability of network resources.
UBR, Unspecified Bit Rate	AAL5	A service that is suitable for applications that are not sensitive to delay, such as file transfer or electronic mail. Traffic is delivered on a best-effort basis.

The behavior of the constant bit rate, real-time variable bit rate, and non-real-time variable bit rate categories can be understood fairly well from their descriptions and the examples that are provided.

Some more explanation is needed to understand the available bit rate and unspecified bit rate service categories.

Available Bit Rate (ABR) Service

As its name suggests, the available bit rate service enables an endpoint to transmit at varying rates, depending on the current availability of resources in the network.

The basic idea is that the sender gets periodic feedback instructions from the network and adjusts its current rate—which is called the *allowed cell rate (ACR)*—up or down. More specifically,

- The sender's transmission rate varies between specified minimum and maximum rates.

- There is a startup rate that is used at initialization as well as after any idle period. This initial rate is set somewhere between the minimum and maximum.

- The sender always is able to transmit at the minimum rate, and can transmit at higher rates if permitted by the network.

- There are prespecified parameters that control the amount by which a rate may be increased or must be decreased.

- Special feedback cells tell the sender whether to increase, decrease, or maintain its transmission rate.

ABR Resource Management Cells

Feedback information is carried in special *resource management (RM) cells.* Figure 6.1 shows how it works. The source periodically generates an RM cell that is returned by the destination. Network nodes adjust the parameters in an RM cell according to the resources that they currently have available.

In addition, if a network node is congested, it can spontaneously generate an RM cell that tells the source to throttle back its rate.

When a source generates an RM cell, it writes the rate at which it would like to transmit data into a field in the cell. A source may increase its rate if the returned RM cell gives it permission to do so.

Figure 6.1 Transmitting resource management cells.

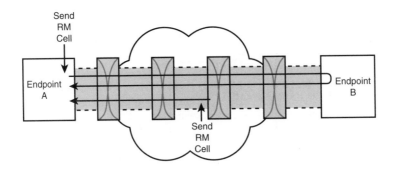

However, any node along the way (including the destination endpoint) can reduce the requested rate or can signal congestion, which tells the sender to throttle back. A source also must reduce its rate

- If it has waited too long since sending an RM cell.

- If no return RM cells have been received during a timeout period.

Resource management cells are easy to recognize because they have a distinctive payload type field whose bits are equal to 110. RM cells for a virtual channel connection have the VPI and VCI of that connection. RM cells for a virtual path connection have the VPI of the path, and are sent with VCI=6.

Unspecified Bit Rate (UBR) Service

The *unspecified bit rate (UBR) service* is a good match for background applications—such as file transfer and electronic mail transfer—that can tolerate variable cell delivery times and occasional long delays.

A provider can offer UBR as a best effort service without any bandwidth or quality of service guarantees. UBR service is a lot like what a subscriber gets today on the Internet. You send your traffic and hope for the best.

Lots of private ATM networks are set up with UBR as the only supported service. UBR is very easy to configure. If end users are happy with the network's performance, there is no reason to fine-tune circuit service categories.

Traffic Contract Parameters

A connection's traffic contract establishes its transmission characteristics and sets target delay and reliability levels. Traffic contract parameters describe features such as the

- Maximum bandwidth that is allowed

- Degree of burstiness

- Maximum time it should take to deliver a cell

- Percentage of cells that may be lost in transmission

The first two items describe transmission characteristics. Quantities that describe transmission characteristics are called *traffic parameters*. The third and fourth relate to delay and reliability. Quantities that relate to delay and reliability are called *quality of service (QoS) parameters*.

The first and most important step in putting together a traffic contract is to choose the service category: CBR, rt-VBR, nrt-VBR, ABR, or UBR. Then, a suitable set of traffic and quality of service parameter values must be selected. In conjunction with this, the network provider must disclose its *conformance definition*, which describes how the network will test your traffic and the action that the network will take for non-conformant cells. The ATM Forum has named and described several standard conformance types.

Table 6.2 lists the traffic and quality of service parameters. The available bit rate service, which uses feedback to set its transmission rate, is very different from the other services and has its own distinct set of traffic parameters.

As the table shows, there are lots of parameters. However, only a selected subset is used for a given service category. Parameters are matched with their service categories in Table 6.3, which appears later in the chapter.

For many of the parameters (such as the peak cell rate), separate values must be specified for each direction of a bidirectional circuit. In some cases, separate values also are applied to two distinct flows of cells:

- The high priority flow, which is made up of cells with cell loss priority equal to 0 (written CLP=0)

- The total flow, whose cells can have cell loss priority 0 or 1 (written CLP=0+1)

Table 6.2	Traffic and Quality of Service Parameters

Type	Parameters
General Traffic Parameters	Peak Cell Rate Sustainable Cell Rate Maximum Burst Size Best Effort indicator Use of tagging
Available Bit Rate Traffic Parameters	ABR Initial Cell Rate Minimum Cell Rate Rate Increase Factor Rate Decrease Factor ABR Transient Buffer Exposure Cumulative RM Fixed Round Trip Time
Quality of Service Parameters	Peak-to-peak Cell Delay Variation Maximum Cell Transfer Delay Cell Loss Ratio

General Traffic Parameters

Values of the peak cell rate, sustainable cell rate, and maximum burst size place limits on the transfer rate and the burstiness of traffic.

- **Peak cell rate (PCR)**—Puts a cap on the highest transmission rate that is allowed for the connection. A traffic source never is supposed to exceed this rate, which is expressed in cells per second.

- **Sustainable cell rate (SCR)**—Analogous to the frame relay committed information rate (CIR). It is the average cell rate for the connection, when measured over a long time scale.

- **Maximum burst size (MBS)**—Limits the number of cells that can be transmitted at the peak rate.

If a traffic contract includes a sustainable cell rate, network switches always should be able to transmit the connection's cells at this rate. A source also should be able to burst traffic at the peak rate for a limited amount of time. Switches support this capability by allocating buffer space to hold the excess cells. If the burst lasts too long, the buffer fills and additional incoming cells are discarded. The maximum burst size is measured in cells and the buffer size is related to this value.

When included, the peak cell rate, sustainable cell rate, and maximum burst size are specified

- In both the forward and backward directions of a bidirectional connection

- For CLP=0 or CLP=0+1 streams of cells, or both

The remaining general traffic parameters describe how traffic is handled. They are

- **Best effort indicator**—Best-effort delivery is supported only for the unspecified bit rate service. (In fact, no other parameters are required for UBR.)

- **Use of tagging**—The tagging parameter indicates whether network switches change the cell loss priority from 0 to 1 for excess traffic. Cells with CLP=1 are discarded in preference to cells with CLP=0.

Available Bit Rate Traffic Parameters

An additional set of traffic parameters is defined for the available bit rate (ABR) service. The *ABR initial cell rate, minimum cell rate, rate increase factor, rate decrease factor*, and *ABR transient buffer exposure* are specified in both the forward and backward directions of a bidirectional connection. These key parameters are defined as follows:

- **ABR initial cell rate**—The rate at which the source may send when it starts up, or after an idle period.

- **Minimum cell rate (MCR)**—The rate at which the source always is allowed to send.

- **Rate increase factor (RIF)**—One of the fractions 1, 1/2, 1/4,...1/32718; caps the amount by which the current allowed cell rate may be increased. The maximum increase is

    (rate increase factor)×(peak cell rate)

- **Rate decrease factor (RDF)**—One of the fractions 1, 1/2, 1/4,...1/32718.

    The transmission rate is decreased by

    (rate decrease factor)×(current allowed cell rate)

    A decrease is applied after a timeout or when congestion is indicated.

- **ABR transient buffer exposure**—A negotiated limit on the number of cells that the source may send during a startup period before the first RM cell returns. The range is from 0 to 16,777,215 cells.

- **Cumulative RM fixed round trip time**—Accumulates the sum of the delays along the route from the source to the destination and back.

Additional ABR parameters that can be specified include the following:

- **Nrm**—Specifies the maximum number of cells a source may send per forward RM cell. (Nrm is a power of 2 and ranges from 2 to 256.)

- **Trm**—A limit on the time between forward RM cells sent by an active source. (The range is from 100×2^7 to 100 milliseconds.)

- **Cutoff decrease factor (CDF)**—Controls the decrease in the current cell rate imposed when backward RM cells either are missing or repeatedly report congestion. (CDF is a power of 2 between 1/64 and 1.)

- **Allowed cell rate decrease time factor (ADTF)**—The time allowed between sending RM cells before the rate must be decreased to the initial cell rate. (The range is from 0.01 to 10.23 seconds.)

Quality of Service Parameters

The previous parameters dealt with setting and controlling the rate of transmission. Quality of service parameters establish goals for reliability and delay. The three quality of service parameters are

- Cell loss ratio (CLR)

- Maximum cell transfer delay (MaxCTD)

- Peak-to-peak cell delay variation (peak-to-peak CDV)

Cell Loss Ratio (CLR)

The cell loss ratio is a measure of reliability. It is equal to the proportion of the cells that are lost. Specifically:

$$CLR = \frac{\text{Lost Cells}}{\text{Total Transmitted Cells}}$$

> **Note**
>
> Cells that belong to a severely errored cell block are not included in the cell error ratio formula. Severely errored cell blocks are described later in this chapter.

The cell loss ratio is computed over the lifetime of the connection for an SVC, or for a stated period for a PVC.

Before examining the parameters that deal with delay, you need to understand how the delay of an individual cell is measured.

Measuring Cell Transfer Delay

The cell transfer delay is the time that it takes to deliver a cell. Figure 6.2 shows how this time is measured. The cell transfer delay for one cell is the difference between the time that the first bit is transmitted from the source and the time that the last bit is received at the destination. Meaningful measurements of delay usually are taken as averages over a time interval.

Figure 6.2   Measuring the cell transfer delay.

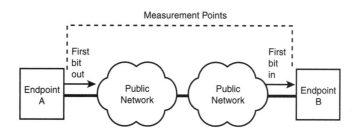

Quality of Service Delay Parameters

The *maximum cell transfer delay* sets a time limit on the amount of time that it takes to deliver cells. The network is supposed to deliver most of the connection's cells within this limit. For example, the cell transfer delay requirement might be that 98 percent of all cells will be delivered within 50 milliseconds.

In an ideal network, cells for a voice, video, or circuit emulation connection would arrive periodically in a predictable manner. In a real network, the time between cell arrivals bounces around.

The *peak-to-peak cell delay variation* measures differences between the ideal periodic cell arrival time and the actual arrival time. It is expressed as the proportion of cells that the network must deliver within a specified interval; for example, "98 percent of all cells must arrive within 20 microseconds of their periodic arrival time."

Values of the peak-to-peak cell delay variation are specified for both the forward and backward direction of a bidirectional circuit. They also are specified for the CLP=0 or CLP=0+1 flows.

Other Quality of Service Measurements

There are some other quality of service measurements that are not used within the network as part of its traffic control process, but are of interest to subscribers, and might be included in service reports. These include

- Mean cell transfer delay

- Cell delay variation tolerance (CDVT)

- Severely errored cell block ratio

- Cell error ratio

The mean cell transfer delay is the average cell transfer delay over a period of time.

It is good for cells to arrive at switches along the way on time, but arriving early can cause problems. A receiver might still be busy processing earlier cells, or may not have enough buffer space when cells crowd in too fast. The cell delay variation tolerance is the biggest early arrival time that the equipment can handle. A cell that is too early will be dropped.

The severely errored cell block ratio indicates how often things go seriously wrong on the network. A *cell block* is a sequence of N cells transmitted consecutively on a specific connection. A cell block is severely errored when more than a threshold level (M) of errored cells, lost cells, or mis-inserted cells are detected for an incoming cell block. The formula is

$$\text{Severely Errored Cell Block Ratio} = \frac{\text{Severely Errored Cell Blocks}}{\text{Total Transmitted Cell Blocks}}$$

The cell error ratio reports less serious problems. It is defined by a very simple computation:

$$\text{Cell Error Ratio} = \frac{\text{Errored Cells}}{\text{Successfully Transferred Cells} + \text{Errored Cells}}$$

Cells that belong to a severely errored cell block are not included in the errored cell count.

Parameters Associated with Service Categories

The ITU-T and the ATM Forum have identified the parameters that are appropriate for use with each service category.

Table 6.3 identifies the traffic and quality of service parameters that are associated with each service category. Some of the parameters are marked optional (O), which means that it is optional to include them in a switched call setup message submitted by a subscriber endpoint. These parameters can be assigned default values by the network.

The only mandatory parameter for a constant bit rate connection is the peak cell rate. Many providers will have default delay and cell loss settings for constant bit rate connections.

The variable bit rate service categories promise a sustainable cell rate and allow bursting up to the peak cell rate. A maximum burst size parameter is required to put a limit on the bursting. The difference between the real-time and non-real-time services is that the maximum total delay and delay variation are controlled for the real-time service.

Apart from the peak cell rate value, the available bit rate parameters all relate to the operation of the feedback mechanism. No limits on delay are promised. The sender controls cell loss by staying within the traffic level set by the network.

The only parameter that is required for the unspecified bit rate service is the best effort indicator. The network can ignore a peak cell rate requested by a subscriber and place its own limit on the transmission rate allowed to the connection.

Table 6.3   Traffic and QoS Parameters Used with Each Service Category

Service Category	Parameters
CBR Constant Bit Rate	Peak Cell Rate Peak-to-peak Cell Delay Variation (O) Maximum Cell Transfer Delay (O) Cell Loss Ratio (O)
rt-VBR Real-Time Variable Bit Rate	Peak Cell Rate Sustainable Cell Rate Maximum Burst Size Tagging (O) Peak-to-peak Cell Delay Variation (O) Maximum Cell Transfer Delay (O) Cell Loss Ratio (O)
nrt-VBR Non-Real-Time Variable Bit Rate	Peak Cell Rate Sustainable Cell Rate Maximum Burst Size Tagging (O) Cell Loss Ratio (O)

continues

Table 6.3   Continued

Service Category	Parameters
ABR Available Bit Rate	Peak Cell Rate Minimum Cell Rate Initial Cell Rate (O) Transient Buffer Exposure (O) Cumulative RM Fixed Round Trip Time (O) Rate Decrease factor (O) Rate Increase Factor (O) Additional Optional Parameters (Nrm, Trm, Cutoff Decrease Factor, and Allowed Cell Rate Decrease Time Factor)
UBR Unspecified Bit Rate	Best Effort Indicator (M) Peak Cell Rate (O) Tagging (O)

Traffic Management

The sections that follow describe two mechanisms that are used to protect a network from excess traffic and assure that the network can meet its traffic contract commitments. These mechanisms are

- **Connection admission control**—Protects a network from unauthorized connections and overload conditions.

- **Usage parameter control**—Acts as a watchdog, preventing endpoints from overloading the network with excessive traffic.

Connection Admission Control (CAC)

New PVC connections are set up by a network administrator, while new SVC connections are requested on demand by an endpoint device. Whenever a new PVC or SVC is requested

- The request must be screened to see whether the subscriber is entitled to set up a new connection with the requested traffic parameters and quality of service parameters.

- The nodes that will participate in the connection must be checked to discover whether they have sufficient free resources to support the connection.

The process of applying these criteria before setting up a connection is called *connection admission control (CAC)*. The way that connection admission control is implemented is network-specific. It depends on the equipment that is used, the way that the equipment is configured, the services that are offered, and local administrative policies.

Most people have experienced connection admission control when using the telephone network. You may have tried to make a long-distance call from a business premise and discovered that it was administratively forbidden. During a holiday, you may have placed a long-distance call to a relative and heard the message: "All circuits are now busy. Please hang up and try your call again later."

Usage Parameter Control (UPC)

A network has to protect itself from excess traffic. *Usage parameter control* is the set of actions taken by the network to

- Monitor traffic to see if it conforms to its contract

- Take action to reduce a stream of cells to a conformant flow

Traffic is tested at the entry switch for a connection. Actions on traffic that is in violation include cell discard and cell tagging. Recall that cell tagging means changing the cell loss priority flag from 0 to 1.

When performed at a network-to-network interface, the usage parameter control function is called *network parameter control* (NPC).

Generic Cell Rate Algorithm (GCRA)

The ITU-T has defined an algorithm called the Generic Cell Rate Algorithm (GCRA) that is used to determine whether the cells of a CBR, rt-VBR, nrt-VBR, or UBR connection conform to their traffic contract.

The idea behind GCRA is fairly simple: A cell is discarded if it arrives too early. Figure 6.3 illustrates roughly how GCRA works.

- Part A of Figure 6.3 shows an ideal traffic stream. Every cell arrives exactly when time interval T expires.

- Part B shows what happens when a cell arrives late. It is conforming and will be transmitted. The expected arrival time for the next cell is set to T units after this arrival time.

- In Part C, a cell arrives early—but not too early. It is conforming and will be transmitted. The expected arrival time for the next cell is the current expected time plus T.

- Finally in Part D, a cell arrives very early—more than a limiting time L before it was supposed to arrive. The cell is nonconforming. It may be tagged or discarded. The expected arrival time is not changed.

Figure 6.3 The Generic Cell Rate Algorithm.

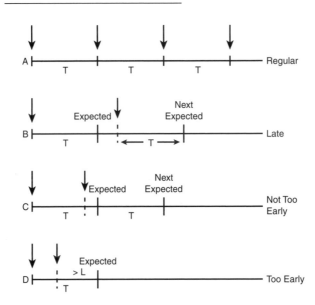

GCRA can be applied twice: once for the CLP=0 stream and then again for the CLP=0+1 stream.

A vendor that uses GCRA for its usage parameter control monitoring function can be sure that the network is testing traffic in an appropriate manner. However, the vendor is free to use any other algorithm to screen traffic, as long as it does not cause traffic contract violations.

ATM Forum Conformance Definitions

The ATM Forum has defined several standard conformance definitions that can be used in traffic contracts. Standard definitions are useful guidelines, but there is no law that forces a service provider to use one of them. A provider can create its own guidelines.

A standard conformance definition

- Identifies parameters that must be specified and traffic flow(s) that will be subjected to the GCRA algorithm
- Indicates whether tagging is used

Currently, there is one standard conformance definition for constant bit rate traffic (called CBR.1), there are three definitions for variable bit rate traffic (VBR.1, VBR.2, and VBR.3), two definitions for unspecified bit rate traffic (UBR.1 and UBR.2), and one definition for available bit rate (ABR) traffic.

Table 6.4 lists the traffic parameters required by each conformance definition. The only difference between UBR.1 and UBR.2 is that the network never changes CLP=0 to CLP=1 for UBR.1, but will "tag" cells for UBR.2.

Table 6.4   Standard Conformance Definitions

Conformance Definition	Required Traffic Parameters
CBR.1	Peak cell rate in cells/second for CLP=0+1 traffic. CDVT in tenths of microseconds.
UBR.1 (No tagging)	Peak cell rate in cells/second for CLP=0+1 traffic. CDVT in tenths of microseconds.
UBR.2 (Tagging)	Peak cell rate in cells/second for CLP=0+1 traffic. CDVT in tenths of microseconds.
VBR.1	Peak cell rate in cells/second for CLP=0+1 traffic. Sustainable cell rate in cells/second for CLP=0+1 traffic. Maximum burst size in cells. CDVT in tenths of microseconds.
VBR.2	Peak cell rate in cells/second for CLP=0+1 traffic. Sustainable cell rate in cells/second for CLP=0 traffic. Maximum burst size in cells. CDVT in tenths of microseconds.
VBR.3	Peak cell rate in cells/second for CLP=0+1 traffic. Sustainable cell rate in cells/second for CLP=0 traffic, excess tagged as CLP=1. Maximum burst size in cells. CDVT in tenths of microseconds.
ABR	Peak cell rate in cells/second. CDVT in tenths of microseconds. Minimum cell rate in cells/second.

Traffic Shaping

Traffic shaping is a method of modifying the stream of cells transferred on a connection in order to improve its behavior. To shape traffic, a switch buffers an incoming burst and then transmits it as a more regular flow. This results in less variation in cell delays, but is likely to increase the average delivery delay.

The left side of Figure 6.4 illustrates a bursty traffic stream. Buffering the burst enables the switch to transmit it in the smoothed manner shown on the right side of Figure 6.4.

Figure 6.4  Traffic shaping.

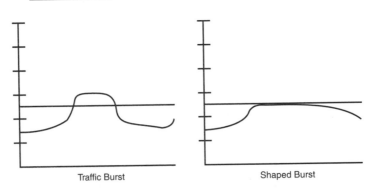

Shaping has two positive effects. It smoothes out bursts, making it less likely that traffic will clump up too much at a later switch, exceed its contract, and experience discards. It also improves network efficiency by presenting switches with more regular streams of traffic. Not all switches need to shape. Shaping often is done by an entry switch. It also can be turned on at strategic points within a network.

An endpoint administrator can improve network performance by configuring endpoint systems to shape the traffic that they send across the user-network interface. Reducing burstiness can prevent big switch queue pileups that lead to delays or even lost cells.

References

The ATM Forum document, *Traffic Management Specification Version 4.0* (1996), contains a detailed description of service categories, traffic and quality of service parameters, traffic contract conformance definitions, and the Generic Cell Rate Algorithm.

The ATM Forum based its document upon the earlier ITU-T document, I.371, *Traffic Control and Congestion Control in B-ISDN*.

CHAPTER 7

Setting Up Switched Connections

ATM switched connections are set up on demand and released when they no longer are needed. Just as for an ordinary telephone call, a user initiates a switched ATM call by communicating with the network and identifying the number to be called. The network selects a route for the call, notifies the called device of the incoming call, and, if the call is accepted, completes the call setup.

An ATM user can

- Request a bidirectional point-to-point virtual channel connection

- Request a bidirectional point-to-point virtual path connection

- Set up a call as the root of a point-to-multipoint connection

- Request that a party be added to a point-to multipoint connection

- Make a request to join an existing point-to-multipoint call as a leaf endpoint

Two ingredients are needed to support switched connections:

- An ATM address numbering plan

- Signaling messages that set up, control, and terminate ATM connections

Several categories of signaling have been defined:

- **User-network interface (UNI) signaling**—The ITU-T Digital Signaling System 2 (DSS2) standard defines the messages exchanged between endpoint devices and their adjacent network switches. (The ATM Forum has added some features to DSS2.)

- **Private switch-to-switch or network-to-network signaling**—Private networks use either the ATM Forum Private Network-Network Interface (PNNI) or proprietary signaling methods. PNNI message exchanges closely mimic UNI message exchanges.

- **Public network signaling**—*Broadband Integrated Services Digital Network User Part* (called *Broadband ISDN* or *B-ISUP*) signaling is an extension of Signaling System No. 7. A public ATM service provider also may use PNNI as a signaling protocol within its network.

- **Public network to public network signaling**—*BISDN Inter Carrier Interface (B-ICI)* specifications describe how network-to-network signaling should be done. B-ICI uses a modified and extended version of SS7. By mutual agreement, carriers also may implement PNNI signaling between their networks.

In all cases, signaling messages are encapsulated in AAL5 frames. Some special functions are added to the ATM Adaptation Layer so that these messages can be delivered reliably.

This chapter describes user-network signaling. PNNI is discussed in Chapter III-9.

ATM Addresses

The switched telephone network could not work without telephone numbers. Similarly, ATM addresses are a necessary ingredient of the ATM switched virtual circuit service. Every ATM system that participates in switched calls needs to be assigned an ATM address.

The ATM Forum has defined two categories of ATM addresses:

- Native E.164 ISDN telecommunications addresses. Ordinary telephone numbers that follow the E.164 format.

- ATM end system addresses (AESAs), whose design is based on ISO *Network Service Access Point (NSAP)* address formats.

Several NSAP address formats were defined for the ISO Open Systems Interconnection (OSI) data network standards. Four NSAP-based formats were adopted for use as AESAs.

Private network ATM addresses have AESA address formats. A public network can use native E.164 addresses, AESA addresses, or both.

Automatic ATM Address Registration

The ATM protocol family includes a very helpful address registration procedure that automates the process of assigning an address to an endpoint device.

For E.164 addresses:

- An ATM switch is configured with the addresses of the endpoints reached through each of its ports.

- When an endpoint device initializes, it learns its address from the switch.

For AESA addresses:

- An ATM switch is configured with an address prefix.

- An endpoint obtains the prefix from the switch, and creates its own unique address by appending a LAN media access control (MAC) address that has been assigned to the endpoint device.

- The endpoint registers its complete address with the switch.

Automated address registration avoids the configuration hassles that have plagued ISDN numbering. See Chapter III-8 for a detailed description of the address registration protocol.

Types of ATM Addresses

The E.164 address format was created by the ITU-T to be used as the ISDN numbering system. E.164 addresses for devices attached to an ATM public network can be up to 15 digits in length. These native E.164 addresses sometimes are referred to as E.164N addresses.

The four types of NSAP-based AESA addresses are

- Addresses that start with an ISO Data Country Code (DCC). These addresses are administered by an official organization within the identified country.

- Addresses that start with an International Code Designator (ICD) that has been registered with the British Standards Institute, the designated ISO ICD registration authority. These addresses are administered by the organization that registered the code.

- E.164 addresses embedded within an NSAP format. These embedded E.164 addresses sometimes are referred to as E.164e addresses.

- Local addresses, used within a network that is not connected to any other network.

NSAP address formats were general and flexible. *ATM end system addresses (AESAs)* follow overall NSAP formats, but they have a well-defined structure. The four formats designed for ATM use are described in the sections that follow.

ATM AESA Address Formats

The ISO address specification allows NSAP addresses to have different lengths. However, ATM end system addresses, which are based on NSAP formats, must have a fixed length of 20 bytes.

An NSAP address starts with an *initial domain part (IDP)* that indicates what the layout of the rest of the address will be. The rest of the address is called the *domain specific part (DSP)*. Figure 7.1 shows the overall format.

Figure 7.1   Overall NSAP address format.

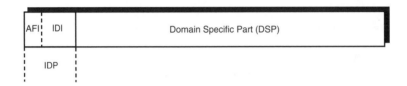

The first byte of the initial domain part is the *authority and format identifier (AFI)*. Except for a local address, the AFI is followed by an *initial domain identifier (IDI)*. The AFI indicates

- The type, format, and size of the IDI that follows

- The authority responsible for allocating IDI values

- The encoding used for the domain specific part (binary, binary encoded decimal, or character)

Together, an AFI and IDI identify the organization that administers the values in the domain specific part. The AFI and IDI values used for ATM NSAP addresses are displayed in Table 7.1.

Figure 7.2 shows the four ATM end system address formats. Note that the IDI for the embedded E.164 format is an 8-byte E.164 address, and that there is no IDI for the local format. A MAC address normally is used as the end system identifier (ESI) portion.

Table 7.1   AFI and IDI Values Used in ATM Addresses

AFI	IDI	Domain Specific Part Encoding
39	ISO Data Country Code (DCC)	Binary bytes
47	International Code Designator (ICD)	Binary bytes
45	Encapsulated E.164 address	Binary bytes
49	Null	Binary bytes

Figure 7.2   ATM end system address formats.

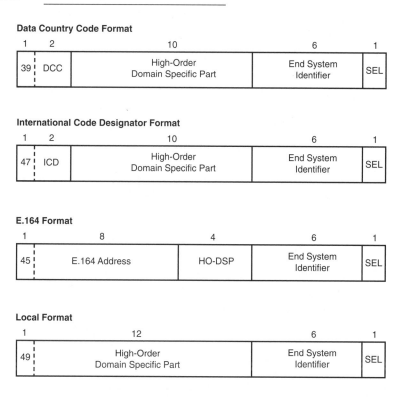

Data Country Code Format

1	2	10	6	1
39	DCC	High-Order Domain Specific Part	End System Identifier	SEL

International Code Designator Format

1	2	10	6	1
47	ICD	High-Order Domain Specific Part	End System Identifier	SEL

E.164 Format

1	8	4	6	1
45	E.164 Address	HO-DSP	End System Identifier	SEL

Local Format

1	12	6	1
49	High-Order Domain Specific Part	End System Identifier	SEL

Note

The digits of an embedded E.164 number are represented in binary coded decimal form. The rightmost four bits are 1111. If the E.164 number is less than 15 digits in length, it is padded on the left with 0000 nibbles.

Use of ISO Data Country Codes

Each country that participates in ISO activities is represented by an official member body and is assigned an ISO Data Country Code. The official member body designs and administers the rest of the NSAP DCC address for that country.

For example, the American National Standards Institute (ANSI) is the U.S. member body, and the U.S. DCC is 0840. ANSI provides a registration service that assigns numeric organization identifiers to U.S. companies. Each U.S. NSAP DCC address starts with

39 0840 (Organization Identifier)

Use of International Code Designators

At one time, an organization that operated a network with international scope, or that wished to design addresses whose format was not mandated by an ISO member body could apply to the British Standards Institute and obtain an ICD code. An NSAP ICD address starts with

47 (Code assigned by the British Standards Institute)

Normally, the owner of an ICD builds a hierarchy of addresses. For example, a private ATM service provider may break the domain specific part of its space into

- Area identifier

- Subscriber identifier

- Number to be assigned by the subscriber

The U.S. government obtained several ICD codes. For example, the U.S. General Services Administration administers the government's OSI network and 0005 is the Government OSI Protocol (GOSIP) ICD. To cite a European example, ICD 0023 is used by the Uninett research network based in Norway.

GOSIP and Uninett addresses have the formats displayed in Table 7.2.

Table 7.2   Examples of ICD-Based Addresses

U.S. GOSIP Fields	Uninett Fields
AFI=47	AFI=47
ICD=0005	ICD=0023
DSP Format Identifier	Version
Administrative Authority	Network
Reserved field	Region
Routing Domain Identifier	Member-ID
Area Identifier	Member-Access-Point
System Identifier	Switch-Number
NSAP Selector	ESI=MAC-Address

Identifiers for Organizations for Telecommunications Addressing

The pool of ICD numbers could be seriously depleted by organizations wishing to own an ATM address hierarchy. The British Standards Institute prevented this by defining one ICD code—X'0124—to be used for telecommunications addresses. This scheme is called

Identifier for Organizations for Telecommunications Addressing (IOTA). This X'0124 code is followed by a three-byte field that contains an IOTA organization identifier. Today, telecommunications organizations apply to the British Standards Institute for an IOTA identifier rather than an ICD. Figure 7.3 shows the format of an ATM end system address with an IOTA identifier field.

Figure 7.3   An ATM ICD end system address with an IOTA identifier field.

International Code Designator Format with IOTA Identifier Format

1	2	3	7 bytes	6 bytes	1
47	0124	Org. Identifier	High-Order Domain Specific Part	End System Identifier	SEL

Use of E.164 AESA Format

A common use for the E.164 AESA format is to create a consistent address format for a private ATM network connected to a public network that uses E.164 addresses. A private switch interface connected to the public network might have a native E.164 address. This address could be used as the IDI for the addresses within the private network. Thus, every address within the private network would start with

45 (E.164 Address)

The remaining high-order domain specific part (HO-DSP) of the address can be broken into a sequence of fields that define an address hierarchy (for example, areas and LANs). The owning organization can set up this hierarchy in any way it wishes. For example:

45 (E.164 Address) (Area) (LAN)

The end system identifier (ESI) in the address uniquely identifies an endpoint. This can be done in any convenient way. The favored method is to use a unique MAC address as the endpoint identifier. The entire address would be

45 (E.164 Address) (Area) (LAN) (MAC Address) (Selector)

An end system can then

• Learn the first 13 bytes of its address from its adjacent switch

• Concatenate its MAC address to generate a globally unique address

The selector (SEL) byte at the end of an NSAP address plays no role in routing a call to an ATM endpoint system. It is included for the convenience of end systems. For example, it could be used to select a specific software component that should process incoming ATM frames.

Group Addresses

Version 4 of the ATM Forum specification defined the use of *group addresses* in its implementation agreements.

Every ATM system must have at least one ATM address that is assigned to only that system. A system also can be assigned one or more group addresses. As the name suggests, the same group address can be given to several systems.

Group addresses have the potential to simplify network configuration by providing an *anycast* service. An anycast group address can be associated with a service function, such as LAN Emulation configuration service. Then, for example,

- Every LAN emulation configuration server can be preconfigured with this group address (in addition to its unique address).

- Each LAN emulation configuration server would register its group address with its adjacent switch. The switch would advertise the location of the server to other switches.

- An endpoint that wished to connect to the nearest LAN emulation configuration server would request a call to the group address.

- The switch would route the call to the *nearest* active server. This server would identify its unicast address during the call setup.

This gives ATM endpoints the ability to find the nearest active server of a given type. Note that this capability supports graceful network recovery in the event of the loss of a server.

The scope of an anycast request can be limited, so the search for an appropriate server is kept as local as security may require.

When the International Standards Organization originally defined AFI values, it restricted the values to binary coded decimal (BCD), which uses four binary bits to express only the decimal digits from 0 to 9. This was fortunate because it was easy for ISO to later assign the other hexadecimal byte values to group addresses. The group address AFIs corresponding to the unicast AFIs used in NSAP addresses are shown in Table 7.3.

Table 7.3	Unicast and Group ATM NSAP AFIs	
Unicast AFI	**Group AFI**	**IDI**
39	X'BD	ISO Data Country Code (DCC)
47	X'C5	International Code Designator (ICD)
45	X'C3	Embedded E.164 address
49	X'C7	Local address

The ATM Forum has obtained an ICD of X'0079, and administers the assignment of group addresses to well-known services. These addresses have the prefix X'C50079. The ATM Forum has assigned LAN emulation configuration servers the group address

C5.0079.000000000000000000000.00A03E000001.00

ATM name system servers, which translate logical system names to ATM addresses, have been assigned the group address

C5.0079.000000000000000000000.00A03E000002.00

The ATM name system is based on the Internet's domain name system (DNS).

Now that you have examined ATM addresses, you are ready to investigate the way switched ATM calls are set up across a user-network interface.

ATM Switched Virtual Circuits

The basic procedure used to set up a switched point-to-point call can be very simple:

- A calling end station sends a setup message to its adjacent switch asking the network to establish a switched virtual circuit with a called endpoint identified by an ATM address.

- The network switch adjacent to the called end station notifies it of the incoming call, and the called end station responds with a message accepting the call.

- Either party can initiate call clearing messages that terminate the call.

Switched ATM calls support a wide array of voice and data services. Hence, at call setup, in addition to providing the ATM address of the called station, a caller specifies the traffic contract parameters that define bandwidth, delay, and reliability characteristics for each direction of the SVC.

The Signaling ATM Adaptation Layer

Signaling messages are transported in AAL5 frames. However, signaling messages are important and should be delivered reliably. To support signaling, the basic AAL5 protocol has been enhanced with some extra features. The expanded AAL Layer is called the *Signaling ATM Adaptation Layer (SAAL)*. SAAL supports user-network signaling, private network signaling, and public network signaling.

An SAAL "user" is a process in an endpoint or a switch. SAAL provides a service to its users that includes the following functions:

- Establishing and terminating a signaling connection

- Delivery of messages in order

- Delivery of messages without loss or duplication

- Controlling the flow of information from the sender by the receiver

Figure 7.4 shows how the signaling function is layered on top of the Signaling ATM Adaptation Layer. The SAAL includes extra functions that are needed to support reliable message delivery. These extra functions are layered on top of the usual AAL5 functions, namely

- Adding a trailer containing a CRC to a data payload before transmission and processing the trailer when data is received. This is done by the common part convergence sublayer—a big title for such a simple job.

- Segmenting an outgoing AAL5 frame into cells, and reassembling the cells into a frame on arrival. This is done by the segmentation and reassembly sublayer.

Figure 7.4   Layering for the signaling function.

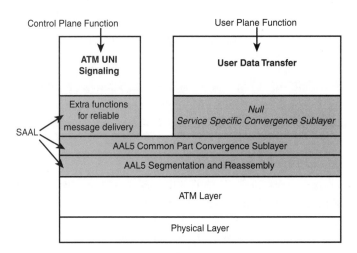

Signaling is classified as a control function. Standards express this by saying that signaling is a *control plane* function. Similarly, the transfer of ordinary user data is called a *user plane* function.

Service Specific Functions for the SAAL

Every ATM function is layered, and every layer has a name. It should not come as a surprise that the extra, service-specific functions needed for the SAAL are sublayered and named, as is shown in Figure 7.5.

| Figure 7.5 | Service specific functions for the SAAL. |

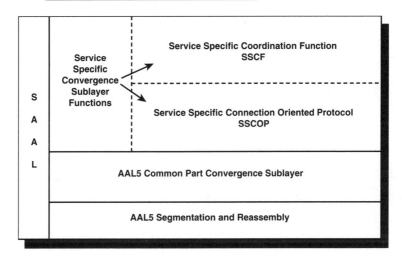

The *Service Specific Connection Oriented Protocol (SSCOP)* is the component that does all the heavy work of supporting the reliable transmission of messages. Although SSCOP was defined because it was needed for signaling, it is a general service and can be used to provide reliable transmission to other applications.

The *Service Specific Coordination Function (SSCF)* provides a simple interface between a process that sends and receives signaling messages and the SSCOP protocol layer. A programming interface to the SSCF is minimal and consists of calls that

- Establish a connection

- Send and receive messages

- Terminate the connection

The SSCF acts as a pipeline between higher layer process and the lower level SSCOP services. It uses only those SSCOP features that are relevant to the needs of the signaling protocol.

Service Specific Connection Oriented Protocol

SSCOP contains the mechanisms that

- Detect and retransmit lost messages

- Impose flow control on the stream of signaling messages

When the endpoint device is a private network switch, it may need to set up large numbers of calls on behalf of many different workstations. Thus, signaling message traffic may be quite brisk. The protocol that performs these functions must be robust and efficient.

The basic SSCOP operations are straightforward:

- To set up a signaling connection, a BEGIN PDU is sent to the partner.

- The partner replies with a BEGIN ACK PDU.

- The partners transmit DATA PDUs.

- An END PDU is sent to terminate the connection.

- The partner replies with an END ACK PDU.

Recovering Lost Messages

The protocol handles data loss efficiently. Messages are numbered and transmitted in order. If a set of incoming messages is numbered 1, 2, 3, and 5, the receiver delivers messages 1, 2, and 3 to its user and stores message 5.

The receiver knows that message 4 is missing and sends an unsolicited status (USTAT) report back to the sender. The USTAT report acknowledges the messages that have been received and states that message 4 is missing. The sender quickly retransmits the missing message(s).

In fact, the receiver can report multiple ranges of missing messages. For example, if 1, 4, and 7 arrive, the receiver can report that the ranges 2—3 and 5—6 are missing.

However, note that this mechanism cannot do the whole job:

- The receiver's USTAT report might itself be lost.

- If messages 1, 2, 3, and 4 were delivered while 5 was lost, and there was a period when no other messages were sent, there could be an unacceptable delay before the receiver discovered that data was missing.

The solution is simple. The sender periodically polls the receiver. The response to a poll is a solicited status (STAT) report that lists any gaps in the received messages and acknowledges the messages that have arrived.

Because data transfer is bidirectional, note that polls and reports actually are transmitted in both directions. Regular polls and reports also provide a keepalive function that indicates whether the signaling connection is up when there is no data that needs to be sent.

Flow Control

A receiver imposes flow control by setting a bound on the biggest message number that it is willing to receive. Numbering always starts at 0, and the first bounds are identified in the BEGIN and BEGIN ACK messages. The limits are updated regularly in USTAT and STAT reports.

Resynchronization Service

In order to recover from an error noted at a higher level, a user of the SSCOP service may need to request that the session be reinitialized. However, if there is a problem with data transfer only in one direction, the user can request that the connection be reinitialized only in that direction.

Resynchronization reinitializes the buffers and counters for one direction, while data transfer in the other direction proceeds normally.

Overview of Signaling Protocol Elements

ITU-T's Digital Signaling System 2 (DSS2) defines the user-network interface procedures and the signaling messages that establish, maintain, and release switched virtual connections.

DSS2 is an extension of *Digital Signaling System 1 (DSS1)*, the user-network signaling protocol for N-ISDN. DSS2 signaling for point-to-point connections was defined in ITU-T standard Q.2931 and was extended to point-to-multipoint connections in Q.2971.

The ATM Forum published a signaling implementation agreement as part of its UNI version 3.1, and later updated and expanded signaling functionality in its *ATM user-network Interface (UNI) Signalling Specification*, Version 4.0.

The SAAL transports signaling messages between peers such as a computer and an ATM switch or a private ATM switch and a public ATM switch.

A switched virtual path or channel connection is established by means of a series of messages exchanged across the user-network interface. For simplicity, a single, static, out-of-band channel often is used for all signaling messages between an endpoint and its adjacent switch. The default UNI signaling channel is identified by VPI=0, VCI=5. The cell payload type field identifies the cells in a signaling message as user data.

Alternatively, signaling messages that set up virtual channel connections within a particular virtual path can be transmitted on a designated signaling channel (currently VCI=5) within that virtual path. This procedure is called *associated signaling*.

Setting Up a Point-to-Point Call

Very few UNI messages need to be exchanged to set up a point-to-point call, although the procedure can be expanded with optional messages that are useful under some circumstances. Figure 7.6 illustrates a simple series of steps that can be followed to set up a call. Basically, a caller sends a SETUP message to request the call and a called party sends a CONNECT to accept. The other messages act as acknowledgments and carry some useful call parameters.

Figure 7.6   Setting up a point-to-point ATM call.

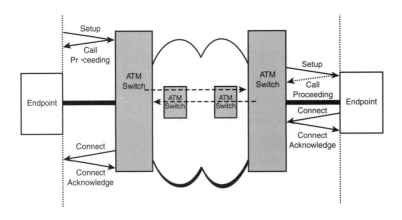

The steps in Figure 7.6 are

1. The caller sends a SETUP message to its network switch.

2. The caller's switch processes the message, responds with a CALL PROCEEDING message, and forwards SETUP information through the network.

3. The called user's switch sends it a SETUP message announcing the call.

    Optionally, the called user can respond to its switch with a CALL PROCEEEDING message, to let the network know that the setup parameters have been received and are being processed. This is done if the called party needs some extra time to prepare its CONNECT message.

4. The called user sends a CONNECT message to its switch to accept the call.

5. The switch responds with a CONNECT ACKNOWLEDGE message and forwards CONNECT information through the network.

6. The caller's switch sends a CONNECT message to the caller to indicate that the call has been accepted.

7. The caller sends a CONNECT ACKNOWLEDGE message to its switch to confirm that it knows that the call has been set up.

Releasing a Point-to-Point Call

The party at either end of a point-to-point call can request the release of the call. Figure 7.7 shows the series of steps. In the figure, the caller initiates the release.

Figure 7.7   Releasing an ATM point-to-point call.

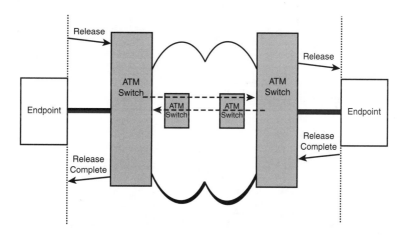

Setting Up a Point-to-Multipoint Call

Recall that currently, a multipoint root sends data to leaf nodes on a one-way connection. When a root starts a point-to-multipoint call, the root connects to its first leaf with the same series of messages that is used for a point-to-point call. The only difference is that a parameter in the SETUP message indicates that this is a point-to-multipoint call.

Figure 7.8 shows a multipoint call being set up to a destination system that is connected to a public network via a private switch. Recall that there is a UNI interface between a private switch and a public switch.

Figure 7.8   Starting a point-to-multipoint call.

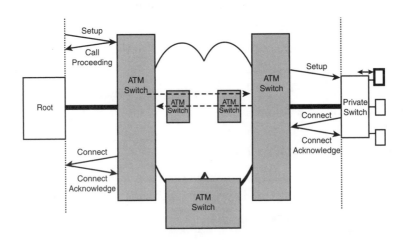

In Figure 7.9, the root adds another party to the call. The second party is located at the same private switch as the first party. The messages consist of an ADD PARTY and ADD PARTY ACK at each UNI. The reason that the messages are so simple is that the destination private switch already knows all the call parameters.

Figure 7.9   Adding a party to a point-to-multipoint call.

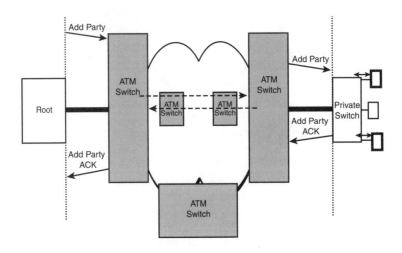

In Figure 7.10, a party at a different location is added to the call. The message exchange at the root remains simple. However, the full series of SETUP, CONNECT, and CONNECT ACKNOWLEDGE messages are needed at the destination UNI in order to establish the parameters for the call.

Figure 7.10   Adding a second party to a point-to-multipoint connection.

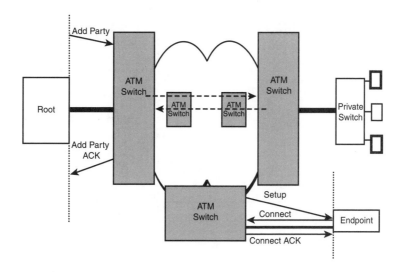

User-Network Signaling Messages

Tables 7.4 through 7.9 describe the message types included in Version 3.1 and Version 4 of the ATM Forum's UNI signaling agreement. In all the tables, message types marked with an asterisk (*) were added to the ATM Forum implementation agreement in Version 4 of the Forum's UNI signaling specification. Each message type has an identifier code that is displayed in the table.

Figures 7.8, 7.9, and 7.10 showed how a root adds nodes to a point-to-multipoint connection. Table 7.9 describes messages that enable a system to make a request to join a point-to-multipoint connection. Depending on the mode of operation that has been established, either the network will automatically add the leaf, or the root will be notified and can decide whether it wants to add the leaf. The addition of the leaf is initiated with a SETUP or ADD LEAF message.

Table 7.4	Point-to-Point Call Establishment Messages	
Hex Code	Message Type	Description
05	SETUP	Sent by a calling user to initiate a call. Also sent by the network to the called user.
02	CALL PROCEEDING	Sent by the network to the calling user to indicate that call establishment has been initiated. Also optionally sent to the network by the called user.
01	ALERTING*	Plays the role of the sound of ringing heard by a telephone caller. Sent by the called user to the network and by the network to the calling user to indicate that called user alerting has been initiated.
03	PROGRESS*	Sent by the user or the network to indicate the progress of a call that involves interworking; for example, with N-ISDN or frame relay.
07	CONNECT	Sent by the called user to the network to indicate acceptance of the call. Also sent by the network to the calling user.
0F	CONNECT ACKNOWLEDGE	Sent by the network to the called user. Also sent by the calling user to the network.

Table 7.5	Call Clearing Messages	
Hex Code	Message Type	Description
4D	RELEASE	Sent by a user to request that a call be cleared. Also sent by the network to indicate that the end-to-end connection is cleared and that the receiving user should send a RELEASE COMPLETE and free the call resources.
5A	RELEASE COMPLETE	Sent by a user that has received a RELEASE. Also sent by the network to indicate that a call has been released and the user should free call resources.

Table 7.6	Call Restart Messages	
Hex Code	Message Type	Description
46	RESTART*	Sent by the user or the network to abort calls due to a serious failure. Asks the recipient to nullify a virtual channel, all virtual channels in a virtual path connection, or all virtual channels controlled by the signaling virtual channel.
4E	RESTART ACKNOWLEDGE*	Acknowledges receipt of a RESTART and indicates that restart processing is complete.

Table 7.7	Miscellaneous Messages	
Hex Code	Message Type	Description
75	STATUS ENQUIRY	Sent by the user or by the network at any time to solicit a STATUS message.
7D	STATUS	Sent by the user or the network in response to a STATUS ENQUIRY message, or at any time to report error conditions.
0E	NOTIFY*	Sent by the user or the network to provide information pertaining to a call.

Table 7.8	Point-to-Multipoint Messages	
Hex Code	Message Type	Description
05	SETUP	Sent by a root to connect to the first called party. The message includes a parameter that indicates that this is a point-to-multipoint call. Also sent to add a party at a UNI that does not already have other parties participating in this call.
80	ADD PARTY	Sent by the root to add a party to an existing call. Sent by the network to add a party to a UNI that already has a participating called party.

continues

Table 7.8	Continued	
Hex Code	**Message Type**	**Description**
81	ADD PARTY ACKNOWLEDGE	Sent by a called party to accept a multipoint call. Sent by the network to notify the root that the ADD PARTY request was successful.
85	PARTY ALERTING*	Sent by a called party to the network and by the network to the root. Indicates that called party alerting has been initiated.
82	ADD PARTY REJECT	Sent to the root by the network if the called party could not be added or the called party did not accept the call.
83	DROP PARTY	Sent to drop a party from a multi-point connection.
84	DROP PARTY ACKNOWLEDGE	Sent in response to a DROP PARTY to indicate that the party has been dropped.

Table 7.9	Leaf Initiated Join Messages	
Hex Code	**Message Type**	**Description**
91	LEAF SETUP REQUEST*	Sent by a user to request permission to join a point-to-multipoint connection. Forwarded to the root if the root will handle the request.
90	LEAF SETUP FAILURE*	Initiated by the root or by the network to indicate failure to join the leaf to the point-to-multipoint connection.

Signaling Message Structure

Examining the contents of signaling messages provides useful insight into how the ATM call setup process works. Understanding the messages is important when call setup is not functioning correctly and you wish to use a network monitor trace as a debugging tool.

The goal of this section is to explain the structure of messages sufficiently so that you can read traces easily. To achieve this goal, a Network Associates Sniffer trace of a SETUP message will be examined in detail.

We'll start with some structural details, and then focus on the substance of the message content.

Fields in a Signaling Message

A signaling message consists of the following fields:

• A protocol discriminator that identifies the content as an ATM DSS2 signaling message

• A parameter named the *call reference value*

• The message type

• The message length

• One or more information elements that contain relevant parameters

The second item requires some explanation. When an endpoint initiates a call, it assigns a locally unique call reference value to the new call. This value is placed in the header of every signaling message relating to the call that is exchanged between the calling endpoint and its adjacent switch.

Why is a call reference needed? An ATM endpoint device might be in the process of setting up and participating in several calls at the same time. The calling device and its adjacent network switch need a local identifier that distinguishes between these calls.

At the other end of the call, the network switch adjacent to the called endpoint makes its own choice of a call reference value. This value is placed in the header of every signaling message relating to the call that is exchanged between the switch and the called endpoint. This value is purely local and is independent of the value used at the calling end.

Figure 7.11 shows the format of an ATM UNI signaling message. The protocol discriminator value, X'09, indicates that an ATM DSS2 signaling message is enclosed. (Recall that a protocol discriminator of X'08 introduces DSS1 messages.)

The second field contains the call reference value. It is coded as a length byte (equal to X'03) followed by three bytes that contain a flag and the call reference value. The flag identifies which end of the signaling channel originated the call reference value.

Note

The side that chose the call reference value sets the flag to 0 in its signaling messages, and the other side sets the flag to 1. The calling party uses flag value 0 at its end of the call. The network uses flag value 0 at the receiving end of the call.

The call reference value is followed by a 2-byte message type field. The first byte contains the message type identifier. The second byte starts with an *extension bit* equal to 1, which indicates that this is the last byte in the message type field. Extension bits are used in a number of parameters. A extension bit equal to 0 means that more follows.

This second byte is called the *message compatibility instruction indicator*. It consists of a flag, two message action bits, and some reserved bits. Usually, the flag and action bits are set to 0 and ignored.

> **Note**
>
> If the flag value in a message compatibility instruction indicator is 1, the message action bits tell a receiver how it should handle an unrecognized element. For a call reference element, action bits 00 mean clear the call, 01 mean discard and ignore the message, and 10 mean discard the message and report status.
>
> The formats of the compatibility instruction indicator bytes that appear in other information elements vary slightly. Many include bits that indicate whether a standard encoding or special encoding is used for the element's parameters. Many have 3-bit action subfields. Actions defined for an element may include discarding the information element and proceeding with the rest of the message.
>
> Fortunately, you should not have to leaf through Q.2931 to find out what the bits say—a good monitor trace will tell you.

Figure 7.11   Fields in a signaling message.

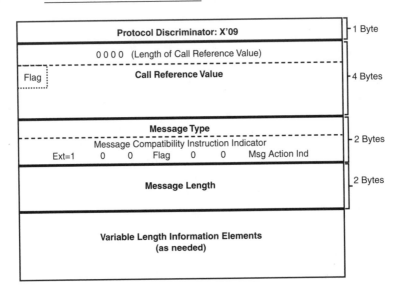

Listing 7.1 shows a trace of the initial fields in a message. When translated to decimal, the call reference value in the trace is 46. A message type of X'05 indicates that this is a SETUP message. The length of the remainder of the message is announced to be 104 bytes.

Listing 7.1	Trace of the Initial Fields in a Signaling Message

```
Network Associates Sniffer Trace
Q2931: Protocol discriminator   = 09
     Q2931: Length of call reference = 3 bytes
     Q2931: Call reference flag     = 0... ....
            (message sent from call reference originator)
     Q2931: Call reference value    = 46
     Q2931: Message type            = 05 (Setup)
     Q2931: Message type Flag/Action = 80
     Q2931:                 ...0 .... = flag
     Q2931:                 .... ..00 = action (Clear call)
     Q2931: Message Length           = 104
```

Signaling Message Information Elements

The information elements in a signaling message contain the parameters—such as the called number and the peak bandwidth required for the call—that are needed in order to set up the connection. An ATM information element typically contains a related group of parameters.

Table 7.10 displays a list of the signaling information elements and the hexadecimal codes that are used to identify them. A different subset of these information elements is required for each type of message.

Table 7.10	Signaling Information Elements

Hex Identifier Code	Information Element
04	Narrowband bearer capability
08	Cause
14	Call state
1E	Progress indicator
27	Notification indicator
42	End-to-end transit delay
4C	Connected number
4D	Connected subaddress

continues

Table 7.10   Continued

Hex Identifier Code	Information Element
54	Endpoint reference
55	Endpoint state
58	ATM adaptation layer parameters
59	ATM traffic descriptor
5A	Connection identifier
5C	Quality of service parameter
5D	Broadband high layer information
5E	Broadband bearer capability
5F	Broadband low-layer information
60	Broadband locking shift
61	Broadband non-locking shift
62	Broadband sending complete
63	Broadband repeat indicator
6C	Calling party number
6D	Calling party subaddress
70	Called party number
71	Called party subaddress
78	Transit network selection
79	Restart indicator
7C	Narrowband low layer compatibility
7D	Narrowband high layer compatibility
7F	Generic identifier transport
81	Minimum acceptable traffic descriptor
82	Alternative ATM traffic descriptor
84	ABR setup parameters
E8	Leaf initiated join call identifier
E9	Leaf initiated join parameters
EA	Leaf sequence number
EB	Connection scope selection
E4	ABR additional parameters
EC	Extended QoS parameters

Information Elements for a SETUP Message

In this section we will examine traces of the information elements in a user-network SETUP message. The important lines in each element are presented in bold print in order to make the traces a little easier to read. The information elements that will be presented are

- ATM adaptation layer parameters

- ATM traffic descriptor

- Broadband bearer capability

- Broadband low-layer information

- Called party number

- Calling party number

- Quality of service parameter

Initial Fields in the Information Elements

The information elements are introduced by three fields:

- Element identifier

- Information element compatibility indicator

- Length of the remaining contents of the element

For example, the *ATM adaptation layer parameters* information element, which is shown below in Listing 7.2, has element identifier value X'58. The message compatibility instruction indicator byte that follows includes a coding standard subfield that indicates that the ITU standardized format is used.

ATM Adaptation Layer Parameters

The ATM adaptation layer parameters in Listing 7.2 indicate that the maximum AAL5 payload size should be set to 9188 bytes in each direction. (The "id" fields identify these parameters.) The AAL service specific convergence sublayer (SSCS) is null, which is normal for a connection that will be used for ordinary data transfer.

Listing 7.2   The ATM Adaptation Layer Information Element

```
Q2931: Info element id       = 58
              (ATM adaptation layer parameters)
      Q2931: Coding Standard/Action = 80
      Q2931:    1... .... =          ext
      Q2931:    .00. .... =          code stand(ITU-T standardized)
      Q2931:    ...0 .... =          flag(not significant)
      Q2931:    .... .000 =          IE instruction field(clear call)
      Q2931: Length of info element = 9 byte(s)
      Q2931:   AAL type       = AAL type 5
      Q2931: Forward max CPCS-SDU
      Q2931:                id  = 140
      Q2931:                size = 9188
      Q2931: Backward max CPCS-SDU
      Q2931:                id  = 129
      Q2931:                size = 9188
      Q2931: SSCS type
      Q2931:   id  = 132
      Q2931:   type = Null
```

ATM Traffic Descriptor Information Element

The ATM traffic descriptor parameters in Listing 7.3 include forward and backward peak cell rates measured in cells per second. Each applies to the total traffic flow (CLP=0+1). A best effort byte is included, which indicates that this should be a UBR connection. The value is reported as decimal 190, which corresponds to X'BE.

Listing 7.3   ATM Traffic Descriptor Parameters

```
Q2931: Info element id       = 59 (ATM traffic descriptor)
      Q2931: Coding Standard/Action = 80
      Q2931:    1... .... =          ext
      Q2931:    .00. .... =          code stand(ITU-T standardized)
      Q2931:    ...0 .... =          flag(not significant)
      Q2931:    .... .000 =          IE instruction field(clear call)
      Q2931: Length of info element = 9 byte(s)
      Q2931: Forward peak cell rate (CLP = 0+1)
      Q2931:                id   = 132
      Q2931:                rate = 370370 cells/sec
      Q2931:                     157036880bps
      Q2931: Backward peak cell rate (CLP = 0+1)
      Q2931:                id   = 133
      Q2931:                rate = 370370 cells/sec
      Q2931:                     157036880bps
      Q2931:   Best effort indicator = 190
```

Broadband Bearer Capability Information Element

The parameters in the broadband bearer capability information element need some explanation.

The ITU-T and the ATM Forum have worked on categorizing different kinds of services over a period of several years. The information elements used to describe services have changed gradually, and the result is comprehensive—but untidy.

The broadband bearer capability information element contains fields that specify the ATM Bearer Class and Service Category for a connection. It also contains another useful field that indicates whether the connection is point-to-point or point-to-multipoint.

Identifying the Bearer Class

The *bearer class* field in the broadband bearer capability information element identifies the Bearer Class for the connection. Chapter III-2 describes the ATM Bearer Classes. Slightly more focused definitions of the Bearer Classes are

- **Class BCOB-A**—Used to request a constant bit rate virtual channel service. The network might perform internetworking to set up this channel. The network might need to examine the AAL information element to perform the interworking function.

- **Class BCOB-C**—Used to request a variable bit rate virtual channel service. The network might perform internetworking to set up this channel. The network might need to examine the AAL information element in order to provide the interworking function.

- **Class BCOB-X**—Provides end-to-end ATM-only service. The connection might be constant or variable bit rate. It is a virtual channel service.

- **Transparent VP**—A virtual path service. The virtual path might be constant or variable bit rate.

Identifying the Service Category

The *ATM transfer capability* field describes the service category. Values can be

- Constant bit rate (CBR)

- CBR with cell loss ratio (CLR) commitment on CLP=0+1

- Real-time variable bit rate (VBR)

- Real-time VBR with CLR commitment on CLP=0+1

- Non-real-time VBR

- Non-real time VBR with CLR commitment on CLP=0+1

- Available bit rate (ABR)

Note that unspecified bit rate (UBR) is missing. This is because ITU defined the categories listed above and the message formats, and UBR was added by the ATM Forum. The best effort parameter described earlier is used to request UBR service.

Broadband Bearer Capability Parameters

Now the complete broadband bearer capability information element can be examined.

The information element trace in Listing 7.4 has identifier X'5E. The bearer class parameter indicates that this connection will have broadband Bearer Class BCOB-X.

The message includes an ATM transfer capability field that requests non-real time VBR. However, because the best effort byte was present in the traffic descriptor, the service will be UBR.

Susceptibility to clipping relates to the problem of losing the beginning or end of a word in voice connections and is not an issue for this data connection. The final parameter indicates that this is a point-to-point connection.

Listing 7.4   Broadband Bearer Capability Parameters

```
Q2931: Info element id       = 5E (Broadband bearer capability)
     Q2931: Coding Standard/Action = 80
     Q2931:      1... .... =          ext
     Q2931:      .00. .... =          code stand(ITU-T standardized)
     Q2931:      ...0 .... =          flag(not significant)
     Q2931:      .... .000 =          IE instruction field(clear call)
     Q2931: Length of info element = 3 byte(s)
     Q2931:   Bearer class        = BCOB-X
     Q2931:   ATM transfer capability= Non-real time VBR
     Q2931:   Suscept to clipping   = Not susceptible to clipping
     Q2931:   User plane conn config = Point-to-point
```

Broadband Low-Layer Information Element

The broadband low-layer information element is not processed by network switches. It contains information for the destination endpoint. It can indicate the type of layer 2 and layer 3 protocol data carried in a frame payload. Listing 7.5 declares that the frame payload carries LLC2 data link frames.

Listing 7.5	Broadband Low-Layer Information Element

```
Q2931: Info element id        = 5F (Broadband low layer information)
     Q2931: Coding Standard/Action = 80
     Q2931:        1... .... =          ext
     Q2931:        .00. .... =          code stand(ITU-T standardized)
     Q2931:        ...0 .... =          flag(not significant)
     Q2931:        .... .000 =          IE instruction field(clear call)
     Q2931: Length of info element = 1 byte(s)
     Q2931:    Layer 2 protocol
     Q2931:        1... .... =   ext
     Q2931:        .10. .... =   layer 2 id
     Q2931:        ...0 1100 = User info layer 2 protocol
                              (LAN logical link control (ISO 8802/2))
```

Called and Calling Party Number Information Elements

The information elements in Listing 7.6 contain the called and calling party numbers. Both numbers are coded using the local AESA format (with AFI 49).

The end system identifier (ESI) field in each ATM address holds a 6-byte MAC address. The Selector byte in each number is set to 0.

The calling party element has a presentation indicator parameter that controls whether the called party will be allowed to see the calling party number.

Listing 7.6	Called and Calling Party Number Information Elements

```
Q2931: Info element id        = 70 (Called party number)
     Q2931: Coding Standard/Action = 80
     Q2931:        1... .... =          ext
     Q2931:        .00. .... =          code stand(ITU-T standardized)
     Q2931:        ...0 .... =          flag(not significant)
     Q2931:        .... .000 =          IE instruction field(clear call)
     Q2931: Length of info element = 21 byte(s)
     Q2931:        1... .... =          ext
     Q2931:        .000 .... =          type of num(Unknown)
     Q2931:        .... 0010 =          addressing/num plan id
                                        (ATM Endsystem Address)
     Q2931: 49:0000:0000 0000 0000 0000 0010:0000A14570FA:00
     Q2931:
     Q2931: Info element id        = 6C (Calling party number)
     Q2931: Coding Standard/Action = 80
     Q2931:        1... .... =          ext
     Q2931:        .00. .... =          code stand(ITU-T standardized)
```

continues

Listing 7.6   Continued

```
Q2931:        ...0 .... =          flag(not significant)
Q2931:        .... .000 =          IE instruction field(clear call)
Q2931: Length of info element = 22 byte(s)
Q2931:        0... .... =          ext
Q2931:        .000 .... =          type of num(Unknown)
Q2931:        .... 0010 =          addressing/num plan id
                                    (ATM Endsystem Address)
Q2931:        1... .... =          ext
Q2931:        .00. .... =          Presentation indicator
                                    (Presentation allowed)
Q2931:        .... ..00 =          Screening indicator
                                    (User-provided, not screened)
Q2931: 49:0000:0000 0000 0000 0000 0010:0000A145706E:00
```

Quality of Service Information Element

The quality of service information element indicates whether performance levels have been set for quality of service traffic contract parameters. In Listing 7.7, the quality of service class in both directions is 0, meaning *unspecified* QoS class. For the unspecified class, no specific cell loss ratio, cell transfer delay, or cell delay variation performance levels are associated with the connection.

Listing 7.7   Quality of Service Information Element

```
Q2931: Info element id       = 5C (Quality of service)
Q2931: Coding Standard/Action = E0
Q2931:        1... .... =          ext
Q2931:        .11. .... =          code stand
        (Standard defined for network)
Q2931:        ...0 .... =          flag(not significant)
Q2931:        .... .000 =          IE instruction field(clear call)
Q2931: Length of info element = 2 byte(s)
Q2931: QoS class
Q2931:   QoS forward  =  QoS class 0 - Unspecified QoS class
Q2931:   Qos backward =  QoS class 0 - Unspecified QoS class
```

Connection Identifier

In Listing 7.8, the sender requests that a specific virtual path connection identifier (VPI) of 0 and virtual channel identifier (VCI) of 32 be used for the connection.

Listing 7.8	Connection Identifier Information Element

```
Q2931: Info element id       = 5A (Connection identifier)
     Q2931: Coding Standard/Action = 80
     Q2931:      1... .... =         ext
     Q2931:      .00. .... =         code stand(ITU-T standardized)
     Q2931:      ...0 .... =         flag(not significant)
     Q2931:      .... .000 =         IE instruction field(clear call)
     Q2931: Length of info element = 5 byte(s)
     Q2931:      1... .... = ext
     Q2931:      .00. .... = spare
     Q2931:      ...0 1... = explicit indication of VPCI
     Q2931:      .... .000 = exclusive VPCI, exclusive VCI
     Q2931:   VPCI = 0
     Q2931:   VCI  = 32
```

Note

There is a small technical difference between the term VPCI used in the listing and the VPI for a connection. If the signaling channel controls a single device interface at the user side, the VPI and VPCI are identical. If there are multiple interfaces, several of them can use the same VPCI number at the same time. The switch will map each of these to a unique VPI on the network side.

References

Relevant documents include

- *ATM Forum Addressing: Reference Guide* (1999)

- *ATM Forum Addressing: User Guide* (1999)

- The ATM Forum *ATM User-Network Interface (UNI) Signalling Specification*, Version 4.0 (1996)

- Chapter 5 of the A*TM Forum User-Network Interface Specification*, Version 3.1 (1994)

- ITU-T Q.2931, *Digital Subscriber Signaling System No. 2 (DSS 2) user-network Interface Layer 3 Specification for Basic Call/Connection Control* (1995)

- ITU-T E.164, *Numbering Plan for the ISDN Era* (1991)

- ISO 8348 *NSAP Addresses*

- ISO 3166 *Country Codes*

- ITU-T Q.2110 *B-ISDN SAAL Service Specific Connection-Oriented Protocol* (SSCOP) (1994)

- ITU-T Q.2130 *B-ISDN SAAL Service Specific Coordination Function (SSCF) for Support of Signaling at the User-Network Interface* (1994)

- ITU-T Q.2971 *B-ISDN DSS2 UNI Layer 3 Specification for Point-to-Multipoint Call/Connection Control*

ATM Network Management

ATM networks deliver critical communications services. Because of the diversity of ATM services, ATM networks are more complicated to configure, manage, and troubleshoot than classic telecommunications and data networks. As a result, standards groups have devoted a lot of attention to ATM network management.

Three different types of management activities will be examined in this chapter.

- **Local management**—Local management defines the way that adjacent devices automatically exchange configuration and status information across a user-network interface.

- **Global management**—Network administrators and operators need to configure, supervise, and troubleshoot network devices. A management station that communicates with devices using the *Simple Network Management Protocol (SNMP)* is the most popular global management tool.

  ISO's *Common Management Interface Protocol (CMIP)* sometimes is preferred to SNMP in the telecommunications public network world. CMIP is an object-oriented protocol, which means it can model the complex inter-relationships between the components of a system far more accurately than SNMP can. However, CMIP is difficult to implement and uses valuable system resources. This chapter will focus on SNMP global management.

- **OAM management cells**—In contrast to SNMP global management, operations, administration, and maintenance (OAM) cells provide a kind of micro management. OAM cells flow through an ATM network picking up valuable information along the way. Their role, the information that they glean, and the way they function are described at the end of this chapter.

SNMP network management stations commonly are used to configure ATM networks and to gather performance information. A second tool, a *network monitor*, is an invaluable aid to network management and troubleshooting. A network monitor can eavesdrop on traffic, watching for errors or dangerous threshold conditions. It can capture traffic that later can be examined to analyze problems.

Integrated Local Management Interface

A very simple set of frame relay Local Management Interface (LMI) functions was described earlier in this book. The LMI functions provide an access device with minimal information on the status of its permanent virtual circuits.

The *Integrated Local Management Interface (ILMI)* defined by the ATM Forum is light years away from the weak and primitive frame relay LMI.

Like the frame relay LMI, ILMI enables an endpoint to check that its link to a switch is active, and to determine the current status of permanent virtual circuits. But ILMI does a lot more.

ILMI is the network administrator's best friend. It supports powerful autoconfiguration functions that automate address assignment and correct incompatibilities between endpoint and switch settings. If an endpoint system is unplugged, moved to a different location, and plugged in, an ILMI interaction with the new adjacent switch prepares the device for action. Little will have to be changed manually other than configuring the endpoint's new permanent virtual path and virtual circuit connections.

> **Note**
>
> ILMI originally stood for *Interim* Local Management Interface because it was believed that ITU-T and ANSI committees would replace it fairly quickly. However, ILMI has matured and has become well entrenched.

Scope of ILMI

The Integrated Local Management Interface enables adjacent devices to exchange configuration and status information. Figure 8.1 shows that the ILMI protocol is used between

- An endpoint system and a public network switch

- An endpoint system and a private network switch

- A private network switch and a public network switch

- Two private network switches

ILMI functions are carried out by software processes called *interface management entities (IMEs)*. A pair of IMEs at opposite ends of an ATM link communicate with one another via ILMI messages in order to negotiate compatible parameters to be used across the ATM link.

Figure 8.1   ILMI communications.

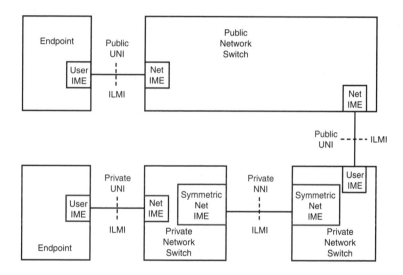

ILMI Structure

ILMI enables an endpoint device or switch to access configuration, status, and performance information at an adjacent device. ILMI data relates to the Physical Layer and the ATM Layer.

ILMI *partners* at each end of a link exchange information via SNMP, which was described in Chapter I-1. ILMI is unusual because of its symmetric behavior:

- An interface management entity in an endpoint or switch is associated with a collection of local *management information base (MIB)* variables that contain configuration and status data.

- Either interface management entity can read its partner's MIB variables (and update some address values) by sending SNMP requests to the adjacent IME.

Expressed in SNMP terminology, every IME plays the role of an SNMP *manager* (sending query and update commands) and an SNMP *agent* (responding to query and update commands).

Furthermore, every IME MIB contains almost the same set of standard variables. There are only a few small differences between the variables at a user endpoint and those at a network node. An ILMI connection between two network node IMEs is completely symmetric. The same set of MIB variables is found at each end of a network-to-network interface.

Figure 8.2 illustrates the ILMI relationship between a user (endpoint) IME and a network IME:

- The network switch can read variables that relate to the endpoint's ATM interface and update some address-specific information.

- The endpoint system can read variables that relate to the network switch's ATM interface and update some address-specific information.

Figure 8.2   Reading and updating MIB variables for the neighbor's interface.

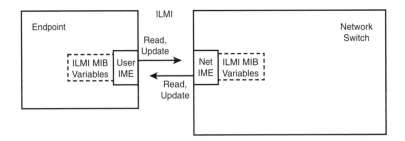

ILMI Functions

Most ATM device and switch vendors already use SNMP-based tools to configure their products, and hence vendors have embraced ILMI enthusiastically. This is very good news for network support staff.

The bane of the existence of a support staffer has been that devices at opposite ends of a wide area circuit have been configured separately—often manually—and by different personnel. Incompatible settings have led to painful debugging sessions and a lot of wasted time. For example, personnel responsible for N-ISDN installations often encounter setup problems.

With ILMI, address configuration can be automated. Also, adjacent devices automatically check up on the compatibility of the settings of many other configuration variables. Some discrepancies are fixed automatically, while others are reported to a network management center.

For example, systems frequently are configured to use only a subset of their VPI and VCI bits for addressing and zero out the rest. An ILMI system will check the values at its adjacent partner and adjust the number of bits that it actually uses to a compatible level.

ILMI MIB Variables

The variables in an ILMI management information base are of interest to anyone who is responsible for configuring or troubleshooting an ATM network, because SNMP and ILMI are key tools in these procedures.

Figure 8.3 shows how the subtree of ILMI MIB variables fits into the larger tree of SNMP network management variables. The groups of variables include

- **System**—Includes basic information, such as the type of hardware and software, the location of the device, and the identity of the person responsible for the device.

- **Physical port**—Includes unique identification for an interface and addresses that can be used for global network management.

- **ATM Layer**—Includes configuration data such as limits on the range of VPI and VCI addresses that are used, and limits on the maximum number of permanent and switched virtual path and virtual circuit connections.

- **Virtual path connection variables**—Provides traffic parameters and the current operational status of each permanent virtual path connection.

- **Virtual channel connections**—Provides traffic parameters and the current operational status of each permanent virtual channel connection.

- **Address registration**—Provides variables that enable a switch to configure the addresses at its adjacent endpoints automatically.

- **Service registry**—Provides the addresses of servers that perform special functions within an ATM network.

Figure 8.3   ATM ILMI MIB variables.

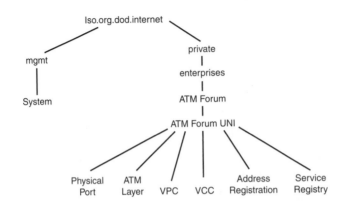

The system variables are defined in the IETF MIB-II standard. The remaining variables are defined in the ATM Forum ILMI MIB document.

An earlier version of the ILMI MIB included a number of variables that now have been declared obsolete. For example, there were several additional physical port variables and there was a group of ATM Layer Statistics variables. Although obsolete variables are listed in the current ATM Forum ILMI MIB document (version 4.0) for the sake of backward compatibility, their definitions state that the variables should not be implemented unless they are required for backward compatibility.

Obsolete variables have been omitted from this chapter.

ILMI Physical Port Variables

The physical port variables provide information about the physical interface at the user-network interface. Variables are listed in Table 8.1. Each ILMI variable has a formal MIB name—for example, *atmfPortMyIfIdentifier* is the formal name of the third variable in Table 8.1. The formal names have been supplemented with simple descriptive phrases that are easier to read.

Table 8.1   Physical Port Variables

Formal Name	Variable	Description
atmfPortIndex	Port index	Set to 0.
atmfPort MyIfName	Local interface name	A text name for the interface.

Formal Name	Variable	Description
atmfPort MyIf Identifier	Local interface number	An index number for the interface, relative to its own device. Every interface on a device is given a different numeric indexing identifier.
atmfMy IpNmAddress	IP network management address	Optionally, an IP address to which a separate network management station can send requests. (IP is not used to carry ILMI messages.)
atmfMy OsiNm NsapAddress	NSAP network management address	Optionally, an ISO NSAP address to which a separate network management station can send requests.
atmfMy System Identifier	System identifier	A 6-byte IEEE MAC address that can be used to uniquely identify the ATM device local to this IME.

Note

Additional variables were defined earlier (for example, the transmission type and media type). Experience showed that they were not useful and they were dropped.

ILMI ATM Layer Variables

The set of ATM Layer ILMI MIB variables for an interface is listed in Table 8.2. Note that several of these variables define important configuration values.

Two of the acronyms in Table 8.2 may be unfamiliar. SVPC stands for *switched virtual path connection* and SVCC stands for *switched virtual channel connection*.

Table 8.2 ATM Layer Variables

Formal Name	Variable	Description
atmfAtmLayer MaxVPCs	Maximum Number of VPCs	Includes both permanent and switched virtual path connections.
atmfAtmLayer MaxVCCs	Maximum Number of VCCs	Includes both permanent and switched virtual channel connections.

continues

Table 8.2 Continued

Formal Name	Variable	Description
atmfAtmLayer Configured VPCs	Number of Configured VPCs	The current number of permanent virtual path connections configured.
atmfAtmLayer Configured VCCs	Number of Configured VCCs	The current number of permanent virtual channel connections configured.
atmfAtmLayer MaxVpiBits	Maximum Number of Active VPI Bits	For example, if the maximum number of active VPI bits is 6, then the maximum VPI number is 63.
atmfAtmLayer MaxVciBits	Maximum Number of Active VCI Bits	Limits the maximum virtual channel identifier.
atmfAtmLayer UniType	ATM UNI Type	Public or private interface.
atmfAtmLayerUniVersion	UNI Signaling version	The latest version of the ATM Forum UNI signaling specification that is supported on this ATM interface.
atmfAtmLayerDeviceType	Device Type	Indicates whether this is an end system or a network node.
atmfAtmLayerIlmiVersion	ILMI Version	The latest version of the ATM Forum ILMI specification that is supported on this ATM interface.
atmfAtmLayer NniSig Version	NNI Signaling Version	The latest version of the ATM Forum PNNI signaling specification that is supported for this ATM interface.
atmfAtmLayerMaxSvpcVpi	Maximum SVPC VPI	Values ranging from 1 to this maximum can be used as the VPI for a switched virtual path connection.
atmfAtmLayerMaxSvccVpi	Maximum SVCC VPI	Values ranging from 0 to this maximum can be used as the VPI for a switched virtual channel connection.
atmfAtmLayerMinSvccVci	Minimum SVCC VCI	Smallest number that can be used as the VCI of a switched virtual channel.

Using ILMI to Resolve ATM Configuration Conflicts

A device reads its neighbor's ATM Layer variables, compares the values with its own, and automatically adjusts the values that actually are used to compatible levels. For example:

- The maximum number of virtual path connections that can be set up across the interface is adjusted to be the smaller of the two configured values.

- The smallest VCI that can be used for a switched virtual channel across the interface is adjusted to be the larger of the two configured values.

Figure 8.4 pictures the range of numbers that may be selected for a switched virtual path connection. Note that a VPI number for a *switched virtual path* connection *must* be taken from the range shown, but the range is not exclusively reserved for this purpose. A VPI in this range might be used as the

- VPI of a permanent virtual path connection

- VPI for a set of virtual channel connections

For the sake of simplicity, VPIs for permanent virtual path connections could be selected out of a separate, higher range of numbers, as shown in Figure 8.4.

Figure 8.4 Ranges for selecting virtual path connection numbers.

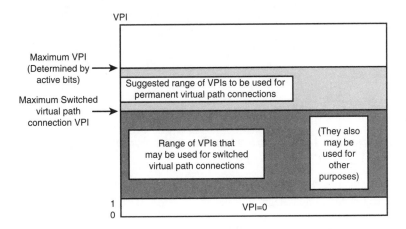

The relationship between the various virtual channel identifier numbering limits is illustrated in Figure 8.5. The range of VPI/VCI numbers that can be used for *switched virtual channel* connections is limited to the dark gray box in the figure. Note that any VPI/VCI combination can be used for a *permanent* virtual channel connection, as long as:

VPI ≤ Maximum VPI

32 ≤ VCI ≤ Maximum VCI

For simplicity, the permanent VCI numbers could be selected from the range 32 ≤ VCI < minimum switched VCC VCI.

Figure 8.5   Ranges for selecting permanent and switched VPI/VCI numbers.

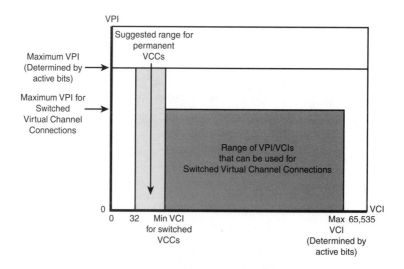

ILMI Parameters for Permanent Virtual Path and Virtual Channel Connections

An ILMI MIB includes key configuration information about every permanent virtual path connection and permanent virtual channel connection at an ILMI interface.

The network uses this information to test the traffic arriving on a connection and discover whether it conforms to its traffic contract. It is important for both ends of an ILMI interface to have compatible connection information.

Traffic at a connection interface is tested according to the conformance definitions that have been assigned to the send and receive directions of the connection. Table 6.4 in Chapter III-6 described the standard conformance definitions and listed the traffic parameters that are required for each. For each connection, the ILMI MIB at an endpoint or network node includes

- The type of conformance definition (if any) that has been associated with each direction of the connection

- The values of the traffic parameters that have been assigned to each direction of the connection

The conformance definition types include

- none
- CBR.1
- UBR.1
- UBR.2

- VBR.1
- VBR.2
- VBR.3
- ABR

The sections that follow describe the ILMI MIB connection tables, which are the

- **Virtual path connection table**—Contains information about CBR, rt-VBR, nrt-VBR, or UBR permanent virtual path connections. The GCRA algorithm or its equivalent is used to test conformance for these service categories.

- **Available bit rate virtual path connection table**—Contains information about ABR permanent virtual path connections. ABR connections are described in a separate table because ABR parameters are very different from the parameters used for the other service categories, and an ABR-specific conformance criterion must be used.

- **Virtual channel connection table**—Contains information about CBR, rt-VBE, nrt-VBR, or UBR permanent virtual channel connections. The GCRA algorithm or its equivalent is used to test conformance for these service categories.

- **Available bit rate virtual channel connection table**—Contains information about ABR permanent virtual channel connections. An ABR-specific conformance criterion must be used.

The ILMI Virtual Path Connection Tables

Table 8.3 contains an entry for each permanent virtual path connection (VPC) whose service category is CBR, rt-VBE, nrt-VBR, or UBR.

Each entry identifies the type of conformance definition and the traffic parameter values for both the transmit and receive directions.

Table 8.3   CBR, VBR, and UBR Permanent Virtual Path Connection Variables

Formal Name	Variable	Description
atmfVpcVpi	VPI Value	VPI for the virtual path connection.
atmfVpc OperStatus	Operational Status	End-to-end status (up or down) if known. If not, then local status (up or down).
atmfVpcTransmit Traffic DescriptorType	Transmit Traffic Descriptor	The conformance definition for the transmit direction.
atmfVpcTransmit Traffic Descriptor Param1-Param5	Transmit Traffic Parameters	Up to five traffic parameters.
atmfVpcReceive Traffic DescriptorType	Receive Traffic Descriptor	The conformance definition for the receive direction.
atmfVpcReceive Traffic Descriptor Param1-Param5	Receive Traffic Parameters	Up to five traffic parameters.
atmfVpcBest EffortIndicator	Best Effort Indicator	Indicator of whether Best Effort is requested for this VPC.
atmfVpc ServiceCategory	Service Category	CBR, rt-VBE, nrt-VBR, or UBR.

The Available Bit Rate (ABR) service provides throughput that varies between prespecified minimum and maximum levels. Transmission starts—and restarts—at a configured initial rate. Subsequently, the level is raised and lowered based on feedback information carried in special Resource Management (RM) cells. ABR parameters include the initial cell rate and parameters that control the resource management protocol. Table 8.4 contains an entry for each permanent virtual path connection whose service category is ABR.

Table 8.4   ABR Permanent Virtual Path Connection Variables

Formal Name	Variable	Description
atmfVpcAbrVpi	VPI	VPI for the virtual path connection.
atmfVpcAbr TransmitIcr	Initial Cell Rate	The initial transmission rate. Also the rate after an idle period.

Formal Name	Variable	Description
atmfVpcAbr TransmitNrm	Maximum number of data cells per forward RM-cell (Nrm)	Maximum number of data cells a source may send between forward resource management cells. Allowed values are: 2, 4, 8, 16, 32, 64, 128, and 256.
atmfVpcAbr TransmitTrm	Maximum time between forward RM-cells (Trm)	Upper bound on the time between forward RM-cells for an active source (in milliseconds).
atmfVpcAbr TransmitCdf	Cutoff Decrease Factor (CDF)	Fraction by which the source transmission rate is decreased when backward RM cells are lost or delayed. Larger values of the fraction cause a faster decrease.
atmfVpcAbr TransmitRif	Rate Increment Factor (RIF)	Fraction by which the source transmission rate increases after receipt of a backward RM cell which indicates no congestion in the network. Larger values permit a faster increase.
atmfVpcAbr TransmitRdf	Rate Decrease Factor (RDF)	Fraction by which the source transmission rate decreases after receipt of a backward RM cell indicating congestion in the network. Larger values cause a faster decrease.
atmfVpcAbr TransmitAdtf	ACR Decrease Time Factor (ADTF)	Allowable cell rate decrease time factor. Allowed time between the transmission of forward RM cells, before the source is required to decrease its transmission rate to the initial rate.
atmfVpcAbr TransmitCrm	RM Cells before Cutoff	The number of forward RM cells that may be sent in the absence of received backward RM cells.

The ILMI Permanent Virtual Channel Connection Tables

Table 8.5 contains an entry for each permanent virtual channel connection (VCC) whose service category is CBR, rt-VBE, nrt-VBR, or UBR.

The channels covered include special connections such as those used for signaling, PNNI, ILMI, and OAM flows.

Table 8.5   CBR, VBR, and UBR Permanent Virtual Channel Connection Variables

Formal Name	Variable	Description
atmfVccVpi	VPI Value	Virtual path identifier for the channel.
atmfVccVci	VCI Value	Virtual circuit identifier for the channel.
atmfVcc OperStatus	Operational Status	End-to-end status (up or down) if known. If not, then local status (up or down).
atmfVccTransmit Traffic DescriptorType	Transmit Traffic Descriptor	The conformance definition for the transmit direction.
atmfVccTransmit Traffic Descriptor Param1-Param5	Transmit Traffic Parameters	Up to five transmit parameters that will be tested for conformance.
atmfVccReceive Traffic DescriptorType	Receive Traffic Descriptor	The conformance definition for the receive direction.
atmfVccReceive Traffic Descriptor Param1-Param5	Receive Traffic Parameters	Up to five receive parameters that will be tested for conformance.
atmfVccBest EffortIndicator	Best Effort	Indicates whether Best Effort is requested for this VCC.
atmfVccTransmit FrameDiscard	Transmit Frame Discard Indication	Indicates that the network should try to discard entire frames in the transmit direction rather than individual cells from a frame.
atmfVccReceive FrameDiscard	Receive Frame Discard Indication	Indicates that the network should try to discard entire frames in the receive direction rather than individual cells from a frame.
atmfVccService Category	Service Category	The Service Category for the VCC.

Just as was the case for the virtual path connection ABR service, parameters that set the initial cell rate and configure the resource management protocol need to be established for each ABR virtual channel connection.

Except for the inclusion of a VCI number, the variables are identical to those in Table 8.4, so some of the descriptive details have been omitted.

Table 8.6   ABR Virtual Channel Connection Variables

Formal Name	Variable	Description
atmfVccAbrVpi	VPI	VPI for the virtual channel connection.
atmfVccAbrVci	VCI	VCI for the virtual channel connection.
atmfVccAbr TransmitIcr	Initial Cell Rate	The initial transmission rate. Also the rate after an idle period.
atmfVccAbr TransmitNrm	Maximum number of data cells per forward RM-cell (Nrm)	Maximum number of data cells a source may send between forward resource management cells.
atmfVccAbr TransmitTrm	Maximum time between forward RM-cells (Trm)	Upper bound on the time between forward RM-cells for an active source (in milliseconds).
atmfVccAbr TransmitCdf	Cutoff Decrease Factor (CDF)	Fraction by which the source transmission rate is decreased when backward RM cells are lost or delayed.
atmfVccAbr TransmitRif	Rate Increment Factor (RIF)	Fraction by which the source transmission rate increases after receipt of a backward RM cell that indicates no congestion in the network.
atmfVccAbr TransmitRdf	Rate Decrease Factor (RDF)	Fraction by which the source transmission rate decreases after receipt of a backward RM cell indicating congestion in the network.
atmfVccAbr TransmitAdtf	ACR Decrease Time Factor (ADTF)	Allowable cell rate decrease time factor.
atmfVccAbr TransmitCrm	RM Cells before Cutoff	The number of forward RM cells that can be sent in the absence of received backward RM cells.

Link Management Traps

In the general network management environment, devices send SNMP *trap* messages to report problems and changes of status. Trap messages also are a convenient way for an ILMI management entity to report important events. When an ILMI interface initializes, it announces its presence with a standard SNMP *coldStart* trap message. The ILMI *atmfVpcChange* and *atmfVccChange* trap messages enable an ILMI management entity to report a newly configured, modified, or deleted VPC or VCC to its partner.

ILMI Address Registration

Automatic address registration is the most valuable function that ILMI provides. A slightly different procedure is used for the two categories of ATM addresses, which are

- 20-byte ATM end system addresses (AESAs), usable within both private networks and public networks

- Up to 15-digit E.164 addresses, used in public networks

AESA addresses consist of a network prefix and a local part. The first 6-byte portion of the local part usually is a unique MAC address. This is followed by a selector byte.

ITU-T E.164 addresses are like telephone numbers. There is no local part within the E.164 format.

The procedure used for automated address registration is straightforward:

- The network side provides either an AESA address prefix or a complete E.164 address.

- For an AESA address prefix, the user side adds the local part that creates a unique address.

- Either side "tells" its partner address information by writing the information into a table in the partner's MIB (using an SNMP request).

Figure 8.6 illustrates this procedure for an AESA address. To fit into the available space, an ellipsis (...) represents 8 bytes of the prefix. The sections that follow spell out the details.

Figure 8.6   Address Registration.

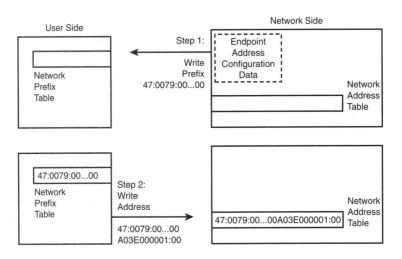

User-Side Network Prefix Table

The user side starts off with an empty network prefix table. At initialization, the network side writes one or more prefixes (or complete E.164 addresses) into the user-side table (via SNMP requests). If the network side assigns ITU-T E.164 ATM addresses, then the user side network prefix table entries contain complete addresses.

The prefixes and E.164 addresses supplied by the network switch come from configuration data that is external to ILMI.

The network side is responsible for maintaining the user-side prefix table. The network side can add new entries and remove obsolete entries at later times.

The user side is not entirely passive. It can decide which of these entries it actually wishes to use. The user side also completes AESA addresses by adding a MAC address and selector.

Network-Side Address Table

The network side IME starts off with an empty address table reserved for the system at the other end of the link that is supervised by this IME. The user side writes acceptable addresses into the network side's table via SNMP requests.

The user side maintains the network-side address table. That is, the user side invokes SNMP requests to add entries to the network-side's address table and to remove obsolete entries.

In addition to holding one or more addresses for the adjacent endpoint, the network side address table includes another variable that indicates the scope of each address. For example, one address might be used only within an organization while another address is used across a public network.

Change and Recovery

A user side system restarts the address registration process whenever it loses ILMI connectivity. To reinitialize, the user side

1. Clears out its network prefix table.

2. Sends a coldstart trap to the network side. The network side reacts by clearing its address table.

3. Reads the network side address table to make sure it is empty. If the network side table is not empty, the user side sends another coldstart trap and tries again.

4. Performs a fresh registration when the tables on both sides are clear.

Devices can be programmed to periodically read the adjacent partner's address table and make sure that the information remains consistent. If not, they can take corrective action, updating the neighbor.

These capabilities take a lot of pain out of installing and moving ATM systems. Of course, switches still need to be manually configured with an address prefix (or prefixes) for each endpoint that will be attached.

Checking if Automatic Registration Is Supported

It is hard to imagine that anyone would prefer tedious and error-prone manual address configuration to ILMI automated registration. However, there might be special circumstances that cause manual configuration to be used by some sites.

To provide for this possibility, the ATM Forum's ILMI specification includes a way for a device to discover if the partner at the other end of the interface supports address registration. The information ("supported" or "unsupported") is stored in an *address registration admin table*. The ILMI standard requires every ATM device to implement this table, which is checked before the automatic registration procedure is initiated.

ILMI Service Registry

Some systems in a network act as special servers. For example, an ATM endpoint system must access a *LAN Emulation configuration server* to join a virtual LAN.

The problem is, where are these special servers? One way that an endpoint can find the answer is by reading a *service registry table* located at its adjacent network switch. This is potentially very useful. Table 8.6 describes the variables in the service registry table.

Each entry in the service registry table corresponds to a system that offers a service. The entry identifies the service and an address that can be used to reach the server. If a server can be reached via multiple ATM addresses, then a separate indexed entry is included for each address.

Table 8.6   The ATM Service Registry Table

Variable	Description
Service ID	An identifier that uniquely identifies a service.
ATM Address	The ATM address at which this service can be reached.
Index	There may be several addresses that can be used to reach an instance of the service. If so, there will be several entries, and this number indexes them.
Parameter	A parameter whose meaning is specific to the particular service identified in this entry.

ILMI Protocol Elements

Currently, version 1 of SNMP is used for ILMI. Version 1 is widely supported by equipment vendors.

ILMI communication between a pair of devices is confined to one predefined permanent virtual circuit—the default is VPI=0, VCI=16. SNMP messages are placed directly into the payloads of AAL5 frames. (AAL3/4 frames could be used, but AAL5 is the prevalent choice.) These messages are important, so the Cell Loss Priority always is set to 0.

Every SNMP message contains a field called the *community name*, which ordinarily is used as a password that is recognized by the destination system. When used for an ILMI message, the community name must be set to "ILMI."

To promote interworking, all implementations must be able to accept SNMP messages containing up to 484 bytes. Individual vendors may support bigger sizes. It is important to configure adjacent devices to support the same size. If a system with a 484-byte limit receives bigger messages from its neighbor during initialization, the initialization will fail.

An IME has to establish ILMI connectivity with its partner, verify connectivity on an ongoing basis, and re-establish communication if it is lost. These functions are carried out by means of SNMP requests that are used as polling messages. An ILMI polling request may ask for any of three variables:

```
sysUpTime
```

```
atmfPortMyIfIdentifier
```

```
atmfMySystemIdentifier
```

The partner is expected to provide a response.

To establish connectivity, a polling message is sent every S seconds (default S=1) until a response is received. Connectivity is then tested every T seconds (default T=5). If no response is received for K consecutive polls (default K=4), then connectivity has been lost. The IME goes back to polling every S seconds.

Listing 8.2 is a trace of an ILMI message that has been sent from an endpoint to the adjacent network switch. Fields of interest are highlighted in bold text. Note that the circuit is VPI=0, VCI=16 and the community name is "ILMI."

The message payload contains an SNMP version 1 *get-request* message asking for the *sysUptime* at the neighboring switch. The SNMP request is carried inside an AAL5 frame.

Listing 8.2   An ILMI Message Sent from an Endpoint to the Adjacent Network Switch

```
Decode from WinPharoah
************************** Frame Number 2 **************************
SUMMARY:
Direction:      TE-Side
 Status:        Good
 AAL:           AAL 5
 VPI:           0
 VCI:           16
 Type:          ILMI
 Summary:       ILMI Operation Get Request

DETAIL:
 ————————AAL5 Common Part Convergence Sublayer————————·
 VPI = 0
 VCI = 16
 Number of padding octets = 41
 AAL5 CPCS Trailer
   User-to-user indicator = 0x00
   Common part indicator (CPI) = 0x00
   CPCS payload length = 47
   Cyclic redundancy check = 0xA21DDA3F
 ————Interim Local Management Interface Specification (ILMI)————
 Type = Sequence
 Octets in length = 2
 Message length = 43
 Type = Integer
 Octets in integer = 1
 Version = 0 (SNMP ver.I)
 Type = OctetString
 Octets in OctetString = 4
 Community = ILMI
 Operation = Get Request
 PDU length = 32
 Type = Integer
 Octets in integer = 4
 Request ID = 1877077822
 Type = Integer
 Octets in integer = 1
 Error status = 0 (No error)
 Type = Integer
 Octets in integer = 1
 Error index = 0
```

```
Type = Sequence
Octets in length = 2
Variable list length = 16
    Type = Sequence
    Octets in length = 2
    Sequence length = 12
    Type = Object identifier
    Octets in identifier = 8
    Object name = 1.3.6.1.2.1.1.3.0 (sysUpTime)
    Object type = NULL
    Object length = 0
    Object value = Null
```

Listing 8.3 shows a Sniffer trace of a series of poll messages sent from a DTE endpoint to a DCE switch. The messages are sent every 3 seconds, and `atmfPortMyIfIdentifier` is used as the polling variable.

Listing 8.3	Sniffer Trace of a Series of Poll Messages

```
1 DTE.0.16 DCE    06:50:12 AM ILMI: Get atmfPortMyIfIdentifier
2 DTE.0.16 DCE    06:50:15 AM ILMI: Get atmfPortMyIfIdentifier
3 DTE.0.16 DCE    06:50:18 AM ILMI: Get atmfPortMyIfIdentifier
4 DTE.0.16 DCE    06:50:21 AM ILMI: Get atmfPortMyIfIdentifier
5 DTE.0.16 DCE    06:50:24 AM ILMI: Get atmfPortMyIfIdentifier
6 DTE.0.16 DCE    06:50:27 AM ILMI: Get atmfPortMyIfIdentifier
7 DTE.0.16 DCE    06:50:30 AM ILMI: Get atmfPortMyIfIdentifier
8 DTE.0.16 DCE    06:50:33 AM ILMI: Get atmfPortMyIfIdentifier
```

Global Network Management

ATM network administration uses one or more management stations and network monitor systems to configure, monitor, and troubleshoot network switches and end devices. Interworking is promoted by defining standard MIBs for this activity.

> **Note**
>
> Recall that this activity is distinct from ILMI, which carries out automated interactions between adjacent devices.

Management variables differ to some degree depending on whether a public switch, private switch, or endpoint system is being managed. In addition, network management systems sometimes access one another for information.

The ATM Forum has labeled all of the global management interactions that occur. These interactions are shown in Figure 8.7. The labels in the figure correspond to the following activities:

- **M1**—Manages an endpoint device.

- **M2**—Manages a private ATM network or switch.

- **M3**—Supports customer network management. A customer can read network configuration, status and performance information, and optionally update its own permanent virtual connections.

- **M4**—Manages a public ATM network.

- **M5**—Supports cooperative management between two public networks.

Figure 8.7   ATM Forum network management model.

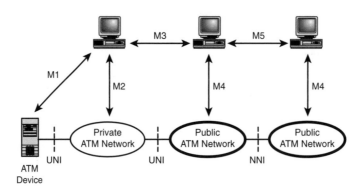

The ATomMIB

IETF RFC 1695 defines a MIB (nicknamed the *ATomMIB*) that is used for SNMP ATM global network administration. This MIB is relevant to M1, M2, M3, and M4 management. The ATM Forum has defined experimental additions to the ATomMIB in a document titled *SNMP M4 Network Element View MIB*.

Figure 8.8 illustrates the interactions between an SNMP management station and switches in a network. An SNMP agent in each switch provides access to RFC 1695 ATomMIB variables. The agent may include a proxy function that enables a network administrator to read ILMI variable values. The SNMP agents in Figure 8.8 provide proxy service to ILMI variables.

An administrator at a network management station can write configuration data into a system, and can read status and performance variables.

| Figure 8.8 | SNMP ATM network administration. |

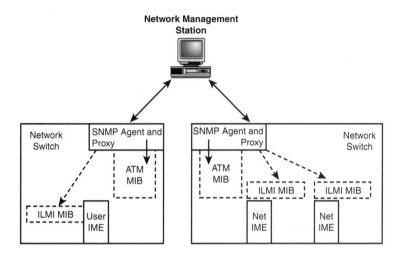

Relationship Between the ATomMIB and the ILMI MIB

Many configuration parameters in the ILMI MIB originate from the ATomMIB.

An administrator writes configuration parameter values—such as the maximum number of virtual path or channel connections for each interface—into the ATomMIB. The SNMP agent in the managed device automatically copies configuration values into the ILMI MIB at each interface.

The names of the copied parameters that are in the ILMI MIB are different from the names of the configuration parameters in the ATomMIB. For example, variables whose ILMI MIB variables are called:

```
atmfAtmLayerMaxVPCs, atmfAtmLayerConfiguredVPCs
```

have ATomMIB names:

```
atmInterfaceMaxVpcs, atmInterfaceConfVpcs
```

ATomMIB Variables

The groups of variables in the ATomMIB are listed here. Examples of variables that belong to each group are indicated. See RFC 1695 for detailed tabulations.

- **ATM interface configuration group**—Maximum number of VPCs and VCCs, maximum VPI and VCI bits used.

- **ATM interface DS3 PLCP group**—Counts of errors and alarms.

- **ATM interface TC Sublayer group**—Counts of loss of cell delineation.

- **ATM interface virtual path link configuration group**—VPI, traffic descriptor, pointer to a cross-connect mapping.

- **ATM interface virtual channel link configuration group**—VPI, VCI, traffic descriptor, pointer to a cross-connect mapping.

- **ATM VP cross-connect group**—Mappings from incoming VPIs to outgoing VPIs.

- **ATM VC cross-connect group**—Mappings from incoming VPI/VCIs to outgoing VPI/VCIs.

- **AAL5 VCC performance statistics group**—Error counts for an AAL5 VCC—for example, CRC errors.

ATM and Network Monitors

A *network monitor* is a network eavesdropping device that is able to view traffic, obtain counts of traffic and errors, raise alarms when thresholds are exceeded, and capture data useful for troubleshooting. A network monitor is an invaluable tool for ATM network management.

A number of ATM network monitoring tools already exist. (A Network Associates Sniffer monitor and a GN Nettest WinPharoah monitor were used to obtain the traces exhibited in Part III, "ATM," of this book.) However, a standard for an ATM remote monitoring (RMON) MIB was not yet complete at the time of this writing. An ATM RMON MIB would enable an SNMP management station to

- Configure a network monitor with ATM error thresholds and alarm settings

- Configure triggers that cause a network monitor to initiate an ATM traffic capture

- Retrieve summary ATM performance information from the monitor

- Receive "inform" messages from the monitor that report ATM errors and alarms

Using OAM Cells for Network Management

Earlier chapters have noted that special operations, administration, and maintenance (OAM) cells carry network diagnostic and test information across an ATM network. OAM cells perform important—although largely hidden—functions.

Four categories of OAM activity have been defined:

- Fault Management

- Performance Monitoring

- Activation/Deactivation

- System Management

There are five levels of OAM functions, labeled F1 to F5. F1, F2, and F3 deal with low-level signal transmission issues. At these low levels, OAM information is carried in the framing bits and bytes of a transmission signal; for example, in DS1 extended superframe (ESF) bits or in SONET overhead bytes.

The sections that follow describe the level F4 and F5 OAM cells. F4 and F5 OAM cells carry information related to ATM paths and channels.

Channels and Payload Types for F4 and F5 Cells

F4 OAM cells are associated with a path segment or an end-to-end path, while F5 OAM cells are associated with a channel segment or an end-to-end channel. A segment consists of one or more consecutive links along the route followed by a virtual path connection or a virtual channel connection.

Table 8.7 reviews the channel and payload type field settings for F4 and F5 OAM cells. The payload type values are binary bits.

Table 8.7   VCIs and Payload Types for OAM Cells

OAM Level	Scope	Channel Used	Payload Type
F4	Virtual Path Segment	3	0a0
F4	End-to-end Virtual Path	4	0a0
F5	Virtual Channel Segment	Monitored Channel	100
F5	End-to-end Virtual Channel	Monitored Channel	101

OAM Cell Formats

The 48-byte payload area in an OAM cell has the format shown in Figure 8.9.

Figure 8.9   OAM cell format.

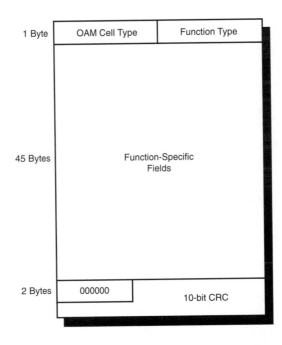

The 4-bit *cell type* indicates whether the cell relates to fault management, performance monitoring, or facility testing. The 4-bit *function type* identifies the specific use. Table 8.8 lists cell-type/function-type pairings.

The 10-bit CRC is calculated on the preceding 46 bytes of cell payload.

Table 8.8   OAM Cell Types and Function Types

OAM Cell Type	ID Bits	OAM Function Type	ID Bits
Fault Management	0001	Alarm Indication Signal (AIS)	0000
		Remote Defect Indicator (RDI)	0001
		Continuity Check	0100
		Loopback	1000
Performance Management	0010	Forward Monitoring	0000
		Backward Reporting	0001

OAM Cell Type	ID Bits	OAM Function Type	ID Bits
Activation/ Deactivation	1000	Performance Monitoring Continuity Check	0000 0001
System Management	1111	Not Standardized	

The sections that follow describe some of these OAM messages. For full details, see ITU-T I.610 and ANSI T1S1.5.

Fault Management

Fault management cells report a problem with a path or channel, and are used to perform loopback tests. These cells provide valuable information used to identify and isolate a trouble spot.

Alarm Indication Signal Cells

A network node generates a virtual path or virtual channel *Alarm Indication Signal (AIS)* cell to alert downstream nodes that a failure has been detected upstream. The failure may be caused by a defect in the underlying physical link, or the loss of a virtual path or channel for some other reason. Each switch along the path or channel processes the AIS cell and becomes aware of the failure.

By default, the 45-byte function-specific part of an AIS cell is filled with a pattern of repeating X'6A bytes. However, the first 17 bytes optionally can consist of

- A defect type code (1 byte)

- A defect location field (16 bytes)

Remote Defect Indicator Cells

On receiving a virtual path or virtual channel AIS, an endpoint returns a virtual path or virtual channel *Remote Defect Indicator (RDI)* cell that notifies upstream nodes that the notification failure has been received.

The 45-byte function-specific part of an RDI cell has the same format as the AIS cell to which it is responding.

Loopback Cells

As its title suggests, a loopback cell is forwarded to an endpoint, which then sends a copy of the cell back toward the source.

Performing loopback tests via OAM cells has a great advantage. There is no need to take a virtual path or virtual channel out of service when performing a loopback test. The OAM loopback cells simply are added to the flow.

Recall that the header of an OAM cell identifies whether it is a path or channel OAM cell. A segment loopback is sent to the end of a path or channel segment. An end-to-end loop-back is returned by the endpoint device for the path or channel.

Figure 8.10 displays the format of a loopback cell:

- The initial byte (00011000) indicates that this is a fault management loopback message.

- The loopback indication is 00000001 on the outward trip and 00000000 when the loopback is returned.

- The sender uses the correlation tag to match a returning loopback with one that was sent.

- The loopback location identifier indicates which point (or points) should send a responding cell. An all-1s value is the default, and indicates the remote endpoint.

- The source can insert an optional loopback source identifier to recognize itself as the originator when the cell returns. The default is all 1s.

Figure 8.10   Format of loopback cells.

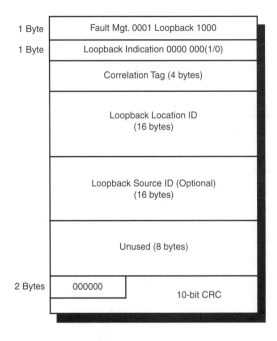

Performance Management

Chapter III-6 described parameters that play an important role in evaluating a connection's reliability and performance. Performance management (PM) cells enable some of these parameters to be measured accurately. Specifically, lost or misinserted cells, bit errors, and (optionally) cell delays can be measured via performance management OAM cells.

An administrator can select a set of paths, path segments, channels, or channel segments for which performance management functions will be executed.

The basic idea is illustrated in Figure 8.11. To monitor a flow of cells, the sending end inserts an OAM performance management cell after each block of user cells. Typical block sizes are 128, 256, 512, and 1,024 cells. The actual number of cells in a block may vary somewhat from the target block size, to avoid delaying user cells. The basic idea is that the sender delimits a block of cells with an OAM cell that indicates how many were included in the block, and the receiver reports back on how many were delivered and whether errors occurred.

Figure 8.11   Monitoring a block of user cells.

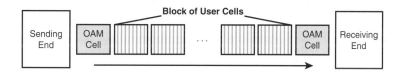

More specifically, in the OAM message, the sender reports the number of user cells in the block that has just completed and includes a parity check computed on the cell payloads. The sender optionally can include a timestamp. The receiver responds with an OAM cell that indicates the number of the block's user cells that it has received, and reports the number of errored parity bits.

Figure 8.11 depicts a one-way flow of cells, but performance management can be activated in both directions. Note that any node along the way can monitor the OAM cells and obtain Performance Management information.

Forward-Monitoring Performance Management Cell Format

Figure 8.12 shows the format of forward monitoring performance management (PM) cells.

Figure 8.12 Format of forward monitoring performance management cells.

Bytes	
1	Perf Mgt. 0010 0000 (Forward)
1	Monitoring Cell Sequence Number
2	Count for all User Cells Sent
2	Block Error Detection Code (BIP-16)
2	Count for User Cells with CLP=0 Sent
4	Optional Time Stamp
29	Unused (Fill with X'6A)
2	Fill with X'6A
1	Fill with X'6A
2	Fill with X'6A
2	000000 / 10-bit CRC

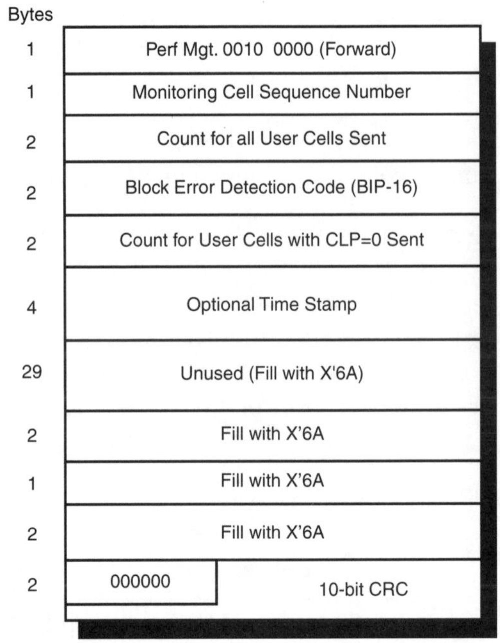

Lost or misinserted performance management cells are detected via the monitoring cell sequence number, which counts up to 255 and then wraps to 0.

The other fields in the cell include

- The current value of the counter for all user cells.

- The current value of the counter for user cells with CLP=0.

- A *block error detection code*, which is an even parity error detection code (BIP-16) computed over the information fields of the just-completed block of user cells.

- Optionally, a timestamp. (If no timestamp is present, the field should be filled with 1 bits.)

Backward-Reporting Performance Management Cell Format

After receiving a forward-reporting OAM cell that terminates a block, the receiving end checks through the fields and then transmits a backward-reporting OAM cell to the sending end. Figure 8.13 shows the format of a backward-reporting performance management (PM) cell.

Figure 8.13   Format of backward-reporting performance management cells.

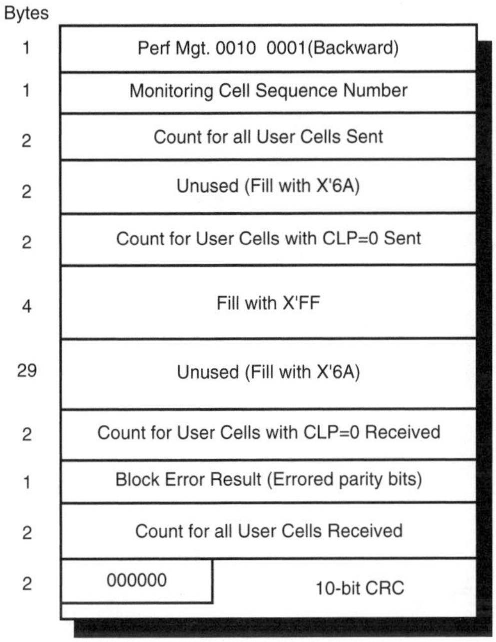

```
Bytes
  1        Perf Mgt. 0010  0001(Backward)

  1        Monitoring Cell Sequence Number

  2        Count for all User Cells Sent

  2        Unused (Fill with X'6A)

  2        Count for User Cells with CLP=0 Sent

  4        Fill with X'FF

 29        Unused (Fill with X'6A)

  2        Count for User Cells with CLP=0 Received

  1        Block Error Result (Errored parity bits)

  2        Count for all User Cells Received

  2     000000              10-bit CRC
```

The fields include:

- Copies of the original counts of all user cells and of user cells with CLP=0 that were carried in the forward monitoring cell

- The local counter values of user cells received and user cells with CLP=0 received, recorded at the receiving end

- If possible, a *block error result* that states the number of errored parity bits

A block error result that makes sense can be computed only if the previous forward OAM cell was not lost and if all user cells were received. Otherwise, the block error result field is filled with 1 bits.

Activation and Deactivation of Performance Management

Activation and deactivation of performance management can be invoked by a network management station or by means of *activation* and *deactivation OAM cells*. Figure 8.14 displays the format of an activation or deactivation cell.

Figure 8.14 The format of an activation or deactivation cell.

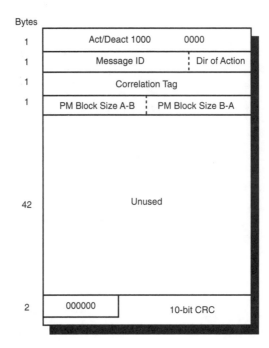

The 6-bit message ID can take on the values:

- Activate (000001)

- Activation confirmed (000010)

- Activation request denied (00011)

- Deactivate (000101)

- Deactivation confirmed (000110)

- Deactivation request denied (000111)

The 2-bit *direction of action code* is meaningful for activate and deactivate commands. It indicates whether performance monitoring should be started or stopped:

- In the transmission direction (denoted A-B) from the node (A) sending the activate or deactivate command (10).

- In the direction (denoted B-A) toward the node sending the activate or deactivate command (01).

- In both directions (11).

The *direction of action field* is set to 00 for other commands.

The other fields are

- A correlation tag that enables the nodes to correlate commands with responses.

- Codes that the activator uses to identify block sizes for the A-B and B-A directions. The field is meaningful in activate and activation confirmed messages, and is set to 0000 in other messages. The block sizes and codes are

1024 (0001)

512 (0010)

256 (0100)

128 (1000)

References

MIB variables relevant to ILMI are defined in

- RFC 1213, *Management Information Base for Network Management of TCP/IP-based internets* (1991), which describes the system variables.

- ATM Forum document, *Integrated Local Management Interface (ILMI) Specification Version 4.0* (1996).

Additional variables that are useful for managing ATM from a management station are defined in

- RFC 1573, *Evolution of the Interfaces Group of MIB-II* (1994).

- RFC 2233, *The Interfaces Group MIB using SMIv2* (1997).

- RFC 1695, *Definitions of Managed Objects for ATM Management Version 8.0 using SMIv2* (1994).

- An experimental extension to RFC 1695, *ATM Forum SNMP M4 Network Element View MIB* (1998).

- The CMIP version of M4 management, *ATM Forum M4 Network View CMIP MIB Specification*, Version 1.0 (1997).

- RFC 1595, *Definitions of Managed Objects for the SONET/SDH Interface Type* (1994).

- RFC 1407, *Definitions of Managed Objects for the DS3/E3 Interface Type* (1993).

- RFC 1406, *Definitions of Managed Objects for the DS1 and E1 Interface* (1993).

- RFC 1514, *Host Resources MIB* (1993).

The M3 Customer Network Management interface is described in ATM Forum document *Customer Network Management (CNM) for ATM Public Network Service (M3 Specification)*, 1994.

Requirements for managing circuit emulation service via CMIP are in the ATM Forum document, *CES Interworking M4 Interface "NE View" Requirements*, Logical and CMIP MIB (1997).

Requirements for AAL management via CMIP are found in ATM Forum document, *AAL Management for the M4 "NE View" Interface* (1997).

The ATM Forum has published a draft ATM RMON MIB, *Remote Monitoring MIB Extensions for ATM Networks* (1997) as document AF-NM-TEST-0080.

There are several other ATM Forum documents that address network management issues. Check the list at the ATM Forum's World Wide Web site for the latest versions.

OAM cells are described in

- ATM Forum ATM User-Network Interface Specification, Version 3.1.

- ITU-T Recommendation, I.610, *B-ISDN Operation and Maintenance Principles and Functions*, July 1995.

- ANSI T1S1.5/94-004, *Broadband ISDN Operations and Maintenance Principles and Functions: Technical Report*, March 1994.

- GR-1248-CORE, *Generic Requirements for Operations of ATM Network Elements*, Bellcore, Issue 2, September 1995.

PNNI Route Selection and Signaling

ATM is being deployed in both public and private networks. Some networks already contain many switches and the number can be expected to grow.

Before a pair of ATM nodes can communicate, a path between them must be set up. The following tasks have to be performed automatically, reliably, and quickly:

- Discovering the best path

- Generating the VPI/VCI table entries in the switches along the path

The ATM Forum has defined its approach to performing these tasks in a series of *PNNI* specifications. *PNNI* stands for both *private network node interface* and *private network-to-network interface*.

PNNI protocols describe the interactions between

- A pair of switches

- A pair of private networks

Figure 9.1 illustrates the scope of the PNNI protocols.

The word *private* in PNNI may be misleading. The PNNI protocols can be used in public telecommunications networks if its administrators desire to do so.

Figure 9.1   Scope of the PNNI protocols.

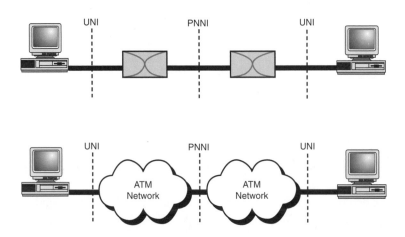

> **Note**
>
> ATM technology is still young and evolving. We can expect vendors to experiment with proprietary protocols and future standards groups to rework the PNNI protocols.
>
> Nonetheless, the current Phase 1 version of PNNI is quite comprehensive. It provides mechanisms that support network self-configuration, construction of large, hierarchical networks, and sharing of information between different networks. It also supports the dynamic generation of routes for specified Service Categories and qualities of service.
>
> Phase 1 PNNI also is very complex. At the time of this writing, vendors have implemented only a small subset of its features.

This chapter presents some major PNNI concepts and mechanisms. Many options have been omitted to keep the discussion simple. For complete details, consult the ATM Forum documents listed at the end of the chapter.

Purpose of PNNI

Suppose that an endpoint device has just sent a SETUP message to an adjacent switch asking it to set up a call. That switch can act very quickly if it knows the complete map (topology) of its network—that is

- The switches in the network

- The links that connect the switches to one another

- Metrics for each link that indicate bandwidth, delay, and reliability features

As illustrated in Figure 9.2, switch A can determine the best path to switch B (and the attached destination endpoint) using its knowledge of how the network is laid out and the various metrics assigned to each link in the network.

Figure 9.2   Selecting a route.

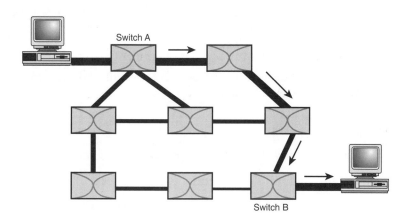

PNNI-capable switches learn a network's topology by exchanging information with other PNNI-capable switches.

Note

A protocol that enables nodes to discover the map of their network is called a *link state* protocol. PNNI is similar in some ways to two existing link state protocols: the IP Open Shortest Path First (OSPF) protocol and the OSI/IP Intermediate System to Intermediate System (IS-IS) protocol.

Learning a network's topology and choosing a path is just one part of PNNI. Switch A in Figure 9.2 also must initiate a process that gets the other switches to agree to set up the path. Each switch must create VPI/VCI entries in its routing table and reserve the resources required to support the flow of traffic. Part of the PNNI specification defines how the information that sets up the path is signaled to the switches along the path.

To understand the basic processes, it is easiest to start with the way that topology discovery and signaling work within small ATM networks. Mechanisms used within large, hierarchical networks will be described at the end of the chapter.

Elements of the PNNI Routing Information Protocol

Switches within a small network use PNNI to develop a detailed map of the network. The switches also learn the bandwidth, delay, and reliability characteristics of each link.

Readers who are familiar with OSPF will feel very much at home with the PNNI mechanisms that are used to build a map and discover link attributes. These mechanisms are described briefly in the sections that follow.

Neighboring switches exchange network topology information across the reserved *PNNI routing control channel* connection with VCC with VPI=0 and VCI=18. Formatted PNNI messages are carried in AAL5 frames.

Hello Messages

Switches periodically exchange Hello messages with their adjacent neighbors. The Hellos

- Enable neighbors to announce their identities to one another

- Provide an ongoing keepalive check that the neighbor—and the link to the neighbor— is still operational

Figure 9.3 illustrates how a node (labeled A.1) learns about nodes A.2, A.3, and A.4 via Hello messages.

Hellos are exchanged periodically. If no Hello is received during a preconfigured number of Hello intervals, the link is declared down.

Figure 9.3   Learning about adjacent nodes via Hello messages.

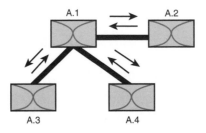

Listing 9.1 shows a Network Associates Sniffer trace of a Hello message. The message has been sent on VPI=0, VCI=18, the connection reserved for PNNI routing topology messages.

The message contains a variable called a *peer group identifier*. This is an ATM address prefix that is used by all nodes in a particular region. The nodes whose addresses start with this prefix belong to a *peer group*.

The 14-byte source node peer group identifier starts with a *level indicator* byte that states how many bits in the string actually matter. In this case, the level indicator is X'48, meaning 72 bits (9 bytes). Thus, the peer group prefix is

X'39 0000 0000 0000 0000

The remaining bytes in the peer group identifier have no significance.

The Hello message also contains *node identifiers* for the sending and receiving systems. Theoretically, administrators can design node identifiers any way they like. However, normally each 22-byte node identifier is made up of a level indicator (X'48), the value X'A0, and the node's ATM address. The node identifiers reveal that both nodes have the same prefix and belong to the same peer group.

> **Note**
>
> A big network can be given a hierarchical structure (which is described later). Identifiers for nodes at a higher level in the hierarchy consist of a level indicator, a 14-byte peer group identifier, the system's 6-byte end system identifier, and a 0 byte.

Every system assigns a port ID number to the physical point of attachment to a link. In Listing 9.1, the port IDs at the local and remote ends of the link between the two neighbors are 3238002698 and 136.

The Hello message sender learned its neighbor's node ID and port ID from the initial Hello message received from the neighbor.

At the end of the listing, the sender states that its *Hello interval* is 15 seconds, which means that it intends to send a Hello every 15 seconds. If its neighbor does not receive any Hellos during a prespecified multiple of this time, the link will be declared dead.

Listing 9.1   Sniffer Trace of a Hello Message

```
PNNI: Routing Hello
ATM: --- ATM Header ---
     ATM:
     ATM: Frame 1 arrived at  15:24:02.0000; frame size is 144 (0090 hex) bytes.
     ATM: Link = DTE
     ATM: Virtual path id = 0
     ATM: Virtual channel id = 18
     ATM:
PROUT: --- PNNI Routing ---
     PROUT:
     PROUT: Packet type          = 1(Hello)
```

continues

Listing 9.1   Continued

```
PROUT: Length                    = 100
PROUT: Protocol version          = 1
PROUT: Newest version supported  = 1
PROUT: Oldest version supported  = 1
PROUT: Reserved                  = 0
PROUT: Flags                     = 0
PROUT: Node ID                   = 48A0390000000000000000020211AA01010101010100
PROUT: ATM endsystem address
PROUT: 39:0000:0000 0000 0000 0202 11AA:010101010101:00
PROUT: Peer Group ID             = 48390000000000000000000000000
PROUT: Remote Node ID            = 48A0390000000000000000020221AA0020DA7F661000
PROUT: Port ID                   = 3238002698
PROUT: Remote Port ID            = 136
PROUT: Hello Interval            = 15
PROUT: Reserved                  = 0
PROUT:
```

Synchronizing Databases

Every switch in a network builds up an identical database that describes the nodes and links that make up the network. The steps in building up this database are

- Exchanging database summaries with an adjacent neighbor

- Requesting database items from an adjacent neighbor

- Receiving and acknowledging database items

- Flooding database items to other nodes

Exchanging Database Summaries

Initially, a node knows only its own interfaces and links. By exchanging Hellos across its links, the node discovers the identity of each adjacent neighbor.

Figure 9.4 illustrates what happens next. In the figure, node A.1 sends neighbor node A.2 summary messages that describe the records currently in its topology database. Node A.2 responds with a summary of its own database.

Figure 9.4   Exchanging database summaries.

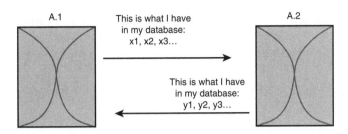

Each database entry is called a *PNNI topology state element* or *PTSE*.

Requesting PNNI Topology State Elements

Each node examines each of its neighbor's summary messages to see whether the neighbor has a database PTSE that it does not yet have, or that is a more recent version of a PTSE that the node already holds. If this is the case, the node requests the element.

As shown in Figure 9.5, node A.1 asks neighbor A.2 for the new or updated PTSEs y2 and y4. When node A.2 responds, node A.1 acknowledges receipt and integrates these elements into its database. At the same time, node A.2 asks for any PTSEs that it needs from node A.1.

Multiple PTSEs are bundled into a *PNNI topology state packet (PTSP)*. When the exchange of PTSPs is complete, the databases at the two nodes are synchronized—that is, they contain identical information.

Figure 9.5   Requesting PNNI topology state elements.

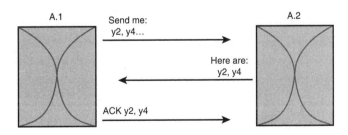

Flooding

Whenever there is an update to network information, a PTSE that reports the update must be propagated through the network. This update process is called *flooding*. The way that it works is

- The node that starts the process sends the PTSE to each of its adjacent neighbors.

- Each recipient sends the PTSE to every adjacent neighbor except for the one from which it was received.

- Each recipient sends an acknowledgment to the source from which it received the PTSE.

- The sender retransmits if an acknowledgment is not received within a timeout period.

The following events trigger a flooding reaction:

- A node creates a new PTSE in its database to describe a new interface that has just been added to the device.

- A node receives a new or updated PTSE.

When flooding is complete, all of the nodes in the network will have identical information in their databases. Any subsequent changes will be flooded through the network to keep all of the databases synchronized.

Periodically, a node refloods the information that it originated to describe its own system and links. To make sure that "stale" data that describes a crashed switch does not remain in network databases, data describing other nodes eventually is "aged out," which means that the information is discarded if it is not refreshed within a timeout period.

Network Topology Database Information

A network topology database contains a variety of parameters that are packaged in different types of *information groups*. One or more groups of a given type is carried in a PTSE. Table 9.1 lists the types.

Table 9.1   PTSE Information Group Types

Type Number	Type	Description
96	Nodal state parameters	Describes properties of a node associated with a given input port/output port pairing.

Type Number	Type	Description
97	Nodal information group	Conveys general information about a node, such as its peer group identifier and its ATM End System Address. Also includes additional information that is used by members of a peer group to elect a peer group leader.
224	Internal reachable ATM addresses information	Advertises the addresses group of directly attached ATM endpoints.
256	Exterior reachable ATM addresses information group	Advertises the addresses of ATM endpoints that can be reached by passing through exterior networks that do not participate in PNNI routing.
288	Horizontal links information group	Advertises links to other nodes within the same peer group.
289	Uplinks	Advertises links to nodes that are outside of the peer group.
640	System capabilities	Advertises standard ATM Forum or proprietary vendor system capabilities.

Nodal Information Group PTSE

Listing 9.2 shows a PTSE that carries a *nodal* information group. The message identifies the originating node, its peer group, and its ATM address, and states that the system is a transit node. A transit node can be traversed to reach other switches.

Additional information that relates to the choice of a leader for its peer group is included.

Listing 9.2   A PTSE Carrying a Nodal Information Group

```
PNNI: Routing PTSP
ATM: --- ATM Header ---
     ATM:
     ATM: Frame 190 arrived at  15:27:16.0648; frame size is 144 (0090 hex)
bytes.
     ATM: Link = DTE
     ATM: Virtual path id = 0
     ATM: Virtual channel id = 18
     ATM:
```

continues

Listing 9.2	Continued

```
PROUT: --- PNNI Routing ---
     PROUT:
     PROUT: Packet type              = 2(PTSP)
     PROUT: Length                   = 112
     PROUT: Protocol version         = 1
     PROUT: Newest version supported = 1
     PROUT: Oldest version supported = 1
     PROUT: Reserved                 = 0
     PROUT: Originating Node ID= 48A0390000000000000000040211AA03030303030300
     PROUT: Node's peer group ID= 48390000000000000000000000000
     PROUT: IE type                  = 64(PTSE)
     PROUT: Length                   = 68
     PROUT: PTSE type                = 97
     PROUT: Reserved                 = 0
     PROUT: PTSE identifier          = 1
     PROUT: PTSE sequence number     = 145
     PROUT: PTSE checksum            = 37088
     PROUT: PTSE remaining lifetime  = 3584
     PROUT: IE type                  = 97(Nodal information group)
     PROUT: Length                   = 48
     PROUT: ATM endsystem address
     PROUT: 39:0000:0000 0000 0000 0402 11AA:030303030303:00
     PROUT: Leadership priority      = 0
     PROUT: Nodal flags
     PROUT:   I am leader            = 0... ....(I am not PGL)
     PROUT:   Restricted transit     = .0.. ....(I am a transit node)
     PROUT:   Nodal representation   = ..0. ....(simple node representation)
     PROUT:   Restricted branching   = ...0 ....(can support additional branch
points)
     PROUT:   Non-transit for PGL    = .... 0...(normal operation)
     PROUT: Preferred PGL node ID    = 000000000000000000000000000000000000000000
```

Internal Reachable ATM Addresses Information Group PTSE

Listing 9.3 displays a PTSE carrying an *internal reachable ATM addresses* information group, which advertises the addresses of directly attached ATM endpoints.

The PTSE carries the originator's node ID and peer group ID. It indicates that the sender can reach all ATM addresses that start with a designated 13-byte prefix.

Note that the PTSE has a remaining lifetime of 3,600 seconds. It will age out if the message originator does not refresh it before that time.

Listing 9.3   A PTSE Carrying an Internal Reachable ATM Addresses Information Group

```
PNNI: Routing PTSP
ATM: --- ATM Header —---
      ATM:
      ATM: Frame 230 arrived at  15:27:37.6840; frame size is 144 (0090 hex)
bytes.
      ATM: Link = DTE
      ATM: Virtual path id = 0
      ATM: Virtual channel id = 18
      ATM:
PROUT: --- PNNI Routing ---
      PROUT:
      PROUT: Packet type          = 2(PTSP)
      PROUT: Length               = 96
      PROUT: Protocol version     = 1
      PROUT: Newest version supported = 1
      PROUT: Oldest version supported = 1
      PROUT: Reserved             = 0
      PROUT: Originating Node ID= 48A03900000000000000020211AA01010101010100
      PROUT: Node's peer group ID= 48390000000000000000000000000
      PROUT: IE type              = 64(PTSE)
      PROUT: Length               = 52
      PROUT: PTSE type            = 224
      PROUT: Reserved             = 0
      PROUT: PTSE identifier      = 2
      PROUT: PTSE sequence number = 67
      PROUT: PTSE checksum        = 51967
      PROUT: PTSE remaining lifetime = 3600
      PROUT: IE type              = 224(Internal reachable ATM addresses)
      PROUT: Length               = 32
      PROUT: Flags                = 32768
      PROUT: Reserved             = 0
      PROUT: Port ID              = 1298231328
      PROUT: Scope of advertisement = 0
      PROUT: Address information length   = 14
      PROUT: Address information count= 1
      PROUT: Prefix length        = 104 bits
      PROUT: Reachable address prefix = 3900000000000000000020211AA
      PROUT: Padding              = 0000
```

Horizontal Links Information Group PTSE

A *horizontal links* information group PTSE carries information that helps a node identify routes that support a given Service Class and quality of service.

Listing 9.4 shows a trace of a PNNI horizontal links PTSE. The message describes a link between the originator and another node. The PTSE identifies the node ID and port ID at both ends of the link.

The PTSE contains two outgoing *resource availability* information groups. The first provides parameter values that apply to outgoing CBR, rt-VBR, and nrt-VBR connections on this link. The second provides parameter values that apply to outgoing ABR and UBR connections on this link.

The resource availability parameters are described below. The first seven parameters appear in Listing 9.4. The remaining two are optional Generic Connection Admission Control (GCAC) parameters. The complete list of nine parameters is

- **Cell transfer delay**—The time required to transmit a cell from its source to its destination.

- **Cell delay variation (CDV)**—A measure of the differences between the expected periodic cell arrival times and the actual arrival times.

- **Cell loss ratio for CLP=0**—The proportion of cells in the CLP=0 stream that are lost.

- **Cell loss ratio for CLP=0+1**—The proportion of cells in the CLP=0+1 stream that are lost.

- **Administrative weight**—A value selected by a network administrator.

- **Maximum cell rate (maxCR)**—The maximum rate usable by connections belonging to a specified Service Category.

- **Available cell rate (AvCR)**—Measures the capacity available for CBR, rt-VBR and nrt-VBR connections, or for the minimum cell rate of an ABR connection.

- **Cell rate margin (CRM)**—Measures the difference between the total bandwidth that has been allocated and the sum of the allocated sustainable cell rates.

- **Variance factor (VF)**—A statistical measurement of the variance of the cell rate margins of all existing connections.

Since parameter values can differ for each direction of traffic flow, they would need to be specified separately for the incoming direction.

Listing 9.4	Trace of a PNNI Horizontal Links PTSE

```
PNNI: Routing PTSP
ATM: --- ATM Header ---
      ATM:
      ATM: Frame 9 arrived at  15:24:16.9762; frame size is 192 (00C0 hex) bytes.
      ATM: Link = DTE
      ATM: Virtual path id = 0
      ATM: Virtual channel id = 18
      ATM:
PROUT: --- PNNI Routing ---
      PROUT:
      PROUT: Packet type           = 2(PTSP)
      PROUT: Length                = 168
      PROUT: Protocol version      = 1
      PROUT: Newest version supported = 1
      PROUT: Oldest version supported = 1
      PROUT: Reserved              = 0
      PROUT: Originating Node ID= 48A0390000000000000000040211AA03030303030300
      PROUT: Node's peer group ID= 4839000000000000000000000000
      PROUT: IE type               = 64(PTSE)
      PROUT: Length                = 124
      PROUT: PTSE type             = 288
      PROUT: Reserved              = 0
      PROUT: PTSE identifier       = 7
      PROUT: PTSE sequence number  = 2
      PROUT: PTSE checksum         = 37608
      PROUT: PTSE remaining lifetime = 3598
      PROUT: IE type               = 288(Horizontal links)
      PROUT: Length                = 104
      PROUT: Flags                 = 32768
      PROUT: Remote node ID        = 48A0390000000000000000030211AA02020202020200
      PROUT: Remote port ID        = 654311427
      PROUT: Local port ID         = 553648129
      PROUT: Aggregation token     = 0
      PROUT: IE type               = 128(Outgoing resource availability)
      PROUT: Length                = 32
      PROUT: RAIG Flags
      PROUT:    CBR                = 1... ....
      PROUT:    rt-VBR             = .1.. ....
      PROUT:    nrt-VBR            = ..1. ....
      PROUT:    ABR                = ...0 ....
      PROUT:    UBR                = .... 0...
      PROUT:    GCAC CLP           = .... ...0
```

continues

Listing 9.4   Continued

```
PROUT: Reserved                     = 0
PROUT: Administrative weight        = 5040
PROUT: Maximum cell rate            = 310731(cells/second)
PROUT: Available cell rate          = 310731(cells/second)
PROUT: Cell transfer delay          = 60(microseconds)
PROUT: Cell delay variation         = 11(microseconds)
PROUT: Cell loss ratio(CLP=0)       = 20
PROUT: Cell loss ratio(CLP=0+1)     = 20
PROUT: IE type                      = 128(Outgoing resource availability)
PROUT: Length                       = 32
PROUT: RAIG Flags
PROUT:    CBR                       = 0... ....
PROUT:    rt-VBR                    = .0.. ....
PROUT:    nrt-VBR                   = ..0. ....
PROUT:    ABR                       = ...1 ....
PROUT:    UBR                       = .... 1...
PROUT:    GCAC CLP                  = .... ...0
PROUT: Reserved                     = 0
PROUT: Administrative weight        = 5040
PROUT: Maximum cell rate            = 365566(cells/second)
PROUT: Available cell rate          = 310731(cells/second)
PROUT: Cell transfer delay          = 60(microseconds)
PROUT: Cell delay variation         = 11(microseconds)
PROUT: Cell loss ratio(CLP=0)       = 20
PROUT: Cell loss ratio(CLP=0+1)     = 20
```

Computing a Path

The topology database gives a source switch the information that it needs to select a suitable path to a destination switch. The source switch includes the path in a SETUP message that is propagated through the nodes listed in the path, toward the destination.

The formatted information element in the SETUP message that contains the path is called a *designated transit list (DTL)*.

Cranking Back

A source node creates a path using the best information that it has available. Sometimes, however, the network may be unable to set up the call along the path described by its designated transit list. Resources may be depleted because many calls are being set up concurrently, or there may be a problem in the network.

A call that cannot be set up along its designated transit list is *cranked back*. This means that the call resources are released in a backward direction until the creator of the designated transit list is reached. At this point, an alternate route can be tried.

PNNI Signaling Messages

PNNI signaling messages are adapted from the UNI signaling messages. Normally, the connection with VPI=0, VCI=5 is used for PNNI signaling messages. PNNI signaling is layered on top of the reliable Signaling ATM Adaptation Layer (SAAL).

Just as is the case for ordinary UNI signaling, other non-standard signaling channels can be used within a network.

Call Setup Messages

Figure 9.6 illustrates the exchange of messages between switches during call setup.

| Figure 9.6 | PNNI call setup messages. |

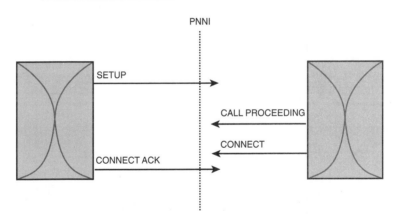

Propagating Call Setup Messages

Figure 9.7 shows how messages propagate through a series of switches.

The process looks simple, but determining whether the Service Category, bandwidth, and QoS values that are requested in a SETUP message can be delivered requires a fair amount of processing. Switches along the way may need to modify the values of bandwidth and quality of service parameters and set them to values that can be delivered.

Figure 9.7   Propagating PNNI call setup messages.

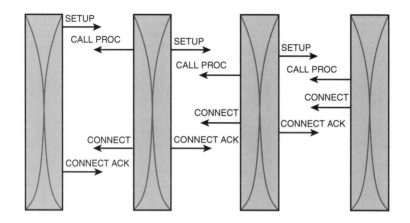

Call Clearing Messages

Figure 9.8 shows the simple exchange of messages between adjacent switches during call clearing. The endpoint device at the left end of the path has initiated call clearing.

Figure 9.8   Call release messages.

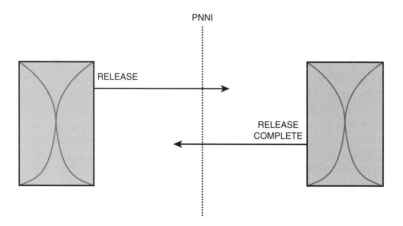

PNNI Hierarchical Routing

All of the switches in a small network can share complete topology information with one another and maintain identical databases.

However, routing based on a complete map of the network will not do the job when

- A network is complex and contains many switches.

- A network connects to other networks.

Large networks need to be broken up into manageable pieces and given a hierarchical structure.

The sections that follow will describe the way that a PNNI hierarchy is set up and the way that switches learn the routing information that they need in order to set up calls.

PNNI Hierarchical Addresses

There is an existing global hierarchy network that is very familiar to us: the telephone system. The physical hierarchy is reflected in hierarchical telephone numbers: Country codes, area codes, and local exchange codes simplify the routing of telephone calls.

PNNI defines a hierarchical structure for ATM networks that also is based on a hierarchical addressing scheme. While telephone system standards have established a fairly rigid numbering hierarchy, PNNI enables a network implementer to design a very flexible multi-level hierarchy. In fact, up to 104 levels of hierarchy can be defined!

Recall that inside a private ATM network, 20-byte ATM end system addresses (AESAs) are assigned to endpoint devices. These AESA addresses were described in Chapter III-7, "Setting Up Switched Connections." Four AESA formats can be used for private ATM addresses. All of these addresses consist of a 13-byte prefix followed by a 6-byte end system identifier and a selector byte, as shown in Figure 9.9. The end system identifier normally is a MAC address.

Figure 9.9   Address prefix and addressing levels.

An ATM addressing hierarchy is built by choosing some number of prefix bits for each level of the hierarchy. (The 104 potential hierarchy levels correspond to the $8 \times 13 = 104$ bits in the address prefix.)

Just as for the telephone system, different prefix field sizes can be used within different networks, or even within regions of a particular network. This may seem strange, but in fact, variable prefix sizes are common in the current international telephone system. For example,

- France has country prefix 33 while Greenland has country prefix 299.

- Bordeaux in France has prefix 33556 while Paris has prefix 331.

Note that the ATM address fields are defined on bit boundaries and consist of binary bits, rather than being expressed as some number of digits. However, network administrators will find that it is a lot easier to administer a network if they break up their addresses on byte boundaries.

Building a Hierarchical Network

To understand how an ATM hierarchy is built, it is helpful to look at diagrams of a sample hierarchical ATM network structure. The diagrams represent a three-level hierarchy created by defining three fixed-size address prefix subfields.

Putting real hexadecimal node addresses into the diagrams would make them very cluttered. The labels shown in Figure 9.10 will be used to represent address prefixes as expressions, such as A.2.3 or B.1.2.

Figure 9.10   A simple scheme for representing address prefixes.

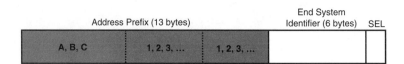

Figure 9.11 depicts a network that has a three-tiered hierarchical structure. All of the nodes within an enclosed region have addresses that start with the same prefix. For example, all addresses in the region labeled C start with a prefix that corresponds to C—just as all telephone numbers in France start with the prefix 33.

All addresses in the region labeled C.2 start with the longer prefix corresponding to C.2— just as all telephone numbers in the Bordeaux region of France start with 33556.

Figure 9.11   A three-level hierarchical network.

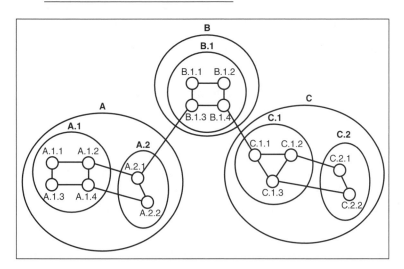

Learning the Network Topology

The method used by PNNI to spread overall topology information can be understood by an analogy. Suppose that there is a group of commissioners responsible for a county's roads. They meet regularly and exchange information, and each of them has detailed knowledge of all the roads in the county. Because they are aware of which roads cross the county border, they know how to get to each adjacent county.

This group needs to work with commissioners in other counties, so they elect a leader who will represent them at state-level meetings. This state-level leader brings back information they did not have before. For example, they learn that if they use road x to cross into adjacent county X, there is a route that will lead them to county Y, which is adjacent to X.

The state-level group wants to work with commissioners from other states, so they elect a leader who will represent them at national-level meetings. The national-level leader learns new information—such as the fact that the best route from state A to state F passes through intermediate states B, C, and D.

The national-level leader shares this information with other state-level leaders in its state. Each state-level leader shares the information with its county-level leaders. Each county-level leader takes this information home and shares it with other commissioners within the county.

In the end, every local commissioner has very detailed information about the local county; less detailed (but very useful) information about the locations of other counties and how to reach them; and information about the other states and how to reach them.

Note that a national-level representative also acts as a state-level representative, a county-level representative, and a local commissioner.

Now we are ready to apply this scenario to the way PNNI switches exchange topology information.

Peer Groups

Nodes that share a common address prefix form a peer group. For example, nodes A.1.1, A.1.2, A.1.3, and A.1.4 in Figure 9.11 have a common prefix (A.1) and form a peer group. The common prefix is the group's peer group identifier. The peer group is the network equivalent of the group of county commissioners.

Nodes in a peer group exchange topology information that gives each of them an identical map of the peer group and of the links that connect the peer group to other peer groups.

Peer Group Leaders

To build a hierarchy, each peer group, like the county commissioners, elects a peer group leader. The election is based on a preconfigured priority parameter, so the outcome can be controlled by the administrator who configures the network nodes.

The black nodes in Figure 9.12 are the ones that have been elected to act as peer group leaders. Each peer group leader has a dual personality:

- It is a lowest-level node.

- It acts as a second-level node that represents its peer group.

Figure 9.12   Peer group leaders acting as second-level nodes.

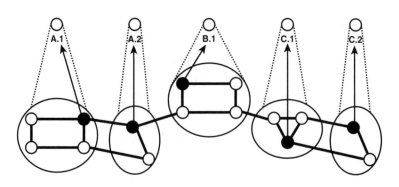

Forming a Second-Level Virtual Network

A *virtual network* is quickly constructed to enable these second-level nodes to communicate with one another. The links in this network consist of switched virtual circuits that are opened between peer group leaders that belong to adjacent peer groups.

The second-level network, analogous to the state-level in the road scenario, is shown in Figure 9.13.

Figure 9.13   The second-level network.

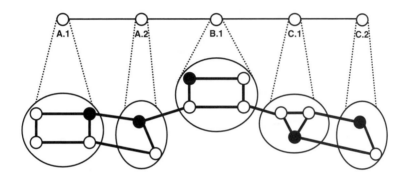

Second-Level Peer Groups

The second-level network is broken into second-level peer groups based on shorter address prefixes. As shown in Figure 9.14, there are three second-level peer groups. For example, the nodes that are the peer group leaders for A.1 and A.2 have a common prefix (A) and belong to a second-level peer group. There also are second-level peer groups for prefixes B and C.

Nodes in a second-level peer group exchange topology information that gives each of them an identical map of this peer group and of the links that connect the peer group to other second-level peer groups.

Each of these peer groups elects a peer group leader. The leaders are represented in Figure 9.14 by the black nodes.

Forming a Third-Level Virtual Network

As shown in Figure 9.15, the second-level peer group leaders form a third-level virtual network in which each represents its peer group. Switched virtual circuits connect A to B and B to C. The nodes in the third-level network are analogous to the national-level commissioners in the road scenario.

Figure 9.14   Second-level peer groups and peer group leaders.

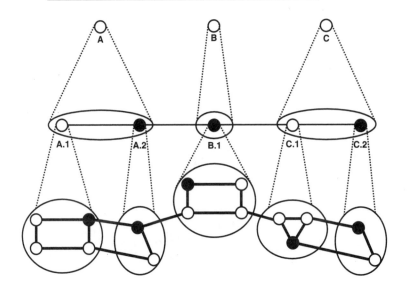

Figure 9.15   The third-level network.

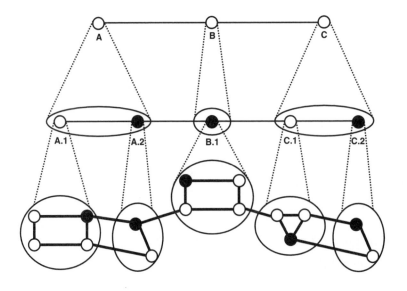

Third-Level Peer Groups

The third level is the highest prefix level for this network, but by convention, A, B, and C are viewed as belonging to a top-level peer group that has a common prefix that is 0 bits long! Figure 9.16 illustrates the third-level peer group that is formed.

Nodes in the third-level peer group exchange topology information that gives each of them an identical map of the peer group.

The group elects a peer group leader, which is represented by the black node. Note that the switch whose complete address prefix is A.2.1 is king of the hill! It is a first-level (A.2.1), second-level (A.2), and third-level (A) peer group leader.

Figure 9.16   Third-level peer group and peer group leader.

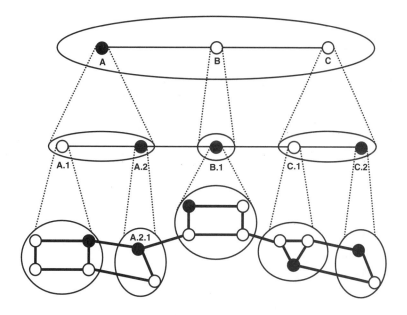

Note

The structures that have been shown are very regular. However, it is not necessary for the peer group tree to have the same number of levels everywhere. In terms of the analogy, a state might be sparsely populated and just have one commissioner who knows all the roads in the state. This commissioner could share her information directly with other state-level representatives.

Purpose of the Peer Group Hierarchy

Nodes at higher levels of the hierarchy have a broader view of the network because of the information they exchange with their upper-level peers. The main function of the higher-level nodes is to summarize what they know and to pass it to lower-level nodes:

- Nodes at the top of the hierarchy have a global view of the network. They know that address prefixes A, B, and C are used in the network, and they know how to reach the parts of the network that contain addresses starting with A, B, or C.

- Each top-level node also is a second-level peer group leader. A top-level node passes the global information to the other nodes in its second-level peer group.

- The second-level nodes combine the global information with what they have learned by exchanging topology information with other second-level nodes.

- Each second-level node is a first-level peer group leader. A second-level node passes the global and second-level information to the other nodes in its first-level peer group.

An example may make this clearer. The peer group leader for A.1 learns that addresses that begin with prefixes B and C can be reached via A.2. It passes the summarized topology information to the other nodes in its bottom-level peer group. This enables nodes A.1.1 and A.1.3 to build the view of the network that is summarized in Figure 9.17.

Figure 9.17   Local view of the global network.

This amount of information is all that A.1.1 or A.1.3 needs in to launch a SETUP request toward any destination in the network.

If A.1.3 has to set up a call to a node connected to switch C.2.2, it can create the designated transit list

A.1.4, A.2, B, C

As the SETUP message advances through the network, additional topology information held at intermediate nodes allows the summarized parts of the path to be replaced with detailed lists of switches. For example,

- A.1.4 knows that it is connected to nodes starting with prefix A.2 via node A.2.2.

- A.2.2 knows the way to reach B through the network represented by A.2: namely via A.2.1 and B.1.3.

- Within B, nodes know how to cross over to C.

If there is a problem with the path, it can be cranked back to an earlier stage for alternate routing.

References

The following documents were published by the ATM Forum Technical Committee:

- *Private Network-Network Interface Specification Version 1.0*, March 1996.

- *Private Network-Network Interface Specification Version 1.0 Addendum (Soft PVC MIB)*, September 1996.

For more insight into link state protocols, see *OSPF: Anatomy of an Internet Routing Protocol*, by John T. Moy (Addison-Wesley).

CHAPTER 10

LAN Emulation

Today's data networks are made up of LANs and point-to-point circuits. The protocol stacks within desktop systems and servers are designed to interface to connectionless LAN environments and serial lines.

ATM is a new and very different connection-oriented technology. The ATM Forum was faced with the problem of finding a way to integrate ATM into the current data network infrastructure quickly. *LAN Emulation (LANE)* was their solution.

LANE consists of a set of mechanisms that enable an ATM workstation to emulate a conventional broadcast LAN system.

LANE is important because it allows current networked application software to operate without change on an ATM workstation. To the software, the running environment looks like it is on top of a LAN protocol stack.

LANE also enables you to build virtual LANs from a mixture of ATM and either Ethernet or Token Ring segments. The virtual LANs may be local or may span a wide area ATM network, as illustrated in Figure 10.1.

LANE Architecture

LANE has to make connection-oriented ATM workstations appear to be connectionless LAN workstations. In other words, a LANE workstation must to be able to

- Send a frame to any other system on the virtual LAN at any time

- Send and receive broadcast and multicast frames

Figure 10.1   Integrating ATM stations into a virtual LAN.

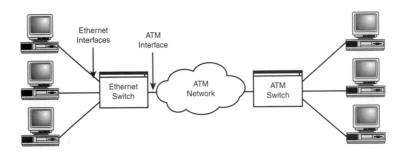

Two components are needed to make this work:

- *LAN Emulation client software* that is part of the device driver software that controls an ATM interface

- The *LAN Emulation Service*, which is implemented by three servers

The first server configures LANE clients when they initialize. The second keeps track of the stations participating in an emulated LAN (ELAN), and the third executes broadcasts and multicasts.

The three servers can be located together within a single ATM switch, can reside in one computer with an ATM interface, or can be spread across two or three ATM systems. The LANE servers will be examined later.

LAN Emulation Clients

Whenever you install a network card, you also must install the card's device driver software, which is provided on a floppy disk or CD-ROM. Network layer software sends and receives data by making standard *send* and *receive* calls to the device driver. For example, NDIS and ODI are familiar "standard" device driver interfaces that enable Windows protocol stacks to pass data to an interface card and receive data from the card. The device driver formats outgoing data into frames and passes them to the LAN hardware interface. It receives incoming frames, removes the data, and passes it to the network layer.

As shown in Figure 10.2, a LAN Emulation client is implemented as a special device driver layer. It performs a number of special LAN Emulation functions in addition to passing data between the network layer above it and the ATM Adaptation Layer below it.

From the point of view of the network layer above it, the LANE client behaves exactly like an Ethernet or Token Ring device driver. Among other things, this means that the LANE interface has to be assigned a MAC address.

Figure 10.2 The role of an LAN Emulation client in an endpoint system.

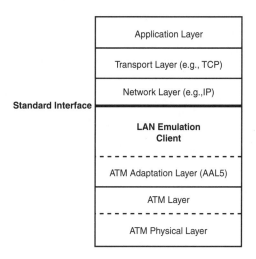

The LAN Emulation client hides the fact that the network hardware actually is an ATM interface card. It transmits Ethernet or Token Ring frames by wrapping them inside AAL5 frames.

Its communications actually are connection-oriented. A LANE client

• Talks to the three LAN Emulation servers via ATM virtual channel connections (VCCs)

• Communicates with other LAN Emulation clients via virtual channel connections

Some or all of these could be permanent virtual connections, but the normal expectation is that switched virtual connections will be used. The rest of this chapter will assume that connections are switched, except where explicitly stated otherwise.

The user-network interface between a LAN Emulation client and its adjacent ATM switch is called the *LAN Emulation user-to-network interface (LUNI)*.

Edge Devices

You can build a virtual LAN that consists of one or more ATM switches and some or all of their attached ATM endpoint devices. However, it often is convenient to build virtual LANs that include a mixture of real LAN devices and ATM LAN Emulation clients.

A device that connects a conventional LAN or WAN environment to an ATM environment is called an *edge device*. An edge device contains one or more LAN Emulation clients. The edge device acts as a middleman, forwarding frames between ATM systems and systems that are attached to a conventional Ethernet or Token Ring LAN. It operates at the data link layer. Thus, it performs a bridging function, not a routing function.

The Ethernet switch in Figure 10.3 has an ATM interface and acts as an edge device. A LAN bridge that has at least one ATM interface also can act as an edge device.

Figure 10.3   Connecting a conventional LAN to LANE clients.

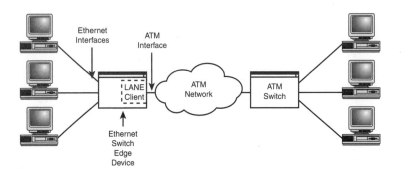

A LAN Emulation client in an edge device acts as a proxy, relaying frames between ATM systems and ordinary LAN systems. Figure 10.4 shows the layering model for an edge device.

Figure 10.4   The role of a LANE client in an edge device.

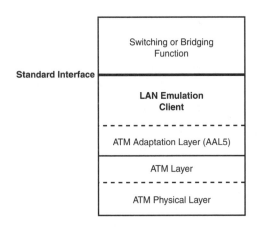

LAN Emulation Client Protocol Elements

The payloads within the AAL5 frames that are transmitted between LANE clients consist of one of the following:

- An Ethernet-II (DIX) frame

- An 802.3/802.2 Ethernet frame

- A Token Ring frame

The Ethernet or Token Ring frame check sequence field is omitted, since the AAL5 frame has a CRC. However, an extra 2-byte header precedes the frame. This contains either X'0000 or a *LAN Emulation client identifier (LECID)* that is assigned to the client when it joins an emulated LAN.

Frame sizes can be larger than normal frame sizes if the emulated LAN includes only ATM systems. (If 802.3/802.2 is used, the length header field in frames of length 1536 or more is set to 0. The real length is determined from the length field in the AAL5 trailer.)

LAN Emulation Service

As shown in Figure 10.5, the LAN Emulation Service is made up of three distinct servers:

- *LAN Emulation Configuration Server (LECS)*—A client connects to this server to find out which emulated LAN it belongs to. The LECS tells the client the address of the LAN Emulation Server that controls its emulated LAN.

- *LAN Emulation Server (LES)*—A LAN Emulation Server acts as mission control for an emulated LAN. All clients register with their LES, which records their ATM and MAC addresses. This enables this server to perform an ongoing address translation function for LANE clients.

- *Broadcast and Unknown Server (BUS)*—The BUS forwards broadcast and multicast frames to and from LANE clients.

Thus, a LAN Emulation client

- Opens a connection to the LAN Emulation Configuration Server (LECS) to get assigned to a virtual LAN.

- Connects to the LAN Emulation Server (LES) to join a virtual LAN. The client relies on the LAN Emulation Server to help it to locate destination systems.

- Connects to the Broadcast and Unknown Server (BUS) and sends and receives broadcast and multicast frames via the broadcast and unknown server.

Figure 10.5   Servers that provide the LAN Emulation Service.

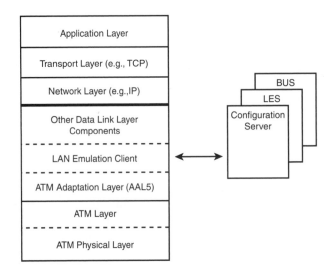

Figure 10.6 displays two emulated LANs. The black workstations belong to LAN 1. The white workstations belong to LAN 2. The application server belongs to both LANs.

All of the LAN Emulation Servers are located within the ATM switch. Only one LAN Emulation Configuration Server is needed. This server tells each LAN Emulation client which LAN Emulation Server to use. Each emulated LAN has its own LAN Emulation Server and BUS.

Figure 10.6   Two emulated LANs.

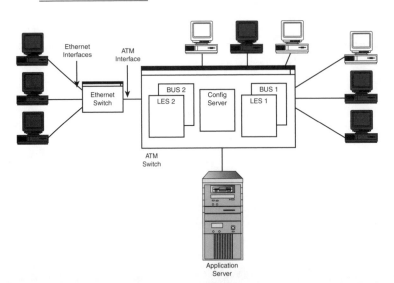

In Figure 10.6, the Ethernet switch is connected to the ATM switch via a local connection. However, if there was a high-speed wide area ATM connection between the two switches, the LAN clients attached to the Ethernet switch could access the application server at rates that would make the server appear to be local to all systems.

Client Initialization via a Configuration Server

Now it is time to take a closer look at the way a LAN Emulation client interacts with the three LAN Emulation Servers. When a LAN Emulation client initializes, its first task is to learn the ATM address of its LAN Emulation Server. This could be manually configured at each LANE system, but centralizing the administration of this chore by using a configuration server makes good sense. However, the client now has to find the configuration server!

Clients could simply be manually configured with the configuration server's ATM address, but the point of using a configuration server is to avoid manual configuration chores. Any of several alternative methods can be used to get the ATM address:

- Determine the configuration server's ATM address from the adjacent switch via ILMI. Recall that ILMI supports a server registration table.

- Open a connection to the following "well-known" ATM group address, which has been reserved for configuration servers:

  X'47007900000000000000000000-00A03E000001-00

  This is an anycast address. The call will be routed to the nearest configuration server.

- Use a special PVC that automatically is connected to the configuration server. This PVC must have VPI=0, VCI=17.

Listing 10.1 shows the beginning of a Network Associates Sniffer trace of a SETUP message used to set up a call to the well-known configuration server address.

The ATM header indicates that the message has been sent on the signaling channel, VPI=0, VCI=5. Messages are numbered, and the SSCOP field contains the initial send sequence number. The SSCOP field is displayed immediately after the ATM header, but for a message, actually is located just before the AAL5 trailer.

The protocol discriminator value, X'09, indicates that this is a Q.2931 signaling message, and the message type is X'05, which shows that it is a SETUP message.

```
SSCOP: SD(Sequence Connection-mode Data)

Q2931: Setup CRN=1 called  =47:0079:0000 0000 0000 0000 0000:A03E000001:00
Q2931:               calling =47:0005:80FF E100 0000 F21C 30D3:Cbltr14A06D6:09


ATM: — —· ATM Header  — —·
     ATM:
     ATM: Frame 190 arrived at  09:17:17.8419; frame size is 144 (0090 hex)
bytes.
     ATM: Link = DTE
     ATM: Virtual path id = 0
     ATM: Virtual channel id = 5
     ATM:
SSCOP: — —· SSCOP  — —·
     SSCOP:
     SSCOP: SD(Sequence Connection-mode Data)
     SSCOP: SD send seq num N(S) = 0
     SSCOP:
Q2931: — —· UNI Signaling  — —·
     Q2931:
     Q2931: Protocol discriminator   = 09
Q2931: Length of call reference = 3 bytes
     Q2931: Call reference flag      = 0... ....(message sent from call reference
➥originator)
     Q2931: Call reference value    = 1
     Q2931: Message type            = 05 (Setup)
.   .   .
```

Interacting with the Configuration Server

The essential data about LANE servers and the clients that should be assigned to each needs to be entered into a configuration server before it can do its job. A configuration server can use a variety of criteria to assign clients to emulated LANs (ELANs), such as a connection port number, the client's MAC address, or the selector byte in the client's AESA address.

A client opens a bidirectional point-to-point connection to the configuration server—and usually closes the connection when the procedure is complete. The interaction between a client and the configuration server is straightforward. The client sends a configure request that includes:

- The client's primary ATM address.

- The LAN type (Ethernet or Token Ring, or to be specified by the server).

- If known, the name of the ELAN that the client wishes to join (or rejoin).

- If known, the maximum frame size to be supported.

Optionally, the client may include:

- The client's LAN MAC address. For a Token Ring environment, a route descriptor can be provided.

- A Layer 3 address.

The response from the configuration server includes:

- The ATM address of the LAN Emulation Server.

- The LAN type (Ethernet or Token Ring).

- If known, the name of the ELAN that the client should join.

- If known, the maximum frame size to be supported.

A client interacts with its configuration server and LAN Emulation Server using special control frames whose format is shown in Figure 10.7.

Table 10.1 describes the fields that are used in control frames. The fields whose names are in boldface print in Figure 10.7 have the same meaning for all control frames. The interpretation of the remaining fields depends on the type of frame. For example, selected fields are unused for some types of frames, and are set to 0.

The Type/Length/Value (TLV) fields contain additional parameters. As the title suggests, each TLV parameter is introduced by a 4-byte type identifier and a length field. The type identifier consists of:

- A 3-byte *organizationally unique identifier (OUI)* that identifies the authority that defined the type number. The ATM Forum has OUI X'00A03E.

- A 1-byte type number.

Figure 10.7   Control frame format.

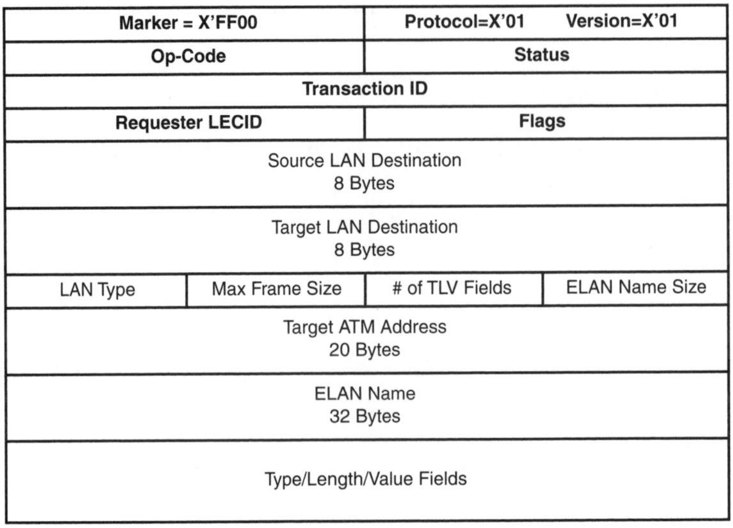

Marker = X'FF00		Protocol=X'01 Version=X'01	
Op-Code		Status	
Transaction ID			
Requester LECID		Flags	
Source LAN Destination 8 Bytes			
Target LAN Destination 8 Bytes			
LAN Type	Max Frame Size	# of TLV Fields	ELAN Name Size
Target ATM Address 20 Bytes			
ELAN Name 32 Bytes			
Type/Length/Value Fields			

Table 10.1   Control Frame Fields

Field	Description
Marker	X'FF00 for a control frame.
Protocol	X'01 for the ATM LANE protocol.
Version	Identifies the ATM LANE protocol version. Currently set to X'01.
Op-Code	Identifies the type of control frame, such as a configuration, join, or ARP request.
Status	Set to X'0000 in requests and successful responses. Reports a problem otherwise.
Transaction-Id	Used to match a response to its request.
Requester-LECID	Provides the LAN Emulation client identifier of the client making a request. (X'0000 if the client's identifier is unknown.)
Flags	Identifies miscellaneous facts, such as whether the sender can support LANE version 2, or whether the sender is a proxy client in an edge device.
Source LAN Destination	When used, can be a MAC address or a Token Ring route descriptor associated with the message source.
Target LAN Destination	When used, can be a MAC address or a Token Ring route descriptor associated with some target system—for example, a system that is the target of a query.
LAN Type	When used, the value is Ethernet or Token Ring. X'00 is unspecified, X'01 is Ethernet, and X'02 is Token Ring.

> **Note**
>
> A Token Ring frame that crosses a bridged Token Ring LAN contains a routing information field (RIF) made up of one or more route descriptors. Each route descriptor consists of a LAN ID (or ring ID) and a bridge number. In some cases, a Token Ring route descriptor must be extracted from a routing information field and used instead of a MAC address in order to route a frame across an emulated LAN.
>
> The phrase *LAN Destination* was chosen to mean either a MAC address or a Token Ring route descriptor.

Listing 10.2 shows a trace of a message sent from a LANE client to a configuration server, requesting the address of a LAN Emulation Server.

The transaction ID in the request is 0. The oddly named "source LAN destination" could contain a client MAC address or a Token Ring Route Descriptor, but the field starts with a tag of X'0000 which means that no value has been provided. The target LAN destination field also is 0. It has no purpose in configuration requests and responses.

The client has entered its ATM address into the source ATM address field and has indicated that it wants to join an Ethernet LAN. The maximum frame size is 1516. A frame of this size can hold a 2-byte LAN Emulation header and a maximum-size Ethernet frame (without a frame check sequence).

The client has provided the 5-byte name (20500) of the emulated LAN that it wishes to join. The target ATM address field is 0, but in the response, this field should contain the address of the LAN Emulation Server. There are no additional TLV parameters in the request.

Listing 10.2   Trace of a Message from a LANE Client to a Configuration Server

```
Network Associates Sniffer Trace
- - - - - - - - - - - - - - - Frame 2 - - - - - - - - - - - - - - -
LANE: CTRL CONFIGURE_REQUEST XID=0 RID=0
ATM: ----- ATM Header -----
     ATM:
     ATM: Frame 1 arrived at  09:17:18.3397; frame size is 144 (0090 hex) bytes.
     ATM: Call reference = 1
     ATM: Link = DTE
     ATM: Virtual path id = 0
     ATM: Virtual channel id = 182
     ATM:
```

continues

Listing 10.2   Continued

```
LECTRL: ----- LAN EMULATION CONTROL FRAME -----
       LECTRL:
       LECTRL: Marker         = FF00
       LECTRL: Protocol       = 01
       LECTRL: Version        = 01
       LECTRL: Opcode         = 0001 (CONFIGURE_REQUEST)
       LECTRL: Status         = 0 (Success)
       LECTRL: Trans ID       = 0
       LECTRL: Request ID     = 0
       LECTRL: Flags          = 0000
       LECTRL: Src LAN Dest   = 0000000000000000
       LECTRL:    Tag         = 0000(not present)
       LECTRL:    MAC Addr    = 000000000000(not present)
       LECTRL: Tar LAN Dest   = 0000000000000000
       LECTRL:    Tag         = 0000(not present)
       LECTRL:    MAC Addr    = 000000000000(not present)
       LECTRL: SRC ATM ADDR   = 47:0005:80FF E100 0000 F21C 30D3:Cbltr14A06D6:09
       LECTRL: LAN-TYPE       = 01 (Ethernet/IEEE 802.3)
       LECTRL: MAX FRAME SIZE= 01 (1516)
       LECTRL: NUMBER TLVs    = 0
       LECTRL: ELAN NAME SIZE= 5
       LECTRL: TARG ATM ADDR = 000000000000000000000000000000000000000000
       LECTRL: ELAN NAME      = "20500"
```

Listing 10.3 shows the corresponding response. The address of a LAN Emulation Server has been entered into the target ATM address field and the configuration server has agreed that the emulated LAN named "20500" is suitable.

The response includes three TLV parameters that configure the client with time-out parameters.

Listing 10.3 The Response to Listing 10.2's Message Request

```
- - - - - - - - - - - - - - - - Frame 2 - - - - - - - - - - - - - - - -
LANE: CTRL CONFIGURE_RESPONSE XID=0 RID=0
ATM: ----- ATM Header -----
     ATM:
     ATM: Frame 2 arrived at  09:17:18.3442; frame size is 144 (0090 hex) bytes.
     ATM: Call reference = 1
     ATM: Link = DCE
     ATM: Virtual path id = 0
     ATM: Virtual channel id = 182
     ATM:
```

```
LECTRL: ----- LAN EMULATION CONTROL FRAME -----
        LECTRL:
        LECTRL: Marker        = FF00
        LECTRL: Protocol      = 01
        LECTRL: Version       = 01
        LECTRL: Opcode        = 0101 (CONFIGURE_RESPONSE)
        LECTRL: Status        = 0 (Success)
        LECTRL: Trans ID      = 0
        LECTRL: Request ID    = 0
        LECTRL: Flags         = 0000
        LECTRL: Src LAN Dest  = 0000000000000000
        LECTRL:    Tag        = 0000(not present)
        LECTRL:    MAC Addr   = 000000000000(not present)
        LECTRL: Tar LAN Dest  = 0000000000000000
        LECTRL:    Tag        = 0000(not present)
        LECTRL:    MAC Addr   = 000000000000(not present)
        LECTRL: SRC ATM ADDR  = 47:0005:80FF E100 0000 F21C 30D3:Cbltr14A06D6:09
        LECTRL: LAN-TYPE      = 01 (Ethernet/IEEE 802.3)
        LECTRL: MAX FRAME SIZE= 01 (1516)
        LECTRL: NUMBER TLVs   = 3
        LECTRL: ELAN NAME SIZE= 5
        LECTRL: TARG ATM ADDR = 47:0005:80FF E100 0000 F21C 30D3:ForeSy1C30D3:52
        LECTRL: ELAN NAME     = "20500"
        LECTRL: TLV OUI       = 00A03E(ATM Forum)
        LECTRL: TLV type      = 01(Control time-out)
        LECTRL: TLV length    = 2
        LECTRL: TLV value     = 10 seconds
        LECTRL: TLV OUI       = 00A03E(ATM Forum)
        LECTRL: TLV type      = 04(VCC time-out period)
        LECTRL: TLV length    = 4
        LECTRL: TLV value     = 1200 seconds
        LECTRL: TLV OUI       = 00A03E(ATM Forum)
        LECTRL: TLV type      = 06(Aging time)
        LECTRL: TLV length    = 4
        LECTRL: TLV value     = 300 seconds
```

The client is now ready to close its connection to the configuration server and move on to the next step.

Unicast and Multicast Server Connections

A client cannot participate in an ELAN until it has gone through an initialization procedure with both its LAN Emulation Server and its Broadcast and Unknown Server.

In both cases, the client opens a bidirectional point-to-point connection to the server. The client uses this connection to send frames to the server.

Then the server normally adds the client to a point-to-multipoint connection for which it is the root.

Note

The latter step is optional in the ATM Forum standards, but is in fact the normal procedure.

In the discussion that follows, it is assumed that the point-to-multipoint connect option is available and is used. The purpose of this connection is to provide a very efficient way of distributing frames that have to go to all systems.

Communicating with the LAN Emulation Server

Figure 10.8 outlines the following steps, which initiate communications between a client and its LAN Emulation Server:

1. The client opens a bidirectional point-to-point connection to the LES.

2. The client sends parameters to the LES in a JOIN REQUEST control frame.

3. The LES sends parameters to the client in a JOIN RESPONSE control frame.

4. The LES adds the client to a point-to-multipoint connection.

Figure 10.8   Setting up communications with the LES.

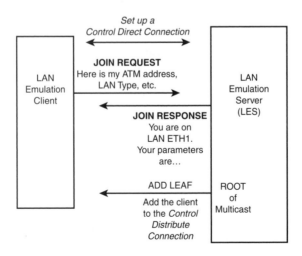

Opening the Control Direct Connection

The bidirectional point-to-point connection opened in the first step is called a *control direct* channel connection. The client will keep this connection open after the initial exchange of control frames is complete, and use it to send frames to the LAN Emulation Server.

Listing 10.4 shows part of a SETUP message used to open a control direct connection to the LAN Emulation Server identified in the configuration step.

Listing 10.4   A SETUP Message Used to Open a Control Direct Connection

```
Network Associates Sniffer Trace
SSCOP: SD(Sequence Connection-mode Data)
Q2931: Setup CRN=5 called  =47:0005:80FF E100 0000 F21C 30D3:ForeSy1C30D3:52
Q2931:             calling =47:0005:80FF E100 0000 F21C 30D3:Cbltr14A06D6:09
ATM: ----- ATM Header -----
     ATM:
     ATM: Frame 218 arrived at  09:17:19.6802; frame size is 144 (0090 hex)
➥bytes.
     ATM: Link = DTE
     ATM: Virtual path id = 0
     ATM: Virtual channel id = 5
     ATM:
SSCOP: ----- SSCOP -----
     SSCOP:
     SSCOP: SD(Sequence Connection-mode Data)
     SSCOP: SD send seq num N(S) = 8
     SSCOP:
Q2931: ----- UNI Signaling -----
     Q2931:
     Q2931: Protocol discriminator  = 09
     Q2931: Length of call reference = 3 bytes
     Q2931: Call reference flag     = 0... ....
            (message sent from call reference originator)
     Q2931: Call reference value    = 5
     Q2931: Message type            = 05 (Setup)
. . .
Q2931:   Bearer class           = BCOB-X
     Q2931:   ATM transfer capability= Non-real time VBR
     Q2931:   Suscept to clipping   = Not susceptible to clipping
     Q2931:   User plane conn config = Point-to-point
. . .
```

The JOIN REQUEST

The JOIN REQUEST that the client sends to the LAN Emulation Server contains

- The client's primary ATM address

- Optionally, a LAN MAC address that the client will use

- The type of LAN (Ethernet, Token Ring, or to be specified by the server)

- If known, the maximum frame size to be supported

- An indication of whether the client acts as a proxy for other remote MAC addresses (that is, the requestor is a switch or bridge edge device)

- If known, the name of the ELAN that the client wishes to join, or which it last joined

Listing 10.5 shows a JOIN REQUEST. Note that the control direct connection on which it is sent has VPI=0 and VCI=186.

The request contains the client's primary ATM address, the type of LAN (Ethernet), the maximum frame size (1516), and the ELAN name (20500).

A simple ATM client can register its MAC address with the server by including it in the *Source LAN Destination* field. This enables the server to respond to address resolution queries that supply the client's MAC address and request the client's ATM address.

The client that sent this JOIN REQUEST did not provide its MAC address. The flags field value (X'0080) indicates that this client is an edge device that acts as a proxy for non-ATM systems. If the server receives an address resolution query that contains an unknown MAC address, the server should forward the query to all of the proxy edge devices. The MAC address may belong to one of the proxied LAN systems.

Listing 10.5   A JOIN REQUEST

```
LANE: CTRL JOIN_REQUEST XID=67108864 RID=0
ATM: ----- ATM Header -----
     ATM:
     ATM: Frame 9 arrived at  09:17:19.8431; frame size is 144 (0090 hex) bytes.
     ATM: Call reference = 5
     ATM: Link = DTE
     ATM: Virtual path id = 0
     ATM: Virtual channel id = 186
     ATM:
LECTRL: ----- LAN EMULATION CONTROL FRAME -----
     LECTRL:
     LECTRL: Marker      = FF00
     LECTRL: Protocol    = 01
```

```
LECTRL: Version       = 01
LECTRL: Opcode        = 0002 (JOIN_REQUEST)
LECTRL: Status        = 0 (Success)
LECTRL: Trans ID      = 67108864
LECTRL: Request ID    = 0
LECTRL: Flags         = 0080 (Proxy Flag)
LECTRL: Src LAN Dest  = 0000000000000000
LECTRL:    Tag        = 0000(not present)
LECTRL:    MAC Addr   = 000000000000(not present)
LECTRL: Tar LAN Dest  = 0000000000000000
LECTRL:    Tag        = 0000(not present)
LECTRL:    MAC Addr   = 000000000000(not present)
LECTRL: SRC ATM ADDR  = 47:0005:80FF E100 0000 F21C 30D3:Cbltr14A06D6:09
LECTRL: LAN-TYPE      = 01 (Ethernet/IEEE 802.3)
LECTRL: MAX FRAME SIZE= 01 (1516)
LECTRL: NUMBER TLVs   = 0
LECTRL: ELAN NAME SIZE= 5
LECTRL: TARG ATM ADDR = 00000000000000000000000000000000000000000
LECTRL: ELAN NAME     = "20500"
```

The JOIN RESPONSE

A server's JOIN RESPONSE contains the same fields as the request. The server must fill in the definitive values for the

- Type of LAN

- Maximum frame size

- Name of the ELAN

The server also assigns a unique numeric identifier—known as the LAN Emulation Client ID (LECID)—to the client. Listing 10.6 displays the server's JOIN RESPONSE. The type of LAN (Ethernet), the maximum frame size (1516), and the ELAN name (20500) are unchanged.

The field that is designated "Request ID" is the requestor identifier—that is, the LECID. Its hexadecimal value, X'000A, has been translated to decimal value 10.

Listing 10.6   A Server's JOIN RESPONSE

```
LANE: CTRL JOIN_RESPONSE XID=67108864 RID=10
ATM: ----- ATM Header -----
    ATM:
    ATM: Frame 13 arrived at  09:17:20.1893; frame size is 144 (0090 hex) bytes.
```

continues

Listing 10.6   Continued

```
        ATM: Call reference = 5
        ATM: Link = DCE
        ATM: Virtual path id = 0
        ATM: Virtual channel id = 186
        ATM:
LECTRL: ----- LAN EMULATION CONTROL FRAME -----
        LECTRL:
        LECTRL: Marker        = FF00
        LECTRL: Protocol      = 01
        LECTRL: Version       = 01
        LECTRL: Opcode        = 0102 (JOIN_RESPONSE)
        LECTRL: Status        = 0 (Success)
        LECTRL: Trans ID      = 67108864
        LECTRL: Request ID    = 10
        LECTRL: Flags         = 0080 (Proxy Flag)
        LECTRL: Src LAN Dest  = 0000000000000000
        LECTRL:   Tag         = 0000(not present)
        LECTRL:   MAC Addr    = 000000000000(not present)
        LECTRL: Tar LAN Dest  = 0000000000000000
        LECTRL:   Tag         = 0000(not present)
        LECTRL:   MAC Addr    = 000000000000(not present)
        LECTRL: SRC ATM ADDR  = 47:0005:80FF E100 0000 F21C 30D3:Cbltr14A06D6:09
        LECTRL: LAN-TYPE      = 01 (Ethernet/IEEE 802.3)
        LECTRL: MAX FRAME SIZE= 01 (1516)
        LECTRL: NUMBER TLVs   = 0
        LECTRL: ELAN NAME SIZE= 5
        LECTRL: TARG ATM ADDR = 000000000000000000000000000000000000000000
        LECTRL: ELAN NAME     = "20500"
```

Opening the Control Distribute Connection

If, as usually is the case, the network supports point-to-multipoint connections, the LAN Emulation Server adds the client to a unidirectional point-to-multipoint *control distribute* virtual channel connection.

Listing 10.7 shows part of the SETUP message received by the client when the LAN Emulation Server establishes a point-to-multipoint control distribute connection. The client probably is being added to an existing connection as a leaf, but the network has transformed the ADD LEAF message into a SETUP before presenting it to the client.

| Listing 10.7 | SETUP Message for a Point-to-Multipoint Control Distribute Connection |

```
SSCOP: SD(Sequence Connection-mode Data)
Q2931: Setup CRN=852 called  =47:0005:80FF E100 0000 F21C 30D3:Cbltr14A06D6:09
Q2931:          calling =47:0005:80FF E100 0000 F21C 30D3:ForeSy1C30D3:52
ATM: ----- ATM Header -----
     ATM:
     ATM: Frame 234 arrived at  09:17:19.8992; frame size is 144 (0090 hex)
➥bytes.
     ATM: Link = DCE
     ATM: Virtual path id = 0
     ATM: Virtual channel id = 5
     ATM:
SSCOP: ----- SSCOP -----
     SSCOP:
     SSCOP: SD(Sequence Connection-mode Data)
     SSCOP: SD send seq num N(S) = 16
     SSCOP:
Q2931: ----- UNI Signaling -----
     Q2931:
     Q2931: Protocol discriminator  = 09
     Q2931: Length of call reference = 3 bytes
     Q2931: Call reference flag      = 0... ....(message sent from call reference
➥originator)
     Q2931: Call reference value     = 852
     Q2931: Message type             = 05 (Setup)
. . .
Q2931: Info element id        = 5E (Broadband bearer capability)
     Q2931: Coding Standard/Action = 80
     Q2931: 1... .... =           ext
     Q2931: .00. .... =           code stand(ITU-T standardized)
     Q2931: ...0 .... =           flag(not significant)
     Q2931: .... .000 =           IE instruction field(clear call)
     Q2931: Length of info element = 3 byte(s)
     Q2931:   Bearer class        = BCOB-X
     Q2931:   ATM transfer capability= Non-real time VBR
     Q2931:   Suscept to clipping  = Not susceptible to clipping
     Q2931:   User plane conn config = Point-to-multipoint
. . .
```

The LAN Emulation Server is responsible for translating MAC addresses to ATM addresses. This translation process is called the *LAN Emulation Address Resolution Protocol (LE-ARP)*.

Since the LAN Emulation Server keeps a record of the ATM addresses and MAC addresses of clients that have joined the LAN, it can use this information to perform MAC-address-to-ATM-address translations for clients. Clients ask for these translations via *LAN Emulation Address Resolution Protocol (LE-ARP)* request messages.

A request might carry the MAC address of a non-ATM LAN station that must be reached via an edge device. In this case, the LES will send the LE-ARP query to all LAN Emulation clients via its multipoint connection. The appropriate proxying edge device will respond.

Registration and Unregistration Control Messages

A single MAC address/ATM address combination can be registered with a LAN Emulation Server during the JOIN interaction. However, a client may have multiple unicast LAN addresses. Or the client may wish to register one or more multicast LAN addresses.

Note that an edge device must not register the volatile LAN addresses for which it acts as a proxy. Only stable addresses should be registered.

The LE_REGISTER_REQUEST and LE_REGISTER_RESPONSE control messages enable a client to register a MAC address or Token Ring route descriptor if the client did not do so during the join process. The client also can use these messages to register additional MAC addresses or route descriptors. A separate message exchange is needed for each additional LAN address, and each LAN address is associated with a client ATM address.

These registration messages have the added benefit that they have space for additional parameters. For example, there is a useful parameter that announces that the client is able to send and receive both Ethernet and Token Ring frames on a single connection to a given ATM address (which is termed an LLC-Muxed-ATM-Address).

After you've registered, you may wish to unregister via an LE_UNREGISTER_ REQUEST/LE_UNREGISTER_RESPONSE interaction. A system that is leaving an emulated LAN should automatically unregister its addresses.

Connecting to the BUS

A LANE client must connect to one more server: the broadcast and unknown server (BUS). The BUS acts as a broadcasting and multicasting middleman.

To get the address of the BUS, a client sends an LE-ARP request for the all-1s broadcast address to the LAN Emulation Server. The server responds with the ATM address of the BUS.

Next:

1. The client opens a bidirectional point-to-point *default multicast send* connection to the BUS.

2. If point-to-multipoint connections are supported, the BUS adds the client to a unidirectional point-to-multipoint *default multicast forward* virtual channel connection for which it is the root.

Broadcast and Unknown Server Functions

Traditional LANs rely heavily on broadcasts and multicasts. Layer 2 and 3 protocols use broadcasts and multicasts to

- Locate other systems

- Transmit bridging or routing information

- Send a message to a group of systems, or to all systems on the LAN

Note that

- A special all-1s MAC address is used to send a broadcast.

- A large set of other special addresses are used for multicasting.

The BUS is very useful. Figure 10.9 illustrates how a LANE client sends broadcast and multicast frames:

1. A LANE client sends a broadcast or multicast frame by forwarding it to the BUS on the *default multicast send* connection.

2. The BUS forwards these messages to appropriate recipients.

The client also can send unicast frames across the connection to the BUS temporarily, until the client learns a partner's ATM address.

Figure 10.9 Sending frames via the BUS.

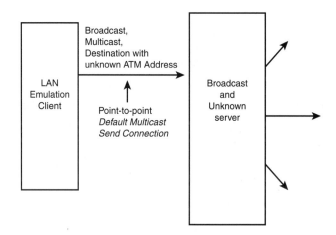

Listing 10.8 shows how a client locates the BUS. The client sends an LE-ARP request to the LAN Emulation Server. The request contains the client's MAC address and ATM address. The target LAN destination MAC address subfield is set to X'FFFFFFFFFFFF, and the broadcast address and the target ATM address are filled with zeros. In the response message, the target ATM address contains the address of the BUS.

Listing 10.8 How a Client Locates the BUS

```
LANE: CTRL ARP_REQUEST XID=134217728 RID=10
ATM: ----- ATM Header -----
      ATM:
      ATM: Frame 17 arrived at  09:17:20.8412; frame size is 144 (0090 hex) bytes.
      ATM: Call reference = 5
      ATM: Link = DTE
      ATM: Virtual path id = 0
      ATM: Virtual channel id = 186
      ATM:
LECTRL: ----- LAN EMULATION CONTROL FRAME -----
      LECTRL:
      LECTRL: Marker       = FF00
      LECTRL: Protocol     = 01
      LECTRL: Version      = 01
      LECTRL: Opcode       = 0006 (ARP_REQUEST)
      LECTRL: Status       = 0 (Success)
      LECTRL: Trans ID     = 134217728
      LECTRL: Request ID   = 10
```

```
      LECTRL: Flags          = 0000
      LECTRL: Src LAN Dest    = 000100001D4A06D6
      LECTRL:   Tag           = 0001(MAC address)
      LECTRL:   MAC Addr      = 00001D4A06D6
      LECTRL: Tar LAN Dest    = 0001FFFFFFFFFFFF
      LECTRL:   Tag           = 0001(MAC address)
      LECTRL:   MAC Addr      = FFFFFFFFFFFF
      LECTRL: SRC ATM ADDR    = 47:0005:80FF E100 0000 F21C 30D3:Cbltr14A06D6:09
      LECTRL: Reserved        = 0000
      LECTRL: NUMBER TLVs     = 0
      LECTRL: Reserved        = 00
      LECTRL: TARG ATM ADDR = 0000000000000000000000000000000000000000
      LECTRL: Reserved        =
0000000000000000000000000000000000000000000000000000000000000000


- - - - - - - - - - - - - - - - - - - - - - - - - - - - - - - - -
LANE: CTRL ARP_RESPONSE XID=134217728 RID=10
ATM: ----- ATM Header -----
      ATM:
      ATM: Frame 18 arrived at  09:17:20.8508; frame size is 144 (0090 hex) bytes.
      ATM: Call reference = 5
      ATM: Link = DCE
      ATM: Virtual path id = 0
      ATM: Virtual channel id = 186
      ATM:
LECTRL: ----- LAN EMULATION CONTROL FRAME -----
      LECTRL:
      LECTRL: Marker         = FF00
      LECTRL: Protocol       = 01
      LECTRL: Version        = 01
      LECTRL: Opcode         = 0106 (ARP_RESPONSE)
      LECTRL: Status         = 0 (Success)
      LECTRL: Trans ID       = 134217728
      LECTRL: Request ID     = 10
      LECTRL: Flags          = 0000
      LECTRL: Src LAN Dest    = 000100001D4A06D6
      LECTRL:   Tag           = 0001(MAC address)
      LECTRL:   MAC Addr      = 00001D4A06D6
      LECTRL: Tar LAN Dest    = 0001FFFFFFFFFFFF
      LECTRL:   Tag           = 0001(MAC address)
      LECTRL:   MAC Addr      = FFFFFFFFFFFF
      LECTRL: SRC ATM ADDR    = 47:0005:80FF E100 0000 F21C 30D3:Cbltr14A06D6:09
      LECTRL: Reserved        = 0000
```

continues

Continued

```
LECTRL: NUMBER TLVs   = 0
LECTRL: Reserved      = 00
LECTRL: TARG ATM ADDR = 47:0005:80FF E100 0000 F21C 30D3:ForeSy1C30D3:62
LECTRL: Reserved      =
0000000000000000000000000000000000000000000000000000000000000000
```

As shown in Figure 10.10, after the client has contacted the BUS, the BUS opens one or more *multicast forward* connections to the client. The client receives multicasts and broadcasts on the *multicast forward* connection(s). The client also can receive unicast frames on a multicast forward connection. These are frames sent by a partner that does not know its ATM address yet.

Figure 10.10 Receiving frames from the BUS.

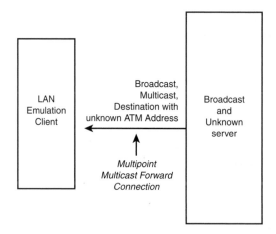

Address Resolution

A LANE client must be able to transmit frames to the MAC address of any system on its LAN. To reach a system identified by a unicast MAC address, the client needs to discover the ATM address of either

- A LANE client with that MAC address

- A LANE edge device that acts as a proxy for a real LAN station that has that MAC address

The steps in communicating with the destination system are

1. The client sends a LE-ARP request to the LAN Emulation Server across the control direct connection, asking for the ATM address that corresponds to the MAC address.

2. The server either forwards the request to an appropriate client or clients, or answers on behalf of the client, using its stored address translations.

3. The requesting client then can open an ATM connection to the destination and exchange frames with it.

The previous section already has shown this function in action. The client discovered the ATM address of the BUS by sending an LE-ARP request to the LAN Emulation Server.

Quick Sends and Flush Messages

A client can send frames to the destination immediately, without performing an LE-ARP and setting up a connection. To do this, the client simply passes the frames to the BUS across the default multicast send connection. If the BUS recognizes the destination MAC address, it will forward the frames directly to the destination. If not, the BUS multicasts the frames to an appropriate set of stations.

After sending some frames in this way, the client may wish to switch methods and open a direct ATM connection to the destination. However, before sending any data on this connection, the client has to make sure that all of the frames have been cleared from the other path.

To do this, the last thing that the client sends down the old path is a special LE_FLUSH_REQUEST. The receiver responds with an LE_FLUSH_RESPONSE, and when this arrives, the client knows that the old path is clear.

Operating with Higher Layer Protocols

Today, most systems communicate across networks using a layer 3 protocol, such as IP. An IP system will initially only be aware of its destination's IP address. It normally broadcasts an ARP message across its LAN, asking the system with the target IP address to answer and provide its MAC address. This is illustrated in Figure 10.11, which shows two systems connected to a LAN switch.

In an ATM environment, after discovering the MAC address of the destination, System A can

• Use the BUS if an exchange of only a few messages is required

• Ask the LANE Server to provide the destination's ATM address if a sustained communications session is required

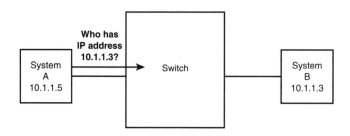

Figure 10.11   Discovering a MAC address.

The IETF has published an RFC called *Classical IP and ARP over ATM* that proposes an alternative. They suggest that a separate *ATMARP Server* be used for IP address to ATM address resolution.

- IP/ATM systems would be preconfigured with the address of this server.

- When a system connects to the server, the server records its IP and ATM addresses in its table.

- Any system that needs an IP to ATM address translation would send a request to this server.

NHRP and MPOA

The IP world is organized as tidy islands that are connected together by routers, as is shown in Figure 10.12. Each island is a *subnet*. A subnet is a set of systems on a LAN that has a common IP address prefix. Usually, all of the systems on a LAN are given addresses with the same prefix and the entire LAN is a single subnet.

Figure 10.12 shows how a station in subnet 1 communicates with a station on subnet 5. All traffic passes through Routers A, B, and C.

When the tidy, localized LANs of the conventional IP environment are replaced with the emulated LANs of the ATM world, this simple picture no longer reflects reality. A station that is attached to an ATM network can add a fresh route to a distant subnet instantaneously by opening a connection to another ATM station.

The IETF and ATM Forum have been wrestling with the opportunities and problems that this situation presents, and have defined two protocols that enable systems to take advantage of ATM shortcuts and speed traffic to its destination.

Figure 10.12 A traditional routed network.

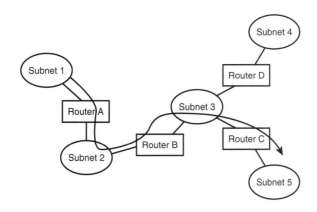

The IETF developed the *Next Hop Resolution Protocol (NHRP)*, which can discover routed shortcuts to network destinations on demand. The ATM Forum's *Multiprotocol Over ATM (MPOA)* specification adapts NHRP to the LANE environment. It is capable of replacing a long routed path with a shorter routed path or a totally switched path.

Note

This section began with a description of IP network topology. MPOA is not IP-specific and can be applied to several other protocols. However, starting with an IP example simplified the discussion.

Next Hop Resolution Protocol

An ATM network is a prime example of a *non-broadcast multi-access network (NBMA)*. What this means is that stations connected to an ATM network have the potential to communicate directly with one another, but unlike a broadcast-style LAN, they cannot shoot off messages to one another any time they like. On an ATM network, a connection has to be set up before systems can communicate.

NHRP enables an ATM host or router to discover the ATM address of a system that is the best next hop on the way to the destination. If the destination is connected to the ATM network, the next hop is the destination itself. Otherwise, the next hop is a router that provides the shortest path to the destination.

Figure 10.13 illustrates the NHRP procedure. ATM Host A wishes to communicate with remote Host B. Host A forwards a NHRP resolution request packet along the conventional route toward Host B. While waiting for a reply, Host A optionally can send data along the conventional path.

The request is handled by *next hop server (NHS)* software modules that are located in routers 1, 2, and 3 in Figure 10.13. The request is forwarded until it reaches a next hop server that can respond. After Host A receives the response, it can open an ATM connection to router 3, which is connected to the ATM network and provides the best access to Host B.

Figure 10.13   Discovering the best next hop.

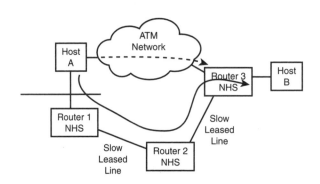

Multiprotocol Over ATM

An MPOA device contains an ATM interface, LAN Emulation software, and MPOA client software. ATM hosts, bridges, and switches can be MPOA devices.

An MPOA device requests *shortcut* information from an MPOA server, which is a router that contains MPOA server software. A shortcut is an ATM virtual channel connection that is used instead of the default routed path. Figure 10.14 illustrates the structure of MPOA devices and servers. The client and server systems are connected to an ATM switch and are LANE stations. Each MPOA server contains a next hop server module.

An MPOA client does not trigger an ATM connection whenever a chunk of data is sent to a new destination. The client will make a request only when it sees a steady traffic flow that could benefit from a shortcut.

A shortcut may terminate at the host destination, or at a router, bridge, or switch that leads to the destination. A router, bridge, or switch would have to forward traffic on to its final target.

Note that MPOA may replace a routed path with a path that is entirely switched, as is shown in Figure 10.15.

Figure 10.14 MPOA devices and server.

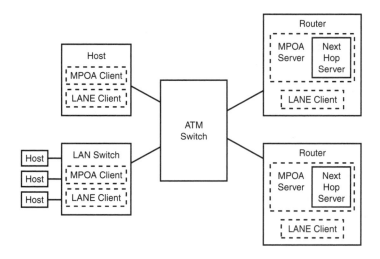

Figure 10.15 An MPOA shortcut.

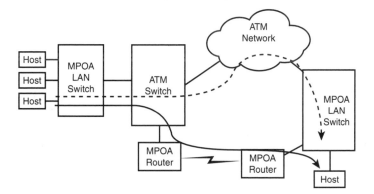

MPOA networks offer the best of both worlds. They allow an existing infrastructure to remain in place—and benefit from high-speed ATM connections.

References

References include

- ATM Forum document *LAN Emulation Over ATM Version 2—LUNI Specification* (1997).

- RFC 2225, Classical *IP and ARP over ATM* (1998).

- RFC 2332, *NBMA Next Hop Resolution Protocol* (1998). NBMA stands for non-broadcast multi-access.

- ATM Forum document *Multi-Protocol Over ATM*, Version 1.0 (1997).

PART **IV**

Appendixes

Standards Bodies

Today, telecommunications and data communications networks are interwoven in a web that wraps around the world. Equipment made by hundreds of vendors plugs into these networks and is expected to interwork with relative ease.

Standardization has been important in enabling this to happen. There are many organizations that play a role in setting telecommunications and data communications standards.

ITU-T

The first wide-scale standardization efforts were devoted to the connecting of the world's telegraph and telephone networks across national boundaries. This was the responsibility of the *International Telegraph and Telephone Consultative Committee (CCITT)*. The name of this organization later was changed to the *International Telecommunications Union— Telecommunication Standardization Sector (ITU-T)*.

The ITU-T led the development of *Integrated Services Digital Network (ISDN)* standards, which introduced a sophisticated signaling system to the telephone network and added end-to-end digital services. Currently, the ITU-T is working on enhancing *broadband ISDN (B-ISDN)*.

The ITU's Web site is

```
http://www.itu.int/
```

ITU-T documents are not free. They can be purchased at the Web site.

ISO

The International Standards Organization (ISO) was created to promote international trade and cooperative advances in science. For a time, its Open Systems Interconnect (OSI) data communications standards generated a great deal of excitement, but today, little of OSI is used except for its pictorial model and some of its address formats.

The International Standards Organization Web site is

```
http://www.iso.ch/
```

ISO documents are not free. They can be purchased through member country organizations. The *American National Standards Institute (ANSI)* is the member organization for the United States.

National and Regional Organizations

The international organizations are supported by national and regional standards organizations. Many standards result from technology submissions made by these organizations.

ANSI

ANSI has contributed to many ITU-T and ISO efforts. ANSI also adapts international standards to North American requirements, sometimes making substantial changes.

ANSI actually is a coordinating organization for dozens of specialized standards organizations and technical committees. For example, the Institute for Electrical and Electronics Engineers (IEEE) and the Electrical Industries Association (EIA) both are ANSI-accredited standards organizations.

The ANSI Web site is

```
http://www.ansi.org/
```

ANSI documents are not free. They can be purchased at the Web site.

A role similar to ANSI's is played by the *European Telecommunications Standards Institute (ETSI)*, which can be found at

```
http://www.etsi.org/
```

ETSI allows individual users to register for free access to documents.

IEEE

The *Institute for Electrical and Electronics Engineers (IEEE)* publishes standards relevant to a broad range of electronic technologies. Readers interested in data communications will be most familiar with the IEEE standards that relate to local area networks. Among other things, the IEEE administers LAN media access control (MAC) addresses.

The IEEE Web site is

```
http://www.ieee.org/
```

IEEE documents are not free. However, you can purchase a subscription that enables you to download documents from the Web site.

IETF

The *Internet Engineering Task Force (IETF)* is responsible for creating and implementing standards for the Internet. Much of their work is related to updating or enlarging the TCP/IP protocol suite.

Preliminary and final IETF standards are published in documents called *Requests For Comments (RFCs)* that are freely available on the Internet. IETF committees also often provide free software implementations of new protocols. Quick development, testing, and rollout are characteristic of Internet protocols.

IETF activities are supervised by members of the *Internet Engineering Steering Group (IESG)*. General strategy and final review of standards is performed by the *Internet Architecture Board (IAB)*.

IETF documents are free, and can be obtained from their Web site:

```
http://www.ietf.org/
```

Many of their documents also are available at other sites across the Internet.

Vendor and User Groups

Several groups have been formed to promote the ease of use and interoperability of communications technologies. These include:

- **The National ISDN Council**—A forum of telecommunications service providers and switch suppliers coordinated by Bellcore. The council defined National ISDN (NI1 and NI2) standards.

  ```
  http://www.bellcore.com/orgs/nic/index.html
  ```

- **The North American ISDN Users' Forum (NIUF)**—An organization that includes user and manufacturer members that cooperate to make sure that ISDN applications and options meet user needs.

  http://www.niuf.nist.gov/misc/niuf.html

- **The Vendor's ISDN Association (VIA)**—A group dedicated to accelerating the deployment of ISDN products, services, and usage.

  http://www.via-isdn.org/

- **The SONET Interoperability Forum**—A group that promotes SONET technology and resolves interoperability problems.

  http://www.atis.org/atis/sif/sifhom.htm

- **The Frame Relay Forum**—An international organization that includes frame relay vendors, service providers, and users. The Forum publishes interoperability specifications.

  http://www.frforum.com/

- **The ATM Forum**—An organization formed to promote the use of ATM. The Forum has published many influential standards documents.

  http://www.atmforum.com/

Other Resources

The British Standards Institute is the source of International Code Designators (ICDs). They can be reached at

http://www.bsi.org.uk/

Information on the IOTA scheme is available from the British Standards Institute at

http://www.bsi.org.uk/disc/iota.html

A useful list of national DCC authorities and contact information is maintained by the Federation of the Electronics Industry, FEI, the ISO country registrar for the UK. This information can be found at

http://www.fei.org.uk/fei/dcc-nsap.htm

Acronym List

AAL	ATM Adaptation Layer
ABR	Available Bit Rate (ATM)
ACM	Address Complete Message (ISDN)
ACR	Allowable Cell Rate (ATM)
ADM	Add-Drop Multiplexer
ADPCM	Adaptive Delta Pulse Code Modulation
ADSL	Asymmetric Digital Subscriber Line
ADTF	Allowed Cell Rate Decrease Time Factor (ATM)
AESA	ATM End System Address
AFI	Authority and Format Identifier (AESA address)
AIS	Alarm Indication Signal (Telephony)
AMI	Alternate Mark Inversion (Telephony)
ANS	ATM Name System
ANSI	American National Standards Institute
AO/DI	Always On/Dynamic ISDN
APPN	Advanced Peer-to-Peer Networking (SNA)
APS	Automatic Protection Switching (SONET)
ARE	All Routes Explorer (LAN)
ARP	Address Resolution Protocol (LAN)
ASP	ATM Service Provider
ATM	Asynchronous Transfer Mode
AU	Administrative Unit (SONET/SDH)
AvCR	Available Cell Rate (ATM)
B3ZS	Bipolar with 3 Zero Substitution (Telephony)
B8ZS	Bipolar 8 Zero Substitution (Telephony)
BAN	Boundary Access Node (SNA)

BASize	Buffer Allocation Size
Bc	Committed Burst Size (Frame relay)
BCD	Binary Coded Decimal
BCOB	Broadband Connection Oriented Bearer (ATM)
Be	Excess Burst Size (Frame relay)
BECN	Backward Explicit Congestion Notification (Frame relay)
BER	Bit Error Rate
BGP	Border Gateway Protocol (TCP/IP)
B-ICI	Broadband ISDN Inter-Carrier Interface (ATM)
BIP	Bit Interleaved Parity
B-ISDN	Broadband ISDN (ATM)
BISSI	Broadband Inter Switching System Interface (ATM)
B-ISUP	Broadband ISDN User's Part (ATM)
B-LLI	Broadband Low Layer Information (ATM)
BLSR	Bidirectional Line Switched Ring (SONET)
BN	Bridge Number (LAN)
BNN	Boundary Network Node (SNA)
BPDU	Bridge Protocol Data Unit (LAN)
BPP	Bridge Port Pair (LAN)
BRI	Basic Rate Interface (ISDN)
BSI	British Standards Institute
BSS	B-ISDN Signaling System
BTAG	Beginning Tag
BUS	Broadcast and Unknown Server (ATM LANE)
C/R	Command/Response
CAC	Connection Admission Control (ATM)
CACH	Call Appearance Call Handling (Telephony)
CAS	Channel Associated Signaling (Telephony)
CBR	Constant Bit-Rate (ATM)
CCITT	International Telegraph and Telephone Consultative Committee
CDF	Cutoff Decrease Factor (ATM)
CDV	Cell Delay Variation (ATM)
CDVT	Cell Delay Variation Tolerance (ATM)
CEPT	Conference of European Postal and Telecommunications
CER	Cell Error Rate (ATM)
CES	Circuite Emulation Service (ATM)
CID	(Sub)channel Identification

CIR	Committed Information Rate (Frame relay)
CLLM	Consolidated Link Layer Management (Frame relay)
CLNP	Connectionless Network Protocol (ISO)
CLP	Cell Loss Priority (ATM)
CLR	Cell Loss Ratio (ATM)
CM	Configuration Management
CMIP	Common Management Information Protocol
CMISE	Common Management Information Service Element
CNM	Customer Network Management
CO	Central Office
CP-AAL	Common Part ATM Adaptation Layer
CPCS	Common Part Convergence Sublayer (ATM)
CPE	Customer Premises Equipment
CPI	Common Part Indicator
CPN	Customer Premises Network
CPR	Constant Packet Rate
CRC	Cyclic Redundancy Check
CRM	Cell Rate Margin (ATM)
CS	Convergence Sublayer (ATM)
CS-ACELP	Conjugate Structure—Algebraic Code Excited Linear Predictive
CSI	Convergence Sublayer Indication (ATM)
CSU	Channel Service Unit
CTD	Cell Transfer Delay
CUG	Closed User Group
DA	Destination MAC address
DACS	Digital Access and Cross Connect System
DCC	Data Country Code
DCE	Data Circuit-terminating Equipment; Data Communications Equipment
DDR	Data Delivery Ratio (Frame relay)
DE	Discard Eligible (Frame relay)
DEMARC	Demarcation Point (Telephony)
DFA	DXI Frame Address
DISC	Disconnect
DIX	Digital, Intel, and Xerox (LAN)
DLCI	Data Link Connection Identifier
DLSw	Data Link Switching (IBM SNA)

DM	Disconnected Mode
DN	Directory Number
DNIC	Data Network Identification Code (X.121 address)
DNS	Domain Name System (Internet)
DQDB	Distributed Queue Dual Bus (SMDS)
DS0	Digital Signal 0
DS1	Digital Signal 1
DS3	Digital Signal 3
DSAP	Destination Service Access Point
DSL	Digital Subscriber Line
DSP	Domain Specific Part (AESA address)
DSS1	Digital Signaling System 1 (ISDN)
DSS2	Digital Signaling System 2 (ATM)
DSU	Data Service Unit
DTE	Data Terminal Equipment
DTL	Designated Transit List (PNNI)
DXI	Data eXchange Interface
EA	Address Extension
E-ADPCM	Discard-Eligible Embedded Adaptive Differential Pulse Code Modulation
ECBR	Errored Cell Block Rate
EFCI	Explicit Forward Congestion Indication
EIA/TIA	Electronic Industries Association/Telecommunications Industry Association
EIR	Excess Information Rate (Frame relay)
EKTS	Electronic Key Telephone Service
ELAN	Emulated Local Area Network
EMC	Electromagnetic Compatibility
EML	Element Management Layer
EPD	Early Packet Discard (ATM)
ES	End System
ESF	Extended Superframe (Telephony)
ESI	End System Identifier
ES-IS	End System to Intermediate System (ISO)
ET	Exchange Termination (ISDN)
ETAG	End Tag
ETSI	European Telecommunications Standards Institute
FCS	Frame Check Sequence

FDDI	Fiber Distributed Data Interface
FDL	Facility Data Link (Telephony)
FDR	Frame Delivery Ratio (Frame relay)
FECN	Forward Explicit Congestion Notification
FID	Format Identification
FRAD	Frame Relay Access Device
FRF	Frame Relay Forum
FRMR	Frame Reject
FRMTBSO	Frame Relay Mean Time Between Service Outages
FRMTTR	Frame Relay Mean Time To Repair
FRVCA	Frame Relay Virtual Connection Availability
FTD	Frame Transfer Delay (Frame relay)
FUNI	Frame-based User-to-Network Interface
Gbps	Gigabits Per Second
GCAC	Generic Connection Admission Control (ATM)
GCRA	Generic Cell Rate Algorithm (ATM)
GFC	Generic Flow Control (ATM)
HDLC	High-level Data Link Control
HEC	Header Error Control (ATM)
HO-DSP	High Order Domain Specific Part (AESA address)
HPR	High Performance Routing (IBM SNA)
HSSI	High Speed Serial Interface
IA5	International ASCII code 5
ICD	International Code Designator (AESA address)
ICR	Initial Cell Rate (ATM)
IDI	Initial Domain Identifier (AESA address)
IDN	International Data Number (X.121 address)
IDP	Initial Domain Part (AESA address)
IDRP	Inter Domain Routing Protocol
IE	Information Element
IEC	Interexchange Carrier (Telephony)
IEC	International Electrotechnical Commission
IEEE	Institute of Electrical and Electronics Engineers
IETF	Internet Engineering Task Force
IG	Information Group
ILMI	Integrated Local Management Interface (ATM)
IME	Interface Management Entities (ATM)

IOC	ISDN Order Codes
IOTA	Identifiers for Organisations for Telecommunications Addressing
IP	Internet Protocol
ISDN	Integrated Services Digital Network
IS-IS	Intermediate System to Intermediate System (ISO)
ISO	International Organization for Standardization
ISUP	ISDN User Part
ITU-T	International Telecommunication Union–Telecommunication, Standardization Sector
IWF	Interworking Function
IWU	Inter Working Unit
IXC	Interexchange Carrier (Telephony)
Kbps	Kilobits per second
LAN	Local Area Network
LANE	LAN Emulation (ATM)
LAPB	Link Access Protocol Balanced
LAPD	Link Access Procedure on the D-channel
LAPF	Link Access Procedures to Frame-Mode Bearer (Frame relay)
LATA	Local Access and Transport Area (Telephony)
LCD	Loss of Cell Delineation (ATM)
LD	LAN Destination
LD-CELP	Low Delay—Code Excited Linear Prediction
LE	LAN Emulation
LE_ARP	LAN Emulation Address Resolution Protocol (ATM LANE)
LEC	LAN Emulation Client (ATM LANE)
LEC	Local Exchange Carrier (Telephony)
LECID	LAN Emulation Client Identifier (ATM LANE)
LECS	LAN Emulation Configuration Server (ATM LANE)
LES	LAN Emulation Server (ATM LANE)
LGN	Logical Group Node
LIJ	Leaf Initiated Join (ATM)
LLC	Logical Link Control (LAN)
LMI	Local Management Interface
LOF	Loss Of Frame
LOP	Loss Of Pointer
LOS	Loss Of Signal
LSB	Least Significant Bit

LT	Line Termination (ISDN)
LUNI	LAN Emulation User-To-Network Interface (ATM LANE)
MAC	Media Access Control (LAN)
maxCR	Maximum Cell Rate (ATM)
maxCTD	Maximum Cell Transfer Delay (ATM)
Mbps	Megabits per second
MBS	Maximum Burst Size (ATM)
MCR	Minimum Cell Rate (ATM)
MHz	Megahertz
MIB	Management Information Base (SNMP)
MIC	Media Interface Connector
MID	Message Identifier (SMDS)
MID	Multiplex Identification (ATM)
MP-MLQ	Multi Pulse Maximum Likelihood Quantizer
MSB	Most Significant Bit
MSOH	Multiplex Section Overhead (SONET)
MTBF	Mean Time Between Failure
MTP	Message Transfer Protocol (SS7)
MTU	Message Transfer Unit
MUX	Multiplexer
NDIS	Network Driver Interface Specification
NE	Network Element
NetBIOS	Network Basic Input Output System
NEXT	Near End Crosstalk
NI	National ISDN
NIST	National Institute of Standards and Technology
NIUF	North American ISDN Users' Forum
NLPID	Network Layer Protocol Identifier (ISO)
NMS	Network Management System
NNI	Network-to-Network Interface
NPC	Network Parameter Control (ATM)
NRM	Network Resource Management (ATM)
nrt-VBR	Non-real time Variable Bit Rate
NRZ	Non-Return to Zero
NSAP	Network Service Access Point
NSR	Non-Source Routed
NT	Network Termination (ISDN)

OAM	Operations, Administration, and Maintenance
OCD	Out of Cell Delineation (ATM)
OCn	Optical Carrier level n (SONET)
ODI	Open Data-Link Interface
OSI	Open Systems Interconnection
OSPF	Open Shortest Path First
OUI	Organizationally Unique Identifier (LANs)
PAD	Packet Assembler/Disassembler
PBX	Public Branch Exchange
PCM	Pulse Code Modulation (Telephony)
PCR	Peak Cell Rate (ATM)
PDU	Protocol Data Unit
PDV	PDU Delay Variation
PG	Peer Group (ATM)
PGL	Peer Group Leader (ATM)
PGLE	Peer Group Leader Election (ATM)
PGSN	Peer Group Summary Node (ATM)
PHY	Physical Layer
PLCP	Physical Layer Convergence Protocol (PLCP)
PMD	Physical Medium Dependent
PNNI	Private Network Node Interface (ATM)
PNNI	Private Network-to-Network Interface (ATM)
POH	Path Overhead (ATM)
POI	Path Overhead Identifier (ATM)
POP	Point Of Presence
POTS	Plain Old Telephone Service
PPD	Partial Packet Discard (ATM)
PPP	Point-to-Point Protocol
PRI	Primary Rate Interface (ISDN)
PSTN	Public Switched Telephone Network
PT	Payload Type (ATM)
PTI	Payload Type Identifier (ATM)
PTSE	PNNI Topology State Element (ATM)
PTSP	PNNI Topology State Packet (ATM)
PVC	Permanent Virtual Circuit
PVCC	Permanent Virtual Channel Connection
PVPC	Permanent Virtual Path Connection

QoS	Quality of Service
RBOC	Regional Bell Operating Company
RC	Routing Control
RCC	Routing Control Channel
RD	Route Descriptor
RDF	Rate Decrease Factor (ATM)
RDI	Remote Defect Indication
REJ	Reject
RFC	Request For Comment (IETF Document Series)
RI	Routing Information
RIF	Rate Increase Factor (ATM)
RII	Routing Information Indicator
RM	Resource Management (ATM)
RNR	Receive Not Ready
RR	Receive Ready
RSOH	Regenerator Section Overhead (SONET)
RT	Routing Type
RTS	Residual Time Stamp (ATM)
rt-VBR	Real time Variable Bit Rate (ATM)
SA	Source MAC address
SAAL	Signaling ATM Adaptation Layer
SABM	Set Asynchronous Balanced Mode
SABME	Set Asynchronous Balanced Mode Extended
SAP	Service Access Point
SAPI	Service Access Point Identifier
SAR	Segmentation And Reassembly (ATM)
SCP	Service Control Point (SS7)
SCR	Sustainable Cell Rate (ATM)
SDH	Synchronous Digital Hierarchy (SONET)
SDLC	Synchronous Data Link Control (SNA)
SDU	Service Data Unit
SEAL	Simple and Efficient Adaptation Layer (ATM)
SECBR	Severely Errored Cell Block Ratio
SEL	Selector
SIF	SONET Interoperability Forum
SIP	SMDS Interface Protocol
SMDS	Switched Multimegabit Data Service

SNA	System Network Architecture
SNAP	Sub-Network Access Protocol (ISO)
SNI	Subscriber-Network Interface (SMDS)
SNMP	Simple Network Management Protocol
SOHO	Small Office Home Office
SONET	Synchronous Optical NETwork
SPE	Synchronous Payload Envelope (SONET)
SPVC	Soft (or Smart) Permanent Virtual Connection
SR	Source Routing (Bridging)
SRF	Specifically Routed Frame
SRL	Structural Return Loss
SRT	Source Routing Transparent (LAN)
SRTS	Synchronous Residual Time Stamp (ATM)
SS6	Signaling System 6
SS7	Signaling System 7
SSAP	Source Service Access Point
SSCF	Service Specific Coordination Function (ATM)
SSCOP	Service Specific Connection Oriented Protocol (ATM)
SSCS	Service Specific Convergence Sublayer (ATM)
SSL	Secure Sockets Layer
SSP	Service Switching Point (SS7)
STE	Spanning Tree Explorer (LAN)
STM	Synchronous Transfer Mode (SONET)
STP	Shielded Twisted Pair
STP	Signal Transfer Point (SS7)
STS	Synchronous Transfer Signal (SONET)
STS-3c	Synchronous Transport Signal 3c (concatenated)
SVC	Switched Virtual Circuit
SVCC	Switched Virtual Channel Connection (ATM)
SVPC	Switched Virtual Path Connection (ATM)
TA	Terminal Adapter (ISDN)
TAXI	Transparent Asynchronous Transmitter/Receiver Interface
TB	Transparent Bridging (LAN)
Tc	Time Interval (Frame relay)
TC	Transmission Convergence (ATM)
TCAP	Transaction Capability Application Part (SS7)
TCP	Transmission Control Protocol

TDM	Time Division Multiplexing
TE	Terminal Equipment
TEI	Terminal Endpoint Identifier (ISDN)
TID	Terminal Identifier (ISDN)
TLV	Type / Length / Value
TMN	Telecommunications Management Network
TSP	Terminal Service Profile (ISDN)
UA	Unnumbered Acknowledgment
UBR	Unspecified Bit Rate (ATM)
ULIA	Uplink Information Attribute
UNI	User-Network Interface
UPC	Usage Parameter Control (ATM)
UPSR	Unidirectional Path Switched Ring (SONET)
USTAT	Unsolicited Status (PNNI)
UTP	Unshielded Twisted Pair
UUI	User-to-User Indication
VBR	Variable Bit Rate (ATM)
VC	Virtual Connection
VCC	Virtual Channel Connection (ATM)
VCI	Virtual Channel Identifier (ATM)
VCL	Virtual Channel Link (ATM)
VF	Variance Factor (ATM)
VFRAD	Voice Frame Relay Access Device
VLAN	Virtual Local Area Network
VoFR	Voice over Frame Relay
VP	Virtual Path (ATM)
VPC	Virtual Path Connection (ATM)
VPCI	Virtual Path Connection Identifier (ATM)
VPI	Virtual Path Identifier (ATM)
VPL	Virtual Path Link (ATM)
VT	Virtual Tributary (SONET)
WDM	Wave Division Multiplexing
XID	Exchange Identification

GLOSSARY

Numeral

2-phase commit A protocol that assures successful completion of transactions, such as funds transfer.

A

AAL-1 ATM Adaptation Layer that manages constant bit rate traffic, such as T1, E1, or Nx64Kbps traffic for ATM transmission.

AAL-2 ATM Adaptation Layer intended for time-sensitive, low bit-rate traffic, such as compressed voice.

AAL3/4 ATM Adaptation Layer that manages data transfer. It is based on SMDS.

AAL5 The simple and efficient ATM Adaptation Layer, usually preferred for data transfer.

ABR initial cell rate The rate at which an ATM ABR source may send when it starts up, or after an idle period.

Access Line A communications line connecting a frame relay access device to a frame relay switch.

Adaptive Differential Pulse Code Modulation (ADPCM) Method that enables voice calls to be carried on 32Kbps digital channels.

Add/Drop Multiplexer A SONET network node that combines and splits signals.

Address Resolution Protocol (ARP) Procedure that discovers the MAC address of a system in order to communicate with it.

Administrative Unit A formatted subunit used within the payload of an ITU-T synchronous transfer module (STM).

Advanced Peer-to-Peer Networking (APPN) An IBM communications protocol that supports peer-to-peer communication.

Alarm Indication Signal (AIS) An all 1s signal that is transmitted by a receiver to notify a sender of the loss of the incoming signal.

Allowed cell rate (ACR) Currently allowed transmission rate for an ATM available bit rate (ABR) circuit.

Allowed cell rate decrease time factor (ADTF) The time allowed between sending RM cells before the rate must be decreased to the initial cell rate.

Alternate Mark Inversion (AMI) A T1 line coding format that transmits ones by alternate positive and negative voltages.

Always On/Dynamic ISDN (AO/DI) A service enables a user to remain continuously connected to an ISDN network and to transparently obtain ISDN bandwidth when it is needed.

Analog For telephones, the conversion of sound wave patterns to analogous electrical wave patterns at one end of a call, and back to sound at the other end.

Associated signaling Procedure in which signaling messages for a call are sent on the same channel used for the call, or on an associated channel on the same line.

Asymmetric Digital Subscriber Line (ADSL) A technology that supports high-speed digital transmission across the local loop.

Asynchronous Transfer Mode (ATM) Method of transmitting information that is organized into cells. The technology that was chosen to implement B-ISDN.

ATM Adaptation Layer Layer that packages data into an appropriate format (such as a data link frame) and then segments the package into cell payloads.

ATM DSU Device that exchanges frames with a router, while providing a UNI interface to an ATM switch.

ATM end system address (AESA) A 20-byte address whose form is based on ISO NSAP formats.

ATM LAN Emulation (LANE) A protocol that enables ATM devices to emulate LAN devices, and to participate in virtual LANs.

ATM Layer Layer responsible for creating cell headers and managing the ATM cell stream.

ATM Physical Layer Layer that performs a number of housekeeping chores and transmits cells onto a physical medium.

Attenuation The reduction of a signal as it traverses a medium.

Authority and format identifier (AFI) The first byte in an ATM end system address. Indicates the type of address that follows.

AutoSPID A method of automating the ISDN terminal initialization process.

Available Bit Rate (ABR) An ATM service that enables an endpoint to transmit at varying rates, depending on the current availability of resources in the network.

B

Bandwidth A measure of the information carrying capacity of a transmission medium.

Basic rate interface (BRI) connects a subscriber to the network across an ordinary local loop.

Basic rate ISDN (BRI) An ISDN interface that extends digital transmission across a local loop to a residential or small business subscriber, and supports a signaling D channel and two bearer B channels.

Bearer Class A (BCOB-A) An ATM constant bit-rate class of service for which the network may perform interworking.

Bearer Class C (BCOB-C) An ATM variable bit-rate class of service for which the network may perform interworking.

Bearer Class X (BCOB-X) An ATM class of service that does not require interworking.

Bidirectional line switched ring (BLSR) A SONET configuration made up of 2 or 4 rings. Half of the capacity is used for normal transmission. The rest is reserved for protection in case part of the facility fails.

Bidirectional procedures A method of exchanging frame relay permanent virtual circuit status information at a network-to-network interface.

Binary Coded Decimal (BCD) A method of encoding decimal digits which uses 4 binary bits to express each decimal digit from 0 to 9.

Bipolar 8 Zero Substitution A method of satisfying the ones-density requirements of T-channel carriers by replacing a string of 8 zeros with a special signal pattern.

B-ISDN intercarrier interface (B-ICI) An ATM Forum interface between public carriers.

Bit Error Rate (BER) A measurement of transmission quality, expressed as the proportion of received bits that are in error.

Bit Interleaved Parity (BIP) An error detection method based on generating a parity summation at the source and checking it at the destination.

Bit Robbing The use of the least significant bit in every sixth DS1 frame for signaling.

Bit-stuffing A procedure in which the transmitting device alters the data bits in a frame before sending them onto the medium, and the receiving device restores them to their original state.

BONDING An inverse multiplexing method that gives multiple channels the appearance of a single, higher-bandwidth communications link.

Boundary Access Node (BAN) A method of carrying SNA traffic across a frame relay network that encloses bridged LAN frames inside frame relay frames.

Boundary Network Node (BNN) A method of carrying SNA traffic across a frame relay network using formats that were defined by the Frame Relay Forum.

Bridge A device that prevents traffic whose source and destination are on the same segment from entering another segment.

Broadband digital cross-connect An ATM product that can multiplex and demultiplex only DS3 and higher level STS (or STM) signals.

Broadband ISDN (B-ISDN) The ITU-T definition of a high-speed digital network based on ATM that can carry voice, video, and data traffic.

Broadband ISDN Inter-Carrier Interface (B-ICI) An ATM Forum specification for the interface between public ATM networks.

Broadband ISDN User's Part (B-ISUP) A protocol used to establish, maintain and release broadband switched network connections across a SS7/ATM network.

Broadcast and unknown server (BUS) A server that enables LANE clients to send and receive broadcast and multicast frames.

Brouter A device that routes some protocols and bridges others.

C

Call Appearance Call Handling (CACH) An ISDN service that supports more than one directory number and allows a user to put a call on hold while continuing with an active call.

Case A service A frame relay service that is not integrated with ISDN.

Case B service A frame relay service that is integrated with ISDN and whose calls are set up using ISDN D-channel signaling.

Cell   ATM Layer protocol data unit (53 bytes in length).

Cell delay variation (CDV)   A measure of cell clumping. That is, a measure of the difference between expected and actual cell arrival times.

Cell delay variation tolerance (CDVT)   A maximum bound on the acceptable amount of cell delay variation.

Cell delineation   The process of determining where each ATM cell begins.

Cell Error Rate (CER)   A measure of the proportion of errored ATM cells.

Cell loss priority bit (CLP)   A bit in the ATM cell header that indicates the relative priority of the cell.

Cell Loss Ratio (CLR)   A QoS parameter that stipulates the reliability of ATM transmission. It is equal to the proportion of the ATM cells that are lost.

Cell rate decoupling   The process of creating a steady stream of cells by inserting dummy cells at the sender and discarding them at the receiver.

Cell rate margin (CRM)   An ATM Generic Connection Admission Control (GCAC) parameter that measures the difference between the total bandwidth that has been allocated and the sum of the allocated sustainable cell rates.

Cell transfer delay   The time that it takes to deliver a cell from its source to its destination.

Central Office (CO)   A local telephone switching office.

Channel   A path along which information flows.

Channel Associated Signaling (CAS)   Channel associated signals are transmitted either within the channel used for the call, or on a separate channel permanently associated with it.

Channel Service Unit/Data Service Unit (CSU/DSU)   A device that terminates the line from the telecommunications network to the customer premise. It performs timing, signal formatting, and loopback functions.

Circuit Emulation Service (CES)   An ATM service category that supports constant bit rate traffic.

Closed loop congestion control   A process that notifies entry point switches that there is congestion in the network and they should throttle back incoming traffic.

Closed user group (CUG)   A set of endpoints whose communication is restricted in some way—for example, to members of the group.

Committed burst size (Bc)   The maximum number of bits that a provider contracts to deliver during a measurement interval.

Committed Information Rate (CIR)
The average rate (in bits per second) at which the network commits to deliver data under normal conditions. The average is measured for a specified time interval.

Common channel signaling The use of separate, dedicated network links for signaling.

Common Management Interface Protocol (CMIP) An ISO network management protocol.

Conformance definition A description of the way an ATM switch will test incoming traffic and the action that it will take for non-conformant cells.

Congested switch A switch that is receiving more cells than it can transmit on output lines and whose queue memory is at or near saturation.

Connection Admission Control (CAC) A procedure that determines whether the network can and will provide the resources requested for a new switched virtual connection. Protects a network from unauthorized connections and overload conditions.

Connection oriented communications Communications characterized by the requirement to set up a fixed circuit for transmission.

Connectionless communications Communication that does not require a prior connection to be set up before data can be transferred.

Connectionless Network Protocol (CLNP) An ISO layer 3 protocol for connectionless delivery of network PDUs.

Consolidated Link Layer Management message (CLLM) A frame relay message that notifies the source of congestion along a transmission path.

Constant Bit Rate (CBR) An ATM Service Category that supports a guaranteed constant bit rate and is suitable for voice or video.

Control plane function A function—such as switching—that is required to support connections, but is not directly involved with data transfer.

Convergence Sublayer (CS) The upper sublayer of the ATM Adaptation Layer.

Cross connection In telephony language, the transfer of traffic arriving on an incoming line to a selected outgoing line in order to build a circuit.

Customer Network Management (CNM) A network service that enables a customer to access network configuration, performance, and error data that relates to the customer's own circuits.

Cyclic Redundancy Check (CRC) A calculation performed at a data source and included with a data frame. The CRC value is checked at the destination and if the value does not match, the frame is discarded.

D

D4 superframe The original packaging that was defined for a DS1 signal. A D4 superframe consists of twelve consecutive DS1 frames.

Data Circuit-terminating Equipment (DCE) A device required in order to access a data network.

Data Delivery Ratio (DDR) For a frame relay circuit, measures the fraction of the transmitted bytes that are successfully delivered.

Data eXchange Interface (DXI) An interface between an ATM endpoint and a special ATM DSU that enables the endpoint to communicate with an ATM network via an ordinary serial interface.

Data Link Connection Identifier (DLCI) A circuit number assigned to each frame relay virtual circuit at a site.

Data link frames Layer 2 protocol data units used in data communications.

Data Link Switching (DLSw) A method of carrying SNA traffic across a network encapsulated within TCP payloads.

Data Network Identification Code (DNIC) The first 4 digits of an X.121 address.

Data Terminal Equipment (DTE) An endpoint device.

Demarcation Point (DEMARC) The boundary between residential wiring and telephone network wiring.

Designated transit list (DTL) For ATM PNNI signaling, a list of nodes that defines a path for a circuit.

Destination Service Access Point (DSAP) A code in a logical link control (LLC) header that indicates the service to which the frame contents should be delivered.

Digital Access and Cross Connect System (DACS) A network device that maps traffic from an incoming line to an outgoing line at either the T1 or individual channel level.

Digital signal 0 (DS0) A 64Kbps digital circuit.

Digital subscriber line (DSL) A technology that supports high speed digital transmission across a local loop.

Digital Subscriber Signaling System 1 (DSS1) The user network signaling protocol for ISDN.

Digital Subscriber Signaling System 2 (DSS2) The user network signaling protocol for B-ISDN networks.

Discard Eligible bit (DE) A bit in the frame relay header that indicates the relative priority of the frame.

Distributed Queue Dual Bus (DQDB) An IEEE access protocol adopted for use with SMDS.

Domain Name System (DNS) A system of directories that translates between computer names and addresses.

Domain Specific Part (DSP) The latter part of an ATM end system address.

E

Early Packet Discard (EPD) Action of a switch that needs to discard AAL5 cells. The switch waits for the start of the next frame and discards that frame in its entirety.

Echo cancellation Method used to support full-duplex communications across an ISDN local loop. If both sides send concurrently, each end of the transmission subtracts its own signal from the combined signal.

Edge-to-edge egress queue measurement For frame relay, a measurement whose scope extends from the point at which a frame enters the network to the point at which the frame enters its exit queue.

Edge-to-edge parameter For frame relay, a measurement whose scope extends from the point at which a frame enters the network to the point at which it exits the network.

Emulated Local Area Network (ELAN) A local area network that includes ATM stations, and possibly ordinary LAN stations. With the help of some extra components, network software in the ATM stations operates as it would for a LAN station.

End System Identifier (ESI) The last six bytes of an ATM end system address, which identifies an individual system. It usually consists of a MAC address.

End-to-end measurements For frame relay, a measurement whose scope extends from the customer's source access device to the destination access device.

Ethertype codes Codes created to identify the different types of traffic carried on an Ethernet LAN.

Event driven procedures A method of exchanging frame relay permanent virtual circuit status information via reliable link across a network-to-network interface.

Excess burst size (Be) The number of excess bits that a frame relay network will attempt to deliver during a measurement interval.

Excess Information Rate (EIR) The excess burst size divided by the time interval.

Exchange Termination (ET) An ISDN termination point at a central office switch.

Explicit Forward Congestion Indication bit (EFCI) A bit that indicates whether the network was congested in the direction of delivery.

Extended Superframe Format (ESF) The preferred packaging for a DS1 signal. An extended superframe consists of 24 consecutive DS1 frames.

F

Facility data link An ESF messaging channel formed from framing bits from 12 of the DS1 frames.

Feature key management protocol An ISDN protocol that enables a user to activate or control a service by pressing a feature key on a telephone set.

Fiber Distributed Data Interface (FDDI) A 100Mbps ring-based local area network.

Flooding A method of propagating routing information to network nodes. Used for ATM PNNI routing.

Forward Explicit Congestion Notification (FECN) A flag in a frame relay header that indicates that congestion was experienced along the path followed by the frame.

Frame A data link layer protocol data unit.

Frame-based User-to-Network Interface (FUNI) A frame-based interface to an ATM network.

Frame Check Sequence (FCS) A field in a data link frame that contains a CRC value.

Frame Delivery Ratio (FDR) A measure of the proportion of frame relay frames that are successfully delivered.

Frame reject (FRMR) An HDLC frame that signals a non-recoverable error.

Frame Relay A layer 2 networking service. Data is carried in frames that have a brief header containing a circuit number (and a few flag bits) and a trailer that contains a frame check sequence.

Frame Relay Access Device (FRAD) A router, bridge, or other special purpose customer device that provides access to a frame relay network.

Frame Relay Mean Time Between Service Outages (FRMTBSO) The average time between frame relay service outages.

Frame Relay Mean Time To Repair (FRMTTR) A measure of the average outage time for a frame relay network.

Frame Relay Virtual Connection Availability (FRVCA) The percentage of the time when there is no fault caused by the provider.

Frame Transfer Delay (FTD) The time required to transport a frame between the entry point and the designated exit boundary point.

Functional protocol An ISDN protocol that enables an intelligent device to activate or control a service by including facility information elements in signaling messages.

G

Generic Cell Rate Algorithm (GCRA) An algorithm used by an ATM switch to determine whether the cells of a CBR, rt-VBR, nrt-VBR, or UBR connection conform to their traffic contract.

Generic Connection Admission Control (GCAC) A process that determines whether a network has enough resources to support a connection.

Generic flow control (GFC) A field in the ATM cell header that can be used for local user functions.

Growth bytes Bytes in a SONET synchronous transfer signal that are reserved for future uses.

H

Header error control (HEC) A field in the ATM cell header that is used to detect cell header errors and optionally correct single-bit cell header errors.

High-level Data Link Control (HDLC) A standard data link protocol defined for use across point-to-point and point-to-multipoint lines.

High Order Domain Specific Part (HO-DSP) The part of an ATM end system address that follows the initial domain part.

I

Identifier for Organizations for Telecommunications Addressing (IOTA) An organizational identifier assigned by a standards organization that can be used as the basis of the organization's ATM network addresses.

Idle cells Cells that are used to pad the flow of ATM cells and are discarded on delivery.

Information Element (IE) A formatted group of parameters in a message (for example, in an ISDN or ATM signaling message).

Initial Cell Rate (ICR) For an ATM ABR connection, the transmission rate used initially, and after idle periods.

Initial Domain Identifier (IDI) A part of an ATM end system address immediately following the initial AFI byte.

Initial Domain Part (IDP) The initial bytes of an ATM end system address.

Integrated Local Management Interface (ILMI) A protocol that defines messages automatically exchanged across an ATM user network or network-to-network interface. ILMI supports automatic ATM address configuration.

Integrated Services Digital Network (ISDN) A standard telecommunications technology that supports switched digital voice and data service, and supports many extra service features.

Interexchange carrier (IEC or IXC) The formal name for a long distance telephone carrier that routes calls whose destination is outside the local exchange carrier's area.

Interface management entities (IME) Software components that execute the ILMI protocol.

International Data Number (IDN) A code that is used in some ATM end system addresses. The code identifies an authority responsible for administering the addresses.

Interworking function (IWF) A component in a system that connects two different types of networks (such as frame relay and ATM) that enables endpoints attached to one network to communicate with endpoints attached to the other network.

Inverse ARP A protocol used to discover the IP address of the partner at the other end of a frame relay connection.

Inverse multiplexer A device that transmits data across several separate channels, but appears to provide access to a single higher-speed channel.

IP datagrams Layer 3 protocol data units carried by IP from source systems to destination systems.

ISDN Order Codes (IOC) A set of predefined features aimed at simplifying the BRI order process. (Also known as ISDN capability packages.)

J–K

Jitter Unwanted variations in a signal rate that cause bits to arrive a little too early or a little too late.

Keypad protocol An ISDN protocol that enables a user to activate or control a service by entering IA5 characters via the device keypad.

Kilobits per second (Kbps) A unit of measure; thousands of bits per second.

L

LAN Emulation (LANE) A set of mechanisms that enable an ATM station to emulate a conventional broadcast LAN system.

LAN Emulation Address Resolution Protocol (LE_ARP) Protocol used by ATM clients to request MAC-address-to-ATM-address translations.

LAN Emulation Client (LEC) Network software in an ATM station that enables the system to perform the LAN emulation protocols.

LAN Emulation client identifier (LECID) An identifier that is assigned to a LAN emulation client when it joins an emulated LAN.

LAN Emulation configuration server (LECS) A configuration server that directs a LAN emulation client to its emulated LAN server.

LAN Emulation server (LES) The server at which a LAN emulation client registers its MAC address, and from which it receives configuration parameters for the emulated LAN.

Leaf Initiated Join (LIJ) A procedure that enables a node to connect to an existing point-to-multipoint connection as a leaf.

Leaves Endpoints of a point-to-multipoint connection.

Line For SONET, a span that does not have a regenerator as an endpoint.

Line Termination (LT) The physical component that terminates an ISDN line at the central office end.

Link Access Procedure on the D-channel (LAPD) A data link protocol used to carry ISDN signaling messages.

Link access procedures to frame-mode bearer (LAPF) Frame relay data link protocol.

Link Access Protocol Balanced (LAPB) A data link protocol defined for X.25.

Link state protocol A protocol that enables nodes to discover the map of their network.

Local loop The copper pair of wires that connects house wiring to a telephone central office.

Local Management Interface (LMI) For ATM, a protocol that enables a user endpoint to determine that status of its permanent virtual circuits.

Logical Link Control 2 (LLC2) A reliable data link protocol that can be used across a local area network.

M

M23 multiplex format A multiplexing format that bit-interleaves groups of four T1s into DS2 signals, and then bit-interleaves seven DS2 signals into a DS3 signal.

Management Information Base (MIB) A collection of SNMP network management variables. A MIB document includes a set of related definitions that are organized into a unit called a MIB Module.

Maximum burst size (MBS) Limits the number of ATM cells that can be transmitted at the peak rate.

Maximum cell rate (maxCR) A Generic Connection Admission Control parameter that specifies the maximum rate usable by connections belonging to a specified Service Category.

Maximum cell transfer delay (maxCTD) A parameter that establishes a limit on the amount of time that it should take to deliver ATM cells.

Media Access Control (MAC) addresses Network interface addresses that are under the control of the IEEE, and consist of 6 hexadecimal bytes. These addresses sometimes are called physical addresses.

Megabits per second (Mbps) Millions of bits per second.

Message Transfer Protocol (MTP) The message protocol used for SS7 messages.

M-frame The formatted DS3 signal unit.

Minimum cell rate (MCR) The rate at which an ATM source always is allowed to send for an available bit rate channel.

Multiplex Section Overhead (MSOH)
The last five rows of overhead bytes in an
ITU-T synchronous transfer module.

Multiplexing The process of combining
two or more communications signals
into a larger signal unit. Alternatively,
interleaving multiple channels onto a
common transmission medium.

N

Narrowband ISDN (N-ISDN)
Another name for ISDN.

National ISDN (NI) A set of standards
for ISDN implementations defined by the
National ISDN Council.

**Network Basic Input Output System
(NetBIOS)** A network programming
interface for LAN software.

**Network Driver Interface Specification
(NDIS)** A network driver interface
commonly used on Microsoft Windows
systems.

**Network Layer Protocol Identifier
(NLPID)** An ISO code that identifies
the protocol being carried in a data link
frame.

Network Parameter Control (NPC)
Usage parameter control that is
performed at a network-to-network
interface.

Network termination type 1 (NT-1) A
device that provides the physical interface
between 2 twisted pair premise wiring and
a basic rate ISDN line.

Nibble A half byte

Non-initializing terminals (NIT)
ISDN terminals that do not require
SPIDs.

**Non-Real-Time Variable Bit Rate
(nrt-VBR)** An ATM Service Category
that delivers a specified average
bandwidth and supports applications
that are not sensitive to delay.

O

Open Shortest Path First (OSPF)
A popular protocol that is used to
learn network topology and maintain
up-to-date knowledge of the status of
network facilities.

Optical carriers (OCs) A line that
carries a SONET signal at a given
bandwidth level.

**Organizationally Unique Identifier
(OUI)** A 3-byte code that identifies
the organization that is responsible for a
2-byte protocol identifier that follows.

Oversubscription The practice of
configuring a set of frame relay circuits
whose combined committed information
rates exceed the available bandwidth of
the access line.

P

Packet Assembler/Disassembler (PAD)
A server that can be accessed by ASCII
terminals and hosts via a direct link or a
dial-up call. The PAD connects these
devices to an X.25 network.

Packet switching A data network technology. Data is packaged in units called packets. A packet is routed to its destination based on information in the packet header.

Partial packet discard (PPD) Action of a switch that needs to discard AAL5 cells. The switch discards the current cell and all of the other remaining cells that belong to the same frame.

Path For SONET, a span whose endpoints are terminals.

Peak cell rate (PCR) A cell rate that a source never may exceed.

Peak-to-peak cell delay variation Measures differences between the ideal periodic cell arrival time and the actual arrival time.

Peer group identifier An ATM address prefix that is used by all network nodes in a particular region.

Peer group nodes The nodes whose addresses start with the peer group identifier prefix.

Permanent virtual circuits (PVCs) Circuits that are preconfigured and set up for an extended period of time.

Plesiochronous network A network whose nodes are allowed to time their signals using separate clock sources with almost the same timing. The networks based on the North American Digital Signal Hierarchy are plesiochronous.

PNNI topology state element (PTSE) A unit of PNNI routing database information.

PNNI topology state packet (PTSP) A message that is used to deliver one or more PTSEs to a neighbor.

Point of presence (POP) A strategically located site that is a point at which subscribers connect to a data network, or telephony local exchange carriers connect to an interexchange carrier.

Point-to-point protocol (PPP) A wide area data link protocol known to many people because it is used for Internet dial-up access.

Primary rate interface (PRI) An ISDN interface that operates across a leased T1 carrier connecting a subscriber to the network.

Private branch exchange (PBX) A private switch that provides telephone service within a business, and also enables internal telephones, fax machines, and modems to connect to the outside world via one or more trunk connections.

Private network node interface (PNNI) ATM network routing and signaling protocols.

Protocol data unit (PDU) A formatted unit of data. Most PDUs consist of a header followed by a data payload. Some PDUs have a trailer that follows the payload.

Protocols Mechanisms and rules used to accomplish intelligible data communications.

Proxy agent For customer network management, an application that relays requests and responses between a customer's management station and a provider's management information.

Q-R

Quality of service (QoS) parameters Parameters that relate to delay and reliability

R reference point An ISDN reference point that identifies the interface between a TE2 and a TA.

Real-Time Variable Bit Rate (rt-VBR) An ATM Service Category that delivers a specified average bandwidth and supports applications that are sensitive to delay and to variations in delay.

Reference points Formal ISDN identifiers for the interfaces between various types of equipment.

Regenerator Section Overhead (RSOH) The first three rows of overhead bytes in an ITU-T synchronous transfer module.

Reject (REJ) frame An HDLC frame used to notify a sender that a frame has been lost or corrupted.

Remote operations An OSI application layer service that supports remote procedure calls.

Requests for Comments (RFCs) Documents published by the Internet Engineering Task Force.

Residual Time Stamp (RTS) A measurement that reveals differences between a local service clock and the ATM network clock.

Resource management (RM) cells ATM cells that support an available bit rate (ABR) connection by providing a traffic source with feedback from the network.

Robbed bit signaling Signaling carried out by using bits taken from each T1 transmission channel. Bit 8 in every 6th frame of a T1 channel is set aside for signaling.

Router A layer 3 device that forwards traffic from link to link until it reaches its destination. Routers cooperate to learn the topology of their network. They can shift the path that data follows based on current network conditions.

S

S/T reference point The interface between an ISDN terminal endpoint type 1 (TE1) and the NT1.

Section The span between any two adjacent nodes.

Secure Sockets Layer (SSL) An application-layer security protocol, widely available in World Wide Web browser and server implementations.

Segment A partial path consisting of one link or several consecutive links along the route.

Segmentation and reassembly (SAR) The ATM Adaptation Layer function that segments frames into 48-byte cell payloads.

Selector byte (SEL) The final byte in an ATM end system address.

Service Access Point (SAP) A point at which data is passed from one layer to the next.

Service Access Point Identifier (SAPI) An identifier that enables incoming PDUs to be passed to the correct higher layer process.

Service Control Point (SCP) An SS7 computer that hosts one or more databases (such as an 800-number database).

Service Data Unit (SDU) A unit of data that is passed down to a lower layer for transmission, or is delivered from the lower layer for reception.

Service Level Agreement (SLA) A formal statement that defines verifiable, quantitative thresholds that define the provider's deliverables, and sets penalties (such as customer credits) that will be imposed when the provider does not meet its target thresholds.

Service Specific Connection Oriented Protocol (SSCOP) An ATM Adaptation Layer protocol used when reliable transmission of messages is required.

Service specific convergence sublayer (SSCS) An ATM Adaptation Layer sublayer that holds any functions that are needed to support a special service, such as interworking with a frame relay network.

Service Specific Coordination Function (SSCF) A service specific portion of the ATM Adaptation Layer that provides any additional functions that are needed at the interface between the service user and the AAL.

Service Switching Point (SSP) A central office or tandem switch that supports SS7 protocol software and can connect to SS7 signaling links.

Set asynchronous balanced mode (SABM) frame HDLC frame that initiates a reliable link when modulo 8 numbering will be used.

Set asynchronous balanced mode extended (SABME) frame Frame that initiates a reliable link when modulo 128 numbering will be used.

Severely Errored Cell Block Ratio (SECBR) The ratio of cell blocks that are severely errored. A cell block is severely errored when more than a threshold level (M) of errored cells, lost cells, or mis-inserted cells are detected for an incoming cell block.

Sharing terminal identifier A 2-digit identifier within an ISDN generic SPID. BRI terminals that have the same capabilities are given the same directory number and the same 2-digit sharing terminal identifier.

Signal Transfer Point (STP) A message switch that routes SS7 message traffic.

Signaling AAL (SAAL) The enhanced AAL5 service that is used for signaling.

Signaling messages Messages exchanged in order to set up or terminate a call, to report a problem, or to establish a special call feature.

Signaling System 7 (SS7) A standardized network signaling system used with ISDN. SS7 can set up calls quickly and provides access to special service databases (such as 800-number service or call charge card service).

Simple and Efficient Adaptation Layer (SEAL) Another name for AAL5.

Simple Network Management Protocol (SNMP) A network management protocol used to read or update device configuration or status variables, read performance information, and carry reports of problems.

SNMP Agent Component in a device that responds to requests from an SNMP network management station and reports problems.

SNMP Manager Component in a management station that sends requests to SNMP agents and receives problem reports.

Soft PVC A permanent virtual circuit whose endpoints are configured manually, but whose route is generated automatically.

SONET Interoperability Forum (SIF) An industry group that was formed to promote SONET technology and resolve interoperability problems.

Source Service Access Point (SSAP) A code in a logical link control (LLC) header that indicates the source of the frame contents.

Subnet A set of systems whose IP addresses start with the same prefix that can communicate directly with one another. Data will not flow through an intermediate router.

Sub-Network Access Protocol (SNAP) subheader A data link frame subheader that identifies the protocol that is carried in the payload.

Subscriber-network interface (SNI) The user network interface between subscriber equipment and an SMDS network.

Sustainable cell rate (SCR) An average cell rate for one direction of a connection, measured over a relatively long time scale.

Switch identification An ISDN feature that enables a customer device to automatically learn the switch type, switch manufacturer, and the National ISDN protocol version supported by the switch.

Switched Multi-megabit Data Service (SMDS) A high speed connectionless public data network service originally offered by Regional Bell Operating Companies (RBOCs).

Switched virtual channel connection (SVCC) A switched ATM channel connection.

Switched virtual circuit (SVC) A circuit set up on demand and terminated at the convenience of the user, much like an ordinary telephone call.

Switched virtual path connection (SVPC) An ATM switched connection that sets up an end-to-end path.

Synchronous Data Link Control (SDLC) An IBM data link protocol that belongs to the HDLC family.

Synchronous Digital Hierarchy (SDH) The ITU-T high speed wide area network multiplexing hierarchy.

Synchronous DS3 M13 multiplex format A multiplexing format that byte interleaves 28 DS1 signals into a DS3 signal payload.

Synchronous Optical Network (SONET) A scalable network transport system that can scale up to very high transmission rates.

Synchronous Payload Envelope (SPE) A formatted unit that carries SONET payload data.

Synchronous Residual Time Stamp (SRTS) method A method that enables a receiving ATM endpoint to reconstruct the timing of a source DS1 or E1 service clock frequency.

Synchronous Transfer Module (STM) A building block signal format used in the ITU-T synchronous digital hierarchy.

Synchronous Transfer Signal (STS) A formatted signal used in SONET transmission.

Synchronous Transfer Signal Nc (STS-Nc) A concatenated format designed to carry bigger SONET payloads. The SPE in an STS-Nc payload area is a single item that is transported and switched as an integral unit.

T

T1 frame A synonym for DS1 frame. A format used to package T1 channels.

Tandem switch A switch that connects to central offices and to other tandem switches. A tandem switch connects a line that is part of a telephone circuit to the next line that will be part of that circuit.

Tc Time Interval The frame relay time interval associated with rate measurements such as the CIR.

T-carrier system The United States transmission system designed to carry voice in digital form.

TCP/IP A suite of data communications protocols.

Terminal Adapter (TA) An adapter that enables a non-ISDN device to interface to an ISDN network.

Terminal Endpoint Identifier (TEI) An ISDN subscriber terminal identifier that is used by the LAPD protocol.

Terminal Equipment type 2 (TE2) Equipment that is not ISDN-ready. A terminal adapter (TA) is needed to connect a TE2 to an ISDN bus.

Terminal Identifier (TID) A 2-digit identifier within an ISDN generic SPID that is used to distinguish between terminals that have the same directory number and sharing terminal identifier.

Terminal Service Profile (TSP) An ISDN service profile that contains configuration data for one or more terminals.

Time division multiplexing (TDM) A multiplexing method for which each information stream is assigned a time slot and data belonging to a stream only may be transmitted during its time slot.

Traffic Contract Information that is associated with an ATM connection. It includes a conformance definition, traffic parameters, and the quality of service.

Traffic parameters Quantities (such as peak cell rate and sustainable cell rate) that describe the transmission characteristics of an ATM connection.

Traffic shaping A method of modifying the stream of cells transferred on an ATM connection in order to improve its behavior.

Transaction Capabilities Application Part (TCAP) A protocol defines the way that an SS7 client interacts with a database server.

Translations Service providers' term for ISDN line settings.

Transmission convergence (TC) The upper sublayer of the ATM physical layer.

Transparent Asynchronous Transmitter/Receiver Interface (TAXI) A method of encoding bits onto a 100Mbps multimode optical fiber.

Transport overhead bytes Overhead bytes in a SONET STS-1 frame.

Trap A message used by an SNMP agent to report a significant event, such as a reboot or a serious error.

Trunks Lines that connect switches together.

U

U reference point The ISDN interface between an NT1 and the telecommunications network.

Unassigned cells Filler cells that are inserted into the cell stream by the ATM Layer.

Unidirectional Path Switched Ring (UPSR) A SONET ring configuration. Nodes are connected by two rings of fiber. The same data is transmitted onto each fiber, but in opposite directions.

Unspecified Bit Rate (UBR) An ATM service category that does not guarantee a specific transmission rate or bound on delay.

Usage Parameter Control (UPC)
The set of actions taken by a network to monitor and control traffic, and to ensure that incoming traffic conforms to its traffic contract.

User plane function The transfer of ordinary user data.

User network interface (UNI) 1) The interface between an ATM endpoint device and an ATM switch. Defines the interactions between an endpoint device and a private network switch, an endpoint device and a public network switch, and a private network switch and a public network switch. 2) The interface between customer premise equipment and network equipment.

V

Variance factor (VF) A Generic Connection Admission Control parameter that is a statistical measurement of the variance of the cell rate margins of all existing connections.

Virtual channel connection (VCC) For ATM, a unidirectional connection.

Virtual channel identifier (VCI) A number in the range 0 to 65,535 that identifies a virtual channel within a given virtual path. VCIs appear in ATM cell headers.

Virtual Circuit A communications circuit that does not occupy a fixed, reserved bandwidth, but shares bandwidth with other virtual circuits.

Virtual Local Area Network (VLAN)
A set of systems that are not physically connected to the same LAN that communicate as if they are connected to a common LAN.

Virtual Path Connection A bundle of virtual channel connections.

Virtual path identifier (VPI) An identifier for a virtual path. VPIs appear in ATM cell headers.

Virtual Private Network (VPN) A network made up of circuits within a provider's network that connect an organization's nodes together. The provider is responsible for maintaining the privacy of the subscriber's data.

Virtual Tributary (VT) A formatted unit within a SONET STS-1 synchronous payload envelope that carries DS1, E1, DS1C, or DS2 signals.

Voice frame relay access device (VFRAD) A device that can multiplex voice, fax, voice-band modem data, and ordinary data across frame relay circuits.

Voice over frame relay (VoFR) A set of Frame Relay Forum interworking standards that define a method of exchanging voice traffic across frame relay circuits.

W–Z

Wave division multiplexing (WDM)
A technique that enables multiple parallel optical signals to be transmitted across one optical fiber using different wavelengths of light.

Wideband digital cross-connect
A product that can multiplex and
demultiplex traffic that includes low
bandwidth streams, such as DS1 or E1.

Zero CIR A frame relay service that
allows a customer to transmit frames
onto the network at any rate up to some
maximum. In some cases, the only limit
is the capacity of the access line.

Index

M

The *Macmillan Technology Series* is a comprehensive and authoritative set of guides to the most important computing standards of today. Each title in this series is aimed at bringing computing professionals closer to the scientists and engineers behind the technological implementations that will change tomorrow's innovations in computing.

Currently available titles in the *Macmillan Technology Series* include:

Gigabit Ethernet Networking
by David G. Cunningham, Ph.D., and William G. Lane, Ph.D.
(ISBN: 1-57870-062-0)

Written by key contributors to the Gigabit Ethernet standard, *Gigabit Ethernet Networking* provides network engineers and architects both the necessary context of the technology and advanced knowledge of its deployment. This book offers critical information to enable readers to make cost-effective decisions about how to design and implement their particular network to meet current traffic loads, and to ensure scalability with future growth.

DSL: Simulation Techniques and Standards Development for
Digital Subscriber Line Systems
by Walter Chen
(ISBN: 1-57870-017-5)

The only book on the market that deals with xDSL technologies at this level, *DSL: Simulation Techniques and Standards Development for Digital Subscriber Line Systems* is ideal for computing professionals who are looking for new high-speed communications technology, who must understand the dynamics of xDSL communications to create compliant applications, or who simply want to better understand this new wave of technology.

ADSL/VDSL Principles
by Dr. Dennis J. Rauschmayer
(ISBN: 1-57870-015-9)

ADSL/VDSL Principles provides the communications and networking engineer with practical explanations, technical detail, and in-depth insight needed to fully implement ADSL and VDSL. Topics that are essential to the successful implementation of these technologies are covered.

LDAP: Programming Directory-Enabled Applications
with Lightweight Directory Access Protocol
by Tim Howes and Mark Smith
(ISBN: 1-57870-000-0)

This book is the essential resource for programmers, software engineers, and network administrators who need to understand and implement LDAP to keep software applications compliant. If you design or program software for network computing or are interested in directory services, *LDAP* is an essential resource to help you understand the LDAP API; learn how to write LDAP programs; understand how to LDAP-enable an existing application; and learn how to use a set of command-line LDAP tools to search and update directory information.

Upcoming titles in the *Macmillan Technology Series* include:

Supporting Service Level Agreements on an IP Network
by Dinesh Verma
(ISBN: 1-57870-146-5)

Virtual Private Networks,
by David Bovee
ISBN: 1-57870-120-1)

Directory Enabled Networking
by John Strassner
(ISBN: 1-57870-140-6)

Understanding the Public Key Infrastructure
by Carlisle Adams and Steve Lloyd
(ISBN: 1-57870-166-x)

SNMP Agents,
by Bob Natale
(ISBN: 1-57870-110-4)